Emerging Trends in Artificial Intelligence Based IoT: Techniques, Applications and Security

Edited by

H.S. Hota
Department of Computer Science, Atal Bihari Vajpayee University, Bilaspur, Chhattisgarh, India

Dinesh K. Sharma
Department of Business, Management and Accounting University of Maryland Eastern Shore, Princess Anne Maryland, USA

Ayan Kumar Das
Department of Computer Science and Engineering Birla Institute of Technology Mesra - Patna Campus, Bihar, India

&

Ditipriya Sinha
Department of Computer Science and Engineering National Institute of Technology, Patna Bihar, India

Emerging Trends in Artificial Intelligence Based IoT: Techniques, Applications and Security

Editors: H.S. Hota, Dinesh K. Sharma, Ayan Kumar Das and Ditipriya Sinha

ISBN (Online): 978-981-5305-06-7

ISBN (Print): 978-981-5305-07-4

ISBN (Paperback): 978-981-5305-08-1

need for a court order if at any point you breach any terms of this License Agreement. In no event will any delay or failure by Bentham Science Publishers in enforcing your compliance with this License Agreement constitute a waiver of any of its rights.

3. You acknowledge that you have read this License Agreement, and agree to be bound by its terms and conditions. To the extent that any other terms and conditions presented on any website of Bentham Science Publishers conflict with, or are inconsistent with, the terms and conditions set out in this License Agreement, you acknowledge that the terms and conditions set out in this License Agreement shall prevail.

Bentham Science Publishers Pte. Ltd.
No. 9 Raffles Place
Office No. 26-01
Singapore 048619
Singapore
Email: subscriptions@benthamscience.net

BENTHAM SCIENCE

CONTENTS

PREFACE

This book intends to increase knowledge regarding emerging techniques of Artificial Intelligence (AI)-based Internet of Things (IoT), its diverse applications, and probable security threats for IoT devices. The Internet of Things (IoT) is a critical component of Industry 4.0 and is sometimes used interchangeably. This is an emerging technology that enables legitimate users to access and monitor the sensors installed in various units in the industry. The smart industry is being developed with the help of IoT. It is used in many applications like smart cities, smart parking, digital healthcare, smart agriculture, smart disaster management, and many more. The data produced by the IoT devices is semi-organized or non-structured, requiring cloud on-demand storage to store that data. The IoT aims to build automated systems so industry and society can proliferate. The number of IoT devices used to implement applications is growing at an exponential rate.

Moreover, device-to-device connectivity makes IoT devices more vulnerable. Thus, secure and authenticated communication is in demand for IoT devices. Furthermore, different AI-based techniques, including fuzzy logic, machine learning, and neural network-based approaches, are proposed for early predicting any severity in the IoT paradigm. Adding an AI-based multi-stage decision-making mechanism also helps optimize the assistive resource distribution where IoT integrates with cloud and fog computing. The resource-constrained IoT devices demand lightweight security schemes to authenticate communicating devices and protect the privacy of industrial data. In the manufacturing industry, the sensor nodes of the IoT network are deployed in a hostile environment. Thus, it is not feasible for the industry to keep track of those devices, and it will be easier for unauthorized users to access the smart devices of the IoT. Thus, this book's editors and contributing authors tried to cover some of the AI-based IoT techniques with an elaborated description of their applications and also propose schemes to prevent vulnerabilities in different security threats.

Chapter 1 overviews blockchain technology for smart IoT, its architecture, security challenges, and applications. This chapter first highlights the introduction of smart IoT with security and privacy concerns for these systems, followed by a detailed systematic analysis of blockchain architecture, its characteristics, consensus algorithms, various platforms, and application areas in smart IoT to analyze the concept and working of blockchain technology. Various benefits and challenges in integrating blockchain with IoT have been analyzed and illustrated.

Chapter 2 describes the role of blockchain in today's financial growth using IoT. Through this analytical survey, the authors have tried to analyze the decentralization that improves consensus success and how these descriptions of blockchain redesign the financial domain and the landscape of rivalry among several crypto-currencies. It has various applications with highly increasing demands for the best solution in a distributed environment using IoT in the present market scenario.

Chapter 3 provides a survey of forest fire surveillance strategies and challenges using the WSN paradigm. The forest is the most beautiful treasure in nature. It always meets the basic needs of the earth's inhabitants. Today, the forests are depleting quickly. The primary cause behind this is forest fires or wildfires. An uncontrollable fire occurs naturally or due to human interruption or any other disturbance caused by nature that may or may not be suppressed by artificial control. Several existing approaches, like wireless sensor networks, machine learning, and remote sensing, are used to identify wildfires. Some researchers are using UAVs to identify forest fires. In most cases, the researchers focus only on prediction using some environmental parameters sensed by the sensors or satellite images. This chapter highlights the various challenges in predicting forest fires in the WSN paradigm.

Chapter 4 proposes an IoT-based intelligent emergency alert system using neural computing and machine learning. Fuels, gases, etc., have prominent uses in our daily lives, households, and industries. However, they often cause severe accidents from gas leakage and fire incidents. The authors have designed a simple system using low-cost devices that sends an SMS *via* a GSM module in case of gas leakage or fire using IoT, neural computing, and ML. The objective of the proposed system is to enhance safety and security and protect properties.

Chapter 5 offers an IoT-enabled framework for secure and transparent digital answer script evaluation using blockchain. The proposed method proved to be beneficial due to its decentralized nature. In the proposed framework, all the steps of evaluation processes are traced and recorded through the blockchain to improve the system's security, transparency, and trustworthiness. This makes it simpler to figure out how a candidate obtained the score that he or she did, providing credibility to the certificate obtained.

Chapter 6 proposes an intelligent farm management system using an IoT-based Agrobot to match pH, temperature, humidity, and soil moisture levels to the levels required for growing crops. Productivity is increased without negatively impacting the soil. This reduced the use of chemical fertilizers by 30% to 75%. This proposed system may help to improve economic and environmentally sustainable crop production.

Chapter 7 provides a novel, unbiased trust establishment mechanism in a cross-domain, cloud-based IoT environment. The authors advocate a trust-dependent authorization model to be implemented in a cloud-dependent IoT environment that also functions as a two-way or dual-mode trust model, considering the requirements of the service giver and taker. In the suggested paradigm, trustworthiness is assessed on both the user and supplier sides. A transaction is only permitted if both trust values exceed a predefined or set threshold.

Chapter 8 uses graphical representation and deep learning to classify IoT malware network traffic. This revolutionary technique of IoT malware traffic analysis uses deep learning and graphical demonstration to detect and categorize new malware more quickly. This will allow us to handle the difficulty that has been presented (zero-day malware). Due to the utilization of deep learning technology, the suggested method for detecting malicious network traffic operates at the package level, significantly reducing the time required for detection and producing encouraging outcomes.

Chapter 9 describes the optimum utilization of modern-day technology for health monitoring with wearable devices using IoT. The Immediate Health Monitoring System uses IoT, enabling it to monitor the patient's temperature along with the oxygen level instantly; this system transmits the same information to the doctor or medical service provider at a distant location. It also enables one to look at the patient's current condition. If the values of the parameters change from the traditional values, then an alert message is given to the medical service provider or the doctor concerned with the patient. This instant health monitoring plan based on IoT helps doctors effortlessly collect real-time numbers at a location far from the patient's location.

Chapter 10 proposes an IoT-enabled automated model for detecting COVID-19 spread using deep learning. The proposed model diagnoses COVID-19 cases quickly and maintains low hardware costs. The proposed model has been tested on 280 COVID-positive and 290 normal patient images taken from two benchmark datasets and has tried to find out the spreading tendency of the virus by getting some actual data from IoT sensor devices in the affected zone. The proposed model achieves an accuracy of 97%. Moreover, cross-validation is applied in this model to avoid over-fitting. This chapter concludes that the proposed model provides insight into the CNN-LSTM+Capsule network used for COVID-19 detection, allowing for richer feature mapping from radiographic images and effectively distinguishing COVID cases from normal ones.

Chapter 11 describes a model for the automated identification of cloud-IoT-based sensitive data in a dataset. Before sharing data with a third party, it is anonymized and de-identified. The detection of data points that have the potential to expose sensitive information can be a tedious task, especially if done manually. Automating the task helps make identification much more manageable when dealing with many small and large data sets. The current solution has been envisaged to help identify potential leakage of sensitive information using an easy-t--implement framework and a solution for detecting potential quasi-identifiers in data.

Chapter 12 proposes an IoT and blockchain-based smart architecture for secure supply chain management. This chapter discusses the architecture of different entities involved in the agriculture supply chain and their roles and interactions with other entities. In this case, smart contracts are used between the farmer and the customer, the farmer and delivery personnel, and the farmer and the quality assurance authorities involved in the agriculture supply chain. It also discusses their roles and interactions with other entities.. The authors built the system using the Remix IDE and Solidity for programming smart contracts.

Chapter 13 suggests the optimization of the application-aware QoS Routing Algorithm (AQRA) and MINA for SDN-based IoT networks that ensure numerous QoS specifications for high-priority IoT applications. The Particle Swarm Optimization (PSO) technique has been applied to get the optimized solution.

Chapter 14 describes IoT-based data security in smart farming systems. The security system is created using a few sensors, like temperature and soil moisture sensors, and the data is encrypted. The sensors transform the plain text into unintelligible cipher text, which is then uploaded to the cloud on the transmitter side. The AES128 key and hash code are used on the transmitter side, which can be used to decode data on the reception side.

The editors would like to express their gratitude to all the reviewers for their outstanding contributions to this book. We sincerely hope that readers enjoy reading these chapters, and we anticipate that they will aid in advancing IoT techniques and implementation research. This book will be a huge success regarding idea exchange, leading to future research collaborations in emerging AI-based IoT techniques and applications.

H.S. Hota
Department of Computer Science
Atal Bihari Vajpayee University
Bilaspur, Chhattisgarh, India

Dinesh K. Sharma
Department of Business, Management and Accounting
University of Maryland Eastern Shore
Princess Anne, Maryland, USA

Ayan Kumar Das
Department of Computer Science and Engineering
Birla Institute of Technology
Mesra - Patna Campus, Bihar, India

&

Ditipriya Sinha
Department of Computer Science and Engineering
National Institute of Technology, Patna
Bihar, India

List of Contributors

Amisha	Department of Electrical Engineering, Deenbandhu Chhotu Ram University of Science and Technology, Murthal, Haryana, India
Aarti	Department of Electrical Engineering, Deenbandhu Chhotu Ram University of Science and Technology, Murthal, Haryana, India
Ayan Kumar Das	Department of Computer Science and Engineering, Birla Institute of Technology, Mesra - Patna Campus, Patna, Bihar, India
Ananya Ganguly	Department of Computer Science, Acharya Jagadish Chanda Bose College, Kolkata, West Bengal, India
Atowar ul Islam	Department of Computer Science and Electronics, University of Science and Technology, Baridua, Meghalaya, India
Amit K. Sharma	Department of Computer Science and Engineering Technology, University of Maryland Eastern Shore, Princess Anne, Maryland, USA
Arvind Rehalia	Department of Information Technology, Bharati Vidyapeeth's College of Engineering, New Delhi, Delhi, India
Arpita Srivastava	Department of Computer Science and Engineering, National Institute of Technology, Patna, Bihar, India
Debdutta Pal	Department of Computer Science and Engineering, Birla Institute of Technology, Mesra - Patna Campus, Patna, Bihar, India
Devadri Bhattacharya	Department of Electronics and Communication Engineering, B.M.S. College of Engineering, Bengaluru, Karnataka, India
G.S. Dhanush	Department of Electronics and Communication Engineering, B.M.S. College of Engineering, Bengaluru, Karnataka, India
G. Kushal	Department of Electronics and Communication Engineering, B.M.S. College of Engineering, Bengaluru, Karnataka, India
H.S. Hota	Department of Computer Science, Atal Bihari Vajpayee University, Bilaspur, Chhattisgarh, India
J.M. Adithya	Department of Electronics and Communication Engineering, B.M.S. College of Engineering, Bengaluru, Karnataka, India
Kaustav Roy	Department of Computer Science and Engineering, Brainware University, Kolkata, India
Kamta Nath Mishra	Department of Computer Science and Engineering, Birla Institute of Technology, Mesra - Patna Campus, Patna, Bihar, India
Milan Kumar Dholey	Department of Computer Science and Engineering, GITAM (Deemed to be University), Visakhapatnam, Andhra Pradesh, India
Manisha Chandrakar	School of Studies in Computer Science and IT, Pt. Ravishankar Shukla University, Raipur, Chhattisgarh, India
M.R. Shrisha	Department of Electronics and Communication Engineering, B.M.S. College of Engineering, Bengaluru, Karnataka, India
Namrata Singh	Department of Computer Science and Engineering, Birla Institute of Technology, Mesra - Patna Campus, Patna, Bihar, India

Nikhil Kaushik	Department of Electronics and Communication Engineering, Lingaya's Vidyapeeth, Faridabad, Haryana, India
Priya Saha	Department of Computer Science and Engineering, ITER, Siksha 'Ó' Anusandhan (Deemed to be University), Bhubaneswar, Odisha, India
Raj Vikram	Department of Computer Science and Engineering, ITER, Siksha O Anusandhan, Bhubneshwar, Odisha, India
Rohtash Dhiman	Department of Electrical Engineering, Deenbandhu Chhotu Ram University of Science and Technology, Murthal, Haryana, India
Rashi	Department of Electrical Engineering, Deenbandhu Chhotu Ram University of Science and Technology, Murthal, Haryana, India
Rishabh Kumar	Department of Computer Science and Engineering, Birla Institute of Technology, Mesra - Patna Campus, Patna, Bihar, India
Radha Tamal Goswami	Department of Electrical Engineering, Techno International New Town, Kolkata, West Bengal, India
Rishikesh	Department of Computer Science and Engineering, National Institute of Technology, Patna, Bihar, India
Raj Vikram	Department of Computer Science and Engineering, ITER, Siksha 'O' Anusandhan, Bhubneshwar, Odisha, India
Sarvpal Singh	Department of Information Technology and Computer Application Engineering, Madan Mohan Malaviya University of Technology, Gorakhpur, Uttar Pradesh, India
Sangeeta Borkakoty	Department of Computer Science and Electronics, University of Science and Technology, Baridua, Meghalaya, India
Sourav Mahapatra	Department of Computer Science and Engineering, National Institute of Technology, Patna, Bihar, India
Souvagya Das	Department of Electrical Engineering, Techno International New Town, Kolkata, West Bengal, India
Sourav Das	Department of Electrical Engineering, Techno International New Town, Kolkata, West Bengal, India
Sayan Biswas	Department of Electrical Engineering, Techno International New Town, Kolkata, West Bengal, India
Swati Dhiman	Department of Electronics and Communication Engineering, Sant Longowal Institute of Engineering and Technology, Longowal, Punjab, India
SVAV Prasad	Department of Electronics and Communication Engineering, Lingaya's Vidyapeeth, Faridabad, Haryana, India
Sanjib Roy	Department of Computer Science and Engineering, Birla Institute of Technology, Mesra - Patna Campus, Patna, Bihar, India
Sudipta Chandra	Abzooba India Infotech Private Limited, Kolkata, West Bangal, India
Soumya Ray	Department of Computer Science and Engineering, Birla Institute of Technology, Mesra - Patna Campus, Patna, Bihar, India
Tarun Dhar Diwan	Govt. E. Raghavendra Rao P.G. Science College, Bilaspur, Chhattisgarh, India

Vikash Kumar   Department of Computer Science and Engineering, ITER, Siksha O Anusandhan, Bhubneshwar, Odisha, India

V. K. Patle   School of Studies in Computer Science and IT, Pt. Ravishankar Shukla University, Raipur, Chhattisgarh, India

A Systematic Study of Blockchain Technology for Smart IoT: Architecture, Security Challenges, and Applications

Namrata Singh[1,*] and **Sarvpal Singh**[2]

[1] *Department of Computer Science and Engineering, Birla Institute of Technology, Mesra - Patna Campus, Bihar, India*

[2] *Department of Information Technology and Computer Application Engineering, Madan Mohan Malaviya University of Technology, Gorakhpur, Uttar Pradesh, India*

Abstract: The growth of the Internet of Things (IoT)-embedded intelligent systems with both the industrial perspective and research enables communication and data transfer among heterogeneous devices in real-time without any physical human intervention. These devices are resource-constrained devices in terms of power and storage. This autonomous and constrained behavior of smart IoT devices leads to privacy and security vulnerabilities. The existing cryptographic techniques for security and privacy preservation are not suitable enough to deal with the issues of these systems. Blockchain technology provides a platform for decentralized computation and secure information sharing in a distributed manner among multiple authoritative participants. These participants do not trust each other but cooperate, coordinate, and collaborate in a rational decision-making process. Blockchain uses a cryptographic environment to secure the data and network. Different characteristics of blockchain technology, such as decentralization, immutability, transparency, security, and reliability, make it the ideal and effective candidate for integration with smart IoT systems. The main objective of this paper is to analyze the use of blockchain technology and its concept in the context of smart IoT to improve capabilities and enhance its security. This paper first highlights the introduction of smart IoT with security and privacy concerns for these systems. This is followed by a detailed systematic analysis of blockchain architecture, its characteristics, consensus algorithms, various platforms, and application areas in smart IoT with the aim of analyzing the concept and workings of blockchain technology. Various benefits and challenges in the integration of blockchain with IoT are then analyzed and illustrated.

Keywords: Blockchain technology, Consensus, Decentralization, Internet of Things, Intelligence, Security, Smart IoT, Smart contract.

---

* **Corresponding author Namrata Singh:** Department of Computer Science and Engineering, Birla Institute of Technology, Mesra - Patna Campus, Bihar, India; E-mail: phdcs10061.20@bitmesra.ac.in

H.S. Hota, Dinesh K. Sharma, Ayan Kumar Das & Ditipriya Sinha (Eds.)

INTRODUCTION

The Internet of Things (IoT) facilitates machine-to-machine communication among various interconnected computing devices, digital machines, objects, and people having the capability of transferring data over the network without any human intervention [2]. The term 'Internet' in IoT refers to connectivity, and 'Things' refers to communicating objects *i.e.*, the collection of web-enabled devices embedded with sensors, processors, microcontrollers, and communicating hardware devices that transfer data from different environments. IoT is responsible for interconnecting these physical and virtual objects in order to provide new services and applications to the users. A large number of interconnected components enables the concept of 'diversity of things', which builds a large-scale network to co-operate with each other for effective sharing of information and enhancing the existing services. It helps in generating novel applications that have the capability to handle real-world problems [9]. The modern development for various applications aims to design intelligence-based IoT objects that have the capability to make autonomous decisions. It enables a broad smart application area covering social and industrial needs. It plays a significant role in building smart environments for different applications, such as smart homes, smart cities, smart healthcare, smart grids, smart factories, and smart industrial equipment [2, 5]. IoT is considered the backbone of the digitized industrial sector as it enables optimized production and cost-reduced manufacturing processes [2].

A notable expansion in the development of smart IoT applications in different areas poses severe challenges that restrict the successful deployment of IoT technology as well as deteriorate the performance of existing systems. One of the major challenges with IoT systems is their complexity, mainly when implemented on a large scale, as IoTtechnology is not a standalone technique but an integration of different information and communication technologies that collaborate with computing and data analytics techniques to achieve the desired smartness [2]. The concept of central server structure is used to integrate networks of scattered IoT devices by interconnecting them with the central server. However, this centralized structure of IoT networks suffers from the difficulty of fulfilling the trust factor *i.e.*, this type of architecture provides unreliable communication, resulting in insecure dataflow [2, 5]. This type of architecture also makes the IoT network susceptible to Byzantine failure [6] and a single point of failure [3, 10]. It deteriorates the performance of whole networks. It urges the requirement of a decentralized IoT platform. Moreover, the increased number of interconnected devices in an IoT system also creates the problem of addressing different devices with unique identification numbers for creating a fully functional IoT [5]. Other major challenges with IoT systems are the limitations of time-constrained and resource-constrained behavior *i.e.*, constraints of processing power, storage capacity, and computational capability in IoT devices that do not allow the deployment of advanced security solutions [2, 3]. The devices and network become utmost critical while deploying large-scale IoT systems with advanced cryptographic techniques in such a constrained environment. Devices in the IoT are interconnected with low-power wireless networks such as LoRa WAN, ZigBee, and Wi-Fi [3]. Each physical or virtual connected device in an IoT system is trackable, and the data generated by them can be retrieved by other users regardless of their location [6]. However, only authorized users are required to have access to the system and resources to deal with various security concerns, such as identity theft, data modification, and leakage of information. The rich communication in IoT devices generates an enormous dataset used for various dependent applications, which demands privacy and security solutions on three levels [4]:

(i) Data level: Real-time sensitive data collected from the physical world.

(ii) Communication level: Interaction among devices in the network.

(iii) Application level: Data processing and interaction between the service provider and service user.

It causes various data security challenges, such as data confidentiality, data integrity, and data availability, in an IoT environment [1, 7]. Each node in an IoT environment is also highly prone to various types of security attacks. Thus, it requires various security measures to protect the IoT environment from different types of attacks, such as Man-in-the-Middle (MITM) attacks, injection attacks, Distributed Denial-of-Service (DDoS) attacks, spoofing, message tampering, and eavesdropping for effective decision-making [8].

A truly decentralized and distributed trust technology is required to alleviate the challenges faced in the successful deployment of IoT systems and to build interoperable security solutions ensuring scalability, privacy, and reliability in an IoT environment [1, 2, 7]. The decentralized architecture alleviates the IoT challenges by reducing the amount of data transfer, improving the services, reducing the operational cost of services, providing resistance against byzantine failure and single point of failure, enhancing protection against security risks and attacks, improving privacy preservation of data, and managing autonomous operations. A standardized peer-to-peer (P2P) is also required for effectively dealing with the huge amount of sensitive data generated from IoT devices and preventing the IoT network from theft and mistrust [6]. P2P is a decentralized network communication model in which each device or node acts as an individual peer and collectively stores and shares the information. Blockchain technology is such a major distributed and decentralized technology thatit can be considered a promising IoT security solution due to its inherent properties *i.e.*, distributed behavior, immutability, data integrity, communication transparency, data availability, node authentication, and cryptographic security [10]. It has obtained the great attention of researchers to successfully deploy advanced IoT technologies and enhance the performance of existing IoT systems by tackling the problems of security, anonymity, traceability, and centralization. Blockchain technology supports P2P communication, which eliminates the concept of a centralized trusted third party, as all the nodes get the same privilege and can act as clients and servers [7]. The nodes in the network do not trust each other and interact with each other by utilizing cryptographic public/private keys to make a decision automatically based on a consensus [5]. Blockchain technology consists of a tamper-resistant or immutable distributed ledger to build a P2P network in which all the transactions collected in chronological order are grouped into blocks. Each node in this type of network has its own copy of information, and the whole system is transparent to every participant *i.e.*, each node has knowledge about the information and corresponding transactions. This unique, transparent, and immutable characteristic inherently establishes trustworthy communication among IoT devices and backend servers [1]. It is helpful in eliminating the problem of a single point of failure as all nodes in the network have the availability of the information to independently verify and validate the transaction in a smart contract. Smart contracts in a blockchain-integrated IoT system are used to enforce the access control mechanism for the identification and detection of unauthorized access to IoT devices [2]. Thus, this technique enables a private and secure communication network between IoT devices and improves the integrity issues in an IoT system. However, various challenges, such as high resource utilization, scalability, high delay, and some interoperability issues, are analyzed while applying blockchain to IoT [4, 20]. Thus, the use of blockchain for developing IoT applications is not always a viable solution. It highly depends upon the nature of applications [6].

SMART IOT

With the advancement of IoT technology, both the number of interconnected IoT devices deployed and the amount of IoT data generated by those devices are growing at a fast pace [11]. It requires real-time analysis of this huge amount of primary data generated by supporting intelligent processing techniques to automate the devices. It also requires knowledge-enhanced advanced data analytics techniques for the successful integration of IoT big data [11]. Collective intelligence and knowledge-enhanced techniques also help in dealing with all the middleware issues related to the interoperability of devices, networking, and data exchange. This advancement has developed a new autonomous IoT environment, namely, smart IoT, by the intelligent interconnection of diverse objects in the physical world, which operates with little or no human intervention in decision-making [12, 13]. A smart IoT enhances the capability of the system by enabling good and timely decision-making and by taking actions to enable intelligent applications [11]. Thus, "Smart IoT is referred to IoT as human agent, human extension and human complement [14]". Smart IoT utilizes low-cost information collection and dissemination devices to facilitate fast-paced intercommunication among different objects at any time and in any place [13]. It makes remote control easier and safer than ever. Smart IoT devices *i.e.*, smart things, are capable enough to dynamically adapt to changing contexts and take actions on the basis of their operating conditions. They are interoperable, self-configurable, and uniquely identifiable (having unique identities) and have the capability of communicating and exchanging data with other devices [15].

BLOCKCHAIN TECHNOLOGY

Blockchain technology was mainly introduced by Satoshi Nakamoto for secure digital currency transactions. Although the basic idea behind blockchain technology has been present since 1991 to support cryptocurrencies, it came into existence in 2008 after a publication, "Bitcoin: A Peer-to-Peer Electronic Cash System" by Satoshi Nakamoto. Bitcoin is the first-generation documentation of blockchain known as "Blockchain 1.0", which employs a public ledger with cryptographically secured financial transactions without any central control. Its functional limitations led to its replacement by Turing-complete Ethereum Virtual Machine (EVM) for the generation of smart contracts, which was known as the second generation of the blockchain network, namely, "Blockchain 2.0". It provided a general-purpose programmable platform with a public ledger for keeping the records of computational results [8, 16]. The smart contract was generated to realize the Decentralized Applications (DApps) and Decentralized Autonomous Organizations (DAOs) that automated the financial applications based on cryptocurrencies by incorporating smart contracts with digital currencies [8, 17]. However, the concept of blockchain technology is not only limited to cryptocurrencies but is also applicable to non-cryptocurrency-based applications. This wider approach of distributed ledger technology that ports all the properties of blockchain used for cryptocurrency-based transactions to other non-cryptocurrency applications where these systems are built on the top of blockchain technology is known as the third generation of Blockchain or "Blockchain 3.0" [8, 16]. In brief, Blockchain 1.0 means "currency", which illustrates the deployment of digital cryptocurrencies in financial applications such as cash transfers, remittances, and digital financial transactions. Blockchain 2.0 refers to "smart contracts", which represent the programmable codes executing automatically to keep the computational record in the public ledger if the predefined set of rules or conditions is met. Blockchain 3.0 refers to "applications" illustrating the applicability of distributed ledger concepts in non-cryptocurrency applications.

Blockchain technology is a distributed and decentralized technology that utilizes a public ledger for recording and storing digital transactions in blocks as a data structure using a one-way cryptographic hash function in chronological order [17]. The use of a cryptographic hash function in the creation of a public ledger ensures the security of the network. Blockchain is a P2P network that maintains a sequential, secure, and incorruptible record of each transaction using a continually growing ledger [18]. The distributed public ledger is a data repository managed in a decentralized way where multiple authoritative domains or participants own the same rights and control over the repository. These participants do not trust each other but can directly communicate among themselves to manage and maintain the repository [17]. Each participant or miner in a blockchain environment has equal power and rights to make decisions. All the participants reach a consensus for decision-making if an update is required to be made to the repository. Various blocks of digitally signed and encrypted transactions are linked with each other chronologically to generate a public ledger that can be accessed only by authorized entities. The cryptographic hash function is used to ensure network security by maintaining a tamper-proof record of data and validating the privacy and authenticity of miners. The consensus algorithm confirms the consistency of the updated public ledger. The commitment protocols after validating transactions ensure that each valid transaction is committed and incorporated in the public ledger within a finite interval of time. Smart contracts are immutable agreements comprised of a public ledger that maintains a trusting relationship among multiple authoritative domains. A smart contract provides the executable logic to generate new facts added to the ledger. A smart contract is software that is self-executing in nature and runs on the Ethereum blockchain when specific criteria or conditions are met [18]. It is a collection of lines of code that lives on the Ethereum blockchain platform at a single location or address. Once the contract is placed on the blockchain, miners may be able to execute it automatically without human intervention [18]. Thus, blockchain technology can be described as a backlinked, decentralized, and distributed database of encrypted records [18]. Backlinked means it is a linked list-like data structure in which each block is linked to another one by considering the hash value of the previous block. Decentralized means that there is no centralized entity, and it is not managed or governed by any third-party organization. A distributed database means that a copy of all the transactions stored in a public ledger is broadcasted to all nodes in the network and is accessible to each of them.

Working

The working of blockchain can be divided into six steps [17]:

(i) Request for a transaction: A user request for a transaction is made;

(ii) Broadcast transaction: The requested transaction is broadcasted to different miner nodes of aP2P network;

(iii) Validation: All nodes in a network participate in validating the transaction using a consensus algorithm. A verified transaction consists of cryptocurrencies, records, contracts, and other information;

(iv) Link creation: Once a transaction is verified, it is linked to another transaction, and a new block can be created for the ledger;

(v) Blockchain network: The new block is added to the existing blockchain network in permanent and unalterable manner;

(vi) Transaction completion: The transaction is considered to be completed after appending new block into the network. (Fig. **1**) illustrates the working procedure of the blockchain [7, 9, 17].

In a blockchain network, *e.g.*, bitcoin, different transactions grouped into blocks are generated and validated by miners who follow a consensus method to achieve the purpose [4]. Miners are the nodes of the blockchain network that are allowed to add transactions to the blocks. Miners compete with each other to win the chance to request a transaction, validate it, and put it into the ledger. It requires solving a mathematical puzzle to be a winner. The winner node or the first miner gets the chance to add a transaction to the ledger and get some financial reward. Only one miner is permitted to add a transaction to the blockchain at a time [7]. Asymmetric public key cryptography is used here in order to assign the cryptographic keys, such as the public key or private key, to each node where the public key is employed to identify a device in the blockchain network, whereas the private key is incorporated for signing the transactions by the device itself or other devices in the network [6]. Whenever a transaction is carried out, the corresponding device signs it using its private key and sends it to the other participant devices of the network in order to verify and disseminate further into the network after verification. The private key serves for integrity and authentication. The public key plays the role of verification of the transaction. Asymmetric cryptography is difficult to find and compute but easier to verify.

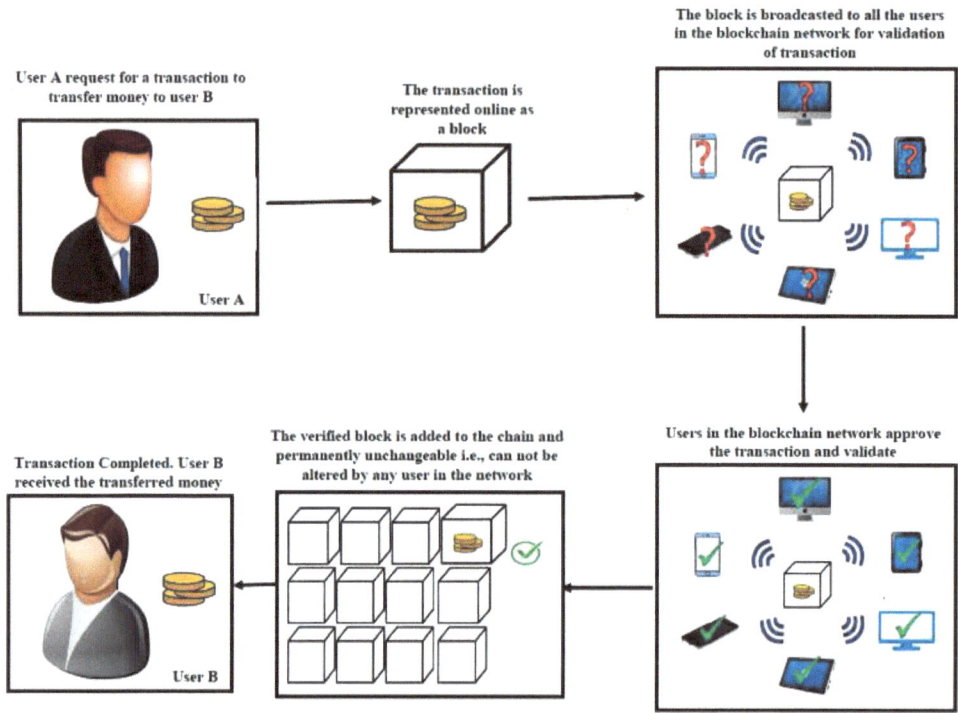

Fig. (1). Working procedure of blockchain for any financial transaction.

Proof of Work (PoW) considers asymmetric public key cryptography, in which every miner tries to solve the SHA-256 cryptographic hash function to find the next block. The process of finding the next block is termed mining [3, 9]. A block is created by the miner only after it is validated by the network. The first block created is known as the genesis block. Every block in a blockchain network contains data and a block header comprising a block version, a hash of the previous block, a hash of the current block, a nonce value, a timestamp, and a Merkle root. Every block is linked with its previous block in a blockchain network using a cryptographic hash pointer in order to generate an immutable chain of blocks [3, 4]. The block version is a four-byte number to indicate the block version number [9]. The nonce value is a four-byte number included in the hashed block in a blockchain and meets difficulty-level restrictions after rehashing. It is used for authentication, which ensures that the old communications cannot be reprocessed,thus preventing a replay attack [7]. The timestamp field of the block is four bytes and is used to record the block creation time [9]. Merkle root encodes the transactions in a single hashed code by repeatedly hashing the hash pair of nodes until only one hash remains [7]. This field is of thirty-two bytes, which represents the hash of all the transactions of that particular block [9]. The data part of the block includes all the inputs and outputs of each transaction. The input contains the output of the previous transaction and a field that contains the signature with the private key of the owner node [7]. (Fig. **2**) represents the general structure of the blockchain, which represents the chain of blocks.

The validation of the block starts when a miner finds a specific nonce value used to solve the mathematical puzzle and broadcasts the block to the network. The other miners use the information of the block and the nonce value associated with it as input to the SHA-256 function in order to verify the block as valid. If the output is found to be less than the target value, the miners consider the block as the valid one and move on to find the next block [3]. The verified block is added to the chain by creating a hash linkage with the previous block and updated or discarded based on the verification [6]. Whenever any invalid block is detected in the blockchain network, it is discarded along with all other blocks linked with it. The credibility of a block depends upon the number of other blocks built upon it. The block achieves higher credibility if comparatively a greater number of blocks are built upon it. This process is termed the cryptocurrency confirmation process in blockchain. A block and transactions associated with it are acceptable after several such confirmations. The ledger contained by all the miners gets updated with this newly added block and permanently exists as a public record in the ledger [9]. A transaction is added to the block only when the majority of miners verify it [9]. These transactions are immutable or non-modifiable. In order to tamper with the recorded data of a transaction, all the blocks containing that transaction are required to be changed in less than ten minutes. It might be possible only with more than half the rate power of the world *i.e.*, to gain 51% of the computing power of the whole blockchain network [3, 7]. The miner finds a specific nonce value for a block that is required to be added to the network for the purpose. It is done in such a manner that the hash value of that block is always less than the corresponding target value. Determining this target value is a computationally very hard and time-consuming process. It is only determined by brute force search, and miners are required to try random nonce values to reach this target value [3].

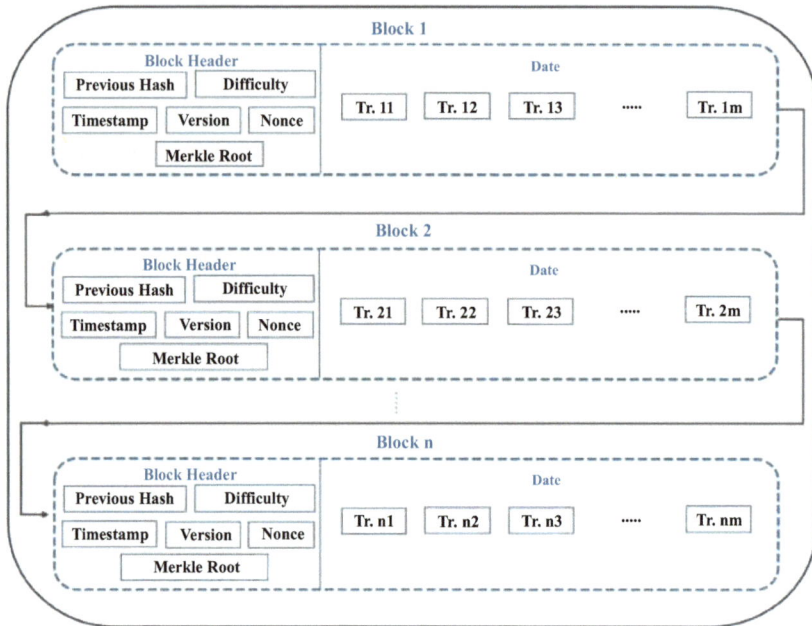

Fig. (2). Structure of Blockchain [2].

Types of Blockchain

Blockchain is categorized as public blockchain, private blockchain, and consortium blockchain. Public blockchain allows data to be accessible to everyone, and everyone can contribute to the consesus process. It is also named permissionless blockchain because no approval is required to join or contribute to the network. Private blockchain allows data to be accessible to only a certain number of nodes. It is managed and governed by a single organization. It is centralized and distributed. It is also known as a permissioned blockchain because the nodes in the network need to be the members of the organization. Only a small number of specified companies and organizations have access to read and participate in the consensus process on a consortium blockchain. It is assumed to be semi-centralized. It is a combination of groups of two or more than two organizations [2, 4, 7 - 9, 17].

Blockchain Platforms

Some of the most promising blockchain platforms, such as Ethereum, Hyperledger fabric, Corda, and IOTA, are illustrated below, which use multiple consensus algorithms to validate the transaction of the network.

Ethereum

It is a permissionless blockchain platform developed using a contract-oriented and high-level language *i.e.*, solidity programming language, which is used for the implementation of smart contracts [3]. Ethereum is an environment of nodes thathavve the capability to replicate and process smart contracts without any central authority [7]. All the nodes necessarily participate in a consensus procedure. Ethereum is designed using "Ethash", which is a derivative of the PoW consensus mechanism. This method is considered comparatively less computationally intensive than the original PoW consensus method due to the use of a directive acyclic graph (DAG). This platform has intrinsic characteristics that enable smart contracts, which makes it customizable and adoptable for various applications [3]. However, there is a plan to migrate this platform to a version named Casper, which uses the Proof of Stake (PoS) consensus method. The block generation process takes ten to twenty seconds, which is comparatively much less than the Ethereum platform, but is still not considered suitable for IoT applications.

Hyperledger Fabric

It is a permissioned blockchain that uses a pluggable method of consensus. The most common consensus method used for it is Practical Byzantine Fault Tolerance (PBFT). Hyperledger Fabric reaches the consensus within hundreds of milliseconds [3]. It is considered suitable for blockchain-based IoT networks due its low latency. However, it lacks the important characteristics of public blockchain *i.e.*, itis highly secure and immutable and has distributed storage of data. In this type of framework, an increment in the number of nodes causes increased network overhead, which results in an increased number of transmitted messages in the PBFT protocol. Thus, Hyperledger Fabric is not considered suitable for large-scale IoT applications [3, 5].

Corda

It is a permissioned blockchain that uses a pluggable method of consensus. It is a decentralized ledger framework in which the special nodes, namely, notary nodes, participate in the consensus procedure. This framework is partially decentralized due to the demand for trusting notaries. This platform is mainly suitable for financial transactions. However, it is not considered feasible for a constrained IoT environment.

IOTA

It is a permissionless distributed ledger framework that uses a consensus mechanism, namely, Tangle. Tangle uses DAG, where vertices represent transactions and edges represent approval [5]. Tangle is a less time-consuming, less computationally intensive, and less complicated consensus procedure. The use of blocks for storing transactions is also not required as every transaction is considered a unique block by itself, and the nodes are required to initially sign the transaction in order to create a transaction. The newly created transaction is known as a "tip" and remains a tip until it approves two randomly chosen previous transactions for adding it to the ledger [3, 5]. The approval of two previous transactions is done by PoW. IOTA is the most suitable and desirable platform for IoT applications due to its fast and scalable characteristics. It is the first cryptocurrency specially designed for IoT applications. It minimizes transaction time as well as network overhead. However, security is adjustable as there is a possibility of some attacks [3]. In IOTA, a cumulative weight is assigned to each transaction on the basis of the number of transactions consecutively associated with it, and there is no requirement for the number of confirmations to ensure the reliability condition. It also does not apply any transactional fee.

Consensus Algorithms

The consensus algorithm describes a procedure to arrive at or agree on common data or the state of the blockchain. Different types of consensus algorithms of blockchain are illustrated below.

Proof of Work (PoW)

Cynthia Dwork and Moni Naor came up with the idea of PoW in 1993. Each node in the blockchain participates in a block mining procedure in which every node competes with each other to solve a mathematical puzzle and reaches an agreement to discover a nonce for the given block. Each node participating in the mining procedure is known as a miner. The miner node, solving the puzzle first, gets the opportunity to broadcast a block into the entire network and add it to the Blockchain network once it is verified by other participant nodes of the network. The miner node, which adds a block to the network, is then rewarded with some amount. The node with the most processing power has a better probability of adding a new block to the network [3, 7, 23]. Although PoW is widely utilized across a variety of platforms, it requires high bandwidth and computational power. Miners have to constantly alter the nonce value until the correct solution is achieved. Thus, a miner needs a lot of computing power to solve this challenge [3, 23]. It is highly susceptible to 51% attack.

Proof of Stake (PoS)

PoS is the second most popular consensus algorithm, which is an alternative technique to PoW. PoS is also cheaper than PoW as it requires less energy, less computational power, and less time to process compared to PoW. In PoS, nodes that get an opportunity for block creation in the network are known as validators. All nodes in the network stake their money for a defined time interval to get an opportunity for new block addition. The node having the greatest stake becomes the validator. The process of becoming a node to be a validator also highly depends on the time duration in which the node stakes its money. The validators are provided with a transaction fee associated with the block. This algorithm saves the computational power and wealth of the validator [3, 7, 23]. This procedure leads to fast, energy-efficient, and secure consensus. It also ensures a low risk of 51% attack. PoS consensus algorithm is widely used for public blockchains where validators are untrusted entities and are anonymously distributed. The most widely used blockchain platform, named Ethereum, is going to switch from PoW to PoS algorithm [23].

Delegated Proof of Stake (DPoS)

Larimer introduced the DPoS consensus algorithm in 2014 to address the problem of the wealthy getting wealthier in the PoS. This is accomplished by electing forgers rather than selecting them based on the number of staked coins they own. In DPoS, a group of nodes containing witnesses to create new blocks and delegates to maintain the network and propose changes *i.e.*, block size, transaction fees, or reward amount, are elected through voting. The voting power of a node depends upon the number of coins it possesses and is proportional to it. Every node can give their vote for more than one witness, with one vote for every witness. After the voting is complete, top M witnesses are selected, with at least 50% of nodes having voted for these witnesses [3]. The main reason for selecting M witnesses rather than selecting one is to avoid a single node getting a chance to mine all the blocks in the blockchain. In this, mining is done using a round-robin algorithm. Each witness gets a turn to mine a block; if it fails, the next witness gets the chance. The list of witnesses is swapped after all of the witnesses in the group have taken their turn, and the round-robin continues [7]. The shuffling is intended to avoid a simple method, which is subject to attack because the next miner is known ahead of time. In this technique, the power lies in the hands of every individual who selects the witnesses. DPoS is a promising technology that promises to achieve high transaction speeds while consuming little energy.

Proof of Importance (PoI)

This algorithm was proposed by the New Economy Movement (NEM) network platform, which uses the XEM cryptocurrency. PoI is the improved or modified version of PoS. It not only selects the nodes on the basis of their economic stake in the system but also on other parameters like the productive network activity of a node. The productive network activity of a node depends on the stake and makes decisions accordingly. It also keeps track of the user's token usage and travel in order to build a level of trust and relevance. Miners are known as harvesters, and mining is known as harvesting in PoI [3]. The miner with the greatest value of significance score within the network is chosen for mining the block. A miner's significance score is computed using three factors: the number of crypto tokens owned by a miner, individuals with whom the miner makes transactions, and the total number and size of transactions made by the miner [3, 7]. A miner must have a certain number of vested tokens, known as the vesting amount, in order to participate in the mining process. The miner significance score will increase with an increase in the number of vested coins. When the miners complete transactions with nodes that have vested tokens, they are rewarded in terms of significance score. Finally, the miner's relevance score is determined by the number of comp-

leted transactions in the previous thirty days, with each transaction amount exceeding a predefined threshold amount.

Practical Byzantine Fault Tolerance (PBFT)

Miguel Castro and Barbara Liskov devised the PBFT consensus in 1999, which was the solution to the Byzantine general's problem. It supposes a Byzantine army is split into different divisions, with each division or group led by a different leader [7]. The generals or leaders of the respective divisions can talk to each other only through a messenger. They plan to attack the enemy by observing its actions. This attack can take place only if all the leaders come to a common decision or agreement. In this group, some of the generals may be traitors whodo not allow all the generals to come up with a common plan. There must be an algorithm provided to the generals to ensure the selection of the same way to proceed by all the honest generals and no ability to persuade the loyal generals to choose a wrong plan of action by a small proportion of traitors [3, 16]. All nodes take part in the voting process in order to add a new block. PBFT ensures that the software system continues working even in node failure or in malicious activity conditions. In this algorithm, the consensus is achieved if more than 2n/3 agree nodes *i.e.*, 66% of the nodes, come to the same decision. In PBFT, all the individuals or nodes in the network have equal power, and there is no concept of mining in it. The protocol is scalability-limited, allowing only a few nodes and requiring the transmission of many messages to obtain consensus.

Proof of Elapsed Time (PoET)

PoET consensus is a lottery-based algorithm that is developed mainly for sawtooth software and allows it to achieve better throughput than any of the other models [7, 23]. In PoET, every node interacting within the blockchain network is considered to be a loyal and trustful entity. Every individual node in the network generates a timer randomly. The node whose timer expires first gets an opportunity to become a leader and is authorized to add a new block [7, 23]. This consensus helps improve the efficiency and reduce network delay as it does not require any computational power. The main motive for the development of PoET was to make the mining process cost-effective and also overcome the problems faced by the PoW algorithm, which was the requirement of high computational power [3]. This consensus protocol is mainly employed in private blockchain networks. Each node in a network has an equal chance of winning as it is an impartial lottery system [23].

Proof of Space (PoSpace)

It is also termed as Proof of Capacity (PoC). This algorithm was devised by Stefan Dziembowski *et al.* in 2015 to overcome the drawbacks or problems faced in PoW. The main idea behind this algorithm is to invest the disk space instead of money or CPU computational power. Users frequently have a substantial amount of free disc space available, making them practically free to use. It is a plotting consensus mechanism [7]. Miners in PoW use processing capacity to select the best solution, whereas in PoSpace, solutions are pre-stored in memory disk drives. The miners create a plot using the storage data. Plotting is the term for this procedure. Miners can participate in the block creation process after the storage data has been plotted. A miner's capacity determines how many solutions he or she can store. As a result, miners with more storage capacity have a higher chance of creating a new block using this approach [3].

Proof of Burn (PoB)

The PoB consensus algorithm was devised by Ian Stewart as an alternative solution to PoW and PoS. This algorithm is also known as PoW [16]. It is used in combination with PoW and PoS to enable block creation and provide network security. PoB is based on the idea of burning coins to reduce energy wastage in PoW [3]. Miners are required to provide proof that they have burnt some money. Burning coins implies the transfer of coins to a particular defined address where the coins are prevented from being used by some cryptographic operations. Once the coins are burned, a transaction takes place for the burning address. The burn transaction is then checked and confirmed in order to determine a burn hash. The computed burn hash is then verified and compared with a pre-defined target. If the burn hash is found to be less than the pre-defined target, the PoB block is created [3, 7]. However, the PoB technique is still vulnerable to 51% attack. The fact that a PoB system is frequently a combination of PoW and PoS makes matters more complicated. A node having a hash power of 51% can attack the system, but it is still not clear what this power is and how it can be measured. It is suitable for Bitcoin design.

Stellar Consensus Protocol (SCP)

SCP was devised by David Mazieres [36]. SCP possesses four crucial qualities: 1. Control is decentralized. Anyone can participate, and there is no central authority dictating who must approve a consensus as it is voting-based. 2. Low latency means there is very little delay. 3. Flexible trust. Users can put their trust in whichever combination of parties they want. 4. Asymptotic security is a term used to describe the security of a system. It is dependent on digital signatures and hash that requires impossibly large computational power [16]. It is a decentralized consensus system in which a node in the blockchain network does not require to trust the whole network, but some trusted nodes are chosen by the node. A group of nodes who trust each other in a network are termed a quorum slice. A quorum is defined as a group of nodes working together to achieve a consensus, whereas a quorum slice is a subset of a quorum that adds a node in its agreement process [3, 23]. SCP consists of two protocols *i.e.*, nomination protocol and ballot protocol. Nomination protocol is the first step, which defines an agreement process based on the submitted new values, namely, candidate values at this time. Each node receives these candidate values and votes for one of them. Thus, it happens that one value wins with majority votes. The nodes in a quorum then deploy the ballot protocol after the successful execution of the nomination protocol. Ballot protocol involves a voting procedure for making a decision on whether to commit or abort the obtained values from the nomination protocol. The uncounted votes are assumed to be irrelevant. However, nodes can get trapped in the states where they are not able to make the decision of aborting or committing a value. Shifting it to a higher-valued ballot and then incorporating it into the next ballot protocol can prevent the defined situation [7, 23].

Proof of Authority (PoAuthority)

The PoAuthority consensus algorithm was developed in 2015. It is a reputation-based algorithm where the reputation of a miner acts as a stake rather than coins. A validator takes on the job of a miner and is known as an authority in

PoAuthority [7, 23]. Validator nodes are responsible for validating data. An authority with a highly good reputation gets an opportunity to be a validator. Each validator node follows a round-robin procedure for generating a block. A validator node offering an incorrect block is considered to be malicious and gains a bad reputation. Validators have complete control over the decisions of the new block [3, 23]. PoAuthority is beneficial due to high-risk tolerance (except when 51% of validators are acting fraudulently), predictable block-generation time, and high transaction rate. It also avoids resource wastage in computation, unlike PoW.

INTEGRATION OF BLOCKCHAIN WITH IOT

Blockchain technology has the capability of tracking billions of interconnected IoT devices, coordinating them to enable the processing of transactions, and eliminating failures and vulnerabilities by making a flexible ecosystem of IoT devices running on it. Blockchain provides security, immutability, transparency, and verifiability in an IoT network. Blockchain is able to maintain an immutable history of smart IoT devices. It also has the capability to enable the autonomous working of intelligent devices and avoid centralized control with the use of smart contracts. IoT also benefits blockchain technology by actively participating in the consensus mechanism. Thus, both the technologies in an integrated environment of blockchain and IoT can benefit each other in a reciprocal manner [7]. Blockchain and IoT are growing rapidly, and the integration of these allows heterogeneous IoT devices to communicate in a decentralized way and provide real-time access to data with enhanced privacy and security. The main objective of the integrated framework is to provide real-time access to data on a defined location in a defined secure format [19]. (Fig. **3**) represents a combination of blockchain and IoT to meet the privacy and security requirements of IoT.

Fig. (3). Blockchain with IoT [19].

The most commonly adopted blockchain-enabled IoT architectures are [4] fully-distributed architecture, gateway-based or hierarchical architecture, and blockchain-as-a-service architecture. Each node in a fully-distributed architecture is a full node. It means that each device in the network communicates directly with other devices to update the blockchain. Public blockchains mostly adopt this type of architecture. However, it shows limitations on computing power, storage, and battery of IoT devices to maintain the blockchain. This type of architecture shows a high risk of security attacks, such as denial-of-service attacks in heterogeneous IoT devices. The gateway-based architecture consists of super nodes *i.e.*, gateways or overlays, in order to control data access mechanism and consensus algorithm performance. Although this kind of architecture is useful in traffic reduction as well as overcoming the issues of constrained IoT devices, it is exposed to some of the security attacks *e.g.*, eclipse attack, when a communication is controlled by any malicious gateway. These malicious activities in nodes are caused by trust concentration on limited nodes. Blockchain-as-a-service architecture considers heterogeneous IoT devices to participate in the network to control the blockchain network. A third-party infrastructure performs all the processing in blockchain to reduce the IoT hardware requirements. This type of architecture is susceptible to malicious activity due to security issues of third parties.

Key Components for the Deployment of IoT-Blockchain Integrated Environment

The deployment of IoT-blockchain integrated architecture requires a focus on some key components [5] defined below.

Identify the Type of IoT Devices

The type of IoT devices can be analyzed on the basis of the type of node, heterogeneity of devices, and owner of devices. Some of the IoT devices are only responsible for sensor functionalities, with the computations only for collecting and sharing the data to a database. In this case, blockchain and edge or gateway-based IoT integrated architecture are considered ideal. However, some IoT devices have capabilities to sense data as well as computational capabilities such as encryption or data processing. In this case, only device architecture can be considered for the application. A full node fully enforces all the blockchain rules and is able to perform computation in a blockchain network. The light node references the trusted copy of the full node in blockchain *i.e.*, transactions in a blockchain network can be made without downloading the full copy of blockchain rules. The heterogeneous devices create interoperability issues in a blockchain-integrated environment, which can be resolved only by standardizing the IoT devices and implementing blockchain. Ownership of devices by different entities requires standardized policies on data.

Identify the Type of Application

IoT devices can be categorized on the basis of the type of application as consumer IoT, enterprise IoT, and industrial IoT. While designing blockchain-based IoT applications, it is required to systematically analyze the characteristics and configurations needed to assess the impact and quality of these with IoT systems.

Identify Data and Storage Requirements

IoT data stored in a blockchain network is identified to specify the type of data and its storage requirement, as it is an important component in designing the IoT-blockchain integrated environment. The data can be sensor data, the identity of a device, cryptographic keys, gateway data, data stored in the cloud, or devices. Blockchain maintains a database *i.e.*, a public ledger, which requires huge storage space. Thus, the concern here is that the huge requirement of storage must be fulfilled with the storage capacity of IoT devices, which must be enough to maintain copies of transactions. Another concern is that IoT devices produce huge amounts of data. Replication of these data to multiple nodes in an IoT-blockchain integrated environment requires huge storage capacity for nodes as well as high-speed data transfer facilities. Reducing unwanted sensor data without replicating it to multiple nodes asks for some intelligence to deal with the storage and real-time transmission issues in this integrated environment.

Identify Security Requirements

Blockchain itself is a potential security solution for IoT. However, the confidentiality of sensitive IoT data should be prevented from unauthorized access based on the sensitivity of data. Blockchain uses asymmetric cryptographic keys to provide security solutions, which require high computational effort to decipher the encrypted data. It asks for quantum-resistant cryptographic techniques for blockchain. Another concern is the reliability of data. Blockchain ensures the reliability of data that is only stored on-chain. If data generated from the IoT source is already found to be malicious, then it will also be malicious throughout the bBlockchain network.

Identify Blockchain Parameters

The identification of optimal consensus, nodes participating in consensus, and an optimal blockchain platform for implementation is necessary for the successful

deployment of a blockchain model, the decision on addition of nodes in the network, and verification of transactions by trusted nodes.

An appropriate selection of blockchain architecture highly depends on the application requirements. Gateway-based architecture is the most preferred choice for the development of different blockchain-IoT integrated architectures as it provides a mid-spectrum approach to both centralized trust and overhead [4]. (Fig. **4**) represents a generic IoT-blockchain integrated environment supporting various IoT devices and infrastructures. The heterogeneous IoT devices presented here range from simple sensor devices, *i.e.*, IoT devices communicating *via* nearby gateways only, to IoT devices having computational and processing capabilities [5]. The integrated environment includes cloud devices, edge devices, gateway devices, and a blockchain network that validates transactions [19]. A unique identification number is provided to each IoT device connected to a network for exchanging data. The gateway devices are responsible for communication purposes and ensure the connection establishment and safety of the network. Networking ensures controlled transmission of data and helps in providing the shortest route among IoT devices. Cloud devices are responsible for the storage and computation of the data. Blockchain consists of a chain of cryptographic blocks of transactions verified by IoT devices in the network. The digital ledger created by storing the data of verified blocks is publicly distributed among all the users.

Smart Contracts for IoT-Blockchain Integrated Environment

An IoT device in a blockchain network broadcasts a transaction to the address of different IoT nodes in order to operate the smart contract. Each smart contract executes on every IoT node automatically and independently in the blockchain network. Thus, a blockchain network acts as a distributed virtual machine as each independent IoT node runs as a virtual machine. Blockchain consensus protocol enforces the execution of smart contracts. Each IoT node in the network starts updating its state on the basis of outcomes received after running and executing a smart contract. This replication procedure benefits the network by providing a great potential for controlling the network in a decentralized way. Once a smart contract is deployed on a blockchain platform such as Ethereum, it automatically runs the smart contract program every time it gets triggered. The IoT node that initiates the execution of the smart contract pays an exceptional amount known as "Gas" for performing the program functions [2]. Gas ensures that the smart contract is obliged by the blockchain network. Gas can be scaled on the basis of the required computational power for performing the contract functions. A smart contract runs only when a transaction calls for it. However, a smart contract can call another one, which, in turn, may call another contract, and so on. Smart contracts can neither be run in the background nor be executed in parallel. Smart contracts are turning into complete systems that can solve any computational problem. Theyalso have the capability to add automation to strengthen the blockchain. Smart contracts are also responsible for managing and recording all IoT interactions to provide secure and reliable processing tools that result in trusted actions. Thus, the smart contract can be surely used to model intelligence-supported IoT applications [2]. Smart contracts basically describe the application logic, and whenever any transaction calls for a particular smart contract, the connected IoT devices send their measurements and data. Moreover, if any flaw exists in the smart contract, it remains in it with no possibility of an update [4]. A logic for disabling the smart contract to avoid the identified bugs may be designed to provide flexibility in the development phase. Although the malicious smart contract still remains in the blockchain network, the logic prevents it from doing any malicious operation.

Blockchain-enabled Smart IoT Applications

This section illustrates various applications for blockchain-enabled smart IoT, such as smart homes, smart transport, smart electronic voting, smart supply chain management, smart healthcare, and smart grid.

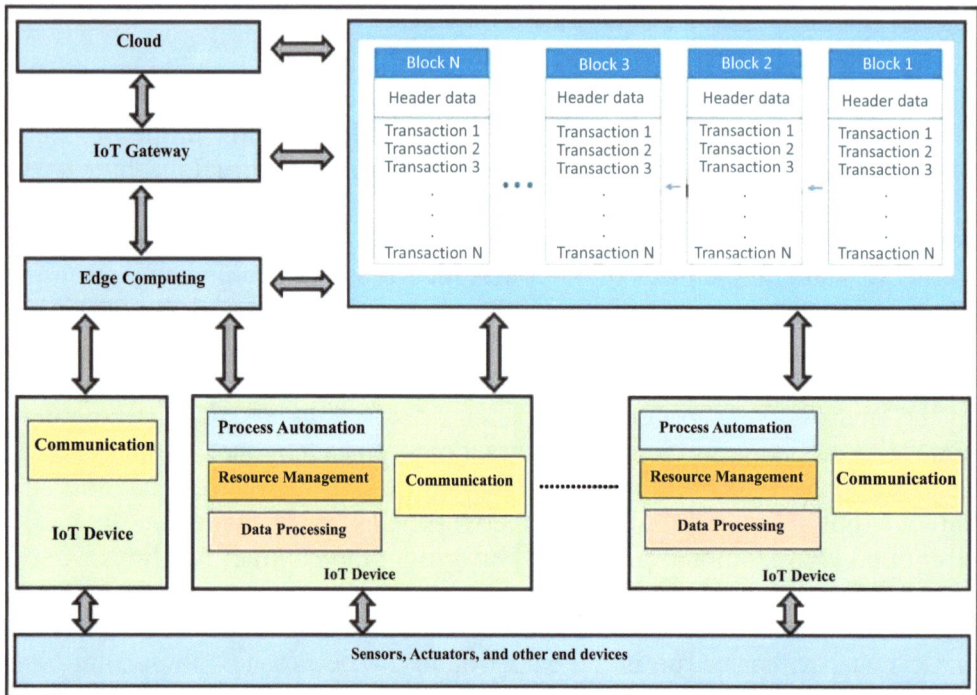

Fig. (4). A generic IoT-blockchain integrated environment [5].

Smart Home

It refers to the sophisticated utilization of various modern technologies such as WSNs, ubiquitous computing, and information and communication technology (ICT)in order to achieve automated control and management of the environment of a home, such as lights, fire alarms, climate, and different entertainment devices. A smart home may also consist of emergency alarms, a security system to detect intrusions, and access control for prevention from cyber-physical threats [7]. A smart home is a revolutionary idea that promises to provide domestic comfort and a better quality of life to enhance living standards by improving energy efficiency, Quality of Service, reliability, safety, and security in a home environment. However, the risk of privacy leakage is possible in a smart home environment as the interconnected IoT devices interact with each other as well as with the local server *via* a local network of home and with remote servers *via* home gateway. Blockchain technology can be considered a promising solution for mitigating this network-level security issue of smart home systems in which the smart contracts ensure secure and trustful communication in an IoT-Blockchain integrated environment [22].

Smart Transport

A smart transport system comprises various advanced computing technologies such as WSNs, modern management ideas to deal with electronic devices, and traffic control techniques for making the transportation system fast, efficient, connected, convenient, economical, profitable, and safe. It involves various intelligent IoT devices such as traffic signal control devices, integrated speed-detection camera systems, automatic recognition of vehicle number plates, real-time traffic monitoring CCTV systems, and management of automated ticket systems. The byzantine fault tolerance characteristics of blockchain can be used in smart transport systems for solving the issue of collaboration and communication in automobiles, the roadside interconnected devices and infrastructures, and the smartphones of pedestrians in a completely distributed way. The double spending resistance characteristics of blockchain can be used in decentralized financial transactions, which helps establish an in-built financial environment for a smart transaction system [22]. In the ride-sharing transport environment, the use of blockchain technology creates a P2P environment that can disrupt the monopoly of corporate-based commercialized transport services such as Ola, Uber, Careem, and Lyft, leading to a more distributed economy.

Smart Electronic Voting

Voting can be defined as a governance process for the election of a representative democratically at the national level, state level, or city level. The reliability of the paper-based voting process totally depends upon the honesty of government officials who conduct the polling. Ballot-based voting has some disadvantages, such as inconsistency, high cost, time-intensive, spurious vote tallying, low voter turnout, and insertion of bogus ballot papers. E-voting or electronic voting procedure allows the voters to vote authentically with the use of biometrics through software platforms. Although e-voting is an effective and authenticated voting process, this approach is highly vulnerable to different cyber-attacks such as tampering attacks at both the user and system level. Blockchain-enabled e-voting is an e-voting procedure in which a wallet with a private key is assigned to each voter for authentication during the polling [22]. A coin is credited to the wallet during each polling that can be used only once in order to cast a vote for a favorable candidate. It can be designed as a system protocol to validate voters who remain anonymous during the final count. Blockchain-based e-voting system is considered tamper-proof on the basis of transparency and immutability characteristics. It is a fast-paced, secure, and transparent counting and an accountability system for voting.

Smart Supply Chain Management

The supply chain can be described as a collaborative system of more than two organizations that are responsible for controlling the commodity flows, knowledge, utilities, and economy from the source entity to the consumer. Supply chain management enhances every supply chain function, from inventory forecasting to demand and supply management. It is required to design a transparent, traceable, and secure supply chain management technique through IoT devices, which is capable of accommodating all the information related to the manufacturing of products along with traceability of everything from plant to consumer. Blockchain technology is an effective solution for supply chain management systems that provides a facility for recording all the specific details of every product during its lifecycle at a single shared distributed ledger in a secured manner, averting entry of bogus products in the market and sharing the information among different entities for optimizing the decision-making procedure. Only authorized respective entities are able to access the relevant information [16, 22].

Smart Healthcare

The healthcare industry is an aggregated and integrated environment of various sectors within the economic system where the information related to the medical history of patients, as well as diagnosis and treatment reports, is required to be shared among different authorized entities. A distributed architecture of blockchain technology is an effective solution for shared medical data management, identity management, transmission control, granting access to authorized entities, and handling security and privacy issues [16]. Various blockchain-intended access control mechanisms can be designed using smart contracts in order to tackle access to information, validation of identities, and privacy concerns. Blockchain-based electronic health records (EHRs) enable real-time storage and updating of each patient's health data based on the identities assigned to them [18, 22]. Blockchain technology is also an effective technique for the management of medical supply chains from manufacturers (factories) to distributors (pharmaceutical stores), in which the provenances of medical products are examined for the detection and prevention of counterfeiting of medicines [22]. Moreover, a blockchain-based supply chain also enables fast, transparent, and cost-efficient delivery of medical products, enhanced traceability of medical products, improved coordination between partners, and better access control to financing.

Smart Grid

A smart grid can be defined as a modern and improvised power grid with the aim of achieving optimized efficiency and reliability. It comprises various smart devices such as sensors, meters, electric appliances, transmission lines, and other intelligent devices that are responsible for producing and distributing electricity with automated control. The primary concern of the smart grid is to enhance traditional electricity distribution systems in order to meet various demands of power supply at an affordable cost. These demands include sufficient power supply, techniques to prevent power loss, improved grid reliability, sustainability, and efficient execution of operations [22]. Low power loss in transmission within the smart grid is due to the generation of power for local consumption. Blockchain helps provide decentralization in a smart grid network by integrating this infrastructure of energy trading in a P2P fashion.

Benefits

Blockchain is an emerging technology that provides necessary solutions in order to overcome the IoT challenges. The growing interest in exploring blockchain-based IoT environments has illustrated some potential benefits of blockchain-IoT integration as described below.

Decentralized and Distributed Framework

The decentralized and distributed features of blockchain technology ensure the removal of a single point of failure in the network [2, 4, 21]. Data is stored in a distributed manner and is protected against failures and tampering of IoT devices.

This type of integrated environment helps in improving scalability and preventing network bottlenecks [2, 4].

Automation and Resource Utilization

Blockchain communication enables automated and direct communication among IoT devices with the use of smart contracts [21]. Smart contracts are also used to facilitate resource utilization by running an algorithm that manages resources and automates payments on completion of requested services [4]. Smart contracts can

also be used in software and hardware updates of IoT devices, upgrading services, initializing requests for repairs, and changing the ownership of IoT devices. Smart contracts also support authenticating IoT devices with the help of specific defined rules associated with their logic. Thus, blockchain helps in empowering the next-generation IoT applications by enabling autonomous services [4, 21].

Tamper-proof Recording and Reliability

The hash linking of blocks in a blockchain network and distributed consensus mechanism ensures the tamper-proof recording of transactions [2]. This creates a trustworthy and reliable environment by providing an immutable transaction consisting of communication history and acquisition of data in a secure way for IoT devices [2, 21].

Data Privacy and Security

The asymmetric encryption technique used in blockchain technology helps store the encrypted IoT data in the form of transactions and validate them using smart contracts. Thus, blockchain communications, as well as IoT data, are securely stored in the form of encrypted and digitally signed transactions [4, 17, 21]. On the other hand, the asymmetric encryption technique ensures that only the authorized IoT nodes *i.e.*, the IoT nodes having private keys, are allowed for data access [2, 4]. This authentication ensures the privacy of IoT data in a blockchain-IoT integrated environment [19].

Transparency

Blockchain ensures the non-tampering or non-removal of the transactions. The timestamped transactions are transparent and traceable to all the participants in a blockchain network in which all participants are authorized to verify each recorded transaction [2, 17].

Challenges

Blockchain technology is generally developed for powerful computers in the paradigm of the internet, and this is not the case with IoT systems. The various challenges associated with the IoT-blockchain integrated environments are defined below.

Resource Constraints

Various consensus algorithms defined in blockchain technology require huge computational power and consume high energy and storage, which is not suitable for low-power IoT devices [20]. The IoT devices in the blockchain network generate huge amounts of real-time bulky data, which makes it inefficient for storing the whole blockchain [4, 21]. IoT devices suffer from very weak network connections, making the network unstable. However, blockchain is designed assuming a stable network connection, which makes the integration of these two technologies infeasible [4].

Scalability

Blockchain technology is not effectively applicable to large-scale IoT applications due to its scalability issue. IoT devices generate huge amounts of real-time data, which demands high storage capacity [19]. Blockchain is able to process a few transactions per second and hence is considered not suitable for storing such a huge amount of data [4, 21]. Although data centralization can be an effective approach to achieving the scalability of IoT, it becomes a great challenge for a decentralized blockchain architecture [21].

Heterogeneity

The heterogeneous IoT devices require some security mechanism for the distribution of resources to end users, which needs intelligence and resources for security purposes [21]. Resource-constrained devices show difficulty in managing the public/private keys used for secure distribution [4].

Data Security

Blockchain has the vulnerability of hijacking the blockchain data by any malicious IoT node for the purpose of delayed broadcasting of blocks [4]. A malicious IoT device can give rise to several security breaches, such as double-spending, jamming, eavesdropping, selfish mining, denial-of-service, and other attacks [20, 21].

Latency

In a blockchain network, the encryption algorithms running for each transaction demand high processing time [21]. Blockchain technology also reduces the responsiveness of the network when an IoT node that requests data is required to wait to reach a decision in a consensus process [20].

CONCLUSION

Blockchain technology is a distributed, decentralized, immutable, transparent, and secure platform thathas proven its promising role in various cryptocurrency applications. The potential characteristics of blockchain technology make it a significant and suitable candidate for integrating it with IoT systems. The integration of these two great technologies would yield potential benefits for next-generation applications by incorporating intelligence into them in order to provide autonomous behavior. This paper presents a detailed systematic study on the integration of IoT systems and blockchain technology as a promising solution to overcome the issues associated with the IoT environment. Firstly, a brief description of smart IoT is presented, followed by a detailed study on blockchain technology, its working, types, platforms, and consensus algorithms. An analysis of the integration of blockchain with IoT and the deployment of an integrated environment through smart contract is then illustrated in order to define its scope of application in smart environments. The potential benefits and challenges of the blockchain-IoT integrated environment are also described with the aim of clearing future research directions.

ACKNOWLEDGEMENTS

The authors would like to thank all the anonymous reviewers and editors for considering the work.

REFERENCES

[1]   E. Bandara, D. Tosh, P. Foytik, S. Shetty, N. Ranasinghe, and K. De Zoysa, "Tikiri - Towards a lightweight blockchain for IoT", In: *Future Generation Computer Systems* vol. 119. , 2021, pp. 154-165.
[http://dx.doi.org/10.1016/j.future.2021.02.006]

[2]   A.A. Sadawi, M.S. Hassan, and M. Ndiaye, "A Survey on the Integration of Blockchain With IoT to Enhance Performance and Eliminate Challenges", *IEEE Access,* vol. 9, pp. 54478-54497, 2021.
[http://dx.doi.org/10.1109/ACCESS.2021.3070555]

[3]   M. Salimitari, M. Chatterjee, Y. Fallah, "A Survey on Consensus Methods in Blockchain for Resource-constrained IoT Networks", In: *Internet of Things*, vol. 11, p. 100212, 2020.,
[http://dx.doi.org/10.36227/techrxiv.12152142]

[4]   V. Dedeoglu, R. Jurdak, G.D. Putra, A. Dorri, and S.S. Kanhere, "A trust architecture for blockchain in IoT", In: *MobiQuitous '19: Proceedings of the 16th EAI International Conference on Mobile and Ubiquitous Systems: Computing, Networking and Services* Association for Computing Machinery (ACM): United States of America, 2021, pp. 190-199.

[5]   D. Pavithran, K. Shaalan, J.N. Al-Karaki, and A. Gawanmeh, "Towards building a blockchain framework for IoT", *Cluster Comput.,* vol. 23, no. 3, pp. 2089-2103, 2020.
[http://dx.doi.org/10.1007/s10586-020-03059-5]

[6]   R. Thakore, R. Vaghashiya, C. Patel, and N. Doshi, "Blockchain - based IoT: A Survey", *Procedia Computer Science,* vol. 155, pp. 704-709, 2019. ISSN 1877-0509.
[http://dx.doi.org/10.1016/j.procs.2019.08.101]

[7]   A. Panarello, N. Tapas, G. Merlino, F. Longo, and A. Puliafito, "Blockchain and IoT Integration: A Systematic Survey", *Sensors,* vol. 18, no. 8, p. 2575, 2018.
[http://dx.doi.org/10.3390/s18082575] [PMID: 30082633]

[8]   M. H. Miraz, "Blockchain of Things (BCoT): The Fusion of Blockchain and IoT Technologies," in *Advanced Applications of Blockchain Technology*, S. Kim and G. Deka, Eds. Singapore: Springer, 2019, pp. 141–159.
[http://dx.doi.org/10.2139/ssrn.3464085]

[9]   H. F. Atlam and G. B. Wills, "Technical aspects of blockchain and IoT," in *Advances in Computers*, vol. 115, S. Kim, G. C. Deka, and P. Zhang, Eds. Academic Press, 2019, pp. 1–39.

[10]   N. Raghav, N. Andola, S. Venkatesan, and S. Verma, "PoEWAL: A lightweight consensus mechanism for blockchain in IoT", In: *Pervasive and Mobile Computing* , vol. 69, no. 9, p. 101291, 2020.,
[http://dx.doi.org/10.1016/j.pmcj.2020.101291]

[11]   A. Sheth, "Internet of Things to Smart IoT Through Semantic, Cognitive, and Perceptual Computing", *IEEE Intell. Syst.,* vol. 31, no. 2, pp. 108-112, 2016.

[http://dx.doi.org/10.1109/MIS.2016.34]

[12]   A. Gyrard, P. Patel, A. Sheth, and M. Serrano, "Building the Web of Knowledge with Smart IoT Applications", *IEEE Intell. Syst.,* vol. 31, no. 5, pp. 83-88, 2016. Available from: https://corescholar.libraries.wright.edu/knoesis/1123
[http://dx.doi.org/10.1109/MIS.2016.81]

[13]   J. Zheng, D. Simplot-Ryl, C. Bisdikian, and H. Mouftah, "The internet of things [Guest Editorial]", *IEEE Commun. Mag.,* vol. 49, no. 11, pp. 30-31, 2011.
[http://dx.doi.org/10.1109/MCOM.2011.6069706]

[14]   R.D. Sriram, and A. Sheth, "Internet of Things Perspectives", *IT Prof.,* vol. 17, no. 3, pp. 60-63, 2015.
[http://dx.doi.org/10.1109/MITP.2015.43]

[15]   S. Madakam, "Internet of Things: Smart Things", *International Journal of Future Computer and Communication,* vol. 4, no. 4, pp. 250-253, 2015.
[http://dx.doi.org/10.7763/IJFCC.2015.V4.395]

[16]   T. Ali Syed, A. Alzahrani, S. Jan, M.S. Siddiqui, A. Nadeem, and T. Alghamdi, "A Comparative Analysis of Blockchain Architecture and its Applications: Problems and Recommendations", *IEEE Access,* vol. 7, pp. 176838-176869, 2019.
[http://dx.doi.org/10.1109/ACCESS.2019.2957660]

[17]   M. Niranjanamurthy, B.N. Nithya, and S. Jagannatha, "Analysis of Blockchain technology: pros, cons and SWOT", *Cluster Comput.,* vol. 22, no. S6, pp. 14743-14757, 2019.
[http://dx.doi.org/10.1007/s10586-018-2387-5]

[18]   A. Hasselgren, K. Kralevska, D. Gligoroski, S.A. Pedersen, and A. Faxvaag, "Blockchain in healthcare and health sciences—A scoping review", In: *International Journal of Medical Informatics* vol. 134. , 2020..
[http://dx.doi.org/10.1016/j.ijmedinf.2019.104040]

[19]   T. Alam, "Blockchain and its role in the Internet of Things (IoT)," International Journal of Scientific Research in Computer Science, Engineering and Information Technology, vol. 5, no. 1, pp. 151–157, 2019.
[http://dx.doi.org/10.32628/CSEIT195137]

[20]   G. S. Ramachandran and B. Krishnamachari, "Blockchain for the IoT: Opportunities and Challenges," arXiv preprint, arXiv:1805.02818, May 2018.
[http://dx.doi.org/10.48550/arXiv.1805.02818]

[21]   M.R. Raza, A. Varol, and W. Hussain, "Blockchain-based IoT: An Overview", *9th International Symposium on Digital Forensics and Security (ISDFS),* pp. 1-6, 2021.
[http://dx.doi.org/10.1109/ISDFS52919.2021.9486360]

[22]   U. Majeed, L.U. Khan, I. Yaqoob, S.M.A. Kazmi, K. Salah, and C.S. Hong, "Blockchain for IoT-based smart cities: Recent advances, requirements, and future challenges", In: *Journal of Network and Computer Applications* vol. 181. , 2021, no. 103007, pp. 1084-8045.
[http://dx.doi.org/10.1016/j.jnca.2021.103007]

[23]   N. Singh, and A.K. Das, "Blockchain of Medical Things: Security Challenges and Applications", In: *Advances in Data-driven Computing and Intelligent Systems. Lecture Notes in Networks and Systems.,* S. Das, S. Saha, C.A. Coello Coello, J.C. Bansal, Eds., vol. 653. Springer: Singapore, 2023..
[http://dx.doi.org/10.1007/978-981-99-0981-0_35]

Role of Blockchain in Today's Financial Growth Using IoT

Milan Kumar Dholey[1], **Priya Saha**[2,*] and **Ananya Ganguly**[3]

[1] *Department of Computer Science and Engineering, GITAM (Deemed to be University), Visakhapatnam, Andhra Pradesh, India*

[2] *Department of Computer Science and Engineering, ITER, Siksha 'Ó' Anusandhan (Deemed to be University), Bhubaneswar, Odisha, India*

[3] *Department of Computer Science, Acharya Jagadish Chanda Bose College, Kolkata, West Bengal, India*

Abstract: Blockchain technology, with its globalized features like a decentralized consensus and tamper-proof immutability, expands the liberty of miners through smart contracts to participate in the Blockchain network. The method of decentralized consensus creation, which involves all relevant alterations in sequence allocation of the informational environment, is a key aspect we will analyze in this survey. Blockchain's redesign of the financial domain protects against the rivalry of several crypto-currencies from various applications in highly demanding areas. It enhances the efficiency and security of today's high-demanding cryptocurrencies. But perhaps most importantly, blockchain plays a vital role in the financial industry, providing a sense of security and stability by maintaining the market's equilibrium and improving economic outcomes. Anti-trust policy inference embattles several blockchain applications, like the extrication of consensus records from a public perspective.

Keywords: Blockchain, Bitcoin, Decentralized, Finance, Cryptocurrencies, Currency, Peer-to-Peer.

INTRODUCTION

Blockchain was first introduced in 2008 by Satoshi Nakamoto [1]. He introduced an electronic-based cryptocurrency named Bitcoin based on the decentralized peer-to-peer construction that creates trust and undoes any problem between customers. The speakers at the Bitcoin Conference in Miami, USA, in January 2015 emphasized the significant advantages of blockchain technology and broadened discussions on the in-depth exploration of blockchain and its diverse

* **Corresponding author Priya Saha:** Department of Computer Science and Engineering, ITER, Siksha 'Ó' Anusandhan (Deemed to be University), Bhubaneswar, Odisha, India; E-mail: moutusipriya92@gmail.com

H.S. Hota, Dinesh K. Sharma, Ayan Kumar Das & Ditipriya Sinha (Eds.)

applications. The conference presented a three-phase development framework for blockchain, with the first phase, Blockchain 1.0, concentrating on e-cash and employing encryption methods linked to Bitcoin. Blockchain 2.0 emphasizes deploying advanced smart contracts in financial and economic markets. This technology includes a variety of instruments such as bonds, stocks, loans, futures, mortgages, intellectual property rights, and numerous other types of agreements. Some global public services are available at the Blockchain 3.0 stage, a fully pioneering claim stage. Thus, blockchain has enormous prospects for every step of our daily lives, *i.e.*, everywhere we use Blockchain. Researchers and experts say that in the future, blockchain will help the financial industry with several successful operations for the interest of the whole society and will be a new Internet revolution. Blockchain will bring changes and open new research directions for researchers. In the global financial system, billions of people use different financial techniques daily. Although this creates the most significant problem due to troublesome paperwork and the cost of regulation acquiescence, it also raises the cost of fees, reducing convenience charges and resulting in the rise of crime-related fraud. The inference is that economically, financial establishments will eventually shift the encumbrance to customers. An appropriate financial system belongs almost entirely to trusted intermediate third parties that can convey transactions of financial claims from one party to another with a charge or at no cost. Licensees are authorized banks; third parties may include other authorized financial institutions. Many developing countries include these third parties, which may be merchant banks, money-deposit banks, progress banks, insurance firms, and individuals. Having more than one monetary institution is a way to build a contest to decrease the price of lending and financial transactions. Many proposals and policy suggestions have tried to minimize the cost of financial transactions. The decrease in financial intermediation costs enabled by blockchain technology removes the need for third-party participation in the mediation process. While earlier studies have highlighted advantages concerning demand and delivery challenges in the financial sector's adoption of blockchain, they have not tackled the regulatory issues that need clarification. This paper is a tribute to the innovation of the financial market.

This book chapter proves the need for improvement in finance and highlights several applications that promote the future of blockchain in the financial domain. Section 2 discusses the background and general fundamental concepts of blockchain technology. In Section 3, we have a brief discussion about decentralized finance. Section 4 provides an understanding of different business models in decentralized finance and their perspectives on blockchain. Section 5 highlights the growth of blockchain in various financial areas along with other crypto-currencies. This article also discusses the future of cryptocurrencies in

Section 6, followed by the limitations of cryptocurrencies in Section 7 and the future scope and conclusion of this analysis.

PRELIMINARY OF BLOCKCHAIN TECHNOLOGY

This section discusses the fundamentals of blockchain and the different topics related to blockchain. This document also introduces the use of consensus algorithms in several ways.

Concept of Blockchain

Blockchain is a distributed, decentralized, publicly accessible ledger in digital mode where transactions are stored chronologically. Records of actions in a blockchain system are not centralized or guarded by any user. People popularly use blockchain in cryptocurrency, such as Bitcoin, in the financial industry. Chronologically, transactions made by blockchains are stored publicly. Any number of people around the globe can view these transaction records and add any new data to the blockchain. Now, there are two types of blockchains: permission-based and permissionless. After gaining access rights to add new information to the blockchain network, users may include new blocks of information in it. Some blockchains are easy to use as they do not need permission to add new blocks to the existing blockchain system. In distributed computing architecture, the information is clubbed into several immutable blocks, keeping all of the records of transactions. Integrating a single block into the blockchain network is achievable. Each block comprises three elements: i) Data relevant to that block, ii) a mathematical algorithm that verifies and extends the sequence from the previous block, and iii) the value linked to the specific block, which enhances the characteristics of blockchain as a distributed database. Particular user interactions with the ledger (transactions) protection are possible by several cryptographic measures tenable by several protocols [5, 6].

The fundamental component of blockchain is a block. Blocks serve as containers for information, encompassing a hash of the newly added block as well as the hash of the preceding block. The distributed blockchain permanently records all the data. People popularly use blockchain in cryptocurrency, such as Bitcoin, in the financial industry.

Immutable

In the case of blockchain, all the transactions are generally written or recorded in a way that is nonerasable, or it is nearly impracticable to remove or rollback; all the exchanges of information or blocks are recorded subsequently in a manner that no one can change, delete, or hide anything [7]. If any changes occur, the hash value also changes, generating another block entirely. Blockchain is defined as an immutable ledger if anything is written in a block that cannot be changed or deleted, though several attacks make it false (Figs. **1** and **2**).

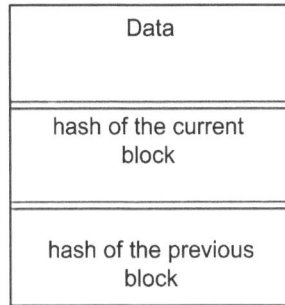

Fig. (1). Structure of blockchain.

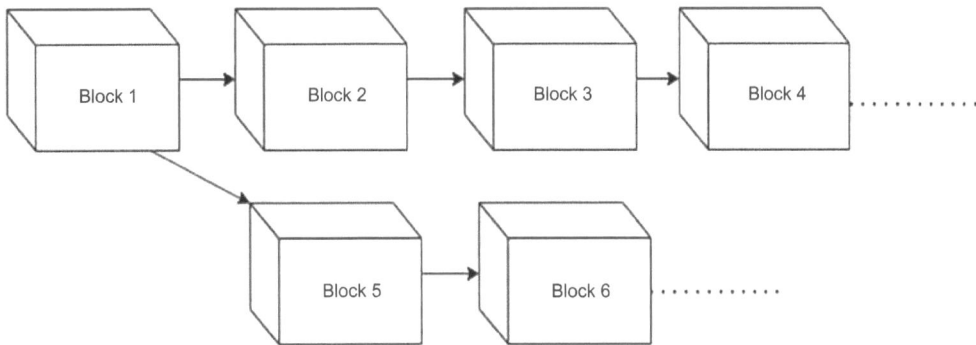

Fig. (2). Transaction's architecture of block.

Mining Pool

A mining pool is a mechanism of grouping computational resources by miners to route the blockchain network. The system is generally used to allocate rewards somewhat based on the amount of work contributed, which helps determine the hash of a block. It recognizes valid partial proofs of work and labels them as "share" members. It finds valid partial proof-of-work and awards them as "share" members. A mining pool solves slower pool generation and frees the resources to receive a constant reward [9 - 11].

Consensus

In a cryptographic competition, the consensus algorithm helps to identify the following block to add to the blockchain system. It is a mathematical expression driving the nodes against the rest of the blocks in blockchain. Any third-party intervention is strictly prohibited as blockchain is a decentralized system. A decentralized mechanism maintains data consistency and reliability. Blockchain [12] involves a distributed consensus method. Several blockchain consensus mechanisms [13] use PoI (Proof-of-Importance), PoS (Proof-of-Stake), DPoS (Delegated Proof-of-Stake), PBFT (Practical Byzantine Fault Tolerance), and PoW (Proof-of-Work). Other consensus mechanisms, such as PoB (Proof-o--Bandwidth) [14], PoI (Proof-of-Importance), PoET (Proof-of-Elapsed Time) [15], PoA (Proof-of-Authority) [16, 17], PoSpace, MBH (Minimum Block Hash), MoT (Measure of Trust), etc., are several uses of different blockchain systems. PoW mechanism is heavily used in the finance industry by Bitcoin and Ethereum. Ethereum uses the PoA mechanism to grant access authority. There are so many consensus mechanisms, but few are very useful in different areas of blockchain. They have some advantages and disadvantages. A brief discussion of this is given here in tabular format (Table **1**).

Table 1. Advantages and disadvantages of individual algorithm.

Consensus Protocols	Advantage	Disadvantages
PoW (Proof of Work)	1. Stable, Safe. 2. High degree of decentralization in open system circuit of blockchain.	1. Low performance involving poor scalability 2. Causing hardware equipment waste
PoS (Proof of Stake)	1. Less energy 2. The degree of decentralization is high in the closed circuit of blockchain.	1. Complex implementation process 2. Security contravene
DPoS (Delegated Proof of Stake)	1. High performance 2 Less energy 3. Finality	1 . The degree of decentralization is high in the closed circuit of blockchain.
PBFT (Practical Byzantine Fault Tolerance)	1. High security 2. Finality 3. Higher performance	1. The degree of decentralization is high in the closed circuit of blockchain.

Peer-to-Peer Architecture

In this type of network, more than one user simultaneously utilizes and provides the foundation of the network. Although all nodes are equal, they can perform different roles within the blockchain ecosystem, like a miner or a "full node" [19]. The entire blockchain resides over a single device that connects the network, making it immutable. We may conclude that as long as the single node with a copy of a blockchain exists, all transactions made over the network will remain the same and intact. It makes it possible to rebuild the network. In Fig. (**3**), a direct connection connects all nodes without requiring any server or central connection. The figure shows that all nodes (maybe computer or mobile) share their data without central control.

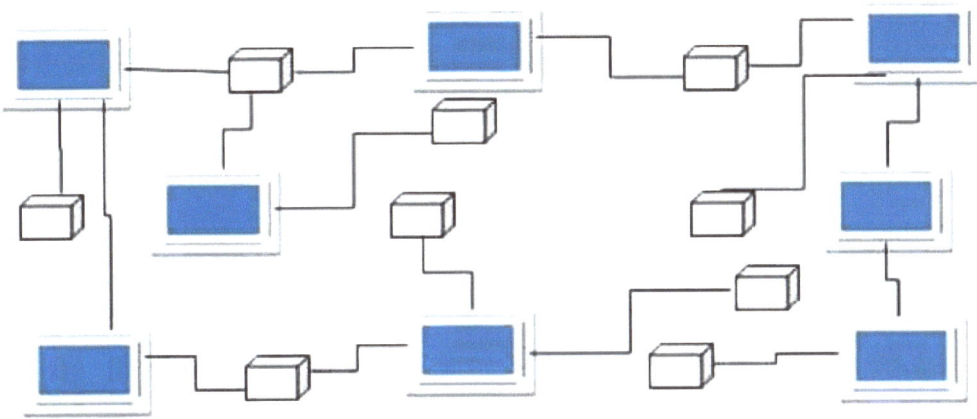

Fig. (3). Peer-to-Peer Architecture.

Advantages of Blockchain

Prioritization of transparency in blockchain as a distributed ledger facilitates information sharing among all nodes. Only after verification of the new block can it be added to the chain. Violation of any third-party intermediation is the most promising prospect for attracting major industries and academics. The building of trust comprises several factors, which are as follows:

- **Transparency:** The boon of intriguing technology makes it possible for every participant of blockchain to view the transaction details. However, a restriction improves transparency so no one can change it. Blockchain anonymity enhances the transparency of transactions.
- **Lower Transactional Costs:**Peer-to-peer transactions, *i.e.*, B2B (Business-to-Business), strictly prohibit the intervention of intermediaries. As there is no intermediary, it is possible to reduce transactional costs over other technologies [6, 23].
- **Make Transaction Faster:**Any other transaction method takes a separate time. However, being a decentralized system, no extra time is needed. When adding a block, all nodes receive the information; hence, the network does not add transaction time to make any transaction. It minimizes transaction time and makes transactions faster [18, 20].
- **Distributed and Decentralized:** Each transaction uses its proof of work and proof of validity for each transaction over the network [6, 21, 23]. As per the property of blockchain, there is no central control, and it is digitally accessible to

all participants. Little change made by any unwanted person will flourish in the entire network, leading to understanding the intruders' attacks on the network.

- **Protected Cryptography**: Blockchain measures authenticity and avoidance of duplicity of data. Maximum trust verification, also known as consensus of the block [23, 24], depends upon the adjacent block to complete the cryptographic parameter checking. A new block is included in the existing system when someone completes it.

Classification of Blockchain According to Requirement

To decrease the scheming and deceitful activities and attain transparency and traceability for every transaction in the system [24], one has to ensure immutability. Only then can the security levels of the blockchain be completed.

Public Blockchain

Without any restriction permission, the public blockchain works very well. All transactions in public blockchain rely on a proof-of-work consensus algorithm. Participants can access the blocks to include new information [24, 25] and participate in the public blockchain without restrictions, making it the most popular.

Private Blockchain

A business strategy to keep information confidential, private blockchain is the best solution. Accessing permission is only given to the central authority, and read-only permissions are given to [25, 26] specified and limited viewers to restrict the access. It is beneficial for growing the internal business strategy.

- **Federated or Consortium Blockchain:** People or organizations mainly control it [25, 26]. There is no possibility for others not participating in the network to access it complimentary. Only after satisfying the verification condition is viewing or accessing the transaction possible.
- **Hybrid Blockchain:** The best attractive characteristics of the three blockchains produce a new mixture. Hybrid blockchain [24, 26] shows better results regarding security to prevent malicious attacks. It allows us to distinguish the data by keeping some information private and some parts open to the public. The comparison of a centralized blockchain with a decentralized network is much more effective in different ways. They do not make any transactions inside their network of community or private nodes; the network can transfer and drift the hash (with or without payload) entirely in a decentralized blockchain like Bitcoin.

- Another essential discussion is about smart contracts, without which blockchain cannot adequately explain. Smart contracts are predefined programs mainly used to enforce negotiation and facilitate the validity of an agreement (contract). The term agreement is a code to ensure a transaction underlying any blockchain platform.

Understanding How Blockchain Works

Now, there are several reasons and multiple features by which we can understand the working procedures of blockchain. Below, we explain the five principles that promote the working process underlying blockchain technology.

- **Distributed Database:** Blockchain solely provides access to each participant of the network. The distributive nature also ensures that no single user will have complete control over the blockchain. Each participant can authenticate and verify transaction details between investors without a mediator.
- **Peer-to-Peer Transmission:** Rather than passing any information to a particular node, it transmits it in the whole networking system. Every node does the same and forwards to all other participating nodes, making it more user-friendly.
- **Transparency with Pseudonymity:** A secured unique alphanumeric address of 30-plus characters verifies each transaction over the system. Each user can see transaction details and their associated value to maintain transparency. The users can keep the property of pseudonymity by not disclosing their identity. Hence, it is optional that users remain anonymous or give their identity to other participating users.
- **Irreversibility of Records:** When a newborn block encounters the existing sequence modification in the public ledger. Successful transactions in the chain ensure that no alteration is possible by any fraudulent person. It will affect the entire chain as all nodes are interlinked. Computational algorithms help store information in a database chronologically and permanently. Any changes made over the system are not allowed once a transaction ends, and it is known to all participating blocks.
- **Computational Logic:** The idea of introducing a distributed ledger aims to support existing computational logic, and as needed, it can be programmed and modified. It eliminates human errors and also consumes valuable time for computation. It provides enthusiasm for building new algorithms and rules triggered by default transactions between the participating nodes. Now, our concern is the utility of blockchain in finance, and here, this finance is decentralized. In the following season, we will discuss the concept of decentralized finance.

BASICS OF IOT TECHNOLOGY

In our daily lives, we use laptops, smartwatches, and handheld embedded devices that rely on the Internet of Things (IoT), which communicates with one another *via* the Internet. The connected devices are sensor-based and have the processing ability to sense the environment. Connected IoT devices decide intelligently and independently to exchange data with other nodes or systems connected over the communication network. The IIoT (Industrial IoT) relies heavily on the Internet of Things (IoT) for everything from energy management to manufacturing goods. Dealing with data collection, analysis, and potentiality checking data from connected devices provides economic benefits. Process control optimizes to achieve automation. Blockchain-based IoT works magnificently and makes cloud computing systems more real-time-centric. Exponential growth in industry and at the academic level is now possible for the IoT platform. However, the adoption of blockchain technology in IoT devices, privacy leakage, and system security have become significant concerns. Current security is vulnerable to resource constraints in the IIoT industry due to the inappropriate use of decentralized topology. As a result, blockchain proposed peer-to-peer network communication using a distributed approach. Billions of connected IoT devices will be able to see all the data exchange and save information, including any updates made over the distributed ledger to keep it transparent. In this way, blockchain establishes a tight connection between customers and business partners.

CONCEPT OF DECENTRALIZED FINANCE

Blockchain technology comes first in the market under decentralized finance or DeFi. To date, the most promising part of blockchain is DeFi. Defi encourages the concept of distributed decentralized networks and open-sourced software for different types of products to ensure financial services. To improve several financial DApps that will work transparently on permission-less blockchain, different peer-to-peer (P2P) protocols are also being developed by using the concept of a decentralized finance system.

Currently, the three most significant functions of DeFi are:

- Creating pecuniary banking services to vacillate the finance system more efficiently.
- Providing P2P or pooled lending platforms to ensure the atomicity of each transaction made by each node.
- Enabling advanced financial machinery such as tokenization platforms, DEX, derivatives, and prediction markets.

Different types of DeFi services are available among the three fields mentioned above. Funding protocols, payment protocols of subscription, software development tools, index construction, and data analysis applications are the most commonly used examples. Compared with traditional financial services, smart contracts make hassle-free transactions possible. It also makes the products and deploys financial applications more secure and less complex. To summarize, the traditional financial system has changed with the introduction of the DeFi movement. A decentralized open-source environment removes the need for intercessors, cuts average costs, and significantly improves security measures.

Decentralization

The centralized finance system of different financial institutions works as an intervening medium, levitating high charges to complete a single transaction [27]. To reduce transaction costs and enhance financial transactions smoothly, intercessors work efficiently. Different renowned centralized financial foundations, like Square, PayPal, and Bank of America have risen to supremacy and misused market power and profits. As a key intercessor, financial institutions try to earn money in a disproportionate ratio to dominate economic activities. However, if the decentralized system makes financial transactions, it is not dependent on any monetary institution and works on distributed peer-to-peer networks.

Innovativeness

The decentralized mode of finance encourages permission-less, permission-based, and combined innovation of the finance economy. A centralized platform may improve modernization and trialing, but its policy makes owners often ask for organizing control and can withdraw access to apply governance control [28]. If platform owners make any unilateral changes, obviously, the negotiator frequently changes emotionally third-party developers' willingness to invest in any innovation. In contrast, a decentralized platform does not require any control that makes open access, improving permissionless innovation. Developers can freely experiment without asking for any prior permission [29]. Permissionless innovation facilities decentralized platforms sanction developers by assuring the hassle-free right of entry, letting inventors make decentralized economics in many unforeseen ways. Today, combinatorial innovation is only possible due to a decentralized finance system. In finance, open sourcing- with permissionless innovation- promotes new products by encouraging freelancer investors.

Interoperability

Surprisingly, distributed decentralized finance enhances interoperability. Centralized investment systems have the propensity to deal in silos, creating transaction hindrances. Concerned financial and monetary institutions tried maintaining their ledgers, incurring a heavy levy. With the evolution of decentralized systems based on open standards, interoperability will become the new standard. Hence, the cumbersome problem of silos and moving capital becomes carefree. High interoperability turns on the potential value of the Internet around the globe. Entrepreneurs and innovators are hugely encouraged to obtain interoperability in decentralized finance. Based projects like Ethereum are the most popular for this interoperability functionality. Polkadot and Cosmos are the most common examples of interoperability relying upon interconnecting with different blockchains.

Borderlessness

Depending on Fiat currencies, a centralized finance system cannot be boundaryless. When a transaction closes with another country, it experiences friction and delays. However, a decentralized distributed finance system can abolish geographic boundaries. The transaction is completed more quickly and with no convenience fee. Moreover, with no requirement of permission from any government or central bank, small investors are easily attracted by relying on borderless transactions of cryptocurrencies. Like writing an email, peer-to-peer networks used by blockchain technology act as a boon of science to humans nowadays, making human life more comfortable to a great extent.

Transparency

Transparency is the key feature of any successful business. In a centralized system, financial institutions have restricted access to their ledgers. Transparency becomes a stake in the public's case. People will stop investing money in any business, stopping the economic growth of any country. In contrast, radical transparency and distributed consensus fully secure public knowledge. It keeps all records of transactions using public ledgers, making it easily viewed and verified across the globe without any hindrance. In this section, we have discussed the concept of decentralized finance, and now, by using this concept, various business models have also developed. Various business models use DiFi or decentralized finance.

BUSINESS MODELS DEVELOPED IN DECENTRALIZED FINANCE

Several business models have been developed based on DiFi or decentralized finance. However, there are several limitations of DiFi till it is highly demanding, and here we will discuss these models.

Decentralized Currencies

Society has been using nationalized fiat currencies for many years. In the past, valuable metals like gold supported currency and central financial organizations solely depended on them. Nowadays, the price of a fiat currency merely compels people's trust within a particular finance economy, enforcement of government, and financial organization. Instead of being issued by any country, bitcoin is the primary decentralized cryptocurrency based on decentralized technology [1]. Traditional currencies issued by popular centralized banks, the supply of bitcoin remains the same and does not depend upon any fiat currency, thus making it anti-inflationary. Nowadays, Bitcoin is considered digital gold for its backing of currency. It is possible to involve Bitcoin without any association of a central controlling system and seamlessly transfer gold across the border through other major decentralized cryptocurrencies like Monero, Zcash, Litecoin, Dash, and Ether, flourishing profusely.

Decentralized Payment Services

Visa, Paypal, and Swift charges are commonly charged high levies to customers, and if internationalized transactions are required, it becomes costly for the people. Although the use of the Internet significantly cuts down the cost of honest kinds of services, the greediness of central financial institutions to earn more profits does not allow them to cut down their costs. Many distributed decentralized payment platforms, such as Libra, push to enable more low-cost, instantaneous, and global payments without any hindrance over traditional payment services. Having low transaction charges, investors also reduce their costs for profit by offering instant, seamless, secure, and irreversible payment services at a much cheaper rate. More importantly, transactions between two users, when free or almost free, unleash a replacement wave of improvement and entrepreneurship. Interestingly, Square, a centralized platform thinks of incorporating the Bitcoin Lightning Network shortly. Like today, Ripple once again broke new ground in decentralized reimbursement services. Nowadays, it is a partner associated with monetary institutions (*e.g.*, MoneyGram) to reinforce the effectiveness of money transfers worldwide.

Decentralized Fundraising

The conventional endeavor of finance frequently experiences significant friction during the fundraising process. Because stockholders only believe and have faith in investing in projects that have a sturdy network, as the fundraising landscape evolves, blockchain technology is pointing in that direction. Decentralized fundraising offers traditional crowdfunding to ICOs. It helps to raise funds from stockholders across the globe, as well as smart contacts for ASCII document validation. Looking closely at the last few years, we can see that ICOs have an outstanding endowment technique that attracts many inventors [28]. Blockchain networks may flourish daily through ICO, enabling many entrepreneurs and investors to cumulate billions of dollars from global pioneers to invest in a business. A utility token typically serves as a token that users can redeem for services or use as a medium of exchange. As cash flow is involved in ICO, some projects may ask for direct ownership issue security tokens. A replacement variant, initial exchange offerings (IEOs) has recently emerged. Similarly, IEOs focus on the trustworthiness of potential projects to authenticate through a cryptocurrency exchange. Cryptocurrency is valuable in impending projects and endorses high-quality exchanges with great reputation.

Decentralized Contracting

Contracts are crucial for markets, firms, and individuals as they facilitate collaborations with other corporations and transactions. Due to many factors like drafting, negotiation, agreements, and sometimes renegotiation, the establishment of contracts is harder. However, with the invention of smart contracts, where agreeing with the pre-specified conditions and the program runs automatically, the complexity and the cost of contracting improve much due to its transparency. Adverse selection, which increases transaction costs, is unaffected by the nature of a peer-to-peer network, which combines immutability, transparency, and programmability [30]. Smart contracts guarantee a reduction in involvedness and cost of contracting through automaticity, immutability, transparency, and programmability.

THE RECENT GROWTH OF BLOCKCHAIN IN DIFFERENT FINANCIAL FIELDS USING IOT

The applications and utilization of blockchain technology are extensive; sometimes, blockchain's application is beyond financial technology because of its distributed, tamper-proof nature. Blockchain is a straightforward medium for automated regulation-based financial transfers; smart contracts are incredibly alluring for financial services, IoT, supply chains, and businesses. Here, we focus on different applications in the economic area, including various types of currency. The amalgamation of IoT, IIoT, and blockchain can improve industrial manufacturing growth, and multiple aspects of human life can reach the next level of digitalization for the Industrial Internet of Things (BIIoT).

Commodity Currency

Commodity money is an intermediate of exchange payments with different native values due to their substitute usage (or prospecting cost). This type of substitute for the price may have both cultural and economic value. A given commodity has to be a suitable candidate in the form of money. Due to the alternative use of cryptocurrency as payment, people must have faith to accept it in future transactions. Any valuable metal is comparable to this type of currency. In this

case, blockchain is the trusted way to transfer where both parties may not rely on each other.

Fiat Currency

Fiat money is the money that is declared a legal tender, which may be issued by any authorized party, like any bank. Any party will use the currency to settle down liabilities endorsed by an agreed statement. We conclude that fiat money has no native value other than paper, and we utilize metals to produce notes and coins.

Blockchain Tools

We can get several tools according to the working area and consensus mechanism. With all these tools, we get different work areas for blockchain technologies. Here, we discuss some well-known tools, as given below.

Bitcoin

The foremost and broadly used decentralized distributed ledger with the maximum market capitalization is Bitcoin. Bitcoin was founded by Satoshi Nakamoto and released in 2009. It is a publicly acceptable scattered ledger where transactions verified by network nodes through cryptocurrency are stored. As a reward for a process called mining, miners created bitcoins. Bitcoin has been both appreciated and criticized. The points critics put forward are its usage in illegal transactions, enormous electricity miners' use, price volatility, and thefts from exchanges.

Litecoin

Charlie Lee founded Litecoin and released it in 2011 using the Scrypt hashing algorithm. Litecoin is a P2P cryptocurrency and non-proprietary software project in open source medium that falls under the license MIT/X11. The evolution of Litecoin after it went live on October 13, 2011 earned the maximum number of coins, making it very popular. A developer decreased the block-generating time of the Bitcoin client by forking its source code by 2.5 minutes. It slightly modifies GUI, and a different hashing algorithm makes it possible. In November 2013, Litecoin experienced massive growth within 24 hours with a 100% leap.

Namecoin

Namecoin also acts as an alternative to decentralized DNS. It was founded by Vincent Durham and released in 2011. To eliminate scaling problems, the developers implemented a mutual proof-of-work (POW) system to ensure the safety of new cryptocurrencies with different use cases. Namecoin is not dependent upon the domain names given by the main governing body, ICANN. Unlike .com or .net domains, the use case of Namecoin's flagship is .bit, which is censorship-resistant to the domain at the topmost level. Peer-to-peer communicationhandles Namecoin's transactions, similar to how Bitcoin balances through the SHA25 algorithm; a proof-of-work mechanism uses this process.

Peercoin

The very first cryptocurrency that used POW and POS functions was Peercoin. Sunny King founded it and released it in 2012. Both systems, including proof-o--stake and proof-of-work, are utilized by Peercoin, a peer-to-peer cryptocurrency, for transactions. In a proof-of-stake system, new coins are generated based on the individual's holdings. It has the effect of making monopolies expensive, and it also distinguishes the risk of monopolies from proof-of-work mining shares. A transaction charge protects junk and spam (instead of being collected by a miner), benefiting the entire network. To convalesce from lost coins and to dampen any advertisement, the currency supply targets growth at 1% per year in the long run for its longevity.

Dogecoin

The Doge meme inspires Dogecoin across the cyber world. Jackson Palmer and Billy Markus founded and released it in 2013, a fast initial coin production schedule. The coins earned traction, and users utilized them as an internet tipping system. The Coin became popular within two weeks with the help of Reddit's social media site. Many popular platforms for social media users permit Dogecoin to be earned as a reward by users in exchange for providing interesting or noteworthy content to a particular site. Dogecoin is also called altcoin. Several parameters distinguish Dogecoin's implementation from that of Litecoin. On December 19, 2013, within 72 hours, Dogecoin leaped nearly 300%, promoting it to a high end.

In contrast with Litecoin, which takes 2.5 minutes block time to add a new block, Dogecoin takes only one minute to do the same. The number is rising with the increased volume of US$0.00026 to US$0.00095 daily. This increase was noticeable when Bitcoin and other cryptocurrencies were reeling from China's decision to forbid Chinese banks from investing in the Bitcoin economy. Dogecoin's block time is 1 minute instead of Litecoin's 2.5 minutes.

Gridcoin

Gridcoin is associated with a lifestyle founded by Rob Halford and released in 2013. Gridcoin (ticker: GRC) is an open-source cryptocurrency securing rewards for volunteer computing performed on the BOINC [4] platform. It hosts over 30 science projects from various scientific disciplines. The proof-of-stake protocol introduced the Gridcoin protocol and ensures it uses minimal resources. The whitepaper of Gridcoin states that idle processing potential (IPP) refers to the product of the processing power of computing devices and the portion of unused processing over time. Individuals direct their IPP of the Gridcoin network to the research projects they deem beneficial, which contain more excellent value in science and research. It aims to provide more excellent resources for efficiently conducting research projects.

Primecoin

Sunny King initially founded Primecoin and released it in 2013. It computed chains of prime numbers (Cunningham and bi-twin chains) and published them in blockchain's public ledger, making them available to scientists, mathematicians, and anyone else. Utilization of energy in multiple ways: Primecoin has achieved it by offering an alternative paradigm of blockchain technology. The Primecoin also meets the criteria for a proof-of-work system and is welcomed by scientists for innovations.

Ripple

Ripple is considered for debt transfer and was founded by Chris Larsen and Jed McCaleb and released in 2013. Open Coin launched Ripple, a company founded by Chris Larsen in 2012. It is a currency and a trustworthy payment gateway for hassle-free cross-border transactions. Ripple users have "wallets" on the Ripple system that they can add value to in any currency using an online exchange backed by a bank. With the property of two parts, the XRP, a mathematically regulated currency unit similar to Bitcoin, and a payment gateway, it works efficiently.

Auroracoin

Auroracoin was introduced as an alternative to replace the Icelandic krona. Baldur Odinsson founded it and released it in 2014. It is a peer-to-peer cryptocurrency. With a proof-of-work algorithm, it was primarily based on Litecoin. Multiple-algorithm architecture depends on Digibyte, a new codebase that was released and pioneered by MyriadCoin. With 50% of the total issuance of Auroracoins by using the Kennitala national identification system, a process copied from the "airdrop," the developer moves to bootstrap network, affecting and introducing cryptocurrencies nationally. Developers introduced a Bitcoin-based currency called Dash. Evan Duffield and Kyle Hagan founded it and released it in 2014. It featured instant transactions, budgeting, decentralized governance, and private transactions. In an average of two and a half minutes, miners created a coin by performing eleven rounds of hashing using a proof-of-work algorithm. Namely, dash cryptocurrencies use the hash function "X11". Using a decentralized voting system, the Dash DAO uses the 10% of what it deceives from mining to endow in DAO.

Mazacoin

The developers derived the fundamental software from another cryptocurrency, Zetacoin. The BTC Oyate Initiative founded it and released it in 2014. The software from which it is derived works on the property of Bitcoin's SHA-256 proof-of-work system. Harris, in 2014, started the development of Mazacoin. In October 2017, a Mashable article on the Oglala Lakota included a video about Harris's efforts to acquire Mazacoin. Mazacoin is an amalgamation of two divergent sociotechnical assemblages:

1) the involvement of a richly traditional indigenous community and

2) the libertarian, elite cryptocurrency technology.

Monero

Monero was a privacy-focused coin that used the crypto note protocol and had improved scalability and decentralization. The Monero Core Team founded it and released it in 2014. An obfuscated public ledger is one in which anybody can broadcast any transactions, but no observing outsider can tell the source, amount, or destinations. Monero uses a proof-of-work mechanism to generate valuable new coins, incentivizing miners to secure the network and validate transactions.

NEM

NEM introduced the Proof of Importance algorithm using the EigenTrust++ reputation system. It was created and released in 2014 by Utopian Future. Implementation of NEM network Eigentrust++, a security clustering algorithm, is used. It monitors the previous behavior of nodes across the network and enriches the reputation of the neighboring cluster. The use of EigenTrust++ based on proof-of-work not only protects data duplicity but also measures the quality of work. Proof of importance (POI) is used in NEM to help calculate the participants' investment in XEM. However, the condition is that the person using NEM must have 10,000 XEM in their balance scores, and all other transactions associated with NEM maximize the NEM network's ability.

Titcoin

A major adult industry award recognized Titcoin through voting. Edward Mansfield and Richard Allen introduced it to the adult world and released it in 2014. The designers exclusively created it for the adult entertainment industry, where users must spend bitcoin to access adult products. Even the browsing history on credit cards is not visible here, with some key modifications that ensure the improvement of transaction speed and network difficulties.

Stellar

Stellar is an open-source, decentralized global financial network. Jed McCaleb founded it and released it in 2014. Users widely use Stellar as a token to exchange money using the Stellar Consensus Protocol. Steller hosts source code on GitHub. It has a protocol used to communicate with other Steller servers. The Stellar Development Foundation controls all three nodes. In addition to 21 different organizations, 66 valid transactions were done. A consensus algorithm uses a quorum slice to complete the information exchange in the network. Mining does not occur here for the transactions. Steller's fee is almost 100 stroops, equivalent to 1/10,000th of a cent or 0.00001 XLM.

Ethereum

Vitalik Buterin founded it and released it in 2015. The difficulty of mining started increasing in November 2016, and by this, Ethereum's difficulty Bomb was programmed from block 200,000. The ice age of Ethereum is termed a Difficulty Bomb. The introduction of this ice age incentivized the Ethereum mechanism network to transition to Proof of Stake (PoS). Once blockchain is ready to shift from Proof of Work (PoW) to using Proof of Stake (PoS), it will experience that transition. However, in February 2019, developers initiated the difficulty bomb.

Nano

Tether claims a 1 to 1 ratio to be backed by USD. Jan Ludovicus van der Velde founded it and released it in 2015. However, in 2017, Tether claimed to uphold all United States dollars in reserve to meet the demand for withdrawal by customers. But it fails to meet any criteria. Tether proposed external audits to make and reserve account holding always transparent to the customers. However, in reality, audits of this type do not exist. Later, in January 2018, Tether stated that hackers stole about $31 million of USD tether tokens from them in November 2017. Later on, researchers found a close connection between the tether hack and the bit stamp attack in January 2015. As a result of theft, trading involving Tether was

banned entirely. The statement also indicated that the developers should implement any hard fork to render all tokens identified as stolen untradeable.

Zcash

Zcash is the first cryptocurrency to use zero-knowledge safety and permissionless financial schemes. It was founded by Zooko Wilcox and released in 2016. Zcash affords private traders the option of selective disclosure, permitting a user to make payment for reviewing purposes. Private traders must decide whether to follow anti-money laundering or violate tax regulations. Dealings are auditable, but revelation is under the participant's control. The company used to host several virtual meetings over the net with law enforcement security agencies in the U.S. to explain these fundamentals to the users.

Bitcoin Cash

Bitcoin improved the block size up to 8 MB. It came out in 2017. Bitcoin Cash, including Bitcoin, uses a proof-of-work algorithm for time division with the introduction of every new block. A hash function describes the movement of each new block. Additionally, Bitcoin and Bitcoin Cash miners aim to generate a new block on average every 10 minutes. The time it takes to complete a transaction on the newly generated block determines the mining difficulty. By increasing the total amount of computational mining power, the mining of data difficulty can keep the block time constant. In contrast, lowering the difficulty of data mining can maintain a constant block time if the mining power decreases. Some blockchain-based cryptocurrencies are mentioned below (Table **2**):

Table 2. Different crypto-currencies and their related details.

Release	Currency	Founder(s)	Transaction Areas	Consensus Mechanism	Notes
2009	Bitcoin	Satoshi Nakamoto [1]	Peer-to-peer	PoW	Decentralized Cryptocurrency is majorly used.
2011	Litecoin	Charlie Lee	Peer-to-peer	PoW	Custom scrypt as a hashing algorithm
2011	Namecoin	Vincent Durham	Peer-to-peer	PoW	Acts as an alternate, distributed DNS.
2012	Peercoin	Sunny King (pseudonym)	Peer-to-peer	PoW & PoS	Uses POW and POS functions as a cryptocurrency for the first time.
2013	Dogecoin	Jackson Palmer, Billy Markus	Peer-to-peer	PoW	Doge memes influence peer-to-peer PoW over the internet.
2013	Gridcoin	Rob Hälford	Peer-to-peer	Decentralized PoS	Used for network computing
2013	Ripple	Chris Larsen & Jed McCaleb	Peer-to-peer	"Consensus"	Involves peer-to-peer debt transfer. It is not dependent on Bitcoin.
2014	Auroracoin	Baldur Odinsson (pseudonym)	Peer-to-peer	PoW	Substitute coinage for Iceland.
2014	Dash	Evan Duffield & Kyle Hagan	Peer-to-peer	PoW & Proof of Service	Dash works efficiently to complete instant dealing, budgeting for distributed governance, and private contacts.
2014	Mazacoin	BTC Oyate Initiative	Peer-to-peer	PoW	The fundamental software is derived from ZetaCoin.
2014	Monero	Moreno Core Teay	Peer-to-peer		

(Table 2) cont.....

Release	Currency	Founder(s)	Transaction Areas	Consensus Mechanism	Notes
2014	NEM	UtopianFuture (pseudonym)	Peer-to-peer	POI	Uses a hybrid public/private blockchain key built from scratch. The algorithm Proof of Importance is considered.
2014	Titcoin	Edward Mansfield & Richard Allen [28]	Peer-to-peer	PoW	Nominated for the first time to use in a major adult pornography business award.
2014	Stellar	Jed McCaleb [28]	Decentralized	Stellar Consensus Protocol (SCP)	Open-source, distributed global transaction methodology.
2015	Ether or "Ethereum"	VitalikButerin	Peer-to-peer	PoW	Provisions Turing-ample smart contracts.
2015	Ethereum Classic	--------	Peer-to-peer	PoW	A substitute version of Ethereum does not include the DAO Hardfork.
2015	Nano	Colin Le Mahien	Peer-to- peer	Open Representative voting	Decentralized, feeless, open-source. It is the very first to use a Block Lattice structure.
2015	Tether	JaLudovicus	Peer-to-peer	PoW	Decentralized, feeless, open-source. Block Lattice structure evolves.
2016	Zcash	Zooko Wilcox	Peer-to-peer	PoW	Permissionless financial system commissioning zero-knowledge safety.
2017	Bitcoin Cash	-	Peer-to-peer	PoW	Ardchild from Bitcoin increased the block size from 1MB to 8MB

THE FUTURE OF MONEY USING BLOCKCHAIN THROUGH IOT

A cryptocurrency is a peer-to-peer communication with a distributive nature for a digital currency that is stored, transferred, and transacted through a decentralized computer network that links all the customers so that no individual user can control the network, as all the transactions are transparent, too. Furthermore, digital money is more secure and trustworthy. Due to its technological support, Bitcoin ensures a public and clear, transparent record of transactions. Moreover, it is also treated as a digital strength to toil in a mode of replacement by using several cryptographic techniques to make transactions more secure. Here, the digital assets or currencies are transferred by following different cryptographic protocols.

Ramping up the involvement of IoT sensor devices in logistics management using radio frequency identification (RFID), home appliances, the e-health sector, and smart cities depends on information and communication technology (ICT). In the E-Business model, smart contracts encourage people to participate in decentralized transaction entities that do not need an intermediary to complete a seamless transaction. Users' addresses remain pseudonymous to avoid privacy leakage and attain blockchain anonymity. However, the system can still determine their identities because users conduct many transactions over the same address. Hence, a new concept of mixing is emerging. In MixNet, shuffled information sharing is done at the recipient end to decrypt transaction details to avoid dishonesty and double-spending. Another idea of an anonymous transaction, zero-cash, uses knowledge of (zk-SNARKs) to hide transaction amounts and the value of exchange coins used by blockchain users.

Supply of Cryptocurrencies

Most decentralized cryptocurrencies have a fixed delivery of tokens in the system; when users gain a reward in cryptocurrency, they add it to the new block. The maximum of transactions depends on the miners' reward points. The supply of cryptocurrency systems uses a decreasing supply as a function of time.

Demand for Cryptocurrencies

With the advancement of technology, the demand for crypto-currencies is increasing rapidly. Blockchain-based cryptocurrencies have become increasingly popular for payment, billing, asset transfer, and saving purposes. Compared to international payment mechanisms, cryptocurrencies provide an efficient payment alternative. Retailers are starting to accept Bitcoin as a secure mode of remittance. Cryptocurrencies may change economic growth in the future depending on the related network advancement and adoption of blockchain to grow it worldwide. The economic environment rises with the increased demand for cryptocurrencies as an alternative to money. Transparent commitment makes cryptocurrencies an everlasting investment asset because of their immutable nature [30].

LIMITS TO DECENTRALIZED FINANCE

Numerous challenges, including fragility, volatility, regulatory uncertainty, and usability, continue to obstruct the full potential of decentralized finance. Several challenges based upon uncertainty, the risk factor of fraud, and acceptance of volatility caused not using the decentralized system to its fullest. First, a decentralized monetary system is often at risk of fraud and the proliferation of untested financial innovations. Cultivating a strong ecosystem encourages responsible modernization and can easily remove fraudulent intercessors. Although stablecoins now resolve this problem by tying themselves to fiat currencies, observers have noted that decentralized finance encourages a tech-centric rather than market-driven approach. Many projects specialize in scientific expansion rather than worthiness and ease of use. Lack of substantial regulatory certainty and scrutiny leads many corporate investors like Facebook to invest in cryptocurrencies rather than decentralized systems, driving many corporate partners not to support a decentralized system. The decentralized finance process must be user-centric and provide genuine value to the user.

Often, they specialize in the characteristics and character of decentralized platforms and distributed trust. Constructive progress is only possible through a transparent regulatory framework. Decentralized finance is specialized to do this smoothly. Several fundamental challenges are more complex, and gradually pulling toward blockchain, decentralized finance will be able to overcome these. There are some ways that we can remove these challenges. Firstly, it publicly distributes all information to every node present in the network to gain trustworthiness and validate information through distributed consensus. Secondly, a distributed trust may jeopardize privacy. Public blockchain easily stores transactions, which means users often misuse it regarding their privacy. Zcash and Monero remove user identity and exchange transaction details to protect user privacy. It makes the approach more concerned about user privacy, leading to data costs because of operational overhead. The immutability of public ledgers and the atomicity property to use smart contracts enhance transparency and build trust, resulting in rigidity and inflexibility. The use of smart contracts that inherit decentralized financial transactions, such as rigidity, inflexibility, and learning potential, has led to the discovery of impeding experimentation. Moreover, decentralized finance may lack accountability because no central entity can take action to congeal transactions, rectify problems, and restore normal operations. Hence, without adequate accountability, decentralized finance will face severe limitations. Decentralized platforms rely on the distributed trust of generally recorded and verified inputs. Lastly, the maneuvers of decentralized finance depend totally on the rule of coding. Not depending upon individual laws or codes is often a plus because it can lessen agency costs. Yet, it may become limited because it will be unsuccessful in controlling human implicit knowledge and domain-specific judgment, which limits what single decentralized finance is ready to do [26].

CONCLUSION AND FUTURE SCOPE

Blockchain is highly advanced, supports infrastructure, and is peer-to-peer in nature. This study focuses on the financial growth and prospects of blockchain technology. Several studies and analyses of different fields of aspects of blockchain, *e.g.*, the algorithm of consensus mechanisms, mining processes, advantages of blockchain, and decentralized financial functionality, reviewed different existing crypto-currencies on blockchain. However, blockchain is a much broader field that extends far beyond Bitcoin. Key features like persistency, peer-to-peer network communication, decentralization, and anonymity change the existing trading system. Blockchain's potential aids stakeholders' efforts to invest in finance more efficiently. Countries like the U.S., Uganda, Nigeria, and Spain have completely prohibited centralized banks from investing in Bitcoin and blockchain transactions. It will make customers worry less about fraud and prevent any negative impact by protecting depositors' money from any risk. The idea proposed in blockchain is to avoid intervention by a centralized organization to regulate financial governance. The remodeling of economic growth is entirely dependent on the boon of blockchain. Optimizing generated data over the physical objects to connect to the Internet using IoT also helps in data analysis. Big data analysis and IoT are inseparable, which helps in data management. For example, suppose blockchain is used in airline ticketing systems to store traveler history details through their airlines. In that case, no one can tamper to steal private information due to the use of asymmetric keys to store information.

REFERENCES

[1] I.O.C. Igwe, "History of the international economy: The Bretton Woods system and its impact on the economic development of developing countries", *Athens Journal of Law,* vol. 4, no. 2, pp. 105-126, 2018.
[http://dx.doi.org/10.30958/ajl.4.2.1]

[2] Kantur, H. and Bamuleseyo, C., How smart contracts can change the insurance industry: Benefits and challenges of using Blockchain technology, 2018.

[3] L. Akoglu, E. Ferrara, M. Deivamani, and R. Baeza-Yates, Eds., *Advances in Data Science: Third International Conference on Intelligent Information Technologies, ICIIT 2018, Chennai, India, December 11–14, 2018, Proceedings*, Communications in Computer and Information Science, vol. 941, Springer, 2019.

[4] S. Aikio, *Blockchain technologies and trust formation in trade finance*, M.S. thesis, Univ. of Oulu, Oulu, Finland, Jun. 2018.

[5] R. Cole, M. Stevenson, and J. Aitken, "Blockchain technology: implications for operations and supply chain management", *Supply Chain Manag.,* vol. 24, no. 4, pp. 469-483, 2019.
[http://dx.doi.org/10.1108/SCM-09-2018-0309]

[6] C. Schlötterer, R. Tobler, R. Kofler, and V. Nolte, "Sequencing pools of individuals — mining genome-wide polymorphism data without big funding", *Nat. Rev. Genet.,* vol. 15, no. 11, pp. 749-763, 2014.
[http://dx.doi.org/10.1038/nrg3803] [PMID: 25246196]

[7] I. Eyal, and E.G. Sirer, "Majority is not enough", *Commun. ACM,* vol. 61, no. 7, pp. 95-102, 2018.
[http://dx.doi.org/10.1145/3212998]

[8] Eyal, Ittay. "The Miner's Dilemma" (PDF). Cornel University. Archived (PDF) from the original on 2017-08-09. Retrieved 2017-05-23., In the IEEE Symposium on Security and Privacy (Oakland), 2015.

[9] X. Li, P. Jiang, T. Chen, X. Luo, and Q. Wen, "A survey on the security of blockchain systems", *Future Gener. Comput. Syst.,* vol. 107, pp. 841-853, 2020.

[10] Z. Liu, N.C. Luong, W. Wang, D. Niyato, P. Wang, Y.C. Liang, and D.I. Kim, "A Survey on Blockchain: A Game Theoretical Perspective", *IEEE Access,* vol. 7, pp. 47615-47643, 2019.
[http://dx.doi.org/10.1109/ACCESS.2019.2909924]

[11] M. Ghosh, M. Richardson, B. Ford, and R. Jansen, *A TorPath to TorCoin: Proof-of-bandwidth altcoins for compensating relays.* Naval Research Laboratory, Washington, DC, 2014.

[12] X. Li, P. Jiang, T. Chen, X. Luo, and Q. Wen, "A survey on the security of blockchain systems", *Future Gener. Comput. Syst.,* 2017.

[13] K. Toyoda, P.T. Mathiopoulos, I. Sasase, and T. Ohtsuki, "A novel blockchain-based product ownership management system (POMS) for anti-counterfeits in the post supply chain", *IEEE Access,* vol. 5, pp. 17465-17477, 2017.
[http://dx.doi.org/10.1109/ACCESS.2017.2720760]

[14] T. Bamert, C. Decker, L. Elsen, R. Wattenhofer, and S. Welten, "Have a Snack, Pay with Bitcoins", *13-th IEEE International Conference on Peer-to-Peer Computing,* 2013

[15] E. Heilman, A. Kendler, A. Zohar, and S. Goldberg, "Eclipse attacks on bitcoin's peer-to-peer network," in Proc. *24th USENIX Security Symposium,* Washington, DC, USA, 2015, pp. 129–144.

[16] J. Golosova, and A. Romanovs, The Advantages and Disadvantages of the Blockchain Technology. In *Proc. 2018 IEEE 6th Workshop on Advances in Information, Electronic and Electrical Engineering (AIEEE),* Vilnius, Lithuania, 2018, pp. 1–6.
[http://dx.doi.org/10.1109/AIEEE.2018.8592253]

[17] J.H. Huh, and K. Seo, "Blockchain-based mobile fingerprint verification and automatic log-in platform for future computing", *J. Supercomput.,* vol. 75, no. 6, pp. 3123-3139, 2019.
[http://dx.doi.org/10.1007/s11227-018-2496-1]

[18] H. Treiblmaier, "The impact of the blockchain on the supply chain: a theory-based research framework and a call for action", *Supply Chain Manag.,* vol. 23, no. 6, pp. 545-559, 2018.
[http://dx.doi.org/10.1108/SCM-01-2018-0029]

[19] *Blockchains & distributed ledger technologies. Available from: https://blockchainhub.net/blockchains-anddistributed-ledger-technologies-in-general/.*

[20] G.J. Benston, and C.W. Smith, "A transactions cost approach to the theory of financial intermediation", *J. Finance,* vol. 31, no. 2, pp. 215-231, 1976.
[http://dx.doi.org/10.2307/2326596]

[21] R. Karlsson Linnér, P. Biroli, E. Kong, S.F.W. Meddens, R. Wedow, M.A. Fontana, M. Lebreton, S.P. Tino, A. Abdellaoui, A.R. Hammerschlag, M.G. Nivard, A. Okbay, C.A. Rietveld, P.N. Timshel, M. Trzaskowski, R. Vlaming, C.L. Zünd, Y. Bao, L. Buzdugan, A.H. Caplin, C.Y. Chen, P. Eibich, P. Fontanillas, J.R. Gonzalez, P.K. Joshi, V. Karhunen, A. Kleinman, R.Z. Levin, C.M. Lill, G.A. Meddens, G. Muntané, S. Sanchez-Roige, F.J. Rooij, E. Taskesen, Y. Wu, F. Zhang, A. Auton, J.D. Boardman, D.W. Clark, A. Conlin, C.C. Dolan, U. Fischbacher, P.J.F. Groenen, K.M. Harris, G. Hasler, A. Hofman, M.A. Ikram, S. Jain, R. Karlsson, R.C. Kessler, M. Kooyman, J. MacKillop, M. Männikkö, C. Morcillo-Suarez, M.B. McQueen, K.M. Schmidt, M.C. Smart, M. Sutter, A.R. Thurik, A.G. Uitterlinden, J. White, H. Wit, J. Yang, L. Bertram, D.I. Boomsma, T. Esko, E. Fehr, D.A. Hinds, M. Johannesson, M. Kumari, D. Laibson, P.K.E. Magnusson, M.N. Meyer, A. Navarro, A.A. Palmer, T.H. Pers, D. Posthuma, D. Schunk, M.B. Stein, R. Svento, H. Tiemeier, P.R.H.J. Timmers, P. Turley,

R.J. Ursano, G.G. Wagner, J.F. Wilson, J. Gratten, J.J. Lee, D. Cesarini, D.J. Benjamin, P.D. Koellinger, and J.P. Beauchamp, "Genome-wide association analyses of risk tolerance and risky behaviors in over 1 million individuals identify hundreds of loci and shared genetic influences", *Nat. Genet.,* vol. 51, no. 2, pp. 245-257, 2019.
[http://dx.doi.org/10.1038/s41588-018-0309-3] [PMID: 30643258]

[22]   G. Parker, M. W. Van Alstyne, and X. Jiang, *Platform ecosystems: How developers invert the firm.* Boston University Questrom School of Business Research Paper, (2861574), 2016.

[23]   B.L. Hallen, and K.M. Eisenhardt, "Catalyzing strategies and efficient tie formation: How entrepreneurial firms obtain investment ties", *Acad. Manage. J.,* vol. 55, no. 1, pp. 35-70, 2012.
[http://dx.doi.org/10.5465/amj.2009.0620]

[24]   X. Guo, C. Chen, and J. Wang, "Sorption of sulfamethoxazole onto six types of microplastics", *Chemosphere,* vol. 228, pp. 300-308, 2019.
[http://dx.doi.org/10.1016/j.chemosphere.2019.04.155] [PMID: 31035168]

[25]   C.M. Vicario, M.A. Salehinejad, K. Felmingham, G. Martino, and M.A. Nitsche, "A systematic review on the therapeutic effectiveness of non-invasive brain stimulation for the treatment of anxiety disorders", *Neurosci. Biobehav. Rev.,* vol. 96, pp. 219-231, 2019.
[http://dx.doi.org/10.1016/j.neubiorev.2018.12.012] [PMID: 30543906]

[26]   C.T. January, L.S. Wann, H. Calkins, L.Y. Chen, J.E. Cigarroa, J.C. Cleveland Jr, P.T. Ellinor, M.D. Ezekowitz, M.E. Field, K.L. Furie, P.A. Heidenreich, K.T. Murray, J.B. Shea, C.M. Tracy, and C.W. Yancy, "2019 AHA/ACC/HRS Focused Update of the 2014 AHA/ACC/HRS Guideline for the Management of Patients With Atrial Fibrillation", *J. Am. Coll. Cardiol.,* vol. 74, no. 1, pp. 104-132, 2019.
[http://dx.doi.org/10.1016/j.jacc.2019.01.011] [PMID: 30703431]

[27]   L. Handoko, H. Xu, G. Li, C.Y. Ngan, E. Chew, M. Schnapp, C.W.H. Lee, C. Ye, J.L.H. Ping, F. Mulawadi, E. Wong, J. Sheng, Y. Zhang, T. Poh, C.S. Chan, G. Kunarso, A. Shahab, G. Bourque, V. Cacheux-Rataboul, W.K. Sung, Y. Ruan, and C.L. Wei, "CTCF-mediated functional chromatin interactome in pluripotent cells", *Nat. Genet.,* vol. 43, no. 7, pp. 630-638, 2011.
[http://dx.doi.org/10.1038/ng.857] [PMID: 21685913]

[28]   T. Shi, D.A. McAllister, K.L. O'Brien, E.A.F. Simoes, S.A. Madhi, B.D. Gessner, F.P. Polack, E. Balsells, S. Acacio, C. Aguayo, I. Alassani, A. Ali, M. Antonio, S. Awasthi, J.O. Awori, E. Azziz-Baumgartner, H.C. Baggett, V.L. Baillie, A. Balmaseda, A. Barahona, S. Basnet, Q. Bassat, W. Basualdo, G. Bigogo, L. Bont, R.F. Breiman, W.A. Brooks, S. Broor, N. Bruce, D. Bruden, P. Buchy, S. Campbell, P. Carosone-Link, M. Chadha, J. Chipeta, M. Chou, W. Clara, C. Cohen, E. de Cuellar, D.A. Dang, B. Dash-yandag, M. Deloria-Knoll, M. Dherani, T. Eap, B.E. Ebruke, M. Echavarria, C.C. de Freitas Lázaro Emediato, R.A. Fasce, D.R. Feikin, L. Feng, A. Gentile, A. Gordon, D. Goswami, S. Goyet, M. Groome, N. Halasa, S. Hirve, N. Homaira, S.R.C. Howie, J. Jara, I. Jroundi, C.B. Kartasasmita, N. Khuri-Bulos, K.L. Kotloff, A. Krishnan, R. Libster, O. Lopez, M.G. Lucero, F. Lucion, S.P. Lupisan, D.N. Marcone, J.P. McCracken, M. Mejia, J.C. Moisi, J.M. Montgomery, D.P. Moore, C. Moraleda, J. Moyes, P. Munywoki, K. Mutyara, M.P. Nicol, D.J. Nokes, P. Nymadawa, M.T. da Costa Oliveira, H. Oshitani, N. Pandey, G. Paranhos-Baccalà, L.N. Phillips, V.S. Picot, M. Rahman, M. Rakoto-Andrianarivelo, Z.A. Rasmussen, B.A. Rath, A. Robinson, C. Romero, G. Russomando, V. Salimi, P. Sawatwong, N. Scheltema, B. Schweiger, J.A.G. Scott, P. Seidenberg, K. Shen, R. Singleton, V. Sotomayor, T.A. Strand, A. Sutanto, M. Sylla, M.D. Tapia, S. Thamthitiwat, E.D. Thomas, R. Tokarz, C. Turner, M. Venter, S. Waicharoen, J. Wang, W. Watthanaworawit, L.M. Yoshida, H. Yu, H.J. Zar, H. Campbell, and H. Nair, "Global, regional, and national disease burden estimates of acute lower respiratory infections due to respiratory syncytial virus in young children in 2015: a systematic review and modelling study", *Lancet,* vol. 390, no. 10098, pp. 946-958, 2017.
[http://dx.doi.org/10.1016/S0140-6736(17)30938-8] [PMID: 28689664]

[29]   A. Bogner, M. Chanson, and A. Meeuw, "A decentralised sharing app running a smart contract on the ethereum blockchain", *Proceedings of the 6th International Conference on the Internet of Things,* 2016pp. 177-178

[http://dx.doi.org/10.1145/2991561.2998465]

[30]   Y. Chen, and C. Bellavitis, "Blockchain disruption and decentralized finance: The rise of decentralized business models", *Journal of Business Venturing Insights,* vol. 13, p. e00151, 2020.
[http://dx.doi.org/10.1016/j.jbvi.2019.e00151]

CHAPTER 3

A Survey of Forest Fire Surveillance Strategy and Challenges Using the WSN Paradigm

Raj Vikram[1,*] and **Vikash Kumar**[1]

[1] *Department of Computer Science and Engineering, ITER, Siksha O Anusandhan, Bhubneshwar, Odisha, India*

Abstract: Nature is the most valuable aspect of humanity. Many civilizations and cultures have flourished in the lap of nature. The forest is the most beautiful treasure in nature. It always fulfills the basic needs of the lives of the earth's dwellers. Today, the forests are depleting quickly. The major cause behind this is forest fires or wildfires. An uncontrollable fire either occurs naturally or due to human interruption or any other disturbance caused by nature that may or may not be suppressed by artificial control. A fire broke out in the Amazon rainforest in 2021 and had a significant impact on this planet. Researchers have measured the impacts of wildfire on the habitats of 14,000 species of plants and animals, finding that 93% to 95% suffered from some consequences of the fires. In 2020, Australia's forest fires caught the world's attention. Wildfires are a major challenge for humans in today's time. Early identification of forest fires is the only way to mitigate the risk of damage.

Researchers are working on various techniques to detect the fire early. Several existing approaches, like wireless sensor networks, machine learning, and remote sensing, are used to identify wildfires. Some researchers are using UAVs to identify forest fires. In most cases, the researchers are focused only on prediction using some environmental parameters sensed by the sensors or images captured by the satellites. This paper highlights the various challenges in the prediction of forest fires using the WSN paradigm.

Keywords: Forest fire, Mobile node, Path generation, Rarefied flow, WSN.

INTRODUCTION

Forest Fires

In addition to destroying millions of acres of land and thousands of acres of forest each year, forest fires around the world are responsible for the destruction of thousands of houses and other buildings. Since the dawn of human civilization,

* **Corresponding author Raj Vikram:** Department of Computer Science and Engineering, ITER, Siksha O Anusandhan, Bhubneshwar, Odisha, India; E-mail: rajvikram@soa.ac.in

H.S. Hota, Dinesh K. Sharma, Ayan Kumar Das & Ditipriya Sinha (Eds.)

there has been a disaster, leading to the loss of life and the destruction of both property and personal belongings.

A number of lives, both human and animal, were lost as a result of forest fires, which contributed to an already existing ecological imbalance. In addition to this, it results in a decrease in the quantity of oxygen that is present in the air. Many individuals are of the opinion that forest fires are one of the key drivers of climate change. If this is the case, it would have catastrophic implications not just for the environment but also for the planet as a whole. There are 118 nations in the world, and forests cover 65 percent of this planet. Forest fires are responsible for the destruction of 19.8 million hectares of land every year [1]. It was anticipated that the number of forest fire occurrences that take place in India would increase by more than 85 percent between the years 2015 and 2019 [2]. In the research that was carried out and released by the Forest Survey of India in the year 2020, it was found that out of a total of 7,12,249 square kilometers of forest area, 1,524,221 square kilometers, or 21.40 percent, is highly sensitive to fire. The Indian states of Chhattisgarh, Madhya Pradesh, Mizoram, and Odisha, as well as the territory of Manipur, are home to some of the most combustible types of [2]. Locating the fire when it is still in its infancy might be helpful in resolving this problem. Researchers are now trying out a variety of alternative strategies [3] for the early identification of forest fires in order to better protect the environment. One of these applications is the detection of forest fires *via* the use of wireless sensor networks (WSN). The study areas that are relevant to this subject are broken down into categories and described in more detail below.

Research Issues

Within the context of a wireless sensor network, some of the difficulties that are connected with monitoring fires are discussed in this study. These difficulties are described in more detail later on. The body of research that already exists identifies a variety of challenges to rapid fire detection in natural environments, which protects both our flora and wildlife as well as the lives of humans. When it comes to the detection of fires, some of these technologies rely on unmanned aerial vehicles (UAVs), while others use the concept of wireless sensor networks (WSNs). The only thing that this piece of writing really focuses on is the difficulties that come with doing research based on the WSN paradigm. The costs associated with deployment are driven up by the inclusion of sensor nodes in forest environments that are equipped with a GPS link. As a consequence of this fact, it is commonly acknowledged that some nodes, which are referred to as GPS-linked nodes, do, in fact, exist, whilst other nodes, which are not GPS-connected nodes, do not. WSN presents a number of difficulties, one of the most significant of which is the difficulty in detecting the position of unknown sensor nodes. Researchers have developed a variety of techniques, some of which do not need a range in order to identify the unknown nodes [11], while others require a range in order to do so [5]. The great majority of them are unable to cut down on the localization inaccuracy of unknown sensor nodes while simultaneously minimizing the amount of unnecessary overhead. One of the challenges that academics working within this paradigm face is figuring out how to rapidly identify the zone in the topography of the forest that is closest to the core of the fire. This is a challenge since the forest covers such a big region.

One step that is absolutely necessary in order to accomplish increased forest zone monitoring is the transmission of a large volume of sensed data from the forest zone in question to the base station. This data is sent from the forest zone in question to the base station. As a direct result of this, it is absolutely necessary to expand the number of sensors that are put in certain areas. Another obstacle that must be conquered in this business is the shortage of energy sources that are accessible by the sensor nodes that are spread out over the forest. This is a barrier that must be addressed.

It is a difficult task for researchers to quickly send data from the area where forest fires are occurring back to the base station so that the forest service can immediately evaluate this data and make predictions about forest fires. However, this is necessary for the forest service to be able to do so. The United States Forest Service can rapidly evaluate this data in order to develop forecasts on forest fires thanks to this.

Both the estimation of the area of the land that has been burned by the flames and the determination of how far the fire has already spread are essential factors to take into account in relation to the forest fire. On the other hand, there are not that many works that are devoted to resolving these difficulties, so this is a disadvantage.

REVIEWS OF CHALLENGES AND DIFFERENT FOREST FIRE DETECTION MECHANISMS IN FOREST FIRE

As the number of instances of forest fires continues to rise, researchers have been motivated to devise an efficient method of monitoring the forest in order to enable the implementation of preventative measures prior to the outbreak of forest fires. In this part, a short discussion takes place on the state-of-the-art strategies that have been offered over the last several years to construct forest fire detection systems [6 - 10], as well as other ways that tackle the many problems that arise during forest fire surveillance. These methodologies are geared at a variety of application domains, including Internet of Things, Wireless Sensor Networks, Cloud, and Fog systems [11 - 14]. These studies take into account not only the challenges of prediction but also the other research-related concerns in WSN, such as the localization of sensors, the energy limits of sensors, and the transfer of data from sensor nodes in forest terrain to the base station.

As mentioned in the first portion of this article, the purpose of this study is to get an understanding of the various Forest Fire Surveillance Strategies as well as the issues that they provide utilizing the WSN paradigm. The use of machine learning, deep learning, and ensemble approaches in the design of forest fire detection methods has been more popular in recent years. These methods are used with the goal of improving the accuracy of fire detection [15, 16] in the forest.

The investigation of the most recent research on the state of the art is divided into five subparts, such as:

• The positioning of sensor nodes within the forest.
• The identification and forecasting of forest fire hotspots.
• Data transmission from sensor nodes positioned across the forest's topography to the base station.
• The creation of trajectory pathways for mobile sensor nodes and the monitoring of their motion with the aid of compressed sensing and GD localization.
• A discussion on various WSN-based forest fire frameworks that are already in place.

Localization of Sensor Nodes

When it comes to wireless sensor networks (WSN), establishing the position of the sensor nodes is one of the most critical challenges. It is possible to determine the position of the sensors with the aid of GPS, but, owing to the complicated nature of the terrain, it would be exceedingly expensive to attach GPS to each sensor node in the forest. In order for those sensor nodes to be able to localize themselves, localization algorithms have also been sent to them even though they are not linked to GPS (unknown nodes). Researchers have come up with a wide range of alternate localization processes in order to bring down the total cost of constructing wireless sensor networks (WSN). This goal is to be accomplished [5]. There are certain techniques that are predicated on the range, while others [4] do not have any limits at all on the range that they are working with. The signals that are connected to the sensor nodes are used in order to localize the sensor nodes when range-based algorithms are utilized. In order to determine the precise location of sensor nodes, these approaches evaluate either the signal intensity or the amount of time that elapses between the sending and receiving of signals. This makes it possible to create a map of the network that is more accurate. The location of the sensor node, on the other hand, may be determined *via* range-free techniques by computing the average hop count value and the distance between it and the sensor node. In this way, the position of the sensor node can be determined.

The many kinds of range-based algorithms, such as TOA [17], TDOA [18], and RSSI [19, 20], are outlined in the following list. Among the several range-free localization methods that are now available, some examples are DVhop [21], Advance DV hop [22], Improved DV hop [23], and LSVM [24]. In order to take part in the DV-Hop [21] localization process, all anchor nodes, as well as any other nodes that are armed with a GPS, are required to transmit a beacon packet. In addition to an identifier, this package is required to have geographic coordinates included. Unknown nodes, or nodes that do not have GPS, determine their coordinates first by calculating the minimum hop count value from anchor nodes, and then they use the least square technique to pinpoint their specific locations. This is done to account for the fact that unknown nodes do not have access to GPS. To ensure that the network as a whole is able to locate all of the nodes, this step is taken. Because DV-Hop calculates distances based on the idea of line-of-sight, the system's potential to localize objects is severely limited by the existence of considerable inaccuracy. This makes it much more difficult for the system to pinpoint the exact location of an item. This inaccuracy has been reduced as a result of the adoption of a more complicated DV-Hop [22] method and the location accuracy has been increased as a result of the deployment of an advanced DV-Hop scheme [23]. The position of unknown nodes shifts whenever the basic or advanced version of the DV-Hop algorithm uses a new set of anchor nodes as a point of reference. This occurs regardless of which version is being utilized. This aspect of the approach is present in both of its iterations. The requirement for accurate localization has been fulfilled by the author of a study [23], who did so by developing the reference anchor selection technique in DV-Hop and a globally optimized solution based on DV-Hop [21], both of which derive hop count for the most appropriate choice of reference anchor [23]. This allowed the author to fulfill the requirement for accurate localization. The authors of a paper [25] suggest employing a range-free localization technique that is based on the support vector machine in order to cut down on the total number of mistakes that occur during the process of localization [25]. (SVM). Another approach to localization is described in the aforementioned reference [24], and it is based on the least square support vector machine (LSVM). This demonstrates that the SVM-based data fusion localization strategy minimizes the amount of inaccuracy that is involved in the identification of the location. [Cause and effect] On the other hand, because of this, an increase in the amount of time that is required to locate unknown nodes in WSN is brought about.

All of the known localization techniques that have been discussed up to this point are either range-based or range-free localization. Researchers almost never employ the range-based localization algorithms since, despite their ability to find sensors with more precision, this strategy is not the most popular choice. The high localization cost of the range-based localization approach is due to the need for extra hardware, which is the root cause of the problem. This hardware is used to find unidentified nodes. This technology is unable to support the creation of large-scale networks. Nevertheless, range-free localization algorithms can only provide an approximation of the location of the sensor node, which results in an increase in the number of localization mistakes. The overview and limitations of the currently available localization strategies in WSN are shown in Table **1**.

Table 1. Literature review of localization in WSN.

Author & Year	Approaches	Summary	Limitation
J. Luomala *et al.*˜2020 [26]	ARBL	Based on trilateration and the choice of reference nodes, an adaptive range-based localization method	Localization error is low, but the computation time is high
T. K. Mohanta *et al.*˜2020 [27]	BFCTO	Advanced localization algorithm with fractional order class topper optimization	Computation time is high
Soumya J Bhat *et al.*˜2020 [28]	DV-maxHop	The H - H optimization-based area minimization integrated with the localization approach for range-free localization with area minimization (HHO-AM)	Localization error is low, but the computation time is high
Miao, Y. *et al.* 2019 [19]	RSSI	Accurate location estimation	A minimum of three anchor nodes are mandatory for sensor node localization
Afzal *et al.* 2018 [25]	SVM	A localization approach using machine learning concept	Localization error is high
L. Gui *et al.* 2018 [23]	Dv-hop	Reference anchor selected for better accuracy	Time computation for reference anchor selection is high
Z. Cui *et al.* 2017 [29]	Cuckoo search, DV-hop	Improves DV-hop performance	Localization computation time is high
Xuejian Zhao *et al.* 2017 [18]	Fermat point model	An outdoor localization algorithm for tracking the adventurer	High localization error
P. Daely *et al.* 2016 [5]	Dragonfly algorithm	Range-based localization with low error	High complexity
W. Yingyou *et al.* 2015 [4]	TCRL algorithm	Examines the link between the distance between neighbor nodes and their junction area.	High complexity

(Table 1) cont.....

Author & Year	Approaches	Summary	Limitation
N Ali Alrajeh *et al.* 2013 [17]	Survey	Analyzes different localization techniques.	NA
E. Cassano *et al.* 2009 [20]	ROC-RSSI and Trilateration Localization Techniques	Comparative study of different localization techniques	NA
Afzal *et al.* 2014 [25]	A learning-based localization algorithm	The suggested solution uses connection data to pinpoint the nodes' locations.	High computation

Forest Fire Detection Model

In the following paragraphs, a wide variety of fire detection models will be broken down into their component parts and studied in more depth. The authors of a study [30] have supplied a system that may be found in their work. This system is known as MFAS, and the study of the relevant literature indicates that it was developed by these writers. This method is detailed in the article that they provided (MANET-based forest fires alert system). This system is comprised of a wide variety of components, the most significant of which are MANET, wireless sensors, middleware software, and a web application that is located on the front end. The MANET-based forest fires alert system is the full name of the exact warning system that we will discuss here. The authors of a paper [31] explain how, in the aftermath of a forest fire, one may determine the percentage of the woods that have been damaged or eradicated as a result of the blaze by calculating the proportion of the forests that have been affected. To do this, one option is to calculate the proportion of the land that has been consumed by fire. In this area, genetic programming was used to construct an intelligent system that is based on data received from metrological equipment, and it was placed in this location. The data for this system was gathered from the various measuring devices. The information used in the creation of this system originated from this site. Real-time data collection is performed by installing a wireless sensor network that is powered by ZigBee in the technique of monitoring forest fires that are described in another study [32]. This makes it possible to collect data in a timeframe that is very close to real time. In a research paper [33], a feed-forward neural network (FFNN), the Naive Bayes algorithm, and a Decision tree were combined in order to provide a novel method of k-means clustering. This method, which was referred to as the hybrid method of k-means clustering, was described as having the following components: The precision with which forest fires can be predicted is one of the key foci of this technique, and the general purpose of the system is to enhance the accuracy of its forecasts. The authors of the paper [34] proposed a method for identifying forest fires using their technology that might be used by the ZigBee network. The writers of an article [35] discussed this approach. Because of this tactic, it will be possible to successfully duplicate some of the network's components, and it will also provide a method for swapping components in order to extend the lifespan of the network. Both of these outcomes will be brought about as a result of the technique. It is possible that the fact that this plan will be put into action will be the cause of both of these advantages. The architecture of the system is made up of a wide variety of distinct components, the hosts, the routers, and the sensor nodes being among the most crucial of these elements. In a paper [36], the author not only gives a model for predicting forest fires but also conducts research on the function that mobile agents play in wireless sensor networks. In addition to this, the author also presents a model for forecasting forest fires. The article that was just described spends a significant amount of material to examine each of these subjects in extraordinary depth. When compared to previous methods that have been used in the past, our strategy for identifying and monitoring the forest fire uses a far smaller amount of energy. An article [37] provides a good illustration of one potential use case for the implementation of a networked machine learning approach, which is the detection of events. In order to carry out an analysis of the data that was provided for this study, the clustering and support vector machine (SVM) methodologies were applied. The author of another paper [38] used an auditory range strategy in order to accomplish the goal of location identification and to send out a warning in the event that there is a fire. In another study [39], waves of sound were used so that both of these responsibilities could be properly completed. Before putting this technique of fire detection to use, the temperature of the area that was the focus of the research was taken into account and noted down. A method that takes data from many sensors and combines it into a single coherent whole is referred to as two-level sensor fusion, and it was first presented in a paper [40]. The method focuses on the detection of events. This strategy is effective in overcoming the network's physical failure because it takes into account the dynamic nature of wireless sensor networks and takes advantage of the connection that these networks provide. In other words, the strategy takes advantage of both the dynamic nature of these networks and the connection that they provide. The pictures that were taken by the Moderate Resolution Imaging Spectroradiometer (MODIS) and used in the building of a model for the progression of forest fires may be found in a study [41]. Additionally, the grey system theory was included in the construction of this model. The authors of another study [42] provide a technique for the detection of flames that is based on machine learning and makes use of a regression. This approach was developed for the purpose of fighting fires. This approach is provided as a potential means of identifying fires that have occurred. One of the most distinguishing features of this method is its consistent capacity to detect the presence of flames. After that, they make use of a decision tree in order to undertake an analysis of the results of the research [43]. A study presents a strategy for constructing a network of wireless hierarchical sensors that would be accessible over the internet. This network would be used to detect forest fires in regions of the forest that are more prone to combustion. These areas of the forest are described as "high-risk". In addition to this, it has components such as fire simulators, geographic information systems, and command centers for the different firefighting operations. Support vector machines (SVM), boosted regression trees, and multivariate adaptive regression splines were used during the construction of the fire prediction model that is described in another study [44]. MARS and BRT are constructed with the help of fourteen distinct sets of fire predictors. These fire predictors are all obtained from plant indices, meteorological elements, environmental parameters, and topographical characteristics in the appropriate proportions. During the process of building the model, each of these factors is taken into account. When evaluating the chance that a fire might start in a certain area, these are the considerations that are taken into account as part of the process. A research study [52] chooses a set of 13 criteria to analyze fire instigation in Chinese forests based on 23 fire hotspots, meteorological data, forest topography, vegetation, infrastructure, and socioeconomic data. The geography of the forest, the vegetation, the infrastructure, and the socioeconomic statistics are all aspects that make up these features. In addition to this, the study makes use of the data that was gathered in the United States [45]. Several of these qualities may be broken down into different categories. According to the information provided in a study [46], one method for predicting the progression of forest fires is to employ a multi-model approach that is divided into two stages. It is possible that this strategy will be adopted in the future. This tactic takes use of the underlying ideas that underlie models that can predict both the growth of wildfires and the course of the weather.

In the present circumstance, information about the climate and the direction of the wind is taken into account in order to develop a prediction regarding the fire. The authors of another study [47] were able to keep track of wildfires and the damage that they caused because of the use of K-means clustering methods. At this point in the procedure, the Neuro-Fuzzy Inference method is used in order to determine the extent to which the forest block is sensitive to detect fires in the forests that surround it. At this point in the process, it will be determined whether or not there are fires in the forests that are in the surrounding area. Table **2**, which may be seen by clicking this link, presents the findings of an investigation of the various approaches that are currently used in the process of locating forest fires.

Table 2. Analysis of forest fire detection approaches.

Proposed Model	Year	Tool	Approaches	Energy Efficiency	Advantage/Summary
A technique that uses wireless sensor networks and machine learning to find forest fires [48]	2022	Python	Regression model	Not mentioned	Detects fire area
A Deep Learning Framework dubbed Fire-Net for Active Forest Fire Detection [49]	2022	Landsat-8 images	CNN algorithm	Not mentioned	Detect and locate the fire area
Early Detection and Smart Monitoring of Forest Fire Using a Hybrid Model [50]	2017	Not mentioned	KNN algorithm	Not mentioned	Find the area that is on fire and mark it.
A Perspective on Using Machine Learning to Detect Forest Fires [42]	2015	Not mentioned	SVM model	Not mentioned	Fire detection time is low
Using Wireless Sensor Networks and Fusion Information Techniques for Forest Fire Detection [50]	2012	programming language known as Enes C and sensor boards known as IRIS motes MTS420/400C.ATmega1281 processor and amib520	Methods of the Dempster-Shafer Type and the Threshold Method	Not mentioned	Efficiently detect forest fire.
An investigation on a MANET-based forest fire surveillance system for Uttarakhand Hills [30]	2012	Not mentioned	Minimum cost forwarding technique	Not mentioned	The forest fire has been seen by the base station.

(Table 2) cont.....

Proposed Model	Year	Tool	Approaches	Energy Efficiency	Advantage/Summary
A forest fire warning system for the Brazilian Amazon [51]	2020	Not mentioned	Fuzzy reasoning based	Not mentioned	A model that was developed by combining wildfire risk indices and wildfire danger indexes together.
Wildfire monitoring [10]	2020	Not mentioned	ANN	Not mentioned	A model influenced by the Internet of Things that was built using neural networks and sensor data.
Model designed using machine-level approach [6]	2015	Not mentioned	SVM model	Not considered	A comparison of several machine learning approaches on the prediction of fires

All of the currently employed fire detection methods are solely concerned with predicting if a forest fire will occur based on recorded information about whether certain forest terrains are part of a fire region or not. To enable a system to operate for a longer period of time, they do not take into account the energy concerns of the sensors.

Routing Between Sensor Nodes and Base Station

It is the task of the data forwarding process, which is an extremely important component of the process of forecasting forest fires, to send sensed data from the forest terrain to the base station. This is a very important step in the process. Within the context of the WSN paradigm, the data forwarding technique must not only be effective in terms of the amount of energy it consumes, but it must also be quick. This is in addition to the requirement that it must be efficient. The authors of a study [52] give a comparison of a range of alternative fault-tolerant routing protocols for detecting forest fires. These protocols include Multilevel, HDMRP, and EAQHSeN [53]. The comparison is made in terms of the network's reaction time and lifetime. HDMRP, EAQHSeN, and Multilevel are some of the protocols that fall under this category. The authors place a special emphasis on the amount of time that any method may continue to work successfully prior to the point at which it no longer performs effectively. In light of the evidence presented, it is reasonable to draw the inference that the HDMRP and EAQHSeN protocols, in comparison to the multilevel protocol, are superior in terms of the efficiency with which they carry out the responsibilities assigned to them. Because WSN makes use of a variety of different routing algorithms, the strain that is put on the network may be more uniformly dispersed, which may result in a longer lifetime for the network. This is one of the benefits that WSN offers. In the event that this tactic is implemented, there is a chance that the sensor nodes that are part of a network will be able to save energy by cooperating with one another. An adaptive clustering approach is proposed for use in dynamic heterogeneous wireless sensor networks, as stated in a study [54]. This recommendation comes from the research that was conducted in another study [55]. LEACH [62], one of the most well-known protocols, was designed with the intention of increasing the lifetime of wireless sensor networks (WSN) by using the clustering approach. This was one of the primary motivations for its creation. This was the impetus behind the decision to create it. This was one of the primary considerations that led to the creation of it in the first place. This protocol does not have the potential to accept mistakes in any form or manner at all, regardless of the form or manner that they take. The authors of a paper [57] only analyzed fault tolerance in the context of communications that take place between the cluster head (CH) and the base station. This is the only circumstance in which they do so. According to the data that is provided in this paper [57], it is the responsibility of each cluster head (CH) to choose a node that will act as the checkpoint node for the cluster that it manages. Every single one of the routing techniques that are analyzed in several studies [57, 58] takes into account the total amount of energy that is consumed as an important factor in their decision-making. The data should be aggregated before being transferred to the base station once the head of the cluster has finished collecting it from the member nodes of the cluster. After the data has been compiled into a single set, it has to be sent to the base station. The author of this paper suggests making use of a method known as "greedy forwarding" in order to efficiently transmit data from the point of origin to the location that will serve as the location that will serve as its final resting place. This will allow for the most effective transmission of data. The authors of the publication [59] present the BEE-SWARM routing protocol as an effective method of regulating energy in a wireless sensor network. The energy-aware buffer management (EABM) routing system that is described in a study [60] has two primary goals: the first is to increase the lifetime of the network, and the second is to decrease the number of data packets that are lost as a result of buffer overflow. Both of these goals are primary goals of the energy-aware buffer management (EABM) routing system. Both of these objectives are interdependent on one another in some way. The authors of the paper [61] provide a technique of energy conservation that takes data into consideration as a means of reducing overall energy use. This is done in order to encourage a data-collecting paradigm in WSN that is effective with regard to the use of available energy sources. The inventor of GPSR [62] is also the person who developed a protocol that performs greedy forwarding on the data as it is being sent. The full name of the protocol that is often referred to by its shortened form, GPSR, is Greedy Perimeter Stateless Routing. The abbreviation GPSR stands for the entire name of the product. For using this protocol, the only factor that is taken into account when deciding whether or not a packet should be sent is the characteristics of an immediate neighbor. This is because this is the only way to determine whether or not a packet should be sent. Another problem that occurs as a direct consequence of it is the need inherent to this technology to pointlessly keep up a planner graph in order to be able to transfer data packets. This is a problem since it is unnecessary. This issue arises as a direct result of it, and it is a problem that emerges as a direct consequence of it. The adoption of GAR [63] was a solution that was used as a cure to go around the challenge that was brought up by GPSR. The Products at Risk (GAR) program ensures that shipments of goods will be delivered to the location specified by the individual who initiated the shipment. This system incorporates the RUT [63] technology into its operation, in addition to the rolling ball approach, in order to facilitate the transmission of data more easily. The GAR [64] method generates better results than the RUT algorithm, but it does have a few drawbacks, such as the fact that it accesses certain superfluous nodes, which is a significant source of energy drainage. Despite these drawbacks, the GAR [64] method generates better results than the RUT algorithm. In spite of these limitations, the GAR [64] technique produces results that are superior to those produced by the RUT algorithm. In spite of these drawbacks, the GAR [70] method generates outcomes that are far more desirable than the RUT algorithm's outputs. The aforementioned issue, which in the past had been resolved by utilizing the rolling ball strategy, served as the impetus for the invention of the BPR [65] method, which was conceived as a different approach to the issue that needed to be resolved. This problem was remedied in the past by using the rolling ball strategy. It has a striking resemblance to the GAR approach in that it avoids going to any nodes until it is absolutely necessary to do so. The approach known as adaptive energy-aware cluster-based routing, which is often abbreviated as AECR (adaptive energy-aware cluster-based routing), is described in a study [66]. Adaptive energy-aware cluster-based is abbreviated as AECR. The alternative method involves producing clusters in a haphazard fashion, but this methodology gives precedence to the generation of clusters with balanced sizes over the production of clusters in a haphazard manner. In order to make the network more effective in terms of the transmission of data as well as the preservation of energy, the process of creating inter-cluster and intra-cluster routing channels is now being carried out on this site. The findings of an investigation into the efficiency of different routing strategies in wireless sensor networks are shown in Table **3**.

Table 3. Analysis of some routing works in WSN.

Author & Year	Methodology	Summary
Mostafa *et al.* [67],	Ant colony	When choosing the optimum data transmission path, the energy level of the sensor nodes and their distance from the base station are taken into account.
Muhammad *et al.* [68],	LEACH	Wireless Sensor Networks: Intelligent On-Demand Clustering Routing Protocol
Rostami *et al.* [69],	Survey	Techniques for clustering in both heterogeneous and homogeneous wSNs
Zhang *et al.* [54]	DHW Ns AVDHs	Developed a dynamic clustering algorithm networks of several wireless sensor types
Farman et al [55]	ANP model	Cluster head selection on 5 parameters
Rango *et al.* [56]	LEACH	A multi-zone monitoring using clusters
Anisi *et al.* [58]	ISEH	In wireless sensor networks, energy harvesting and battery-powered routing are used.
Mann *et al.* [59]	Swarm intelligence	Packet delivery, throughput, and network life enhanced
Jayarajan *et al.* [60]	EABM	Before sending the next hop data to the cluster, memory emptiness and energy level are taken into account.
Diwakaran *et al.* [61]	ARIMA, PCA	By using this technique, a significant amount of redundant data transfer is stopped.
Yang *et al.* [68]	GPSR	The concept of minimum angle is intro- duced as the criterion of the optimal next hop node.
Yaakob *et al.* [65]	BPR, Fuzzy	Using a dual rolling ball approach, dynamically avoid the contaminated nodes.
Haseeb *et al.* [70]	AECR	It prevents random clusters and creates balanced-sized clusters depending on the distribution of the nodes.
Yang *et al.* [64]	CCPEA, HDWSNs	It defines a clone operator to minimize the communication energy consumption of HDWSNs.
Moussa *et al.* [71]	HDMRP, EAQHSeN	A comparison of several routing protocols is conducted for forest fire identification, which examines the network lifespan and reaction time.

All the existing techniques are only focused on the data transfer from source to destination. The main issue of quick data delivery with energy conservation is still a challenging task for researchers.

Trajectory Path Generation for Mobile Sensor Nodes and Tracking with Compressed Sensing and GD Localization

In a forest, mobile sensors can be used to gather and send more sensed data from fire affected areas to the base station for further analysis. It quickly assists the base station in analyzing the sensed data during forest fire prediction. Tracking and movement of mobile nodes are challenging tasks in the WSN field. This section describes some existing mobile node movement techniques in WSN. It is divided into two subsections:

• Trajectory generation for mobile sensor node

• Compressed Sensing and GD Localization

Trajectory Generation for Mobile Sensor Node

In WSN, sensors are an incredibly important component that plays an important role. It is possible for it to roam about or it might stay in one area. As part of their ongoing endeavor, the researchers are putting in a lot of effort to develop an optimal trajectory path for mobile sensors. The random walk [72], the space-time prism, and the Brownian bridge movement models [73] are some of the essential approaches that are used for the generation of random trajectory pathways. Other important methods include the random number generator. The RTG is built on the combination of these concepts, which serve as its basis. The authors of a study [74] propose a route planning method for moveable anchor nodes that use both the static and the dynamic scheme. This technique is intended for use in the design of routes. Real-time route planning for mobile sensors in an operational zone has been made available by the authors of another study [75]. The amount of time necessary to build a route for mobile sensors will be reduced significantly if this planning is carried out properly. The authors of a paper [76] offer a method for selecting routes for mobile sensor nodes that take advantage of a public transportation system. While data is being gathered, this process helps guarantee that a suitable amount of land is covered, which is helpful. In another paper [77], an algorithm for target tracking is described; this algorithm uses a regression tree approach and filtering methods that make use of an RSSI metric [78]. The authors of an article [79] constructed a model to describe the mobility pattern of a target trajectory by using a number of filtering algorithms to the data in order to do so. There is various studies on many different current trajectory schemes for mobile sensor nodes in Ad Hoc WSN, which are mentioned in a paper [80]. Some of these schemes are PBDGF [81], JMRLE [82], and ESMM [80]. The authors of another study [84] address the issues that are presented by broken wireless channels and the limited lifetime of the network while monitoring mobile sensor nodes as part of the procedure. On the other side, an illustration of a mobile charging node may be seen in a paper [85]. This mobile charger node is used to both charge the wireless sensor nodes at multiple places and find the unknown nodes by utilizing the unique Time of Charge (TOC) sequences. This is accomplished by employing the mobile charger node.

Compressed Sensing and GD Localization

Making sure that mobile nodes are followed as they travel along the trajectory route is another tough component of the task. Two methods, compressed sensing and generalized decentralized localization, are used to track the movement of mobile nodes inside a network. The first method uses compressed data, while the second method uses generalized data. The mobility of mobile nodes may be monitored in a variety of different ways using these two approaches. In this article, a number of different current methods that are based on compressed sensing and that are employed in the WSN paradigm are broken down and explained. The authors of a study [86] proposed a compressed sensing architecture for Ad Hoc WSN in order to reduce the amount of energy that is needed by the network. This would allow the network to function more efficiently. Compressed sensing is the methodology that the authors of another study [87] used in order to discover nodes in their Ad Hoc WSN. They believed that this is the most efficient method. It regards position as a sparse signal that can be reconstructed using approaches that make use of compressed sensing. Additionally, it views this as a feature that should be taken into account. The authors of a publication [88] present a localization technique that is based on Received Signal Strength (RSS). To adjust the accuracy of the localization method, they use multiplicative distance-correction factor (MDCF). In order to achieve the goal of data compression collecting inside a sensor network, a Joint Sparsity model has been developed. This model was developed by using the concepts described in the distribution compressive sensing theory in order to better understand the data [89]. A study suggests using a method for the safe collection of data called compressive sensing (SeDC), which also has the added benefit of lowering the overall computing expense of the network. The authors give several recommendations, one of which is that this method should be used. Random Walk (RW) and Compressive Sensing (CS) are two of the ideas that are covered in the article [90], which aim to lessen the amount of energy that is used by WSN networks. The article also strives to lower the amount of energy that is used by WSN networks. The goal of the research is to reduce, as much as possible, the quantity of energy that is used. According to the information presented in a study [91], the use of sensor networks makes it feasible to detect localization in addition to a significant number of other types of occurrences. The implementation of a technique that makes use of compressed signal data has made this feasible. This has been made possible thanks to the development of this method. An approach that makes use of both the TOA [70] signal and the GD localization [92] method has been proposed by the authors of a study [93] as a way for more accurately monitoring moving objects. This approach makes use of both the TOA [70] signal and the method of GD localization [92]. In this approach, signals are sampled in a manner that is both consistent and erratic, and after that, the signals are reconstructed by the use of a standard linear interpolation.

Forest Fire Detection Framework

As a result of the current climate in which we live, keeping an eye out for forest fires is an inescapable concern for mankind. The researchers are coming up with a large number of different ideas as to the ways in which this particular goal may be accomplished. In the next part, you will find information about many Internet of Things (IoT) based forest fire frameworks that are generating the most attention right now. These frameworks are now receiving a lot of attention because of their usefulness.

The authors of an article [94] provide a framework for the Internet of Things that may be used for the detection of forest fires. This construction has the potential to save a great number of unnecessary fatalities. The creators of another paper [95] employ high-tech sensors and equipment that are linked to the Internet of Things in order to monitor and secure not just their own property but also the neighboring forests. This allows them to keep an eye on both areas at once. The authors of an article [96], which was written by the persons who came up with the concept, recommend utilizing a data fusion approach as a means of fire detection. This recommendation can be found in the publication. Sensors are used to monitor both the temperature and the relative humidity, and after that, the copula principle is used in order to determine the nature of the relationship that exists between the two parameters that were measured. Both the temperature and the relative humidity may be determined using the sensors. For the purpose of determining whether or not this method is successful, a dataset including information that was gathered in real time was used. In order to collect data for the monitoring of forest fires, the authors of an article [97] constructed WSN architecture. This is accomplished by referring to the overall context of the piece. It is made up of sensors that are able to read both the temperature and the humidity in the air at the same time wherever it is positioned. The authors of a book [98] provide a disaster management system that is built on fog technology and the Internet of Things. This system is described in the book (IoT). The authors of a article [99] propose a wireless sensor network (WSN)-based emergency warning system that makes use of sensors to implement the data mining approach for the purpose of detecting forest fires. In addition, the authors state that the WSN-based system should be equipped with a data mining approach. The use of this strategy would be suitable given the setting provided by the title of the book. The authors of a research [100] propose using a low-power wireless ground sensor network (LPWGSN) as a strategy for reducing the amount of energy that is used by sensors. This recommendation comes in the form of a technology. Creating a network out of the connections between the sensors would be able to achieve this goal. This information is offered in the aforementioned article. Within their research, the authors of a paper [101] describe a self-organizing, fault-tolerance model for the early detection of forest fires. In order to monitor wildfires in the future, the creators of a study [102] developed a smart smoke alarm that is based on ZigBee technology. In a study [103], an effective and time-sensitive GA is demonstrated for the purpose of calibrating the uncertainty of the data input in a forest fire model, which ultimately leads to an efficient use of computing resources. The purpose of this GA is to calibrate the uncertainty of the data input. This is done with the intention of calibrating the degree of uncertainty associated with the data that is entered. The purpose of this more generic assignment is to calibrate the degree of uncertainty that is connected to the data that was provided. This specific activity was carried out in order to achieve the goals that were initially established for the undertaking. The authors refer to what is established in an article [104] as an integrated forest fire danger assessment system for Austria. This system was established in Austria. This system is also known as an Integrated Fixed-Disk System (Integrated Forest Fire Danger Assessment System). The data obtained from the daily fire weather index is used as the basis for this method. In addition to this, they are in the midst of creating a hazard map for the whole of the state that will describe the likely causes of human-caused fires. This map will cover the entire state. The authors of [105]another paper propose a fog-assisted system that is enabled by the Internet of Things and consumes very little energy for the precise early prediction of forest fires. This system is facilitated by the Internet of Things at Ionian University. The writers of a paper [106] delivered a presentation in which they demonstrated a prototype for wildfire monitoring that puts an emphasis on response time. In the presentation, they also discussed the article. They discussed the significance of having a quick answer in their conversation. On the other hand [107], another study provides a diagram that depicts the basic structure of a system for monitoring wildfires. The Internet of Things (IoT) and cloud computing both play important roles in the functioning of this system. The authors of a paper [108] devised a system for the tracking of events across a dispersed environment. The writers of another paper [109] used wireless sensor networks as the primary source of data for their systems. This section gives an overall summary of the organizational structure.

The comparative study between existing schemes is described in Table **4**.

Table 4. Analysis of some forest fire detection frameworks.

Proposed Model	Year	Tool	Approaches	Energy Efficiency	Advantage/Summary
Forest fire spread model [109]	2018	ArcGIS, ENVI	Grey system theory	Not mentioned	MODIS photos are being utilized as data, and access to them is free.
Early Alarming System in Forest Fire Using Ad-Hoc Network and Microcontroller [110]	2013	Hardware-based ccs compiler, Proteus simulato turbo c.	Real-time automation provided with rR, TOS	Not mentioned	The proposed system is cost-effective.
Integrated IoT-Fog-Cloud energy-efficient framework [108]	2019	Amazon EC2 cloud	ANOVA SARIMA	Considered	An architecture based on the Internet of Things that was created using sensor data in order to anticipate the susceptibility level of wildfires.
Forest fire spread model [109]	2018	ENVI, ArcGIS	Grey system theory	Not mentioned	A model that was developed by fusing information obtained from remote sensing satellites (MODIS)
Framework for forest fire monitoring [94]	2020	Not mentioned	6low-pan/RF/4G/5G	Not considered	An architecture for the Internet of Things that is built on fog and is created using sensor data.
The European Alps' comprehensive forest fire risk assessment system [104]	2019	Amazon EC2 cloud	Web GISprototype	Not considered	For the purpose of forest monitoring, an Integrated Forest Danger Assessment System (IFDS) has been developed using the data from a fire weather index, hazard human activity, and a fuel type map.
Fog-assisted IoT-enabled scalable architecture for wildfire monitoring [89]	2018	Not mentioned	SARIMA-Multilayer perceptron	Considered	A system for the detection of forest fires based on the Internet of Things, fog computing, and cloud computing concepts.

CONCLUSION

This chapter provides a brief analysis of recent approaches covering different aspects of forest fire monitoring in the WSN paradigm. It provides a broader range of state-of-the-arts that include the various issues of monitoring forest fire.

It has outlined different studies under sections Localization of sensor nodes (section 2.1), Forest fire detection model (section 2.2), Routing between sensor nodes and base station (section 2.3), Trajectory path generation for mobile sensor nodes and Tracking with compressed sensing and GD localization (section 2.4), and different Forest fire detection frameworks (section 2.5).

Methods reviewed in section 2.1 mainly cover range-free and range-based localization approaches. Most of these techniques are used to reduce the localization error of sensor nodes. From Table **1**, it is seen that these techniques are complex and have high computational costs.

In section 2.2, different forest fire detection techniques are discussed. Most of these techniques have low accuracy and a low response time. These techniques also do not consider any energy issues of the sensor nodes as well as quick delivery of sensed data from forest terrain to the base station.

In section 2.3, various data transfer protocols are discussed. These routing protocols are analyzed with different parameters like packet delivery ratio, network lifetime, and energy consumed by the sensors.

In section 2.4, different techniques for the movement of mobile sensor nodes are discussed. Mobile nodes from low active and medium active zones move forward nearer the high active zone. As a result, the quick data delivery of sensor nodes from the high active forest zone to the base station will be assured by the proposed model.

At last, in section 2.5, different frameworks for forest fire detection are discussed. It is observed from Table **4** that most of them do not consider the energy issue of sensors and quick data delivery of sensed data from forest terrain to the base station.

It can be concluded that a complete framework for forest fire monitoring is required that addresses these aforementioned issues. Based on abovementioned research issues obtained after reviewing the existing works, the thesis's contribution is presented.

REFERENCES

[1]   State agency. Victoria emergency Australia.[Online],

[2]   Forest survey report. Forest department India, 2021 [Online],

[3]   V. Chowdary, and M.K. Gupta, "Automatic forest fire detection and monitoring techniques: a survey", *Proceedings of ICICCD 2017,* pp. 1111-1117, 2018.
[http://dx.doi.org/10.1007/978-981-10-5903-2_116]

[4]   W. Yingyou, L. Zhi, M. Yinghui, and Z. Dazhe, "A two-stage range-free localization method for wireless sensor networks", *Int. J. Distrib. Sens. Netw.,* vol. 11, no. 2, p. 908417, 2015.
[http://dx.doi.org/10.1155/2015/908417]

[5]   P.T. Daely, and S.Y. Shin, "Range based wireless node localization using dragonfly algorithm", *Eighth International Conference on Ubiquitous and Future Networks (ICUFN),* pp. 1012-1015, 2016.
[http://dx.doi.org/10.1109/ICUFN.2016.7536950]

[6]   A. Kansal, Y. Singh, N. Kumar, and V. Mohindru, "Detection of forest fires using machine learning technique: A perspective", *Third International Conference on Image Information Processing (ICIIP),* pp. 241-245, 2015.
[http://dx.doi.org/10.1109/ICIIP.2015.7414773]

[7]   A. Kansal, Y. Singh, N. Kumar, and V. Mohindru, "Detection of forest fires using machine learning technique: A perspective", *Third International Conference on Image Information Processing (ICIIP),* pp. 241-245, 2015.
[http://dx.doi.org/10.1109/ICIIP.2015.7414773]

[8]   K. Trivedi, and A.K. Srivastava, "An energy efficient framework for detection and monitoring of forest fire using mobile agent in wireless sensor networks", *International Conference on Computational Intelligence and Computing Research,* pp. 1-4, 2014.
[http://dx.doi.org/10.1109/ICCIC.2014.7238433]

[9]   C. Lv, J. Wang, and F. Zhang, "Forest fire spread model based on the grey system theory", *J. Supercomput.,* vol. 76, no. 5, pp. 3602-3614, 2020.
[http://dx.doi.org/10.1007/s11227-018-2560-x]

[10] H. Kaur, S.K. Sood, and M. Bhatia, "Cloud-assisted green IoT-enabled comprehensive framework for wildfire monitoring", *Cluster Comput.,* vol. 23, no. 2, pp. 1149-1162, 2020.
[http://dx.doi.org/10.1007/s10586-019-02981-7]

[11] H. Adab, K.D. Kanniah, and K. Solaimani, "Modeling forest fire risk in the northeast of Iran using remote sensing and GIS techniques", *Nat. Hazards,* vol. 65, no. 3, pp. 1723-1743, 2013.
[http://dx.doi.org/10.1007/s11069-012-0450-8]

[12] H. Kaur, and S.K. Sood, "Fog-assisted IoT-enabled scalable network infrastructure for wildfire surveillance", *J. Netw. Comput. Appl.,* vol. 144, pp. 171-183, 2019.
[http://dx.doi.org/10.1016/j.jnca.2019.07.005]

[13] P. Cortez and A. Morais, "A data mining approach to predict forest fires using meteorological data," in *New Trends in Artificial Intelligence: Proceedings of the 13th Portuguese Conference on Artificial Intelligence (EPIA 2007)*, Guimarães, Portugal, 2007, pp. 512–523.

[14] H. Sharma, A. Haque, and Z.A. Jaffery, "Maximization of wireless sensor network lifetime using solar energy harvesting for smart agriculture monitoring", *Ad Hoc Netw.,* vol. 94, p. 101966, 2019.
[http://dx.doi.org/10.1016/j.adhoc.2019.101966]

[15] B.T. Pham, A. Jaafari, M. Avand, N. Al-Ansari, T. Dinh Du, H.P.H. Yen, T.V. Phong, D.H. Nguyen, H.V. Le, D. Mafi-Gholami, I. Prakash, H. Thi Thuy, and T.T. Tuyen, "Performance evaluation of machine learning methods for forest fire modeling and prediction", *Symmetry (Basel),* vol. 12, no. 6, p. 1022, 2020.
[http://dx.doi.org/10.3390/sym12061022]

[16]   Z. Jiao, Y. Zhang, J. Xin, L. Mu, Y. Yi, H. Liu, and D. Liu, "A deep learning based forest fire detection approach using UAV and YOLOv3", *1st International Conference on Industrial Artificial Intelligence (IAI),* pp. 1-5, 2019.
[http://dx.doi.org/10.1109/ICIAI.2019.8850815]

[17]   N.A. Alrajeh, M. Bashir, and B. Shams, "Localization techniques in wireless sensor networks", *Int. J. Distrib. Sens. Netw.,* vol. 9, no. 6, p. 304628, 2013.
[http://dx.doi.org/10.1155/2013/304628]

[18]   X. Zhao, X. Zhang, Z. Sun, and P. Wang, "New wireless sensor network localization algorithm for outdoor adventure", *IEEE Access,* vol. 6, pp. 13191-13199, 2018.
[http://dx.doi.org/10.1109/ACCESS.2018.2813082]

[19]   Y. Miao, H. Wu, and L. Zhang, "The accurate location estimation of sensor node using received signal strength measurements in large-scale farmland", *J. Sens.,* vol. 2018, pp. 1-10, 2018.
[http://dx.doi.org/10.1155/2018/2325863]

[20]   E. Cassano, F. Florio, F. De Rango, and S. Marano, "A performance comparison between ROC-RSSI and trilateration localization techniques for WPAN sensor networks in a real outdoor testbed", *Wireless Telecommunications Symposium,* pp. 1-8, 2009.
[http://dx.doi.org/10.1109/WTS.2009.5068988]

[21]   S. Kumar, and D.K. Lobiyal, "Novel DV-Hop localization algorithm for wireless sensor networks", *Telecomm. Syst.,* vol. 64, no. 3, pp. 509-524, 2017.
[http://dx.doi.org/10.1007/s11235-016-0189-8]

[22]   Y. Chen, X. Li, Y. Ding, J. Xu, and Z. Liu, "An improved DV-Hop localization algorithm for wireless sensor networks", *13th IEEE Conference on Industrial Electronics and Applications (ICIEA),* pp. 1831-1836, 2018.

[23]   L. Gui, X. Zhang, Q. Ding, F. Shu, and A. Wei, "Reference anchor selection and global optimized solution for DV-hop localization in wireless sensor networks", *Wirel. Pers. Commun.,* vol. 96, no. 4, pp. 5995-6005, 2017.
[http://dx.doi.org/10.1007/s11277-017-4459-x]

[24]   F. Zhu, and J. Wei, "Localization algorithm in wireless sensor networks based on improved support vector machine", *Journal of Nanoelectronics and Optoelectronics,* vol. 12, no. 5, pp. 452-459, 2017.
[http://dx.doi.org/10.1166/jno.2017.2049]

[25]   S. Afzal, and H. Beigy, "A localization algorithm for large scale mobile wireless sensor networks: a learning approach", *J. Supercomput.,* vol. 69, no. 1, pp. 98-120, 2014.
[http://dx.doi.org/10.1007/s11227-014-1129-6]

[26]   J. Luomala, and I. Hakala, "Adaptive range-based localization algorithm based on trilateration and reference node selection for outdoor wireless sensor networks", *Comput. Netw.,* vol. 210, p. 108865, 2022.
[http://dx.doi.org/10.1016/j.comnet.2022.108865]

[27]   T.K. Mohanta, and D.K. Das, "Advanced localization algorithm for wireless sensor networks using fractional order class topper optimization", *J. Supercomput.,* vol. 78, no. 8, pp. 10405-10433, 2022.
[http://dx.doi.org/10.1007/s11227-021-04278-2]

[28]   S.J. Bhat, and S.K. Venkata, "An optimization based localization with area minimization for heterogeneous wireless sensor networks in anisotropic fields", *Comput. Netw.,* vol. 179, p. 107371, 2020.
[http://dx.doi.org/10.1016/j.comnet.2020.107371]

[29]   Z. Cui, B. Sun, G. Wang, Y. Xue, and J. Chen, "A novel oriented cuckoo search algorithm to improve DV-Hop performance for cyber–physical systems", *J. Parallel Distrib. Comput.,* vol. 103, pp. 42-52, 2017.
[http://dx.doi.org/10.1016/j.jpdc.2016.10.011]

[30]   M.N. Khetwal, and M. Ishrat, "A study of forest-fire surveillance system based on MANET for Uttarakhand Hills", *Pragyan.,* vol. 10, pp. 36-39, 2012.

[31]   M. Castelli, L. Vanneschi, and A. Popovič, "Predicting burned areas of forest fires: an artificial intelligence approach", *Fire Ecol.,* vol. 11, no. 1, pp. 106-118, 2015.
[http://dx.doi.org/10.4996/fireecology.1101106]

[32]   U. Ganesh, M. Anand, S. Arun, M. Dinesh, P. Gunaseelan, and R. Karthik, "Forest fire detection using optimized solar-powered Zigbee wireless sensor networks", *Int. J. Sci. Eng. Res.,* vol. 4, no. 6, pp. 586-596, 2013.

[33]   C.M. Wu, R.S. Chang, P.I. Lee, and J.H. Yen, "An innovative scheme for increasing connectivity and life of ZigBee networks", *J. Supercomput.,* vol. 65, no. 1, pp. 136-153, 2013.
[http://dx.doi.org/10.1007/s11227-011-0696-z]

[34]   C.M. Wu, R.S. Chang, P.I. Lee, and J.H. Yen, "An innovative scheme for increasing connectivity and life of ZigBee networks", *J. Supercomput.,* vol. 65, no. 1, pp. 136-153, 2013.
[http://dx.doi.org/10.1007/s11227-011-0696-z]

[35]   P. Zou, and Y. Liu, "An efficient data fusion approach for event detection in heterogeneous wireless sensor networks", *Appl. Math. Inf. Sci.,* vol. 9, no. 1, pp. 517-526, 2015.
[http://dx.doi.org/10.12785/amis/090160]

[36]   K. Trivedi, and A.K. Srivastava, "An energy efficient framework for detection and monitoring of forest fire using mobile agent in wireless sensor networks", *International Conference on Computational Intelligence and Computing Research,* pp. 1-4, 2014.
[http://dx.doi.org/10.1109/ICCIC.2014.7238433]

[37]   S. Gaglio, G.L. Re, G. Martorella, and D. Peri, "A symbolic distributed event detection scheme for Wireless Sensor Networks", *21st International Conference on Emerging Technologies and Factory Automation (ETFA),* pp. 1-4, 2016.
[http://dx.doi.org/10.1109/ETFA.2016.7733685]

[38]   V. Pande, W. Elmannai, and K. M. Elleithy, "Optimized algorithm for fire detection over WSN using Micaz motes," Dept. of Computer Science and Engineering, University of Bridgeport, CT, USA.

[39]   B.A. Sundari, and A.S. Thanamani, "An efficient feature selection technique using supervised fuzzy information theory", *Int. J. Comput. Appl.,* vol. 85, no. 19, 2014.

[40]   P. Zou, and Y. Liu, "An efficient data fusion approach for event detection in heterogeneous wireless sensor networks", *Appl. Math. Inf. Sci.,* vol. 9, no. 1, pp. 517-526, 2015.
[http://dx.doi.org/10.12785/amis/090160]

[41]   C. Lv, J. Wang, and F. Zhang, "Forest fire spread model based on the grey system theory", *J. Supercomput.,* vol. 76, no. 5, pp. 3602-3614, 2020.
[http://dx.doi.org/10.1007/s11227-018-2560-x]

[42]   D. Sinha, R. Kumari, and S. Tripathi, "Semisupervised classification based clustering approach in WSN for forest fire detection", *Wirel. Pers. Commun.,* vol. 109, no. 4, pp. 2561-2605, 2019.
[http://dx.doi.org/10.1007/s11277-019-06697-0]

[43]   A. Molina-Pico, D. Cuesta-Frau, A. Araujo, J. Alejandre, and A. Rozas, "Forest monitoring and wildland early fire detection by a hierarchical wireless sensor network", *J. Sens.,* vol. 2016, pp. 1-8, 2016.
[http://dx.doi.org/10.1155/2016/8325845]

[44]   B. Kalantar, N. Ueda, M.O. Idrees, S. Janizadeh, K. Ahmadi, and F. Shabani, "Forest fire susceptibility prediction based on machine learning models with resampling algorithms on remote sensing data", *Remote Sens. (Basel),* vol. 12, no. 22, p. 3682, 2020.
[http://dx.doi.org/10.3390/rs12223682]

[45]   G.E. Espinoza Diaz, "Implementación del sistema de información geográfica para la gestión de

incendios forestales del parque arqueológico de Machupicchu", *Bachelor's thesis, Escuela Profesional de Ingeniería Ambiental, Universidad César Vallejo, Cusco, Peru,* 2021.

[46] A Jilbab, and A Bourouhou, "Hybridized model for early detection and smart monitoring of forest fire", *Transactions on Machine Learning and Artificial Intelligence,* vol. 5, no. 4, 2017..

[47] H. Kaur, and S.K. Sood, "Adaptive Neuro Fuzzy Inference System (ANFIS) based wildfire risk assessment", *J. Exp. Theor. Artif. Intell.,* vol. 31, no. 4, pp. 599-619, 2019.
[http://dx.doi.org/10.1080/0952813X.2019.1591523]

[48] U. Dampage, L. Bandaranayake, R. Wanasinghe, K. Kottahachchi, and B. Jayasanka, "Forest fire detection system using wireless sensor networks and machine learning", *Sci. Rep.,* vol. 12, no. 1, p. 46, 2022.
[http://dx.doi.org/10.1038/s41598-021-03882-9] [PMID: 34996960]

[49] S.T. Seydi, V. Saeidi, B. Kalantar, N. Ueda, and A.A. Halin, "Fire-Net: A deep learning framework for active forest fire detection", *J. Sens.,* vol. 2022, pp. 1-14, 2022.
[http://dx.doi.org/10.1155/2022/8044390]

[50] A. Díaz-Ramírez, L.A. Tafoya, J.A. Atempa, and P. Mejía-Alvarez, "Wireless sensor networks and fusion information methods for forest fire detection", *Procedia Technol.,* vol. 3, pp. 69-79, 2012.
[http://dx.doi.org/10.1016/j.protcy.2012.03.008]

[51] I.D.B. Silva, M.E. Valle, L.C. Barros, and J.F.C.A. Meyer, "A wildfire warning system applied to the state of Acre in the Brazilian Amazon", *Appl. Soft Comput.,* vol. 89, p. 106075, 2020.
[http://dx.doi.org/10.1016/j.asoc.2020.106075]

[52] N. Moussa, A. El Belrhiti El Alaoui, and C. Chaudet, "A novel approach of WSN routing protocols comparison for forest fire detection", *Wirel. Netw.,* vol. 26, no. 3, pp. 1857-1867, 2020.
[http://dx.doi.org/10.1007/s11276-018-1872-3]

[53] S.K. Malik, M. Dave, S.K. Dhurandher, I. Woungang, and L. Barolli, "An ant-based QoS-aware routing protocol for heterogeneous wireless sensor networks", *Soft Comput.,* vol. 21, no. 21, pp. 6225-6236, 2017.
[http://dx.doi.org/10.1007/s00500-016-2347-z]

[54] J. Zhang, and J. Chen, "An adaptive clustering algorithm for dynamic heterogeneous wireless sensor networks", *Wirel. Netw.,* vol. 25, no. 1, pp. 455-470, 2019.
[http://dx.doi.org/10.1007/s11276-017-1648-1]

[55] H. Farman, H. Javed, B. Jan, J. Ahmad, S. Ali, F.N. Khalil, and M. Khan, "Analytical network process based optimum cluster head selection in wireless sensor network", *PLoS One,* vol. 12, no. 7, p. e0180848, 2017.
[http://dx.doi.org/10.1371/journal.pone.0180848] [PMID: 28719616]

[56] F. De Rango, N. Palmieri, and S. Ranieri, "Spatial correlation based low energy aware clustering (leach) in a wireless sensor networks", *Advances in Electrical and Electronic Engineering,* vol. 13, no. 4, pp. 350-358, 2015.
[http://dx.doi.org/10.15598/aeee.v13i4.1496]

[57] M.N. Cheraghlou, A. Khadem-Zadeh, and M. Haghparast, "Increasing lifetime and fault tolerance capability in wireless sensor networks by providing a novel management framework", *Wirel. Pers. Commun.,* vol. 92, no. 2, pp. 603-622, 2017.
[http://dx.doi.org/10.1007/s11277-016-3559-3]

[58] M.H. Anisi, G. Abdul-Salaam, M.Y.I. Idris, A.W.A. Wahab, and I. Ahmedy, "Energy harvesting and battery power based routing in wireless sensor networks", *Wirel. Netw.,* vol. 23, no. 1, pp. 249-266, 2017.
[http://dx.doi.org/10.1007/s11276-015-1150-6]

[59] P.S. Mann, and S. Singh, "Energy-efficient hierarchical routing for wireless sensor networks: a swarm intelligence approach", *Wirel. Pers. Commun.,* vol. 92, no. 2, pp. 785-805, 2017.

[http://dx.doi.org/10.1007/s11277-016-3577-1]

[60]   P. Jayarajan, G.R. Kanagachidambaresan, T.V.P. Sundararajan, K. Sakthipandi, R. Maheswar, and A. Karthikeyan, "An energy-aware buffer management (EABM) routing protocol for WSN", *J. Supercomput.,* vol. 76, no. 6, pp. 4543-4555, 2020.
[http://dx.doi.org/10.1007/s11227-018-2582-4]

[61]   S. Diwakaran, B. Perumal, and K. Vimala Devi, "A cluster prediction model-based data collection for energy efficient wireless sensor network", *J. Supercomput.,* vol. 75, no. 6, pp. 3302-3316, 2019.
[http://dx.doi.org/10.1007/s11227-018-2437-z]

[62]   X. Yang, M. Li, Z. Qian, and T. Di, "Improvement of GPSR protocol in vehicular ad hoc network", *IEEE Access,* vol. 6, pp. 39515-39524, 2018.
[http://dx.doi.org/10.1109/ACCESS.2018.2853112]

[63]   Das AK, Chaki R. "Localization based Anti-Void Clustering Approach (LAVCA) for Energy Efficient Routing in Wireless Sensor Network" *Computer Information Systems and Industrial Management: 16th IFIP TC8 International Conference, CISIM* Bialystok, Poland, Proceeding, Springer International Publishing, 2017 pp. 290-302.

[64]   J. Yang, F. Liu, and J. Cao, "Greedy discrete particle swarm optimization based routing protocol for cluster-based wireless sensor networks," *Journal of Ambient Intelligence and Humanized Computing*, vol. 10, no. 9, pp. 3475–3480, 2019.

[65]   N. Yaakob, I. Khalil, H. Kumarage, M. Atiquzzaman, and Z. Tari, "By-passing infected areas in wireless sensor networks using BPR", *IEEE Trans. Comput.,* vol. 64, no. 6, p. 1, 2014.
[http://dx.doi.org/10.1109/TC.2014.2345400]

[66]   K. Haseeb, K.A. Bakar, A.H. Abdullah, and T. Darwish, "Adaptive energy aware cluster-based routing protocol for wireless sensor networks", *Wirel. Netw.,* vol. 23, no. 6, pp. 1953-1966, 2017.
[http://dx.doi.org/10.1007/s11276-016-1269-0]

[67]   M.E.A. Ibrahim, and A.E.S. Ahmed, "Energy-aware intelligent hybrid routing protocol for wireless sensor networks", *Concurr. Comput.,* vol. 34, no. 3, p. e6601, 2022.
[http://dx.doi.org/10.1002/cpe.6601]

[68]   M.A. Khan, and A.A. Awan, "Intelligent on demand clustering routing protocol for wireless sensor networks", *Wirel. Commun. Mob. Comput.,* vol. 2022, pp. 1-10, 2022.
[http://dx.doi.org/10.1155/2022/7356733]

[69]   A.S. Rostami, M. Badkoobe, F. Mohanna, H. keshavarz, A.A.R. Hosseinabadi, and A.K. Sangaiah, "Survey on clustering in heterogeneous and homogeneous wireless sensor networks", *J. Supercomput.,* vol. 74, no. 1, pp. 277-323, 2018.
[http://dx.doi.org/10.1007/s11227-017-2128-1]

[70]   J. Hamie, B. Denis, R. D'Errico, and C. Richard, "On-body TOA-based ranging error model for motion capture applications within wearable UWB networks", *J. Ambient Intell. Humaniz. Comput.,* vol. 6, no. 5, pp. 603-612, 2015.
[http://dx.doi.org/10.1007/s12652-013-0215-6]

[71]   N. Moussa, A. El Belrhiti El Alaoui, and C. Chaudet, "A novel approach of WSN routing protocols comparison for forest fire detection", *Wirel. Netw.,* vol. 26, no. 3, pp. 1857-1867, 2020.
[http://dx.doi.org/10.1007/s11276-018-1872-3]

[72]   Y. Yoshimura, R. Sinatra, A. Krebs, and C. Ratti, "Analysis of visitors' mobility patterns through random walk in the Louvre Museum", *J. Ambient Intell. Humaniz. Comput.,* vol. 15, no. 9, pp. 1643-1658, 2024.

[73]   G. Technitis, W. Othman, K. Safi, and R. Weibel, "From A to B, randomly: a point-to-point random trajectory generator for animal movement", *Int. J. Geogr. Inf. Sci.,* vol. 29, no. 6, pp. 912-934, 2015.
[http://dx.doi.org/10.1080/13658816.2014.999682]

[74]   E. Erdemir, and T.E. Tuncer, "Path planning for mobile-anchor based wireless sensor network

localization: Static and dynamic schemes", *Ad Hoc Netw.,* vol. 77, pp. 1-10, 2018.
[http://dx.doi.org/10.1016/j.adhoc.2018.04.005]

[75] Y. Kim, W. Jung, and H. Bang, "Real-time path planning to dispatch a mobile sensor into an operational area", *Inf. Fusion,* vol. 45, pp. 27-37, 2019.
[http://dx.doi.org/10.1016/j.inffus.2018.01.010]

[76] O. Saukh, D. Hasenfratz, and L. Thiele, "Route selection for mobile sensor nodes on public transport networks", *J. Ambient Intell. Humaniz. Comput.,* vol. 5, no. 3, pp. 307-321, 2014.
[http://dx.doi.org/10.1007/s12652-012-0170-7]

[77] H. Ahmadi, F. Viani, and R. Bouallegue, "An accurate prediction method for moving target localization and tracking in wireless sensor networks", *Ad Hoc Netw.,* vol. 70, pp. 14-22, 2018.
[http://dx.doi.org/10.1016/j.adhoc.2017.11.008]

[78] J.S. Bilodeau, A. Bouzouane, B. Bouchard, and S. Gaboury, "An experimental comparative study of RSSI-based positioning algorithms for passive RFID localization in smart environments", *J. Ambient Intell. Humaniz. Comput.,* vol. 9, no. 5, pp. 1327-1343, 2018.
[http://dx.doi.org/10.1007/s12652-017-0531-3]

[79] S. Misra, S. Singh, M. Khatua, and M.S. Obaidat, "Extracting mobility pattern from target trajectory in wireless sensor networks", *Int. J. Commun. Syst.,* vol. 28, no. 2, pp. 213-230, 2015.
[http://dx.doi.org/10.1002/dac.2649]

[80] S.K. Singh, and P. Kumar, "A comprehensive survey on trajectory schemes for data collection using mobile elements in WSNs", *J. Ambient Intell. Humaniz. Comput.,* vol. 11, no. 1, pp. 291-312, 2020.
[http://dx.doi.org/10.1007/s12652-019-01268-4]

[81] S. Say, H. Inata, J. Liu, and S. Shimamoto, "Priority-based data gathering framework in UAV-assisted wireless sensor networks", *IEEE Sens. J.,* vol. 16, no. 14, pp. 5785-5794, 2016.
[http://dx.doi.org/10.1109/JSEN.2016.2568260]

[82] J. Luo, and J.P. Hubaux, "Joint mobility and routing for lifetime elongation in wireless sensor networks", *Proceedings IEEE 24th Annual Joint Conference of the IEEE Computer and Communications Societies,* vol. 3, pp. 1735-1746, 2005.

[83] Y. Gu, F. Ren, Y. Ji, and J. Li, "The evolution of sink mobility management in wireless sensor networks: A survey", *IEEE Commun. Surv. Tutor.,* vol. 18, no. 1, pp. 507-524, 2016.
[http://dx.doi.org/10.1109/COMST.2015.2388779]

[84] Y. Qi, P. Cheng, J. Bai, J. Chen, A. Guenard, Y.Q. Song, and Z. Shi, "Energy-efficient target tracking by mobile sensors with limited sensing range", *IEEE Trans. Ind. Electron.,* vol. 63, no. 11, pp. 6949-6961, 2016.
[http://dx.doi.org/10.1109/TIE.2016.2584000]

[85] Y Shu, P Cheng, Y Gu, J Chen, and T. He, "Localizing wireless rechargeable sensors with time of charge", *ACM transactions on sensor networks (TOSN),* vol. 11, no. 3, pp. 1-22, 2015.

[86] W. Chen, and I.J. Wassell, "Energy-efficient signal acquisition in wireless sensor networks: a compressive sensing framework", *IET Wirel. Sens. Syst.,* vol. 2, no. 1, pp. 1-8, 2012.
[http://dx.doi.org/10.1049/iet-wss.2011.0009]

[87] Y. Wei, W. Li, and T. Chen, "Node localization algorithm for wireless sensor networks using compressive sensing theory", *Pers. Ubiquitous Comput.,* vol. 20, no. 5, pp. 809-819, 2016.
[http://dx.doi.org/10.1007/s00779-016-0951-7]

[88] L. Gui, M. Yang, P. Fang, and S. Yang, "RSS☐based indoor localisation using MDCF", *IET Wirel. Sens. Syst.,* vol. 7, no. 4, pp. 98-104, 2017.
[http://dx.doi.org/10.1049/iet-wss.2016.0085]

[89] P. Zhang, S. Wang, K. Guo, and J. Wang, "A secure data collection scheme based on compressive sensing in wireless sensor networks", *Ad Hoc Netw.,* vol. 70, pp. 73-84, 2018.
[http://dx.doi.org/10.1016/j.adhoc.2017.11.011]

[90]   M.T. Nguyen, and K.A. Teague, "Compressive sensing based random walk routing in wireless sensor networks", *Ad Hoc Netw.,* vol. 54, pp. 99-110, 2017.
       [http://dx.doi.org/10.1016/j.adhoc.2016.10.009]

[91]   R. Jiang, Y. Zhu, T. Liu, and Q. Chen, "Compressive detection and localization of multiple heterogeneous events in sensor networks", *Ad Hoc Netw.,* vol. 65, pp. 65-77, 2017.
       [http://dx.doi.org/10.1016/j.adhoc.2017.08.001]

[92]   N.A.S. Alwan, and A.S. Mahmood, "Distributed gradient descent localization in wireless sensor networks", *Arab. J. Sci. Eng.,* vol. 40, no. 3, pp. 893-899, 2015.
       [http://dx.doi.org/10.1007/s13369-014-1552-2]

[93]   N.A.S. Alwan, and Z.M. Hussain, "Compressive sensing with chaotic sequences: An application to localization in wireless sensor networks", *Wirel. Pers. Commun.,* vol. 105, no. 3, pp. 941-950, 2019.
       [http://dx.doi.org/10.1007/s11277-019-06129-z]

[94]   S. Srividhya, and S. Sankaranarayanan, "IoT–fog enabled framework for forest fire management system", *fourth world conference on smart trends in systems, security and sustainability (WorldS4),* pp. 273-276, 2020.
       [http://dx.doi.org/10.1109/WorldS450073.2020.9210328]

[95]   F. Cui, "Deployment and integration of smart sensors with IoT devices detecting fire disasters in huge forest environment", *Comput. Commun.,* vol. 150, pp. 818-827, 2020.
       [http://dx.doi.org/10.1016/j.comcom.2019.11.051]

[96]   S.H. Javadi, and A. Mohammadi, "Fire detection by fusing correlated measurements", *J. Ambient Intell. Humaniz. Comput.,* vol. 10, no. 4, pp. 1443-1451, 2019.
       [http://dx.doi.org/10.1007/s12652-017-0584-3]

[97]   A.R. Ulucinar, I. Korpeoglu, and A.E. Cetin, "A Wi-Fi cluster based wireless sensor network application and deployment for wildfire detection", *Int. J. Distrib. Sens. Netw.,* vol. 10, no. 10, p. 651957, 2014.
       [http://dx.doi.org/10.1155/2014/651957]

[98]   A. Aljumah, A. Kaur, M. Bhatia, and T. Ahamed Ahanger, "Internet of things-fog computing-based framework for smart disaster management", *Trans. Emerg. Telecommun. Technol.,* vol. 32, no. 8, p. e4078, 2021.
       [http://dx.doi.org/10.1002/ett.4078]

[99]   M. Saoudi, A. Bounceur, R. Euler, and T. Kechadi, "Data mining techniques applied to wireless sensor networks for early forest fire detection", *Proceedings of the International Conference on Internet of things and Cloud Computing,* pp. 1-7, 2016.
       [http://dx.doi.org/10.1145/2896387.2900323]

[100] Z Feng, Z Zhao, S Chen, and H. Zhang, "Research on Multi-Factor Forest Fire Prediction Model Using Machine Learning Method in China". *ResearchGate, Beijing Forestry University, China,* 2020.

[101] F.T. Giuntini, D.M. Beder, and J. Ueyama, "Exploiting self-organization and fault tolerance in wireless sensor networks: A case study on wildfire detection application", *Int. J. Distrib. Sens. Netw.,* vol. 13, no. 4, 2017.
       [http://dx.doi.org/10.1177/1550147717704120]

[102] Q. Wu, J. Cao, C. Zhou, J. Huang, Z. Li, S.M. Cheng, J. Cheng, and G. Pan, "Intelligent smoke alarm system with wireless sensor network using ZigBee", *Wirel. Commun. Mob. Comput.,* vol. 2018, no. 1, p. 8235127, 2018.
       [http://dx.doi.org/10.1155/2018/8235127]

[103] T. Artés, A. Cencerrado, A. Cortés, and T. Margalef, "Enhancing computational efficiency on forest fire forecasting by time-aware Genetic Algorithms", *J. Supercomput.,* vol. 71, no. 5, pp. 1869-1881, 2015.
       [http://dx.doi.org/10.1007/s11227-014-1365-9]

[104] M.M. Müller, L. Vilà-Vilardell, and H. Vacik, "Towards an integrated forest fire danger assessment system for the European Alps", *Ecol. Inform.,* vol. 60, p. 101151, 2020.
[http://dx.doi.org/10.1016/j.ecoinf.2020.101151]

[105] "An insight to forest fire detection techniques using wireless sensor networks", *4th International conference on signal processing, computing and control (ISPCC),* pp. 647-653, 2017.
[http://dx.doi.org/10.1109/ISPCC.2017.8269757]

[106] A. Tsipis, A. Papamichail, I. Angelis, G. Koufoudakis, G. Tsoumanis, and K. Oikonomou, "An alertness-adjustable cloud/fog IoT solution for timely environmental monitoring based on wildfire risk forecasting", *Energies,* vol. 13, no. 14, p. 3693, 2020.
[http://dx.doi.org/10.3390/en13143693]

[107] H. Kaur, and S.K. Sood, "Soft-computing-centric framework for wildfire monitoring, prediction and forecasting", *Soft Comput.,* vol. 24, no. 13, pp. 9651-9661, 2020.
[http://dx.doi.org/10.1007/s00500-019-04477-3]

[108] N. Dziengel, M. Seiffert, M. Ziegert, S. Adler, S. Pfeiffer, and J. Schiller, "Deployment and evaluation of a fully applicable distributed event detection system in Wireless Sensor Networks", *Ad Hoc Netw.,* vol. 37, pp. 160-182, 2016.
[http://dx.doi.org/10.1016/j.adhoc.2015.08.017]

[109] C. Lv, J. Wang, and F. Zhang, "Forest fire spread model based on the grey system theory", *J. Supercomput.,* vol. 76, no. 5, pp. 3602-3614, 2020.
[http://dx.doi.org/10.1007/s11227-018-2560-x]

[110] S. Philomina, "Ad-hoc network and microcontroller remote for early warning system in forest fire control. International Journal of Advanced Research in Electrical", *Electronics and Instrumentation Engineering.,* vol. 2, no. 6, pp. 2127-2132, 2013.

[111] H. Kaur, and S.K. Sood, "Energy-efficient IoT-fog-cloud architectural paradigm for real-time wildfire prediction and forecasting", *IEEE Syst. J.,* vol. 14, no. 2, pp. 2003-2011, 2020.
[http://dx.doi.org/10.1109/JSYST.2019.2923635]

CHAPTER 4

IoT-Based Intelligent Emergency Alert System Using Neural Computing and Machine Learning

Sangeeta Borkakoty[1,*], **Atowar ul Islam**[1] and **Rakesh K. Sharma**[2]

[1] *Department of Computer Science and Electronics, University of Science and Technology, Meghalaya, Baridua, India*

[2] *Department of Computer Science and Engineering Technology, University of Maryland Eastern Shore, Princess Anne, Maryland, USA*

Abstract: Fuels, gases, and other such substances are widely used in domestic and industrial settings daily. However, they frequently result in significant mishaps like fires and gas leaks. If prompt notification is received, such accidents can be avoided. Installing a gas leakage and fire incident detection system in strategic locations is one approach to achieve this. Here, we demonstrate the construction of a straightforward system that sends an SMS using a GSM module in the event of a fire or gas leak. Additionally, a temperature sensor simultaneously detects the temperature of that difficult circumstance and transmits information to a web server. This is achieved with the use of the Internet of Things (IoT), neural computing, and machine learning. We employ a system with multi-sensing and interaction with the current centralized M2M (Machine-to-Machine) home network and external networks in place of discrete units with basic functionality (such as the Internet). Then, using machine learning, we apply a data mining technique to the sensed data and find anomalous changes for early risk prediction. The system's goals are to increase security and safety and safeguard properties.

Keywords: Alert system, IoT, Machine learning, Neural network, Risk prediction.

INTRODUCTION

Dr. Walter Snelling invented LPG in 1910 [24]. According to his theory, natural gas might be compressed when under pressure. A non-renewable energy source, LPG, is made by processing natural gas. It contains both saturated and unsaturated hydrocarbons and combines commercial propane and commercial butane [1]. LPG's adaptability may be used for various purposes, including heating, lighting,

---

* **Corresponding author Sangeeta Borkakoty:** Department of Computer Science and Electronics, University of Science and Technology, Meghalaya, Baridua, India; E-mail: s.borkakoty06@gmail.com

H.S. Hota, Dinesh K. Sharma, Ayan Kumar Das & Ditipriya Sinha (Eds.)

and transportation fuel [25]. LPG demand is also growing exponentially every day. However, because LPG is combustible, it seeps from faulty equipment over time, resulting in hazardous gas leaks. This raises the possibility of a fire and might even cause an explosion. In recent years, more fatalities have been caused by gas cylinder explosions. Breathing in these fumes or smoke might cause serious respiratory problems [2]. Therefore, a system for detecting and preventing LPG leakage is urgently needed. A chemically infused paper that changed color when exposed to the gas was used to detect the presence of gas before electronic household gas detectors were developed in the 1980s and 1990s [26]. These risks can be reduced by developing warning technologies like smoke detectors [3]. However, there may be situations where a gas leak happens when the house is vacant or a kid, an older adult, or a person with a disability is alone. In these cases, the individual may not be able to react to the risk promptly or at all.

In this work, we offer a prototype for an Intelligent Emergency Alert System that will send a text message alert to a predetermined list of numbers in the event of an emergency. We employ the concepts of neural computing and machine learning to construct a prediction model that can estimate the level of danger based on monitoring and examining particular environmental parameters. We employ sensors to monitor the site's environment continuously. The system is equipped to send an SMS alert right away when particular risk criteria are reached thanks to an Internet of Things IoT-based design [35].

ARCHITECTURE AND DATA FLOW OF THE PROTOTYPE

The prototype uses the following sensors

- DHT-11 sensor [4], which measures air temperature and humidity.
- MQ-2 sensor for measuring CO, smoke, and LPG levels [5].
- LM35 sensor [6] for flame level detection.

The range of the factors is summarized in Table **1** [36].

Table 1. Summary of sensors and environmental factors with ranges.

S. No.	Factor	Unit	Sensor	Normal Range	Extreme Range
1	Temperature	Celsius	DHT-11	$25 - 32$ °C	60 °C (as allowed by the sensor)
2	Humidity	Percentage	DHT-11	$60 - 70\%$	0%
3	Smoke	Parts-per-million (PPM)	MQ-2	$0 - 100$ PPM	10,000 PPM
4	LPG	Parts-per-million (PPM)	MQ-2	$0 - 30$ PPM	10,000 PPM
5	CO	Parts-per-million (PPM)	MQ-2	$0 - 50$ PPM	10,000 PPM

(Table 1) cont.....

S. No.	Factor	Unit	Sensor	Normal Range	Extreme Range
6	Flame	Flame Level	LM35	400 – 500 flame level	10,000 flame level

Components of the System

The hardware components and protocols of our system include [23]:

- **Arduino Uno R3:** The open-source Arduino Uno R3 [7] microcontroller board is based on the Microchip ATmega328P microprocessor [37]. Various expansion boards and other circuits can be connected to this board's digital and analog I/O pins. There are 14 digital I/O pins and six analog I/O pins on the Arduino Uno R3 board [38]. The Arduino IDE can be used to program it through a type-B USB connector [39]. The board features several communication ports that can be used to connect to computers, other Arduino or microcontroller boards, or other devices.
- **Raspberry Pi 3:** Small single-board computer (SBC) Raspberry Pi 3 [9] is the size of a credit card. It was developed by the Raspberry Pi Foundation in association with Broadcom. Due to its adaptability, open architecture, and low cost, the Raspberry Pi 3 is used in a variety of applications, including robotics, Internet of Things (IoT)-based projects, weather monitoring, and forecasting.
- **Zigbee protocol:** A wireless technology called Zigbee was created as an open, international standard. It takes care of the requirements for cheap, low-power wireless IoT networks. The Zigbee protocol runs on the IEEE 802.15.4 physical radio specification. It uses unlicensed frequencies, including 2.4 GHz, 900 MHz, and 868 MHz. The Zigbee protocol is designed to operate effectively in noisy RF settings, which are common in commercial and industrial applications. Additionally, the Zigbee standard guarantees the compatibility of goods made by various producers. The ability to monitor and operate numerous devices, including smartphones and tablets, on a LAN or WAN, including the Internet, is made possible when the Zigbee network is connected to the IP domain.
- **Arduino GSM Shield:** The global standard for mobile phones is GSM [28] - "Global System for Mobile Communications." Essentially a GSM modem, the Arduino GSM shield enables voice calls, SMS sending and receiving, and internet connectivity for Arduino boards. The Arduino GSM library is used to achieve this.
- **M2M Gateway:** One or more locally networked devices are connected to a wired or wireless broadband connection by an M2M gateway [29]. The gateway runs on virtual machines with one or more CPU cores and can host a variety of networking stacks and applications.

Block Diagram of the Prototype

The block diagram of our prototype is depicted in Fig. (**1**).

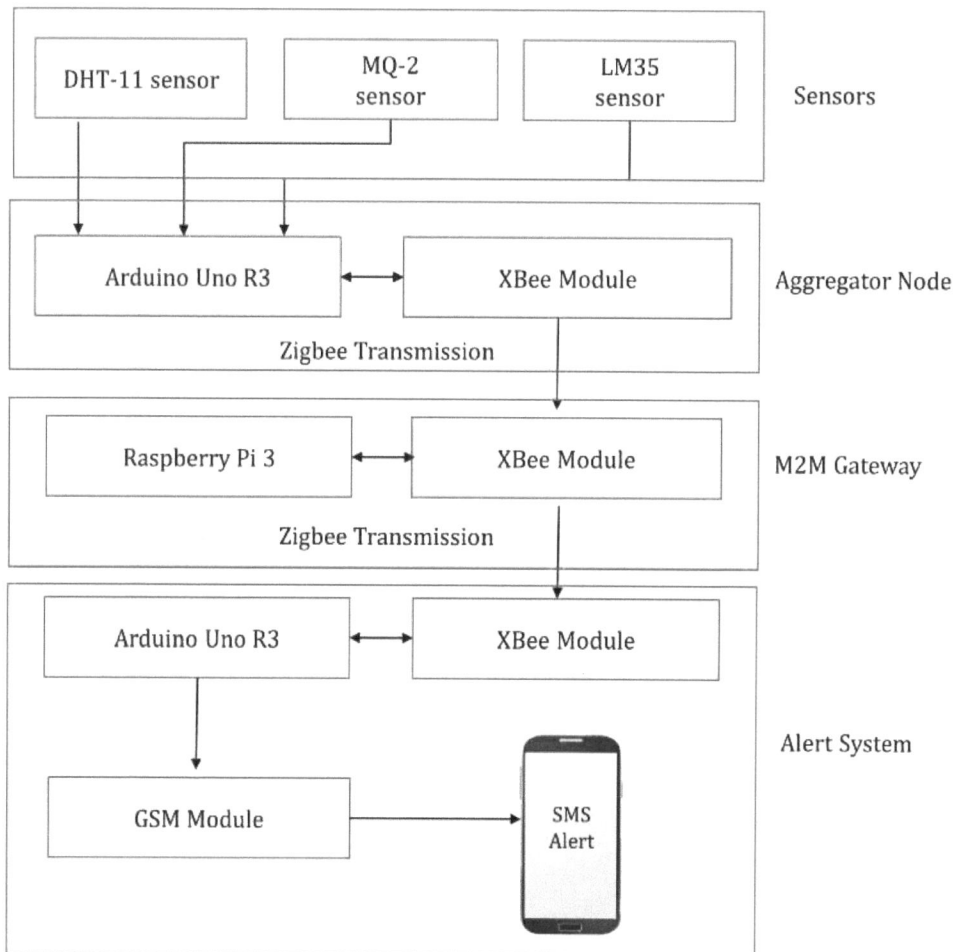

Fig. (1). Block diagram of the prototype.

- An Arduino Uno R3 is used to compile the sensor data. The Zigbee protocol is used for inter-device communication (Zigbee protocol [8]).
- A Raspberry Pi 3 device is employed as our M2M (Machine-to-Machine) gateway [10], which receives the detected data.
- For the Alert System, a second Arduino Uno R3 device is utilized. The Alert System sends Warning SMS Alert to a predetermined list of mobile numbers using a GSM Shield [27].

Dataflow of the System

The data flow of our setup is shown in Fig. (**2**).

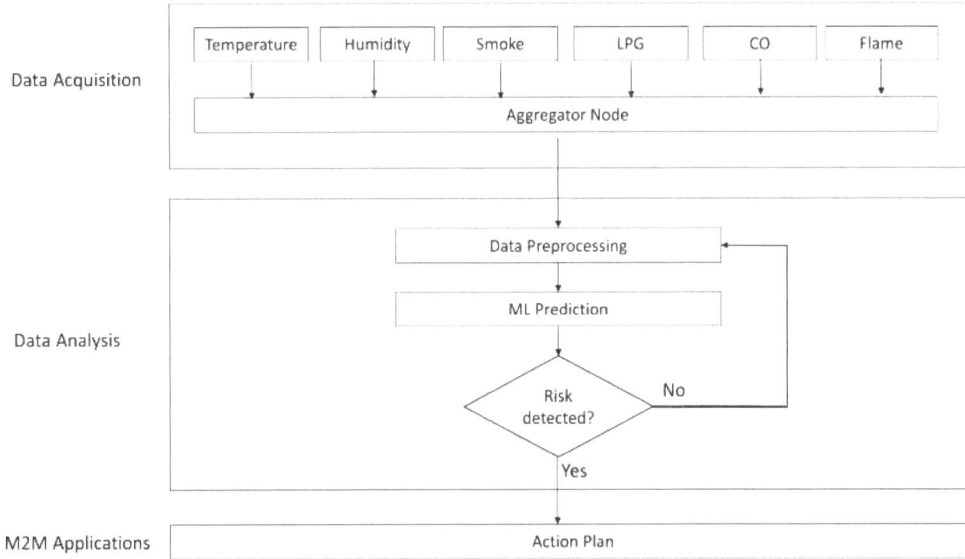

Fig. (2). Dataflow of the setup.

There are three layers in our data flow:

- **Data Acquisition Layer:** These are the sensors used to collect the data. Six factors must be considered for the study's objectives: air temperature, air humidity, smoke, liquefied petroleum gas (LPG), carbon monoxide (CO) level, and flame intensity. The aggregation node receives the data from the sensors and combines it before sending it to the gateway.
- **Data Analysis Layer:** This layer will forecast environmental changes and identify abnormal situations based on the input received. We have utilized machine learning to create a model that can forecast risk levels rather than depending on predefined threshold values for our parameters.
- **M2M Application Layer:** The third layer is activated if a risk is found. For this, we have established an action plan that includes a warning system and activating M2M systems.

NEURAL NETWORK MODEL FOR RISK PREDICTION

The core concept of our model is to use deep neural networks to enhance reliability by intelligent processing. A deep neural network (DNN) [11] is an artificial neural network (ANN) [30] with multiple hidden layers between the input and output layers. Complex non-linear relationships can be modeled by DNNs. A neural network's fundamental objective is to collect inputs, process them through increasingly sophisticated calculations, and then produce an output that may be applied to real-world issues. We have a flow of sequential data, an output, and an input in a deep neural network.

To improve fire detection accuracy, we have used a radial basis function (RBF) network [12]. Radial basis function networks are ANNs that employ radial basis functions [31] as activation functions. A neuron's activation status is determined by an activation function [32]. This function determines whether a specific neuron's contribution to the network is necessary for making a prediction using mathematical operations. The activation function's goal is to create a node's output from a collection of input values.

The approximation multi-variable functions known as radial basis functions are created by combining linear terms based on a single univariate function. The network output is a linear combination of the inputs' radial basis functions and the parameters of the neuron units [40].

RBF networks have several benefits, including simple design, efficient generalization, high input noise tolerance, and online learning capability. RBF networks can be used to construct flexible control systems due to their characteristics.

The structure of our RBF network is shown in Fig. (**3**).

Our RBF network has an input layer, a single hidden layer, and an output layer.

Input Layer

The input layer does not perform any computation. It just feeds the input data into the special hidden layer of the RBF network.

Hidden Layer

The hidden layer receives the input. It is possible that the pattern in this situation cannot be linearly separated. According to Cover's theorem [13], this layer subsequently changes the separability of patterns into a new space that is more linearly separable. This theorem states that a pattern is more likely to be linearly separable if it can be translated nonlinearly into a higher-dimensional space. Comparisons with prototype vectors, which are vectors from the training set, are used in the hidden layer calculations.

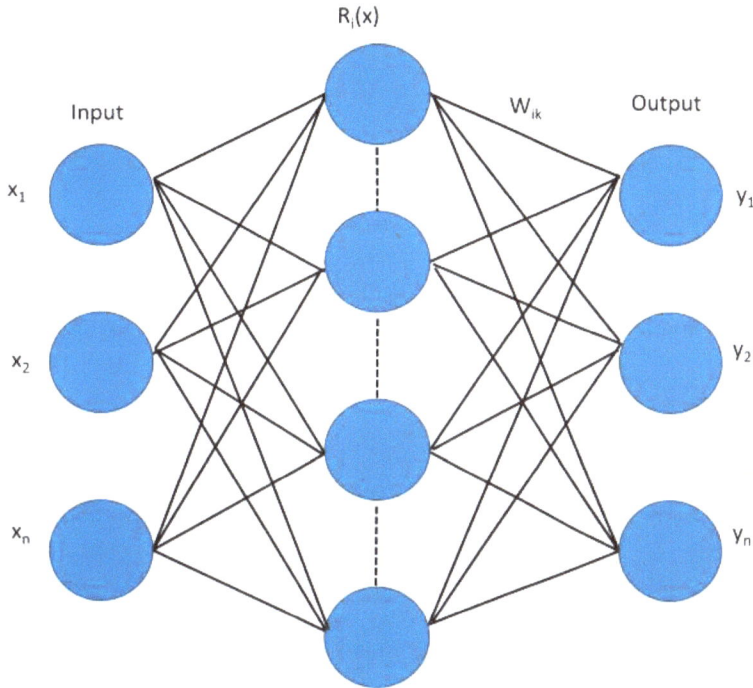

Fig. (3). RBF Network.

In mathematical terms, the computation taking place inside the hidden layer can be denoted as:

$$\phi_i = e^{\left(-\frac{||\underline{X}-u_i||^2}{2.\sigma_i^2}\right)}$$

Where,

$\underline{X}$ - input vector

$\underline{\mu}$ - i[th] neuron's prototype vector

σ - i[th] neuron's bandwidth

ϕ - i[th] neuron's output

Output Layer

The computations are carried out as they would be in a typical artificial neural network inside the output layer. The input vector and the weight vector are combined linearly. Mathematically, it can be written as:

$$y = \sum_{i}^{n} w_i \phi_i$$

Where,

w_i - weight connection

ϕ – the hidden layer's i^{th} neuron's output

y - prediction layer

TRAINING THE MODEL

We employed a two-phase hybrid learning approach in our network model. To include machine learning in our system, we acquired an open dataset. Around 15,000 sample readings from the sensors we used in our investigation are included in the dataset. The information was collected in typical and abnormal circumstances, mimicking a gas leak and a following fire.

This dataset can be used as a starting point for forecasting aberrant patterns under adverse circumstances. The model was trained on 80% of the dataset and tested on the remaining 20%.

We used both supervised [33] and unsupervised [34] learning techniques on our dataset.

When we train the machine using labeled data, it is called supervised learning. This indicates that the correct answer has already been assigned to some data. The machine is provided with a fresh set of data for the supervised learning algorithm to assess the training data and produce an accurate output from the labeled data.

Unsupervised learning teaches a machine to use data that has yet to be categorized or labeled. Based on that knowledge, the algorithm is free to take action without supervision. The algorithm's job is to categorize the unsorted data according to patterns, similarities, and differences.

Phase 1

The first phase of unsupervised self-organizing learning employs the K-means clustering technique [14]. Based on clustering the radial basis function nodes in the hidden layer and the distance between the centers, the best data center and the rate of expansion of the hidden nodes are determined. In this instance, k points are initialized at random. These are referred to as cluster centroids or means. After that, we assign each item to the nearest mean and update the mean's coordinates, which are the sums of all the items previously categorized in that cluster. Finally, after a predetermined number of iterations, we have our clusters.

Phase 2

In the second stage, the output layer weights are trained using supervised learning. We have classified our dataset into four levels:

(i) No risk

(ii) moderate risk

(iii) high risk

(iv) very high risk

To analyze our dataset, we used Python and various machine learning algorithms:

- Linear Regression (LR)
- K-Nearest Neighbor (KNN)
- Classification and Regression Trees (CART)
- Gaussian Naïve Bayes (NB)
- Support Vector Machines (SVM)

Linear Regression (LR)

Linear regression is a machine learning algorithm [15] based on the supervised learning methodology. It carries out a regression operation. Generally, linear regression forecasts some outcomes and finds relationships between variables. Linear regression makes predictions about the value of the dependent variable y based on the independent variable x that is provided. Hence, this approach establishes a linear connection between the input variable (x) and the output variable (y).

The hypothesis function for Linear Regression is as follows:

$$y = \theta_1 + \theta_2.x$$

Where,

x - input training data

y - dependent value

θ_1 - intercept

θ_2 - coefficient of x

Once we have chosen the ideal values of θ_1 and θ_2, we obtain the best-fit line. Hence, the value of y will be predicted depending on the input value of x when we use our model to make predictions.

K-Nearest Neighbor (KNN)

One of the simplest machine learning methods is K-Nearest Neighbor [16]. It is based on the technique of supervised learning. This algorithm places the new case in the category that matches the available categories the most by assuming similarity between the new case/data and existing cases. A new data point is classified using the KNN algorithm depending on how similar it is to previously classified data. As a result, using the KNN algorithm, new data can be quickly categorized into a specific category [41].

For example, let us consider the scatter graph in Fig. (4).

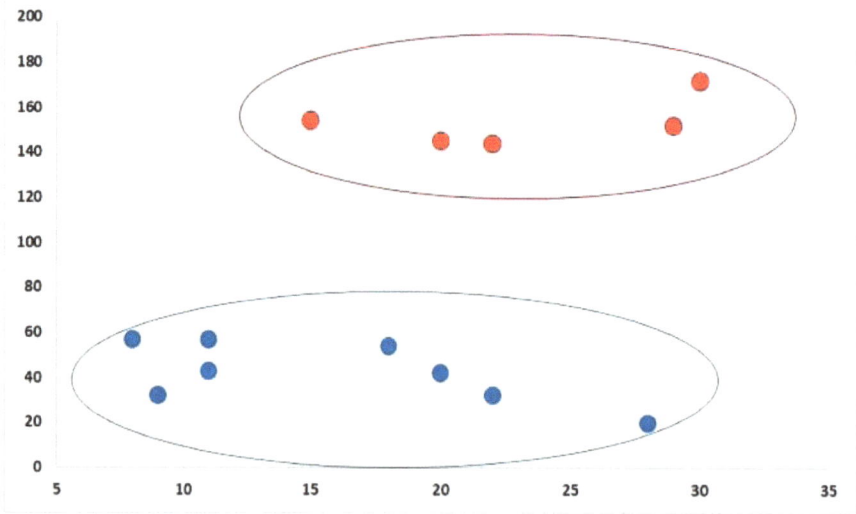

Fig. (4). K-nearest neighbor clusters.

The figure shows that the data has formed two clusters or groups – Red and Blue. As a result, by determining which group a point's nearest neighbor belongs to, we may assign any unclassified point. This suggests that a point's likelihood of being categorized as "Red" increases the closer it is to a group of "Red" points and vice versa.

Classification and Regression Trees (CART)

Classification and Regression Trees (CART) [17] is a type of predictive algorithm. This algorithm demonstrates how the values of the target variable can be predicted from those of other variables. It functions as a decision tree, with each fork splitting into a predictor variable and each node ending with a prediction for the target variable.

The decision tree's nodes are divided into sub-nodes based on an attribute's threshold value. As the training set, the root node is used. The best attribute and threshold value are then taken into account, and it is divided into two. Additionally, the subsets are divided further using the same reasoning. This splitting procedure continues until the last pure subset is discovered in the tree or the developing tree reaches its maximum number of leaves. This is depicted in Fig. (**5**).

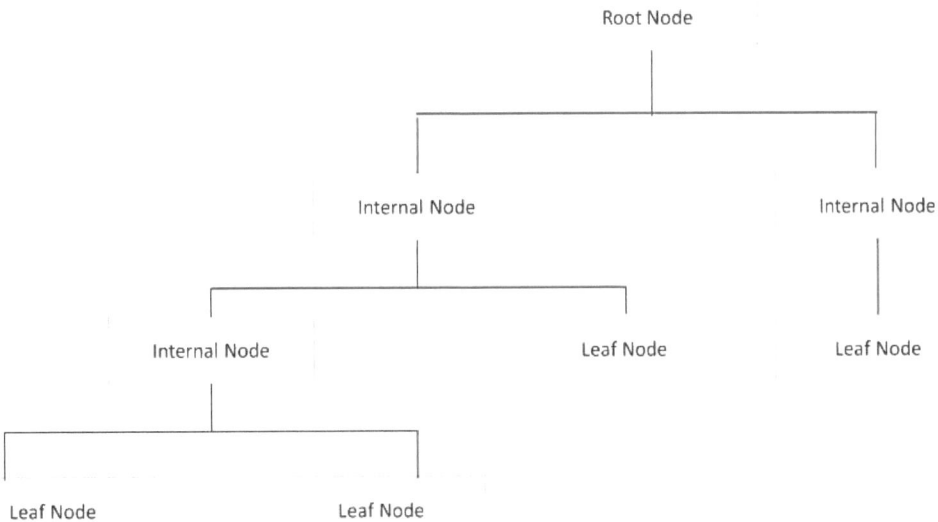

Fig. (5). Classification and Regression trees (CART).

The CART algorithm uses Gini Impurity [18] to divide the dataset into decision trees. The Gini index determines the subnodes' optimal homogeneity to achieve this.

The squared probabilities of each class are added to create the Gini index. It determines the likelihood that a specific variable will be incorrectly classified when selected at random, as well as a Gini coefficient variant. It uses categorical variables and yields results of "success" or "failure."

The Gini index has a value that varies from 0 to 1 [42].

- Value 0 – all the elements are of a particular class, or only one class exists.
- Value 1 – all the elements are distributed randomly across various classes
- Value 0.5 – all the elements are uniformly distributed into the classes

Mathematically, the Gini Impurity can be depicted as:

$$Gini = 1 - \sum \sum_{i=1}^{n} (pi)^2$$

Where,

pi - the probability of an object being classified to a particular class.

Gaussian Naive Bayes (NB)

The Gaussian Naive Bayes algorithm is based on Naive Bayes classifiers [19]. Naive Bayes classifiers are a group of classification algorithms. They are based on Bayes' Theorem [20]. Every pair of traits being classed is independent, which is the key idea here.

Our training dataset is divided into two parts:

- **Feature matrix:** The dataset's vectors (rows), each of which holds the value of dependent characteristics, are all contained in the feature matrix.
- **Response vector:** The value of the class variable (prediction or output) for each row of the feature matrix is contained in the response vector.

The core tenet of Naive Bayes is that each characteristic contributes equally and independently to the result.

It is assumed in Gaussian Naive Bayes that each feature's continuous values are randomly distributed using a Gaussian distribution [21] (often referred to as a normal distribution). When this is graphed, the result is a bell-shaped, symmetrical curve centered on the mean of the feature values. The likelihood of the features is thought to be Gaussian.

Hence, the conditional probability is given by:

$$P(y) = \frac{1}{\sqrt{2\pi\sigma_y^2}} \exp\ exp\ (-\frac{(x_i - \mu_y)^2}{2\sigma_y^2})$$

Support Vector Machines (SVM)

The goal of the Support Vector Machines (SVM) [22] approach is to determine the ideal decision boundary or line for categorizing an *n*-dimensional space. As a consequence, it will be easy to add more data points in the future and place them in the relevant categories. A hyperplane is this best-case decision boundary. When creating the hyperplane, SVM picks the extreme points and vectors. Support vectors describe these extreme circumstances. Fig. (**6**) illustrates this.

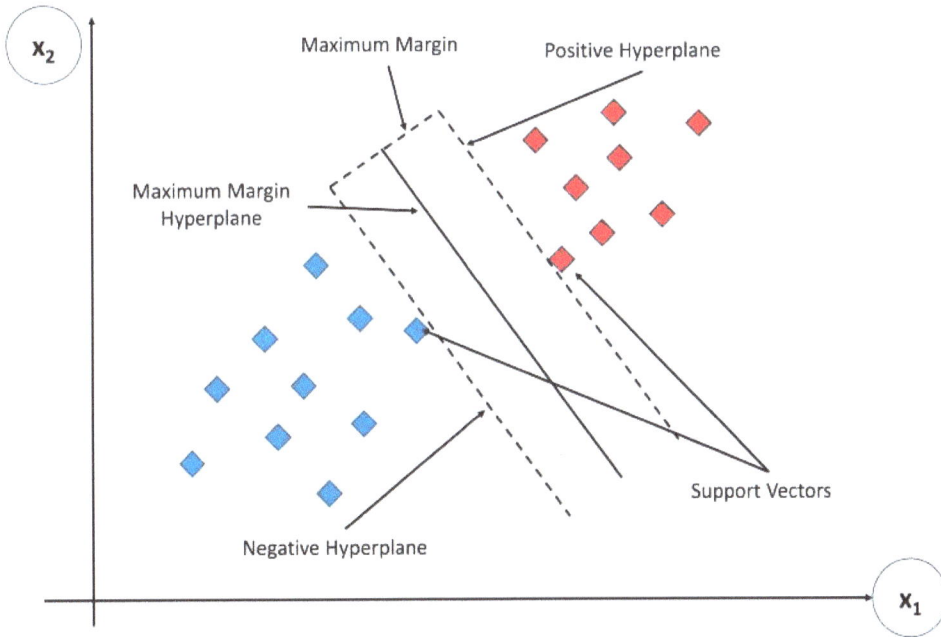

Fig. (6). Support vectors.

ALGORITHM ACCURACY

We tested the algorithms in ten rounds and recorded the accuracy scores, as depicted in Table **2**.

Table 2. Accuracy scores of algorithms for ten rounds of testing.

Algorithm	Round 1	Round 2	Round 3	Round4	Round 5	Round 6	Round 7	Round 8	Round 9	Round 10
LR	0.956410	0.962390	0.951510	0.958780	0.968150	0.962570	0.950590	0.958550	0.952450	0.963980
KNN	0.982360	0.982900	0.986440	0.987700	0.982680	0.983560	0.981050	0.980520	0.982800	0.986690
CART	0.995980	0.992890	0.994070	0.991800	0.997670	0.994700	0.996410	0.999890	0.991130	0.993480
NB	0.933680	0.943870	0.959120	0.937590	0.945370	0.950770	0.952940	0.939240	0.960000	0.933440
SVM	0.967750	0.967230	0.967670	0.962550	0.971180	0.960630	0.973650	0.973470	0.970890	0.962150

Fig. (**7**) shows a box plot of the accuracy scores of applying the different algorithms on our dataset.

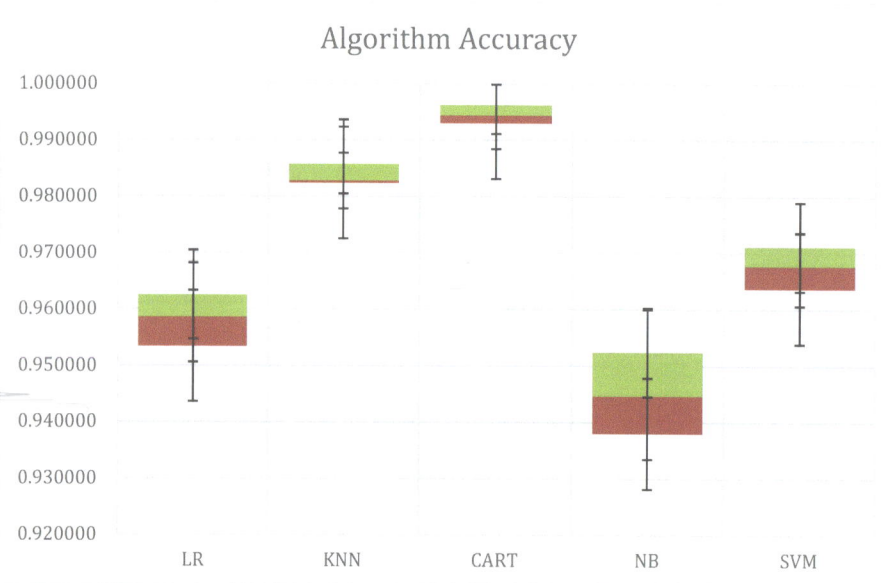

Fig. (7). Algorithm accuracy.

The figure shows that classification and regression trees (cart) gives the highest score. This indicates that we can use this algorithm to enhance our machine-learning model further.

CONCLUSION

This research presents a system for early fire danger prediction caused by LPG leakage. The approach involves the use of the Internet of Things (IoT), neural networks, and machine learning algorithms. In the future, we can collect real-world, live data to improve our prediction model further and investigate alternative machine-learning techniques. We can also investigate the potential for real-time system monitoring *via* web and mobile apps with reporting capabilities. The system may be integrated with cloud services for improved real-time analysis.

In order to decrease false positives, we can also improve the accuracy of the data collected by the sensors. Due to harsh environmental conditions or failure, sensors can measure incorrect data or fail to collect data.

ACKNOWLEDGEMENTS

The authors would like to express their heartfelt gratitude to the editors for reviewing the manuscript critically.

REFERENCES

[1]   A. Demirbas, "Fuel properties of hydrogen, liquefied petroleum gas (LPG), and compressed natural gas (CNG) for transportation", *Energy Sources,* vol. 24, no. 7, pp. 601-610, 2002.
[http://dx.doi.org/10.1080/00908312.2002.11877434]

[2]   M. Gorguner, and M. Akgun, "Acute inhalation injury", *Eurasian J. Med.,* vol. 42, no. 1, pp. 28-35, 2010.
[http://dx.doi.org/10.5152/eajm.2010.09] [PMID: 25610115]

[3]   C. Garbacz, "Smoke detector effectiveness and the value of saving a life", *Econ. Lett.,* vol. 31, no. 3, pp. 281-286, 1989.
[http://dx.doi.org/10.1016/0165-1765(89)90015-3]

[4]   D. Srivastava, A. Kesarwani, and S. Dubey, "Measurement of Temperature and Humidity by using Arduino Tool and DHT11", *International Research Journal of Engineering and Technology,* vol. 5, no. 12, pp. 876-878, 2018.

[5]   R.C. Pandey, M. Verma, L.K. Sahu, and S. Deshmukh, "Internet of things (IOT) based gas leakage monitoring and alerting system with MQ-2 sensor", *International Journal of Engineering Development and Research.,* vol. 5, no. 2, pp. 2135-2137, 2017.

[6]   B Oyebola, and O. Toluwani, "LM35 Based digital room temperature meter: a simple demonstration", *Equatorial Journal of Computational and Theoretical Science,* vol. 2, no. 1, 2017..

[7]   R.H. Kumar, A.U. Roopa, and D.P. Sathiya, "Arduino ATMEGA-328 microcontroller", *Int. J. Innov. Res. Electr. Electron. Instrum. Control Eng.,* vol. 3, no. 4, pp. 27-29, 2015.

[8]   MS Pan, and YC Tseng, "ZigBee and their applications", 3 *Sensor networks and configuration: Fundamentals, standards, platforms, and applications,* pp. 349-368, 2007.
[http://dx.doi.org/10.1007/3-540-37366-7_16]

[9]   M. Maksimović, V. Vujović, N. Davidović, V. Milošević, and B. Perišić, "Raspberry Pi as Internet of things hardware: performances and constraints", 3 *Design Issues,* vol. 3, no. 8, pp. 1-6, 2014.

[10]   J. Hosek, P. Masek, D. Kovac, and F. Kröpfl, "The centerpiece of future home", 3 *6th International Congress on Ultra Modern Telecommunications and Control Systems and Workshops (ICUMT),* pp. 190-197, 2014.

[11]   A. Canziani, A. Paszke, and E. Culurciello, "An analysis of deep neural network models for practical applications", *arXiv preprint arXiv,* 2016.

[12] Y, Wang H, Zhang B, Du KL. Wu, "Using radial basis function networks for function approximation and classification", *International Scholarly Research Notices.,* vol. 2012, no. 1, p. 324194, 2012.

[13] Samuelson F, Brown DG. Application of Cover's theorem to the evaluation of the performance of CI observers. In The 2011 International Joint Conference on Neural Networks 2011 Jul 31 (pp. 1020-1026). IEEE.

[14] A. Likas, N. Vlassis, and J.J. Verbeek, "The global k-means clustering algorithm", *Pattern Recognit.,* vol. 36, no. 2, pp. 451-461, 2003.
[http://dx.doi.org/10.1016/S0031-3203(02)00060-2]

[15] X. Su, X. Yan, and C.L. Tsai, "Linear regression", *Wiley Interdiscip. Rev. Comput. Stat.,* vol. 4, no. 3, pp. 275-294, 2012.
[http://dx.doi.org/10.1002/wics.1198]

[16] L. Peterson, "K-nearest neighbor", *Scholarpedia J.,* vol. 4, no. 2, p. 1883, 2009.
[http://dx.doi.org/10.4249/scholarpedia.1883]

[17] W.Y. Loh, "Classification and regression trees", *Wiley Interdiscip. Rev. Data Min. Knowl. Discov.,* vol. 1, no. 1, pp. 14-23, 2011.
[http://dx.doi.org/10.1002/widm.8]

[18] Y. Yuan, L. Wu, and X. Zhang, "Gini-Impurity index analysis", *IEEE Trans. Inf. Forensics Security,* vol. 16, pp. 3154-3169, 2021.
[http://dx.doi.org/10.1109/TIFS.2021.3076932]

[19] G.I. Webb, E. Keogh, and R. Miikkulainen, "Naïve Bayes", *Encyclopedia of machine learning,* vol. 15, pp. 713-714, 2010.

[20] D. Berrar, "Bayes' theorem and naive Bayes classifier", *Encyclopedia of Bioinformatics and Computational Biology: ABC of Bioinformatics,* vol. 403, p. 412, 2018.

[21] E. W. Weisstein, "Normal distribution," *MathWorld,* 2002.

[22] M.A. Hearst, S.T. Dumais, E. Osuna, J. Platt, and B. Scholkopf, "Support vector machines", *IEEE Intell. Syst. Their Appl.,* vol. 13, no. 4, pp. 18-28, 1998.
[http://dx.doi.org/10.1109/5254.708428]

[23] A. Ul Islam, S. Borkakoty, D. Kalita, P. Sarma, D. Sharmah, and M. Islam, "Designing web interface and LPG safety kit as an Arduino-based LPG monitoring & alert system," *J. East China Univ. Sci. Technol.,* vol. 65, no. 3, pp. 20–25, 2022.

[24] F. Synák, K. Čulík, V. Rievaj, and J. Gaňa, "Liquefied petroleum gas as an alternative fuel", *Transp. Res. Procedia,* vol. 40, pp. 527-534, 2019.
[http://dx.doi.org/10.1016/j.trpro.2019.07.076]

[25] X. Qian, R. Zhang, Q. Zhang, M. Yuan, and Y. Zhao, "Cause analysis of the large-scale LPG explosion accident based on key investigation technology: A Case Study", *ACS Omega,* vol. 6, no. 31, pp. 20644-20656, 2021.
[http://dx.doi.org/10.1021/acsomega.1c02837] [PMID: 34396010]

[26] F. Sauli, "Gas detectors: achievements and trends", *Nucl. Instrum. Methods Phys. Res. A,* vol. 461, no. 1-3, pp. 47-54, 2001.
[http://dx.doi.org/10.1016/S0168-9002(00)01165-7]

[27] H.K. Patel, T. Mody, and A. Goyal, "Arduino based smart energy meter using GSM", *4th International Conference on Internet of Things: Smart Innovation and Usages (IoT-SIU),* pp. 1-6, 2019.
[http://dx.doi.org/10.1109/IoT-SIU.2019.8777490]

[28] M. Rahnema, "Overview of the GSM system and protocol architecture", *IEEE Commun. Mag.,* vol. 31, no. 4, pp. 92-100, 1993.
[http://dx.doi.org/10.1109/35.210402]

[29]   M. Chen, J. Wan, S. Gonzalez, X. Liao, and V.C.M. Leung, "A survey of recent developments in home M2M networks", *IEEE Commun. Surv. Tutor.,* vol. 16, no. 1, pp. 98-114, 2014.
[http://dx.doi.org/10.1109/SURV.2013.110113.00249]

[30]   A.K. Jain, Jianchang Mao, and K.M. Mohiuddin, "Artificial neural networks: a tutorial", *Computer,* vol. 29, no. 3, pp. 31-44, 1996.
[http://dx.doi.org/10.1109/2.485891]

[31]   B. Mulgrew, "Applying radial basis functions", *IEEE Signal Process. Mag.,* vol. 13, no. 2, pp. 50-65, 1996.
[http://dx.doi.org/10.1109/79.487041]

[32]   S. Sharma, S. Sharma, and A. Athaiya, "Activation functions in neural networks", *Towards Data Sci.,* vol. 6, no. 12, pp. 310-316, 2017.

[33]   T. Jiang, J.L. Gradus, and A.J. Rosellini, "Supervised machine learning: a brief primer", *Behav. Ther.,* vol. 51, no. 5, pp. 675-687, 2020.
[http://dx.doi.org/10.1016/j.beth.2020.05.002] [PMID: 32800297]

[34]   R. Gentleman and V. J. Carey, "Unsupervised machine learning," in *Bioconductor Case Studies*, F. Hahne, W. Huber, R. Gentleman, S. Falcon, and V. J. Carey, Eds. New York, NY, USA: Springer, 2008, pp. 137–157.

[35]   C.Z. Radulescu, and M. Radulescu, "A Hybrid Multi-Criteria Approach to the Vendor Selection Problem for Sensor-Based Medical Devices", *Sensors,* vol. 23, no. 2, p. 764, 2023.
[http://dx.doi.org/10.3390/s23020764] [PMID: 36679559]

[36]   H. Supriyono, S. Anton, U. Fadlilah, and K. Harismah, "Portable machine with android application display for measuring CO and HC of vehicle exhaust gas", *J. Phys. Conf. Ser.,* vol. 1524, no. 1, p. 012110, 2020.
[http://dx.doi.org/10.1088/1742-6596/1524/1/012110]

[37]   S. Shrestha, V.K. Anne, and R. Chaitanya, "IoT based smart gas management system", *3rd International Conference on Trends in Electronics and Informatics (ICOEI),* pp. 550-555, 2019.
[http://dx.doi.org/10.1109/ICOEI.2019.8862639]

[38]   K. Monalisha, and T.S. Kirthana, "IoT based Safety System for Women", *6th International Conference on Communication and Electronics Systems (ICCES),* pp. 731-736, 2021.

[39]   A.K. Majhi, S. Dash, and C.K. Barik, "Arduino based smart home automation", *ACCENTS Transactions on Information Security,* vol. 6, no. 22, pp. 7-12, 2021.
[http://dx.doi.org/10.19101/TIS.2021.621001]

[40]   S.S. Chandrayan, K. Singh, and A.K. Bhoi, "Atmospheric Weather Fluctuation Prediction Using Machine Learning", *Proceeding of CISC 2021,* pp. 431-443, 2022.
[http://dx.doi.org/10.1007/978-981-16-8763-1_35]

[41]   A.R. Mangalam, S. Singh, C. Lalremtluanga, P. Kumar, R. Das, J. Basu, and S. Chatterjee, "Emotion Recognition from Mizo Speech: A Signal Processing Approach", *IEEE International Conference on Distributed Computing and Electrical Circuits and Electronics (ICDCECE),* pp. 1-6, 2022.
[http://dx.doi.org/10.1109/ICDCECE53908.2022.9793078]

[42]   Y. Yuan, L. Wu, and X. Zhang, "Gini-Impurity index analysis", *IEEE Trans. Inf. Forensics Security,* vol. 16, pp. 3154-3169, 2021.
[http://dx.doi.org/10.1109/TIFS.2021.3076932]

CHAPTER 5

IoT-Enabled Framework for Secure and Transparent Digital Answer Script Evaluation Using Blockchain

Sourav Mahapatra[1,*], Souvagya Das[2], Sourav Das[2] and Sayan Biswas[2]

[1] Department of Computer Science and Engineering, National Institute of Technology, Patna, Bihar, India

[2] Department of Electrical Engineering, Techno International New Town, Kolkata, West Bengal, India

Abstract: Evaluation of answer scripts is an essential component of any test or educational institution to measure learner outcomes. In a digital script evaluation system, write-up scripts are scanned and uploaded to the central server and assigned to the evaluator for grading. A fair, consistent, unbiased, and error-free evaluation protects an examination system's integrity and is essential for all educational institutions. Most of the applications available in the market were concerned with certificate administration. For an examination system, security, transparency, accessibility, and trust are the major factors that can easily be audited when a blockchain infrastructure is followed. There are a few challenges found in adopting blockchain technology in this field, like scalability, cost of adaption, trust in technology, etc. It is intended to create a totally transparent and effective examination and reward system that may be utilized to replace the traditional system. This chapter presents a self-sustaining educational environment on top of a blockchain for fair assessment. The proposed method proved to be quite beneficial due to its decentralized nature. In our framework, all the steps of evaluation processes are traced and recorded through blockchain to improve the security, transparency, and trustfulness of the system. This makes it simpler to figure out how a candidate obtained the score that he or she did, providing credibility to the gained certificate.

Keywords: Blockchain, Decentralized, Digital evaluation, E-gradation, Online examination, Smart contract, Trustfulness, Transparency.

INTRODUCTION

Education refers to the process that promotes continuous learning through the assembling of knowledge, information, skills, and abilities to develop moral and

---
** **Corresponding author Sourav Mahapatra:** Department of Computer Science and Engineering, National Institute of Technology, Patna, Bihar, India; E-mail: souravm.phd20.cs@nitp.ac.in*

H.S. Hota, Dinesh K. Sharma, Ayan Kumar Das & Ditipriya Sinha (Eds.)

ethical values, facilitating decision making through reasoning, logical thinking, and interpreting. In today's digital world, education is no longer portrayed as taking place within the four walls of the classroom. People can be educated from any corner of the world with the help of ICTE. You may also utilize ICTE in student evaluation processes. Quality of education empowers a person socially, mentally, physically, and emotionally. Education plays a vital role in every field, such as agriculture, medical science, business, politics, economics, etc., which encourages us to develop a nation. The purpose of educational evaluation is to judge the potential of individuals in educational phenomena. Assessment is needed for an educational organization to provide quality education and to achieve its mission and vision. With the significant shifts from test-oriented education to quality education and stewardship education to creative experience, as well as the emergence of new curriculum concepts, education and teaching techniques pose new challenges for educational innovation and teaching evaluation methods [1]. As an alternative to present quality assurance procedures, trust is required for 'intelligent accountability' through networking and trust-building for an organization [2]. Academicians from all around the world are continuously trying to develop and investigate education and teaching assessment systems that may meet the needs of current educational development. Education and teaching assessment techniques are evolving and innovating in the direction of diversity, science, objectivity, and rationality.

The examination is a tool used in the educational system to assess pupils and rank them using a consistent yardstick. An institute operates a repository to maintain its assessment records for a substantial tenure for verification of academic credentials and beneficial and effective improvements. One major issue with this kind of system has consistently been that it is always controlled under one central agency and typically operated with scant to or no transparency. Reviewing an answer script or generating a transcript is a lengthy process in the traditional system and is subject to concerns and misgivings about the legitimacy of the transcript, which students may produce to others. It is also a tedious and resource-consuming job for the mother organization to keep all the records for future verification.

For an e-exam process, the reliability and authenticity of the examinee's e-gadget must be ensured before any data is stored in the blockchain. There are several roadblocks to sorting, evaluating, and preserving the growing volume of paper scripts in paper-based exams. Moreover, there is a lack of transparency in their gradation system. The on-screen evaluation aims to transform the way evaluations are done and reviewed digitally with rapid outcomes. Onscreen marking is a revolution in the digital evaluation system, which reduces the cost, time, storage, and distribution complications.

Digital evaluation of answer scripts helps in:

• Reducing the burden of logistic activity.
• QR, which can mask the identity and other details of the students.
• Centralized control dashboard tracking of the overall progress.
• Managing examiner and moderator as well as the resulting analytics of students' performances.
• Auto-calculating results to speed up the result publication.

In an online education and certification course, the organization uses ICTE for demonstration and evaluation purposes, which involves numerous IoT devices to support the system. Verification, authentication, and access to these tools are important when we are concerned with evaluation processes. Device authentication is essential for maintaining data integrity and removing malicious devices trying to connect to the network. Fog Computing (FC) is essential for reducing the latency of getting data from sensitive applications and also authenticating the devices by a cryptographic computation. Certain technologies, such as IoT, Cloud Computing (CC), and FC, have a single point of failure, which means that the systems might collapse quickly. IoT, Fog, and blockchain infrastructure can mitigate the above-mentioned challenges and secure them by storing them in the blockchain. In terms of security and availability, blockchain technology improves IoT challenges in a peer-to-peer network.

Our study aims to address the shortcomings of the traditional issues by developing an effective modern examination and rewarding system based on blockchain technology that is less biased and more responsible. The FC has been introduced to reduce latency and increase the service quality of IoT by processing data locally at the edge. IoT devices can benefit from blockchain in terms of establishing trust and facilitating efficient data transfer without requiring network interventions. Blockchains are used to create distributed, tamperproof, and secure systems. Smart contracts are used to automate participant interactions as well as the execution of data from things or any other resources. Our framework essentially replaces the present examination and evaluation system with a transparent and distributed examination and evaluation process. This system can account for all the evaluation steps cleared by a student, and a blockchain wallet will be provided, which stores all certificates and transcripts. Any third-party verification is also possible through the smart contract designed to access the chain. The smart contracts in blockchain technology will secure security and trust, as well as reduce time and monetary costs.

The rest of the chapter is presented as follows. In section II, a brief survey of related works is presented with their limitation and motivation of the work. The technical background for the proposed framework is presented in section III. After that, the description of the proposed model is demonstrated in section IV with code sniff. Section V highlights the manifesto of this research for its acceptability. The work is summarized in sections VI and VII, and the scope of the research is highlighted.

RELATED WORK

In the era of Industrial Revolution 4.0, new technologies like AI, smart automation, machine learning, cloud services, etc., have emerged in our educational system to enhance automation and advancement. Education 4.0 refers to the process of learning, which involves Industrial Revolution 4.0, concentrating on modern technologies to promote smart automation. Collaboration of blockchain technology with the education system can bring revolution in the education sector with the potential feature to overcome the challenging disruption wave of Industrial Revolution 4.0 [3]. An insight into the utilization of blockchain in the education system is elaborated in "The Blockchain Manifesto" by Untung Rahardja *et al.* The adaptation of blockchain technology in the business sector has greatly impacted the industry [4, 5].

Existing problems in the education system, like academic credential fraud, student's inability to choose an optimal career field, non-homogenous student groups, and unauthorized dispersal of copyrighted educational material across the internet, can be diminished by respective proposals of blockchain-based degree verification systems and student record keeping and performance tracking and copyright management system [6]. "The Blockchain Challenge for Higher Education Institutions" by H. Haugsbakken and I. Langseth focuses on whether blockchain technology can be deployed in higher education to democratize and automate the learning process, reducing bureaucratic costs [7]. Untung Rahardja *et al.* proposed a blockchain framework by using AI to overcome well-known issues of tertiary education and improve the quality of education [8]. Cadelina Cassandra *et al.*, in their research, suggested an innovative solution to secure diplomas and transcripts from the forgery of university transcript documents [9]. D. J. Peurach highlighted that the first step towards a transparent and technologically smart education system is initiated with decentralization [10].

It is evident from analyzing the above studies that the solutions of academic credential and certification fraud, unauthorized dispersal of copyrighted educational materials, student inability to choose optimal career fields, non-homogenous student groups, and issues of tertiary education are already proposed in education. Similarly, testing and evaluation are crucial parts of the education system thatneed to be digitalized. The evaluation process must be fast, accurate, secure, and transparent to improve the quality of education. There is a necessity to fill the gap in the evaluation system, which is not presented yet. The suggested architecture uses smart contracts to automatically receive, track, protect, and store data from Things to blockchain.

TECHNICAL BACKGROUND

What is Blockchain?

Blockchain is one of the most emerging technologies that can bring revolution to the modern world. Blockchain gained its popularity through the invention of Bitcoin, the first digital currency created by pseudo name Satoshi Nakamoto in 2008. Now, Bitcoin is the most popular and valuable cryptocurrency in the current market. Blockchain means a sequence of blocks containing data (for example, transactions, records, timestamps, nonce, a hash of the previous block, etc.) from a chain. Blockchain is a decentralized, immutable, distributive ledger technology (DLT) that works in a peer-to-peer (P2P) network that stores records (Fig. **1**). Blockchain guarantees a high level of security through cryptographic hash and consensus algorithm (proof of work, proof of stake, etc.). Whenever new transactions take place, validation is done by consensus of every participant present in the network. Once transactions are validated, they get permanently stored in the block and are added to the growing blockchain. After the addition of a block in the chain, it cannot be modified, which ensures its immutability. Every participant present in the network has access to the updated ledger. Thus, blockchain ensures security and transparency.

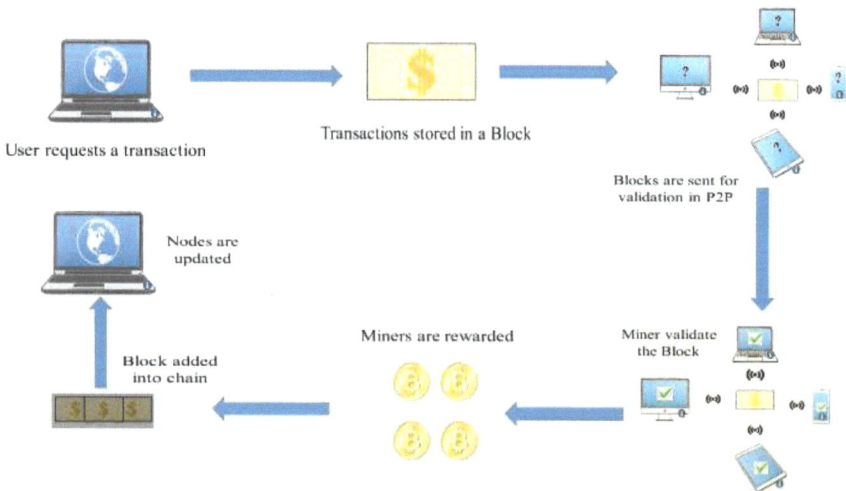

Fig. (1). Working principle of blockchain.

What is a Smart Contract?

Smart contracts are deployed in the blockchain, which can be defined as a set of rules that will be executed automatically when all the conditions are satisfied. Thus, smart contracts ensure fast and secure transactions.

Development Tools Solidity & Remix

Solidity is one of the most famous high-level programming languages for designing and constructing smart contracts in the blockchain platform. It is basically an object-oriented programming language. Solidity shares a lot of similarities with different programming languages like C++, Python, JavaScript, etc. It supports inheritance, abstraction, libraries, etc. Solidity is the main language for blockchain running platforms.

Remix IDE is a platform where smart contracts are written for blockchain development work. Remix IDE compiles the smart contract and deploys it to Ethereum.

Ethereum is basically a blockchain-based software platform that enables the feature of smart contracts. It is mostly known for its cryptocurrency, ether (ETH).

What is Consensus?

Consensus algorithms are adopted in blockchain networks to obtain agreement among diverse, dispersed nodes to validate transaction. These techniques are intended to accomplish dependability in a network with various users or nodes. Proof of work (PoW) or Proof of Stake (PoS) consensus mechanisms safeguard the network and prohibit unauthorized users from validating fraudulent transactions.

Proof of Stake

Validators are identified based on the computation of their stake, which is computationally lighter than POW. Validators are compensated, or their stake keeps growing in proportion to the number of blocks uploaded to the blockchain.

We have developed our smart contract using Solidity and deployed it in the Ethereum platform through Remix, as represented in Fig. (**2**).

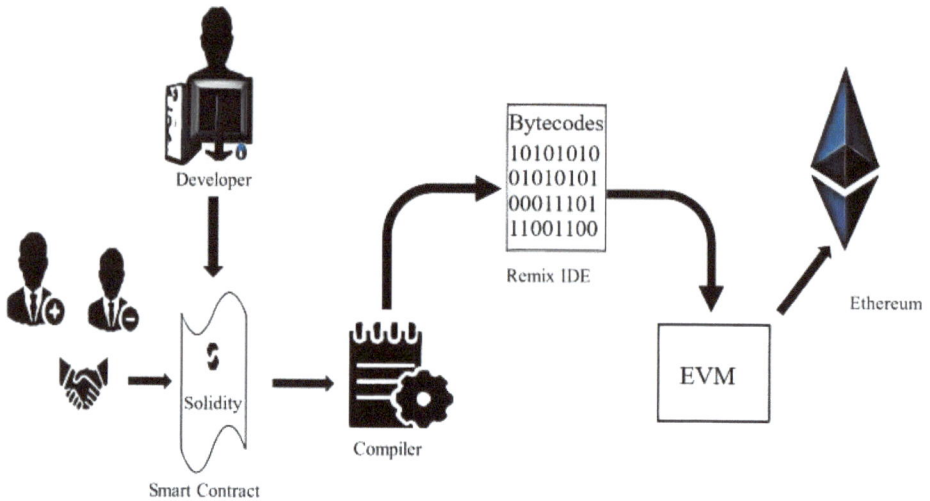

Fig. (2). Platform for the implementation of blockchain technology.

IoT-based Blockchain Architecture for Smart Evaluation

Because of Internet and IoT improvements, digital evaluation infrastructure provides higher detection accuracy, services, and ease of access than traditional systems. An enormous volume of data is generated from IoT throughout the world, causing issues with processing, distributing, and storing data and traffic. FC has been introduced between Things and Cloud space (Fig. **3**). FC has therefore been utilized to reduce the processing time of diversified data transit between Things by processing the majority of data closer to CC. However, this solution relies on centralized design, which is inapplicable to IoT and renders it very prone to attack, crash, and single point of failure, as well as it is less scalable. As a result, peer-to-peer blockchain is the greatest IoT solution for this market since it increases data safety, storage, and processing by aggregating. In order to share and transmit exam records in a tamper-proof way across the network, an IoT-based blockchain is suggested. The framework uses smart contracts to automatically receive, track, protect, and store data from Things to the blockchain.

PROPOSED MODEL

The ongoing research established the factual requirement of the digital evaluation system. This research proposed a model of a digital evaluation system where inputs are from different ICTE devices (IoT's) connected, and the information is semi-processed through the Fog layer and finally stored in the form of distributed ledger in the blockchain. Smart contracts will provide access control over the information stored.

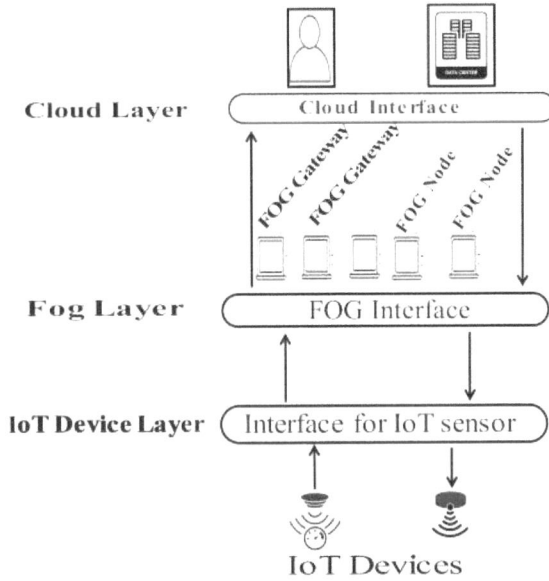

Fig. (3). IoT-fog-cloud architecture.

There are two aspects of this framework:

• First, the authentication of the information collected from heterogeneous devices

• Second, storing it in a distributed peer-to-peer reliable communication.

User Authentication: Before the user interacts with the system, his/her smart device needs to be registered and verified with the system. To authenticate the device and for secure communication, cryptographic key distribution happens through secure organization and secure control/monitoring protocol. Once the device is recognized and its authentication is in the chain, students and examiners can perform their operation accordingly. Fog node communicates blockchain for storing their data into the chain and protects the confidentiality, authenticity, and veracity of the transmitted IoT data. Every communication that takes place is verified automatically, and its secure hash is recorded into the chain.

The steps and functionality involved in storing answer scripts and evaluation of scripts inside the chain are explained in Fig. (**4**).

Following are the entities (Table **1**) taking part in this system to record the required information into the chain.

Table 1. List of entities taking part in the chain.

studentName	Student Name
stdId	Student Id No.
subjectCode	Specific code of any paper as per the university rules.
fees	Student has to pay a particular amount of fees to appear in the examination.
entryFees	Entry fees for the examination.
studentNo.	Total no. of students present in the blockchain
Entry	Tabular representation of student status, whether present in the blockchain
Exist	Tabular representation of studentNo. corresponds to its stdId
teacherName	Teacher Name
teachRequestId	Teacher Id
number	To check a student's script teacher requests a no. to specify the student

Below is a case study of a university examination process through which a demonstration of the activity of the proposed framework is implemented.

Suppose a university conducts a paper-based or online examination. Now, the answer will be evaluated by the digital evaluation system as described below.

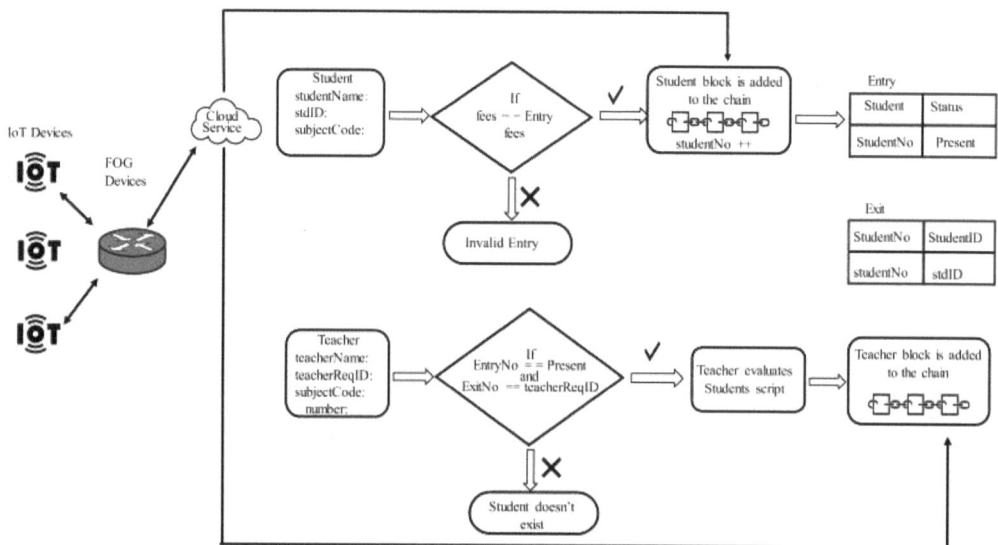

Fig. (4). Flow diagram of the model.

- **Student's Exam Registration:** Every student with a unique student ID under the university can register themselves in this portal. During the submission of the answer script, the student specifies the subject code (Fig. **5**).

```
studentEntry(string memory name, uint id, string memory subjectCode)
```

Fig. (5). Implementation of student entry.

Now, students need to pay a certain amount of fee to appear in the exam. If the fee is equal to the entry fee of the examination (Fig. **6**), then the student is allowed to submit the script.

```
if ( msg . value ==1 ether )
```

Fig. (6). Implementation of fee payment.

Hence, after verification through a smart contract, a new block consisting of the answer script with other information is added to the chain. The student is recorded as present in the entry table, and the student ID is recorded in the exist table corresponding to the respective student number.

Similarly, if the student's fee is not equal to the entry fee, the student is not allowed to submit the script. Hence, no block will be added to the chain. In this case, neither the student number will increase nor the student will be recorded in the entry and exist table. In this way, every student can submit their answer scripts abiding by the rules (Fig. **7**).

```
studentNumber = studentNumber + 1 ;
present [ studentNember ] = true ;
exist [studentNember ] = student ;
chain.push ( student ) ;
```

Fig. (7). Implementation of student's record.

- **Answer Script Evaluation:** To check the student's answer scripts, teachers need to specify the name, teacher request ID, and subject code of the paper, and the number will be verified by the smart contract (Fig. **8**).

```
teacherEntry(string memory name, uint number, uint id, string memory subjectCode)
```

Fig. (8). Implementation of teacher entry.

If the number exists in the entry table and the student ID corresponding to this number from the exist table is equal to the teacher request ID, then the teacher can evaluate the requested student's answer script (Fig. **9**). After that, the teacher will add the grade card to the block and receive compensation.

```
if ( present [ number ]  &&  exist [ number ].id == id )
```

Fig. (9). Implementation of student's existence.

Therefore, the teacher's block will be added to the chain. Otherwise, the student requested by the teacher does not exist in the chain. Hence, teacher's entry is prohibited.

PERFORMANCE ISSUES RESOLVED

The credibility of the proposed model can be represented in the form of the Agile Manifesto. The Agile Manifesto can be described as a primary picture of advantages over the prior technology. In Fig. (**10**) shown below, "CR Over CRUD" suggests that the proposed approach has the advantages of creating and reading contexts where the present model has the disadvantage of being altered by unknown parties.

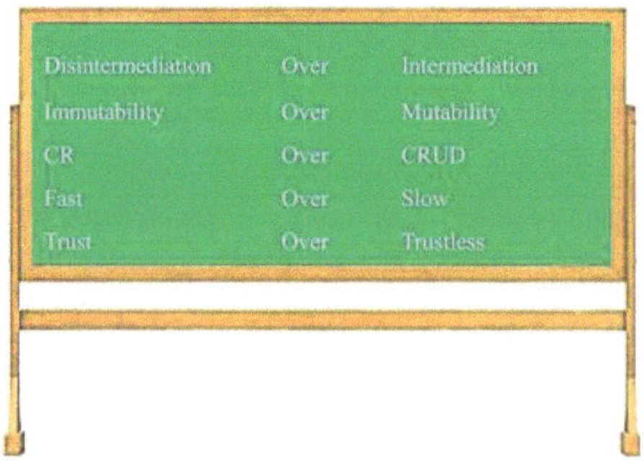

Disintermediation	Over	Intermediation
Immutability	Over	Mutability
CR	Over	CRUD
Fast	Over	Slow
Trust	Over	Trustless

Fig. (10). Agile manifesto of proposed model.

Disintermediation: The proposed model removes third parties and makes it more independent of the existing manual system. Thus, it establishes disintermediation.

Immutability: Blockchain has the magnificent property of immutability, which states that once data is recorded in the blockchain then it will never be modified or deleted. Hence, the proposed model ensures protection against forgery.

CR: The existing system uses CRUD (Create, Read, Update, and Delete) operations, whereas the proposed model uses only CR (Create and Read) operations to ensure security.

Fast: Deployment of smart contracts automates the execution of the process once conditions are satisfied. Automation makes the process faster than the present system.

Trust: Trust is one of the pillars in the development of education. Universities need to choose a trustful system for their students on the basis of their present learning status. Blockchain is a peer-to-peer network that ensures trust by creating a block where data can neither be deleted nor mutated. Therefore, it is the most faithful system that can be utilized in the education sector.

CONCLUSION

The goal of this article is to show how to utilize blockchain to conduct decentralized examinations and improve the evaluation of examination records. With this framework, we addressed the lack of information in the present examination system, which can be eliminated and provides openness and trustworthiness by documenting examination information on the unchangeable public blockchain. It is learned from the COVID-19 pandemic that providing services has become an even larger problem. Mostly, in the case of the institutional test process, authorities cannot rely on remote decentralized examination only because of an untrusted environment. This research work aimed to provide a decentralized, trusted, and transparent environment where a fair test can be conducted. This approach can improve the teaching and learning process and also mitigate critical situations like COVID-19. In the globalization of education, smart contracts and cryptographic security open scope for the researcher to develop an ecosystem where knowledge can be spread trustfully and fair evaluation is possible. This research suggests that the major benefits of smart contracts are openness and trust. Moreover, data protection and privacy, resource management, and decision-making processes can help develop a good ecosystem for educational institutions.

FUTURE SCOPE

The current study offers the framework for adopting a blockchain in the realm of academic education. A scalable web interface is demanded for IPFS connectivity and user accessibility. The scalability of the framework is not tested for different blockchain platforms. There is a scope to migrate our work from Ethereum to Hyperledger [11] to reduce the transaction cost imposed by Ethereum.

ACKNOWLEDGEMENTS

We are thankful to the editors for their expertise and assistance throughout all aspects of our study and for their help in writing the manuscript.

REFERENCES

[1]   Duoyi Hu, "The Development Thread and Innovation Trend of Educational Teaching Evolution Method," In: 2nd International Conference on Computers, Information Processings and Advanced Education (CIPAE 2021), 2021.

[2]   Pasi Sahlberg, "Rethinking accountability in a knowledge society". Journal of Educational Change, 11, 45 – 61, 2010.

[3]   Untung Rahardja, Qurotul Aini, MD Asri Ngadi, Marviola Hardini and Fitra Putri Oganda, "The Blockchain Manifesto," In: 2nd International Conference on Cybernetics and Intelligent System (ICORIS), 2020.
[http://dx.doi.org/10.31763/ijele.v3i3.283]

[4]   Anak Agung Sagung Mas Anastassia Nawang Asri and Gede Sri Darma, "Revealing the Digital Leadership Spurs in 4.0 Industrial Revolution". International Journal of Business, Economics À Management, 3(1), 93-100, 2020.

[5]   Ninda Lutfiani, Qurotul Aini, Untung Rahardja, Lidya Wijayanti, Efa Ayu Nabila, and Mohammed Iftequar Ali, "Transformation of blockchain and opportunities for education 4.0," International Journal of Education and Learning, Vol. 3, No. 3, pp. 222-231, December 2020.

[6]   Manzoor Ahmed Hashmani , Aisha Zahid Junejo , Abdullah Abdulrehman Alabdulatif and Syed Hasan Adil, "Blockchain in Education – Trackability and Traceability, " In : International Conference on Computational Intelligence (ICCI), 2020.
[http://dx.doi.org/10.1109/CITSM47753.2019.8965380]

[7]   Halvdan Haugsbakken, and Inger Langseth, "The Blockchain Challenge for Higher Education Institutions," European Journal of Education, Vol. 2, Issue 3, December 2019.

[8]   Untung Rahardja, Achmad Nizar Hidayanto, Taqwa Hariguna, Qurotul Aini, "Design Framework on Tertiary Education System in Indonesia Using Blockchain Technology," In: The 7th International Conference on Cyber and IT Service Management (CITSM), 2019.
[http://dx.doi.org/10.3102/0013189X16670898]

[9]   C. Cassandra, H. A. E. Widjaja, H. Prabowo, E. Fernando, and Y. U. Chandra, "A Blockchain Technology-Based for University Teaching and Learning Processes," In: International Conference on Information Management and Technology (ICIMTech), 2020, pp. 244–247.
[http://dx.doi.org/10.1007/s10833-008-9098-2]

[10]   Donald J. Peurach "Innovating at the Nexus of Impact and Improvement: Leading Educational Improvement Networks," Sage Journals, Vol. 45, Issue 7, September 26, 2016.

[11]   Aidin R., "A Coin Marketplace Implementation on Blockchain Using the Hyperledger Platform," September 2018.

CHAPTER 6

Intelligent Farm Management System Using IoT-Based Agrobot

Rohtash Dhiman[1,*], **Aarti**[1], **Rashi**[1], **Amisha**[1] and **Swati Dhiman**[2]

[1] *Department of Electrical Engineering, Deenbandhu Chhotu Ram University of Science and Technology, Murthal, Haryana, India*

[2] *Department of Electronics and Communication Engineering, Sant Longowal Institute of Engineering and Technology, Longowal, Punjab, India*

Abstract: The unwanted and excessive use of pesticides and fertilizers creates health hazards and makes the soil unproductive. Only a small portion of the crop catches disease, but the farmers spray the pesticides evenly over the entire field, resulting in wastage and overuse of pesticides. They are not aware of the exact composition of the soil. Certain nutrients, pH levels, moisture, and fertility support a certain kind of crop. All of these problems have been observed in the nearby villages of District Sonepat (Haryana), such as in the villages of Bhigan and Murthal. Robots with sensors to match the levels of pH, temperature, humidity, and soil moisture to the levels required for growing crops are used in the present research to identify the best crop for a given soil. The sensors are connected to Raspberry Pi to send the data to ThingSpeak, which compares the sensed data with the standard data and gives the user the required information. A drone hovering over the field clicks the pictures of the field to be used by the intelligent image processing system for disease detection. The productivity can be increased without adversely affecting the soil. This will reduce the use of chemical fertilizers by 30% to 75% and create economic and environmentally sustainable crop production. The equipment manufacturing companies are potential buyers for the patent of the proposed technology. Marketing of this technology may be done in partnership with fertilizer suppliers.

Keywords: Drone, Disease, Fertilizers, Farming, Humidity, Pesticides, Productivity, Temperature, Robot.

INTRODUCTION

In order to address these issues, the authors present a method for boosting farmers' output that is based on robots and drones. It is an innovative idea that would completely alter the current approach's ideology in the direction of farming. Robots can minimize crop failure and increase productivity exponentially by

* **Corresponding author Rohtash Dhiman:** Department of Electrical Engineering, Deenbandhu Chhotu Ram University of Science and Technology, Murthal, Haryana, India; E-mail: Rohtash.ee@dcrustm.org

H.S. Hota, Dinesh K. Sharma, Ayan Kumar Das & Ditipriya Sinha (Eds.)

monitoring the moisture and nutrient content of the soil at regular intervals. This data will be provided to the farmers through an app to ensure they plan accordingly. Once the crop is sown, a hovering drone will capture pictures of the produce at regular intervals, and these will be compared to the already available data through image processing techniques to ensure disease-free crops.

The authors propose a solution based upon a synergetic approach between hardware and software to cope with the problems. A robot equipped with 4 different types of sensors and Raspberry Pi acting as an on-board computer is used to observe the soil continuously. It collects data on levels of pH, humidity, temperature, and nutrients and performs a computational process with the standard levels required to grow crops to give important indications and suggestions to farmers. By doing this, the proposed system is able to recognize the top suitable crop for the soil under consideration. A drone is used to collect images from the fields at regular intervals during the growth of crops to find the beginning of any disease. The disease is identified at the beginning and the required dose of insecticide and pesticide is sprayed in the affected area only. The monitoring is continued for any possible spread of disease at a later time. The hovering drone, at continuous intervals, sends pictures to the proposed intelligent image processing scheme. Finding sick crops and solving productivity issues at the same time result in the type of transformation the country is seeking, tripling farmer incomes.

LITERATURE SURVEY

Agriculture robots have unique technological and technical challenges that are not normally encountered by indoor robotic systems since they work both outdoors and on uneven terrain. These research initiatives were focused on these distinct agricultural concerns. Further examination of these publications revealed that the following issues attracted the attention of researchers:

(i) Image processing specific to agriculture and handling rough terrain

(ii) sensors

(iii) navigation in rough terrain, natural lighting, handling wheel slip, its effects on the performance of image processing, the effects of vegetation on the localization of operations consistency of tractor-trailer activity, mechanical design, and other concerns studied by researchers.

Agriculture robotics, amidst this success and recent advancements in robotics, is still in its infancy. No industrial-scale or large-scale agricultural operations using agriculture robots have been reported [1]. The following researchers understood that agriculture robots needed to become applicable in order for that to happen, so they worked to improve their robots.

In a study [2], a multifunctional agricultural robot was presented. The two primary goals from the start were designing the robot and developing a cloud-based system to connect it to the farmers' mobile devices. They used readily available tools and equipment to build their robot internally for less than $2,000, and they were able to manage it wirelessly [2]. The intriguing aspect of their research was that they were able to pinpoint the characteristics of an effective agriculture robot, which included not only being fully mobile but also being wireless, cloud-based, and connected to a mobile device [2]. A study [3] proposed the Greenhouse Partner Robot System. The authors created an agricultural network of support to promote collaboration between humans and robots, concentrating on the management of pests and crop harvesting [3]. A four-wheeled mobile trolley with tracker sensors was introduced, which could move around the greenhouse on its own using a guidance line and tracker sensors. For managing the harvesting and insect control operations, the carts also have a control range with a joystick, a control panel, and an RFID tag reader [3].

While the team member operates its control panel to carry out the necessary agricultural tasks, the robot moves around the greenhouse on its own [3]. A functional prototype of the Agribot agricultural robot, capable of performing a variety of agricultural activities, was developed by Amer *et al.*. The robot could easily move in any direction thanks to its hexpad physical design as well as its walking mechanism [4]. Their robot connects to the internet *via* WiFi, and a laptop on board makes a WiFi connection. The robot and its operator are connected *via* this link. Additionally, the robot can link to many robots *via* WiFi and coordinate goals [4]. Emmi *et al,* added numerous electronic systems to agro-based robots to improve their functionality, but it also made them larger, heavier, more expensive, and less reliable. They suggested that in order for an agro-based robot to succeed, complexity as well as functionality must be balanced [5].

Shete and Naik [6] state that robotics in the agricultural industry, with its execution based on the idea of precision farming, is the most recent emerging technology in recent years. Reducing labor-intensive, repetitive farming chores and increasing yield productivity through precision farming are the main forces behind the automation of agricultural processes. These robots are made according to a certain process, taking into account particular elements of the farming environment in which they will be utilized. These elements and the different approaches that were explored were summarized by the writers. Also shown is a prototype for an autonomous agro-based robot that is only intended for tasks related to planting seeds. The LPC2148 microcontroller drives this four-wheeled vehicle. Its operation is based on smart agriculture, which enables effective seed sowing at the right depth as well as the distance between crops and their rows, depending on the type of crop. According to E. Praveen Kumar and S. Mohan [7], the efficiency of developed agriculture needs to be increased in novel ways. To decrease and target energy inputs more effectively as compared to the past, one strategy is to make use of the information technologies that are currently available in the form of more intelligent robots. Although smart agriculture has shown the benefits of this approach, we can now switch to a new creation of equipment.

Amer *et al.* [4, 6] proposed an entirely new line of farming equipment based on tiny, intelligent robots that can perform tasks correctly when performed in the proper location, at the proper time, and in the proper manner thanks to the development of autonomous system architectures. Autonomous farming robots that can acknowledge, spray, and pick specific grains of wheat and rice may become a reality soon. Other fields, such as robotic surgery as well as other applications in medicine, might also benefit from the process. By connecting the robot and PC with GSM and Lab View software, the concept of designing an agro-based robot can be realized. Oil testing, according to Shah Alamgir and Israt Jahan [8], is crucial for modern agriculture in order to maximize output, safeguard the environment from excessive fertilizer use, and conserve resources while producing food. The aim of this analysis was to create an autonomous smartphone for agriculture with a soil sampling device.

To ascertain the characteristics, composition, or nutrient concentration of the soil, soil samples are analyzed. Simple, portable field testing kits are available for smallholder farmers. However, the automated framework with a soil sampler would also be the greatest option for huge farmland where plants are farmed across hundreds of hectares. Using state-of-the-art production and management methods that use all the information acquired about specific regions and crop types is known as precision farming.

The aforementioned robot can improve data acquisition efficiency in terms of resources and costs. The machine's onboard systems can retrieve data about the soil's characteristics from the field, allowing farmers to react to sudden changes in real time. An effective production process is made possible by data technologies and soil collection systems. The use of robots on farmlands is linked to the ongoing digitization of all aspects of our lives, including agriculture. Salleh *et al.* [9] presented the review of agro-based robots and looked into the potential causes of this phenomenon, this time concentrating on viability and practicability. The authors came to the conclusion that practical agro-based robots depend on robotics advancements as well as on the existence of the support infrastructure after conducting a thorough review and analysis.

The infrastructure consists of a platform for software communication and reuse, an efficient framework for HRI (Human-Robot Interaction) between robots and agricultural members, and all other services and technologies needed by agro-based machines when they are operating. Without such infrastructure, agricultural robots, no matter how advanced in design, would remain unfeasible and impractical. Agriculture robots are, however, both uneconomical and envious due to the high technological and administrative price of constructing such type of infrastructure. In light of this, the paper comes to the conclusion that the key to developing the necessary support infrastructure for agriculture robots in a novel, economical, and reliable manner is essential for practical agriculture robotics. Wang and Feng [10, 11] crafted a tomato smart picking robot to enhance the robotic cultivation of fresh tomatoes and decrease the amount of manual work. The picking machine included a carrying platform, a control system, a picking gripper, and a vision positioning unit. The picking robot's operational procedure was updated in accordance with the operating principles of each component. Their color model for image segmentation was used to improve the recognition precision. To avoid damaging the fruits, the picking end-grasping effectors' component was replaced with sacs stuffed with constant pressure air. The vision positioning module and the gripper module performed well, according to the picking robot's performance test. A single tomato harvest cycle took about 24 seconds to complete, and it was successful 83.9 percent of the time.

Fig. (1) depicts the challenges of implementing an agriculture robot. As a result of a detailed survey of relevant literature, it can be concluded that overcoming the technological obstacles involved in creating the support infrastructure required by agriculture robots is essential for their practical implementation issues with connecting, using HRI tools, and sharing and reusing software, to name a few. In order to accomplish this, a fresh concept is required to address these technological issues, assist in the establishment of the necessary infrastructure, and ultimately support the adoption of useful farming robots.

PROBLEM FARMERS ARE FACING

A requirement of contemporary farming is the evaluation of soil conditions prior to crop selection. In addition to being uneconomical and potentially harmful to health, the excessive and unwarranted use of fertilizers and pesticides is also rendering the land unusable. Although only a small portion of crops contract the disease, farmers spray pesticides all over the field, wasting money and resources and frequently causing fatalities because the person applying the chemicals is also indirectly breathing them in. In order to save their crops, farmers borrow money for fertilizer and pesticides. When they eventually can no longer afford the loan, they commit suicide as a result of their mounting debt. To address the severe issues of farmers mentioned above, agricultural automation can be a blessing in the present time of IoT. The authors look at different approaches for the purpose. Three options are typically available when performing an agricultural task.

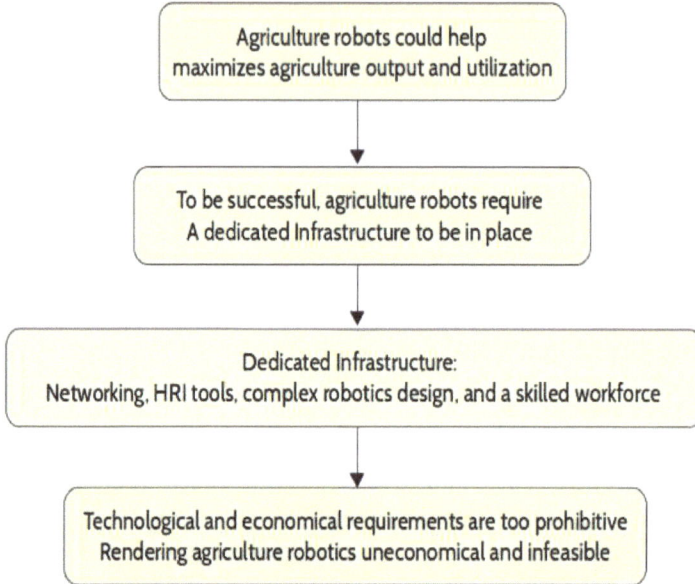

Fig. (1). The challenge of implementing agriculture robot.

- Manual work
- "Blind machine" (*i.e.* a machine devoid of sensors)
- Automated devices

Table **1** provides a summary of these three options' qualities.

Table 1. Basic characteristics.

-	Production Efficiency	Running Initially	Investment Cost
MANUAL WORK	less	less	more
BLIND MACHINE	more	more	less
ROBOT	less	more	less

A summary of favorable and unfavorable factors is presented in this section.

Favorable Factors

The following are favorable factors for agricultural automation and IoT-enabled systems:

Economic and Socioeconomic Aspects

In order to maintain their competitiveness in the market, farmers today must constantly deal with issues related to production costs. Therefore, they furnish his land with machinery that will yield a quick return on investment and address the complex issue of seasonal labor. Innovation is no longer hindered by the farmer's accustomed routine temperament. There are many instances where a farmer invents or enhances his own production of equipment.

Many jobs are seasonal, and it is now considered unacceptable in industrialized nations to employ temporary, unskilled labor during the harvest season. Another justification for automation is the unfavorable environment that farming chemicals produce, leading to the statement that "vegetable fields are no place for humans". Additionally, only machines will have the accuracy to prevent waste in activities like chemical spraying, fertilizer or pesticide distribution, and crop irrigation when there is a lack of land, water, power, and other resources.

Technical Aspects

A favorable environment has been created for the advancement of agricultural equipment by recent industrial advancement. Electronic parts used in automated machines are getting better at what they do while still getting cheaper. This holds true for data processors, sensors, and actuators. The CCD camera, which is increasingly used in the area of artificial vision, may serve as an illustration.

Similar to this, the development of specialized signal processors has made it possible to compute at about 10 Mlps per second. The computing power of agricultural equipment in the late 1980s may be comparable to that of large data centers today.

Automation-focused labs have grown more interested in the idea of using their expertise to improve agricultural machinery over the past ten years, which has led to the development of fresh ideas for new technology. Additionally, CAD effectively addresses the complexity of these machines, reducing the time required for implementation and increasing their accessibility to less highly specialized industrial manufacturers.

Unfavorable Factors

The unfavorable factors are discussed below:

Financial Aspects

The modern farmer, who has historically been renowned for his wisdom and vast wealth, is frequently in debt. This suggests a number of challenges when it comes to large investments, particularly in the case of small areas, which make up the vast majority (the United States only has four major industries that manufacture cars, but there are about 2 million farming land).

Agriculture still typically involves generating affordable products over a large area, like potatoes. Slow financial return is due to agricultural machinery's seasonal use.

Technical Aspects

Despite plant and animal breeders' best efforts, agricultural products still come in a wide range of sizes, colors, and shapes, so an agricultural robot must travel great distances and handle them.

Fragile objects require careful handling due to their fragility. The robot must be able to withstand environmental factors in the open field, such as light, dust particles, inclement weather, air, fog, *etc.*

This suggests the utilization of advanced technologies, which raises the machine's cost.

Industrial Aspects

These very complex machines require the design and construction of an extremely competent team of workers. Sadly, this is not usually the case with farm equipment, where there will inevitably be a push for technological advancement in the coming years. Additionally, it should be kept in mind that the industry is currently dealing with a serious emergency. It is becoming more and more obvious that agricultural automation requires standardizing the structure, communication links, and networks.

Differences in the Operation of Indusctrial & Agricultural Robots

The proliferation of incompatible components creates anarchy and only slows down design progress. Industrial and agricultural robots are supposed to operate in totally different types of environments and conditions.

Therefore, the authors find it appropriate to sum up these differences here. The main differences are as given below:

Environment

The robot must withstand poor weather, particles, a variety of barriers, *etc.*, when crops are growing in an open field. Additionally, the ground may have various features such as rakes, slopes, uncomfortable ground, grass, *etc.* Robots are typically not exposed to such a wide variety of situations in industrial settings. In order to maintain its integrity and prevent any harm from malfunctioning, the robot must be outfitted with a redundant multisensory system because the agricultural area is so unpredictable.

Handling an Object

Handling an object, such as a young plant or soft fruit, requires care because they are often fragile. They can range widely in size, shape, and color. Additionally, using machines around animals can provoke unpredictable and dangerous reactions like fear or aggression.

When shearing sheep, for instance, the animal must sometimes be restrained from moving. The animal may react more cooperatively in other situations, such as when milking cows. These issues are not brought on by this nature's fragility or unpredictability in business.

Accessibility of the Items

Fruit is frequently tucked away among branches and covered in leaves, making it challenging to find and collect. Some vegetables must be plucked from the ground. A good example of a delicate item that needs to be inserted relatively deeply into its mound of soil is white asparagus.

The Seasonal Nature of Farm Work

Several farm tasks are done in a relatively short amount of time. As a result, machine rates of return are frequently slower than in industry.

Unspecialized Consumer

Even though these devices are complicated, using them should not be difficult for the consumer. The majority of the farm equipment is typically maintained and repaired by the farmer. It will be more challenging to accomplish this if sophisticated machinery malfunctions, which will unavoidably occur during the busiest season of the year.

Therefore, the authors conclude that the requirements for the design of agricultural robots are different from those of industrial robots. The main applications of farm robots are summed up below:

The introduction of robots in agriculture will lead to a number of issues with regard to how agricultural work is organized. Teams of robots will need to work together to complete various tasks due to their low productivity, necessitating the development of machine-machine and man-machine communications infrastructure.

The power available on modern tractors today can be equal to 100 horsepower. It should be noted that over a lengthy period of time, a field laborer is equivalent to about one-tenth of a horsepower. Thus, devices like verticality, wheel skids, and shock sensors are required to be installed on the machines in order to identify breakdowns in their typical operation or deviations in their surroundings.

The machineries, therefore, present significant risks in the event of failure. It is likely that new circumstances like these will result in appropriate legislation.

In order to have a view of how much insecticides, pesticides, and fertilizers are consumed by the farms in India, the authors present tabular data accessed from online sources in Tables **2** and **3**.

Table 2. Consumption of pesticides in India (state-wise).

S No.	State	Total Pesticides Consumed
1	Uttar Pradesh	39948
2	Punjab	29235
3	Haryana	21908
4	Maharashtra	16480
5	Rajasthan	15239
6	Gujrat	13420
7	Tamil Nadu	12851
	All India	210600

Table 3. Pesticides used.

S No.	Pesticide (Technical Grade)	Quantity Consumed (Metric Tonnes)
1	Sulfur (fungicide)	16424
2	Endosulfan (insecticide)	15537
3	Mancozeb (fungicide)	11067

(Table 3) cont.....

S No.	Pesticide (Technical Grade)	Quantity Consumed (Metric Tonnes)
4	Phorate (insecticide)	10763
5	Methyl Parathion (insecticide)	08408
6	Monocrotophos (insecticide)	08209
7	Cypermethrin (insecticide)	07309
8	Isoproturon (herbicide)	07163
9	Chlorpyrifos (insecticide)	07163
10	Malathion (insecticide)	07103
11	Carbendazium (fungicide)	06767
12	Butachlor (herbicide)	06750
13	Quinalphos (insecticide)	06329
14	Copper oxychloride	06055
15	Dichlorvos (insecticide)	05833

The authors carried out a farm survey, interviewed farmers in the villages of district Sonipat in Haryana state, and observed all these problems at ground level. The major crop we observed is tomato in villages like Bhigan, Murthal, Tajpur, Revli, *etc.* If the farmers get to know which part of the farm is catching the disease, they can spray the pesticides accordingly and will get two benefits: their soil quality will remain stable and money will be saved. Knowing about soil conditions and indicating which crop is best suited to their farms will help them in choosing the appropriate crop.

MATERIALS USED

The materials used to create a lab-scale prototype of the suggested robot are shown in this section. The authors have developed a lab-scale gadget and are currently working on a farm-scale version. The materials utilized for the lab-scale prototype are as follows:

The Raspberry Pi Foundation created the Raspberry Pi, a tiny single-board computer, in the UK to encourage computer science education in classrooms and underdeveloped nations. For applications such as robotics, the original concept has become far more prevalent than expected outside of its intended market (see Fig. **2**). Among its features is a CPU speed range of 700 MHz to 1.2 GHz.

Fig. (2). Raspberry Pi.

- Onboard memory (RAM) can range in capacity from 256 MB to 1 GB.
- USB and 1 slots are not the same.
- HDMI, composite video output, and a 3.5mm phone jack.
- Low-level output is provided by GPIO pins that support widely used protocols, such as I2C (inter-integrated circuit).
- Ethernet 8 Position 8 Contact (8P8C).

Python

For computer programming, Python is a high-level, interpreted programming language. Python offers a wide range of GUI (Graphical User Interface) programming choices. When it comes to GUI methods, tk inter is the most often utilized. Python's Tk GUI toolkit features a standard Python interface. The simplest and fastest tools for creating GUI programs are Python and Tk Inter. It is easy to design a GUI with tk inter.

Python Functions

- Python's straightforward syntax, minimal keywords, and clear-cut construction help one to learn it. This enables the pupil to acquire the language rapidly.
- Simple to understand: Python code is highly readable and concisely defined.
- Easily maintained: Python's code is not too difficult to keep up with.
- A sizable standard library: On UNIX, Windows, and Macintosh, a large percentage of the Python library is highly portable and cross-platform compatible.
- Interactive Mode: Live testing and code snippet debugging are both possible in the interactive mode that Python supports.
- Portability: Python has the same user interface across all hardware platforms and can be used on a wide range of hardware platforms.

- Extendable: Low-level modules are compatible with the Python interpreter. These modules allow programmers to improve or change their equipment to make them more functional.
- Databases: All significant commercial databases have Python interfaces available.
- GUI Programming: A variation of system calls, libraries, and Windows-based operating systems, such as Windows MFC, Macintosh, and the Unix X Window system, are supported by Python for the development and porting of GUI applications.

Power Supply or Battery

The farming robot can be operated by a power source or battery. DC motors need 12V to run, and the type of processor/controller used for the controller will vary. Therefore, a DC motor is driven by a 12V battery.

DC Motor Driver (L293D)

We have employed a DC motor driver by the name of L293D to drive a DC motor. It is a high voltage, high current device that is monolithic. There are four channel drivers inside a 16-lead plastic package. There are four centered pins connected together for the heat sink.

DC Motor

DC motors have been used to drive applications like the wheels on a robot. These 12V DC motors require motor driver L293D operation. Two or one L293D can drive DC motors.

Relay Paired with a Driver

Relays are electromagnetic switches that have four terminals: a coil, a common terminal, a terminal that is normally closed, and a terminal that is normally open. With the aid of relays, one circuit can switch another, potentially completely independent, circuit. Relays can be used, for example, to switch a low-voltage battery circuit's 230V AC main circuit. There is a mechanical and magnetic connection, but no electrical connection, between the two circuits in the relay.

Soil Moisture Sensor

Utilizing capacitive sensing, which alters capacitance in response to the amount of water present in the soil, gauges the moisture level of the soil. The obtained capacitance is converted to volts, ranging from 1.3V to 3.2V at the most. The advantage of capacitive soil moisture sensors is that they have a longer lifespan because they are made of corrosive and corrosion-resistant materials. Moreover, a 3-pin sensing interface is supported (shown in Fig. **3**).

Temperature Sensor

This sensor measures temperature and humidity digitally. The air temperature and humidity will be measured using this sensor. The output pin receives a digital signal that is sent by the device using a humidity sensor to track the surrounding wind. While it is not particularly complicated, getting the data requires close attention. The sensor readings are, therefore, frequently up to two seconds old anytime we are using the library. This sensor's limitation is that it can only provide us with updated information every two seconds (shown in Fig. **4**).

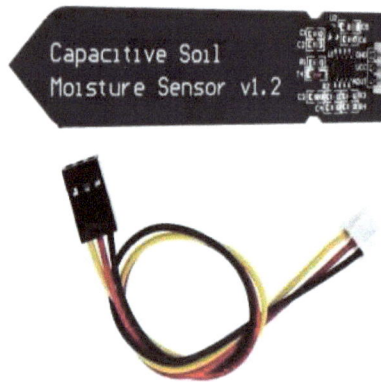

Fig. (3). Soil moisture sensor.

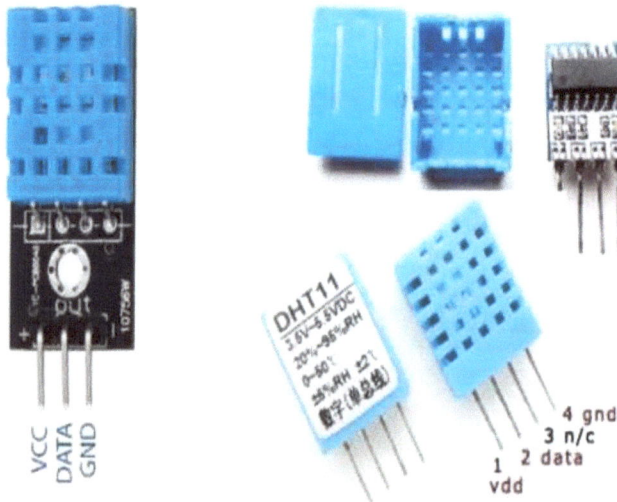

Fig. (4). DHT11 humidity temperature sensor.

SOLUTION AND WORKING

This section presents the working prototype of the proposed solution. The solution is using an approach based on IoT (Internet of Things). The prototype robot was designed, fabricated, and programmed by a team of authors in the laboratories of the university authors were working with. The drone kit was bought and assembled by the authors. This section presents a brief description of the working of the solution.

Internet of Things (IoT)

The IoT is made up of various modules and sensors that enable automation, *i.e.*, the removal of human interaction from the process of operating an object. It is made up of different hardware and software combinations that enable things to operate remotely/ automatically. In order to detect changes and remotely control objects, IoT uses sensing devices. This direct integration of physical realm presence into computer-based systems improves efficiency, precision, and economic benefit while reducing human involvement. The technology gives an overview of computer-based systems, which also include advancements like smart grids, smart roads, home automation, *etc.*, when the Internet of Things is fitted with sensors. Human reach can be difficult in some locations. With the aid of IoT, these processes are automated, reducing both the need for human labor and expense. In the present research and development project, the authors used the IoT framework in the proposed prototype.

This project uses a Raspberry Pi-based IoT-based smart agricultural aid system. Raspberry Pi acts as an on-board computer in the proposed system. The improvement of nations that are entirely dependent on agriculture is greatly influenced by the agriculture sector. The country's progress slows down as a result of agricultural problems. Sensible agriculture, which modernizes outdated agricultural practices or methods, is the finest solution to this issue. Therefore, the strategy is to advance our agriculture through the use of various automation techniques and IoT-based technologies. With the aid of the Internet of Things, we can monitor crop growth appropriately, choose the best crops, and implement automatic irrigation, among other things. An improved agricultural assistance system built on a Raspberry Pi is suggested to modernize and boost crop productivity in the field. Using some cutting-edge sensors that are readily available on the market, we are creating an Internet of Things (IoT) intelligent Agriculture Aid System in our project. To gauge the amount of moisture in the soil, a capacitive-type soil moisture sensor is needed.

A humidity and temperature sensor is used to gauge humidity and air temperature, respectively. The soil's toxicity can be determined using a pH sensor (Table **4**). It assists farmers in determining whether their crops are receiving the right nutrients or not. The robot, connected with different types of sensors, monitors the soil continuously by roaming around the farm. It matches the levels of pH, temperature, humidity, and soil moisture with the standard levels required to grow crops. By doing this, we can determine the crop that is most suited to that soil. The sensors are connected to a Raspberry Pi, which sends the data to ThingSpeak, which compares the sensed data to the standard data and provides us with all of the necessary information. A drone floats above the field, taking images and informing us about the diseases contracted by the crops. We can also learn about the trees or plants in the area, allowing us to spray the appropriate amount of fertilizer and pesticides over the field. Fig. (**5**) depicts the T/H sensor data updation, while Sensor values updation in chart is shown in Fig. (**6**).

Table 4. T/H sensor data's updation.

Temperature	Humidity
22	45
22	40
22	45
21	45
21	45
20	40
21	45
22	45
21	45

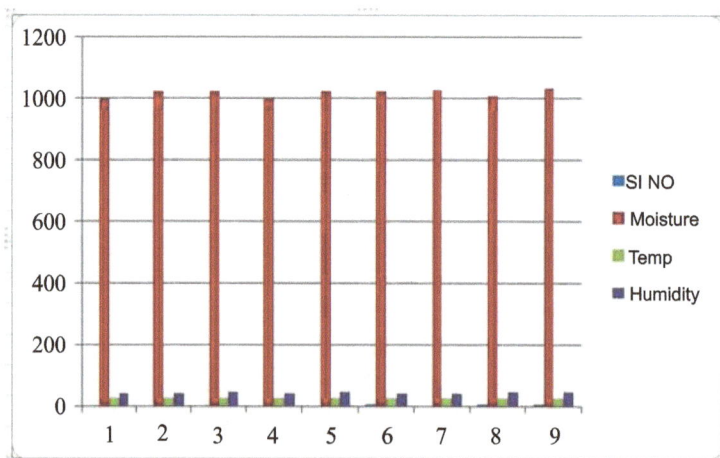

Fig. (5). Sensor values updation in the chart.

Data we received from raspberry Pi is shown in Fig. (**7**). The components used and the photograph of prototype are shown in Figs. (**8** and **9**), respectively.

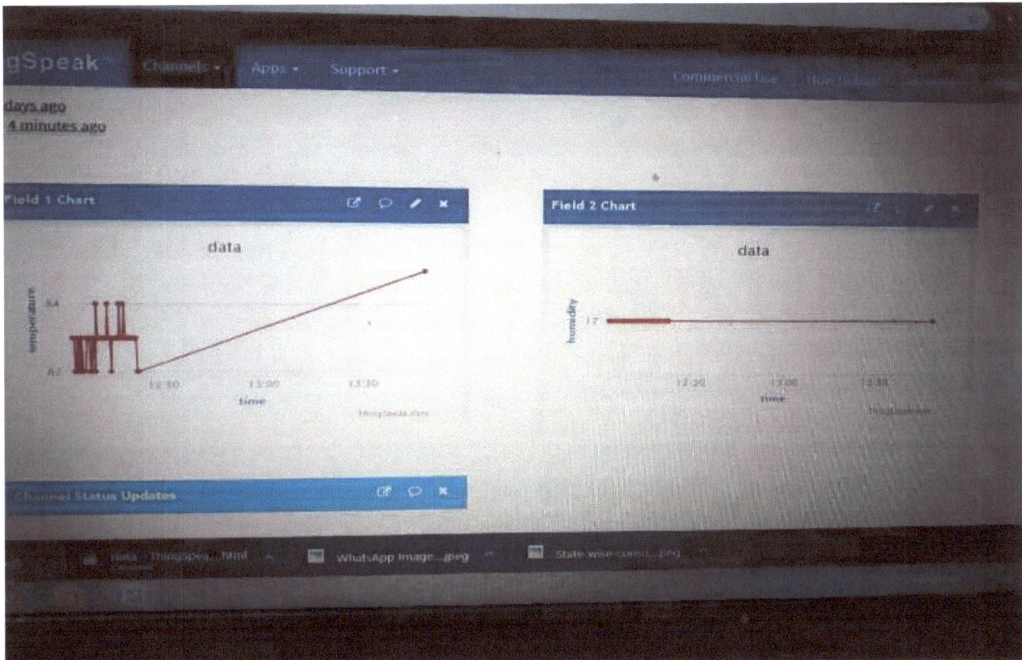

Fig. (6). Data Received.

The following are the salient features of the devised prototype robotic system:

- Acquiring knowledge about soil components beforehand.
- Indication of the appropriate crop based on soil data collected.
- Early detection of diseases through visual monitoring at continuous intervals by drone.
- Prevention from any disease in the crop by suggesting a target area and appropriate pesticide.
- Use of renewable solar power.
- It will assist in increasing the quality and quantity of produce.

Fig. (7). Material used.

Fig. (8). Prototype.

CONCLUSION AND FUTURE DIRECTIONS

The advancement of contemporary farming technology has a significant impact on the growth of agriculture. Agriculture is the primary economic engine of a developing nation like India. It will be a component of the long-term agricultural development plan. Two key advantages of applying IoT to crop production are making efficient use of the resources at hand and guaranteeing the precision, stability, and efficiency of agricultural production. The authors of the current research and development project suggested an intelligent system that uses an Internet of Things-enabled robot to sense soil parameters, a drone to continuously monitor crops visually, and a drone to indicate which crop is best for the farm's soil. The drone also indicates the emergence of any diseases, which suggests the use of fertilizers and pesticides.

The robot senses the soil parameters, and the on-board computer interacts with the ThingSpeak website to give a suggestion about the appropriate crop to be grown in the field. The hovering drone is made to carry out visual inspections through a camera and intelligent image processing system, thereby detecting the emergence of any disease in the field. The identified area by this visual monitoring is suggested by the system to be sprayed with appropriate pesticide/insecticide. In this manner, the farmer uses only the optimum amount of pesticide/insecticide in the affected area.

The future scope of the proposed system includes the development of farm-scale robotic devices. Also, the authors are in the process of researching a long flight time robot with heavy payloads to make the drone capable of spraying pesticides and fertilizers in an optimum and need0based way. In the future, more features will be added to the proposed solution through Internet of Things (IoT) systems, which will become increasingly precise, quick, stable, and cost-effective as technology improves. With continuous research and development, these systems will become a part of farms in India in the near future.

CONSENT FOR PUBLICATON

Authors express and give their consent for publication.

ACKNOWLEDGEMENTS

The authors acknowledge their institutes for providing research facilities.

REFERENCES

[1]   Frank   Tobe.   The   Robotreport.   Are   ag   robots   ready?.   Available   from https://www.therobotreport.com/are-ag-robots-ready-27-companies-profiled/

[2]   H. Durmus, E.O. Gunes, M. Kirci, and B.B. Ustundag, "The design of general purpose autonomous agricultural mobile-robot", *Fourth International Conference on Agro-Geoinformatics (Agro-geoinformatics)*, pp. 49-53, 2015.

[3]   K. Kashiwazaki, Y. Sugahara, J. Iwasaki, K. Kosuge, S. Kumazawa, and T. Yamashita, "Greenhouse Partner Robot System," in *Proc. ISR 2010 (41st Int. Symp. Robotics) and ROBOTIK 2010 (6th German Conf. Robotics)*, Munich, Germany, 2010, pp. 184–191.

[4]   G. Amer, S.M.M. Mudassir, and M.A. Malik, "Design and operation of Wi-Fi agribot integrated system", *International Conference on Industrial Instrumentation and Control (ICIC)*, pp. 207-12, 2015.
        [http://dx.doi.org/10.1109/IIC.2015.7150739]

[5]   L. Emmi, M. Gonzalez-de-Soto, G. Pajares, and P. Gonzalez-de-Santos, "New trends in robotics for agriculture: integration and assessment of a real fleet of robots", *ScientificWorldJournal,* vol. 2014, pp.

1-21, 2014.
[http://dx.doi.org/10.1155/2014/404059] [PMID: 25143976]

[6]   N. S. Naik, V. V. Shete and S. R. Danve, "Precision agriculture robot for seeding function," *2016 International Conference on Inventive Computation Technologies (ICICT)*, Coimbatore, India, 2016, pp. 1-3

[7]   F.A. Auat Cheein, and R. Carelli, "Agricultural Robotics: Unmanned Robotic Service Units in Agricultural Tasks", *IEEE Ind. Electron. Mag.*, vol. 7, no. 3, pp. 48-58, 2013.
[http://dx.doi.org/10.1109/MIE.2013.2252957]

[8]   S. Yaghoubi, N. A. Akbarzadeh, S. S. Bazargani, S. S. Bazargani, M. Bamizan, M. Irani Asl, "Autonomous Robots for Agricultural Tasks and Farm Assignment and Future Trends in Agro Robots", *International Journal of Mechanical & Mechatronics Engineering IJMME-IJENS.*, vol. 13, no. 3, pp. 1-6, 2013.

[9]   Pavan C., "DrBS Wi-fi Robot For Video Monitoring & Surveillance System", *Int. J. Sci. Eng. Res.*, vol. 3, no. 8, pp. 1247-1250, 2012.

[10]   T. Bakker, K. van Asselt, J. Bontsema, J. Müller, and G. van Straten, "A path following algorithm for mobile robots", *Auton. Robots,* vol. 29, no. 1, pp. 85-97, 2010.
[http://dx.doi.org/10.1007/s10514-010-9182-3]

[11]   Q. Feng, X. Wang, G. Wang, and Z. Li, "Design and test of tomatoes harvesting robot", *International Conference on Information and Automation,* pp. 949-52, 2015.
[http://dx.doi.org/10.1109/ICInfA.2015.7279423]

CHAPTER 7

A Novel Unbiased Trust Establishment Mechanism in a Cross-Domain Cloud-Based IoT Environment

Kaustav Roy[1,*], **Debdutta Pal**[2], **Ayan Kumar Das**[2] and **Amit K. Sharma**[3]

[1] *Department of Computer Science and Engineering, Brainware University, Kolkata, India*

[2] *Department of Computer Science and Engineering, Birla Institute of Technology, Mesra - Patna Campus, Bihar, India*

[3] *Department of Computer Science and Engineering Technology, University of Maryland Eastern Shore, Princess Anne, Maryland, USA*

Abstract: Establishing a secure and safe trust system for a dispersed cloud-based IoT environment is very tough. Nowadays, the differences between cloud and IoT are blurring, and they are increasingly being applied together in several applications. A robust trust establishment model is the need of the hour. In this paper, we are advocating a trust-dependent authorization model to be implemented in a cloud-dependant IoT environment that also functions as a two-way or dual-mode trust model, taking into account the requirements of service giver and taker. In the suggested paradigm, trustworthiness is assessed on both the user and supplier sides. A transaction is only permitted if both trust values exceed a predefined or set threshold. We cannot entirely rely on the recommender's comments to determine how trustworthy a node or entity is. Therefore, the primary presumption in this situation is that a small number of hostile entities may provide false information about other entities. In the actual world, we can anticipate several malevolent actors attempting to sabotage the efficient operation of the cloud system by providing misleading reports and feedback, and the IoT ecosystem is ultimately dependent on the cloud for data processing and allied services, which generally consists of an application layer, network layer, and sensor layer. A new phrase for gauging this inaccurate or biased reporting is included in the model. In addition, the ongoing transactions are made more trustworthy by removing skewed feedback from both the user and supplier end. We also put forward a rule that allows trust values to be dynamically modified and active nodes to be given more weightage when determining trust.

Keywords: Cloud-based IoT environment, Feedback, Trust, Virtual organization.

** **Corresponding author Kaustav Roy:** Department of Computer Science and Engineering, Brainware University, Kolkata, India; E-mail: kr.cs@brainwareuniversity.ac.in*

H.S. Hota, Dinesh K. Sharma, Ayan Kumar Das & Ditipriya Sinha (Eds.)

INTRODUCTION

The always-evolving, multifaceted behavior of the cloud computing environment is a matter of great concern for the environment's consumers. The emergence of cloud-based IoT applications has made the situation much more complex. The mingling of several autonomous domains or workgroups consisting of context-aware nodes of the IoT environment having autonomous rights or administration poses severe problems in terms of management. The lack of consistent authorization processes among the cross-domain environments based on the trust levels of particular nodes has worsened the situation further. In such circumstances, the emergence of access control based on roles and its reliance on node trustworthiness have recently attracted significant attention, where context signifies the role or purpose of an individual user in the network setup.

The basis of computational grids and cloud-based IoT systems is the formation of virtual organizations comprising multiple physical organizations. Global management and local autonomy must be practiced in those virtual organizations to establish proper access control. Users may be granted varying rights or permissions at distinct local domains according to cloud access control policies that can be implemented centrally. Based on their positions or functions, users will receive role rankings. It is necessary to set up a trustworthy environment and to limit the user's needs using appropriate authorization techniques. As a result, a mechanism should create an equality of roles of a particular user among the various domains. An appropriate authorization policy must be implemented to approve or reject client service requests. This paper will present a model where a mechanism has been laid out to construct a reliable cloud computing-based IoT environment.

The shortcomings of the present research work in the said domain are as follows:

• A major obstacle in the current research is the reliance on certificate authorities and complex cryptographic techniques, which take time and effort.

• Finding appropriate, adjustable trust values for nodes in a dynamic cloud IoT environment.

The novelty of this paper can be summed up as follows:

• Incorporating a dynamic trust updating method with a novel access control mechanism.

• A dual-mode trust model is being developed that is impartial and weighs the reputations of the client and the service provider equally.

The remaining parts of the chapter contain the following sections. Section 2 discusses existing literature. Section 3 illustrates a functional model of the domain-specific organization. A dual-mode credibility model is described in Section 4. Section 5 demonstrates the performance diagnosis, and Section 6 concludes the chapter.

LITERATURE REVIEW

The findings of the current research works are as follows:

In a study [1], the authors have put forth a federated cloud trust management paradigm that uses three distinct techniques to calculate trust: SLA parameters for trust, customer feedback, and user feedback. They have included the idea of a trust engine in their architecture, which will undoubtedly make processing more complex. Additionally, SLA can be used to gauge performance levels, but it is unreliable for gauging the dependability of individual nodes in a cloud context.

In another study [2], the authors have drawn attention to the problems in establishing confidence in a cross-cloud federated context. For the cloud network's composite and mutual trust evaluation, novel approaches have been presented. The main problems in such a setting are resource awareness and unilateral trust delegation. For a productive and reliable environment, the nature of the federation and the traits of the trust management system must coincide.

In a paper [3], the authors have proposed a simple, logic-based trust determination algorithm for a networked cloud computing environment. Uncertainty and imperfect information can be modeled and analyzed using subjective logic and a form of mathematical logic. It can be used to express one participant's level of trust in another. They also proposed an inter-trust algorithm with local and global levels and a total trust value.

In another paper [4], the authors have offered a trust assessment and evaluation-based access control system. The display of a multi-attribute-based trust model, which centered on direct trust, risk estimation of trust, feedback trust, awarding a penalty, and obligation trust, highlights the seriousness of long-lasting relationships.

In a research work [5], the authors have proposed a zero-trust technique in a cloud setting. "Never trust, always verify" is the guiding principle of the zero-trust strategy. In the zero trust approach, every traffic is regarded as being untrusted. It aids in preventing data breaches brought on by the abuse of rights given to specific nodes.

CROSS-DOMAIN ORGANIZATION

An important consideration when there are numerous domains involved is cross-domain authorization. Making up access control policies can be complicated as IoT considers multiple devices. After collecting data, sensor devices send it to cloud domains for processing, which can then be transferred to other domains [6]. The cloud computing infrastructure communicates data transfer and receiving operations from the IoT environment. Many domains may have their own set of rules and laws for granting resource access. The role of a node can vary greatly between domains. There is a genuine need for some degree of equality between the roles [7]. A trust-based strategy has been identified as this case's best course of action.

Access control, depending on the roles, plays a crucial function. The model proposes a unique organization of multiple domains where appropriate access control policy focussing mainly on establishing a biased free trust model needs to be implemented.

The multi-domain organization includes the following relevant components (Fig. **1**):

- Two sample domains are work groups, an accumulation of nodes that are being used for data processing by the underlying IoT network setup.
- Two credential-checking servers for the individual domains or workgroups.
- Two rating servers for storing detailed information (role rankings of individual nodes).
- A redirection server is also present, which is needed when requests span multiple domains.

TWO-WAY OR DUAL-MODE TRUST COMPUTING MECHANISM

The proposed methodology estimates node reputation by considering other nodes' recommendations. Feedback is obtained, and a statistical way of finding a correlation among the obtained feedback values is implemented to avoid favoritism. Trust comes under two headings: direct trust and indirect trust [8]. Between the two types, direct trust is more important. It is computed based on earlier transactions between the service consumer and provider. Indirect trust is computed depending on feedback scores that are being accumulated from neighboring entities in their domain or different domains. Specific attributes by similarity, activity, specificity, and inactivity are used to determine the credibility of the promoter's opinion [9]. A concept of a predefined threshold parameter is also there, which must be satisfied to proceed with the transaction [10] ultimately. Not only the service requester but the service provider also checks the credibility of the requester in the said model, thus forming a two-way checking mechanism. After collecting the data, IoT sensor nodes send it to the cloud environment, which is only processed by legitimate or trustworthy nodes.

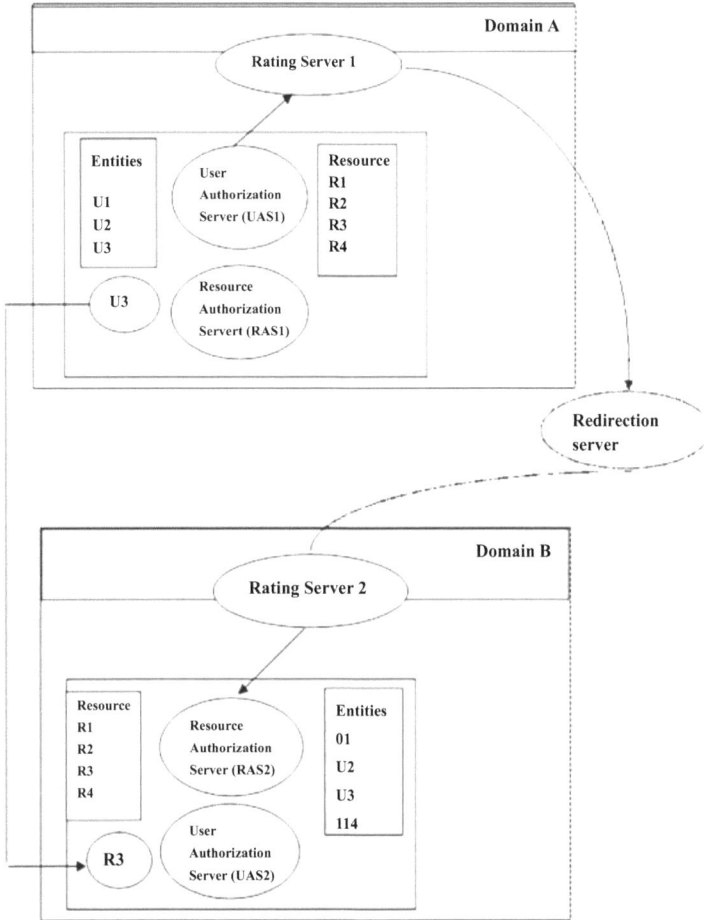

Fig. (1). Requests spanning multiple domains in cloud-based IoT setup.

Trust Calculation

Let us assume A is a client and B is a service provider. In such a scenario, A needs to find out whether B is the right candidate to choose to satisfy its needs or not.

The total trust is given here as follows:

$$Direct\ Trust = \frac{Total\ no\ of\ successful\ transactions\ within\ a\ time\ period\ T}{No\ of\ submitted\ jobs\ within\ the\ time\ period\ T} \tag{1}$$

$$Indirect\ Trust = \frac{(1-CR)*average\ feedback\ received\ from\ the\ same\ domain}{Credibility\ factor} \tag{2}$$

where the Credibility factor = 0.50, which is a constant, and the score of credibility is given by CR.

Past transaction records between provider and consumer play a crucial role in this model. Indirect trust is also calculated based on referrer feedback. Here, we are implementing Spearman's rank correlation method with slight modifications to determine the rank co-relation of feedback values obtained from neighboring nodes of a given node. A positive co-relation value nearing 1 prevents any distortion or biases. The reliability of recommender feedback is made much more intense or robust. The same measures are being followed from the provider side, as shown in Figs. (**2** and **3**).

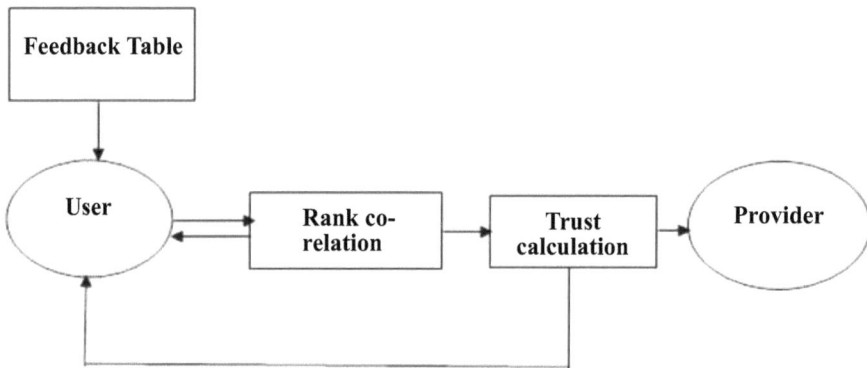

Fig. (2). The user asking for the provider's feedback.

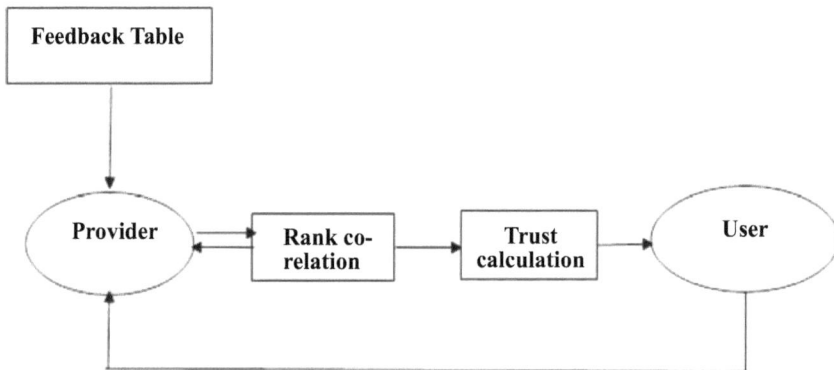

Fig. (3). Provider asking for user's feedback.

Several equations are being used in the proposed work, which are as under:

$$similarity = 1 - \frac{6\sum d_i^2}{n(n^2-1)} \tag{3}$$

where d signifies the difference in recommender feedback and n = collection of all nodes.

$$activeness = \frac{Number\ of\ transactions\ by\ recommendor}{Total\ number\ of\ transactions\ by\ all\ recommenders} \tag{4}$$

$$specificity = \frac{Number\ of\ transactions\ with\ initator}{Total\ number\ of\ transactions\ with\ all\ other\ hosts} \tag{5}$$

$$idleness = 1 - \frac{Total\ number\ of\ successful\ transactions\ within\ time\ period\ T}{Number\ of\ submitted\ jobs\ within\ time\ period\ T} \tag{6}$$

$$Credibility = m * similarity + n * activeness + o * specificity + p * idleness \tag{7}$$

where m>n>o>p and m+n+o+p=1

Neighborhood recommendation scores are collected, rank correlations are estimated, and inputs are chosen to be accepted or not. A positive rank co-relation value is very much essential for choosing the intended recipient. Total trust is then estimated. A provider is selected if its overall trust score exceeds the minimum acceptable value. Otherwise, the whole procedure is executed again to choose another reputed node for availing service.

Concept of credibility feedback calculation: Suppose two nodes, X and Y, are there. X wants a transaction with node Y to perform a specific task. The target entity's activities during direct transactions are used to determine the direct trust. Then, to determine Y's reliability, it asks other nodes operating in the same domain about its credibility in the form of reputation feedback collection.

Host Y may be a new entity: Let us assume that node y is a brand-new node that has only recently been added to the environment and, as a result, is due to transact with any other nodes. A predetermined initial value that x uses—which might be minimal —determines how x transacts with y. For the first time, y will be given non-harmful materials. The job will be provided to y if its reputation score exceeds some optimal value. If not, it is going to be turned down. The reputation table will be modified following the transaction on the client's advice. A depreciation value must be calculated for each entity's reputation over time. If there is little or no interaction between hosts over time, a host's rapport in relation to neighbor hosts usually deteriorates substantially. Host z adjusts its reputation information relative to host y by taking the depreciation value into account on receiving a credibility request (from host x) on host y. It then provides the modified result to the requestor.

$$\text{rep } y/z = \text{terminal value} + (\text{terminal value} - \text{elementary value}) * \text{depreciation value} \qquad (8)$$

where depreciation value varies over time. Considering t as the current time and t0 as the time of the last transaction, the computation of depreciation value will be as under:

$$\text{Depreciation value} = 1 \text{ if } t - t0 < 1 \text{ month} \qquad (9)$$

$$\text{Depreciation value} = 0.75 \text{ if } 1 < t - t0 < 2 \text{ months} \qquad (10)$$

$$\text{Depreciation value} = 0.5 \text{ if } 2 < t - t0 < 3 \text{ months} \qquad (11)$$

$$\text{Depreciation value} = 0 \text{ if } t - t0 > 3 \text{ months and the final value is the past value} \qquad (12)$$

$$\text{elementary value} = u * \text{direct trust} + v * \text{indirect trust} \quad \text{where } u, v \text{ are constants, } u+v=1 \qquad (13)$$

Workflow Diagram

The flowchart for the suggested model is shown in detail in Fig. (**4**). The decision to use entity Y's services may be made by user X. The user or initiator then determines the provider's dependability by compiling neighborhood opinions about its offerings. In order to assess the validity of such feedback values, rank correlation techniques are used. The combined trust scores are then computed, and the resource provider is contacted for assistance if they exceed a particular threshold value. After that, it is the provider's turn to decide whether the user or requestor can be trusted by performing all the steps outlined in the workflow from its side. The transaction can begin if the user and the provider are happy with their mutual trust.

RESULTS ANALYSIS AND INVESTIGATION

In order to perform the results analysis, we have chosen a sample group of three requestor nodes and ten recommender nodes who will each provide thoughtful feedback on the other requestors. As shown in the following Table **1**, at time instant t1, we have some fictitious values in the form of recommendation ratings (ranging from 1 to 10) for the three entities.

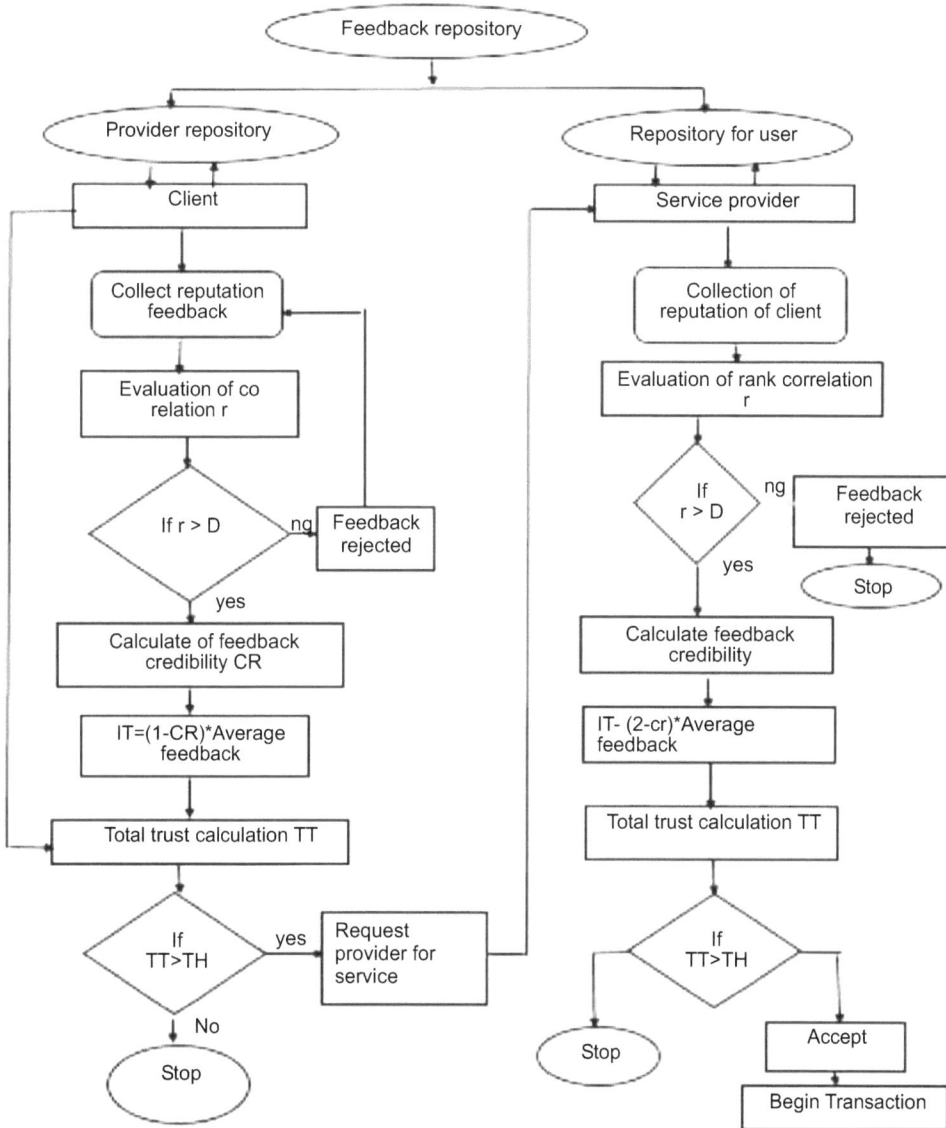

Fig. (4). Flow diagram.

Table 1. Feedback scores at time instant t1.

-	RC1	RC2	RC3	RC4	RC5	RC6	RC7	RC8	RC9	RC10
Entity 1	2	1	0	2	3	1	1	2	1	1
Entity 2	0	1	2	1	1	2	1	3	1	1
Entity 3	4	1	1	2	0	1	1	0	2	4

The outcomes obtained from visualizing the rank co-relations using modified Spearman's formula suggest that there is a strong likelihood that the value of rank co-efficient will be discarded and that the accompanying reputation score will not be seriously considered if the variation of feedback concerning a single item is significant.

Rank coefficients are shown in Fig. (5) above for a certain time instant, t1. The link is weaker and surely to be disregarded the closer the co-relation value is to 0. The association and dependability of the node increase as the value gets near to 1. According to the graph above, the second entity is the one that has the best reputation among the three, making it the ideal entity for client nodes to request any services.

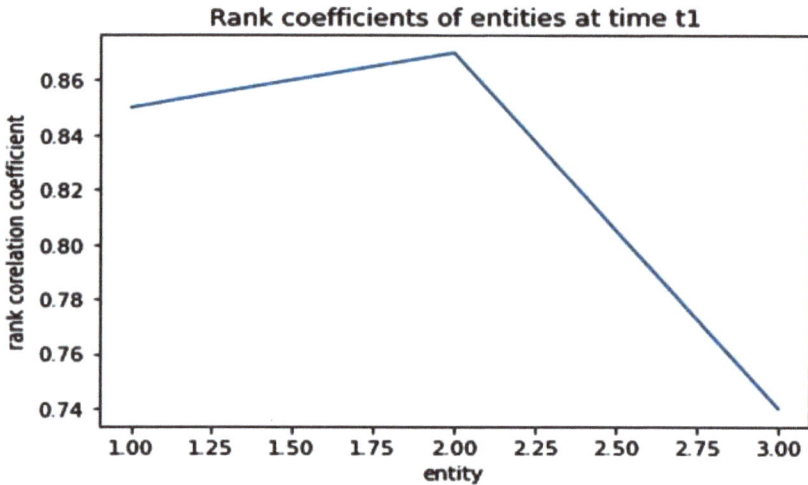

Fig. (5). Illustration of rank coefficients at an instant.

Fig. (6) above shows the rank coefficients shown in relation to two distinct time slots, t1 and t2. The rank coefficients can change significantly over time, and a node will unquestionably be less trustworthy if there are significant discrepancies in the recommenders' assessments of it. As a result, the requestor will not ask it to perform the requested service (Table 2).

Table 2. Feedback scores at time instant t2.

-	RC1	RC2	RC3	RC4	RC5	RC6	RC7	RC8	RC9	RC10
Entity 1	5	3	4	3	2	4	1	3	0	2
Entity 2	2	3	4	4	1	0	2	0	3	1
Entity 3	6	1	4	5	0	7	2	3	2	3

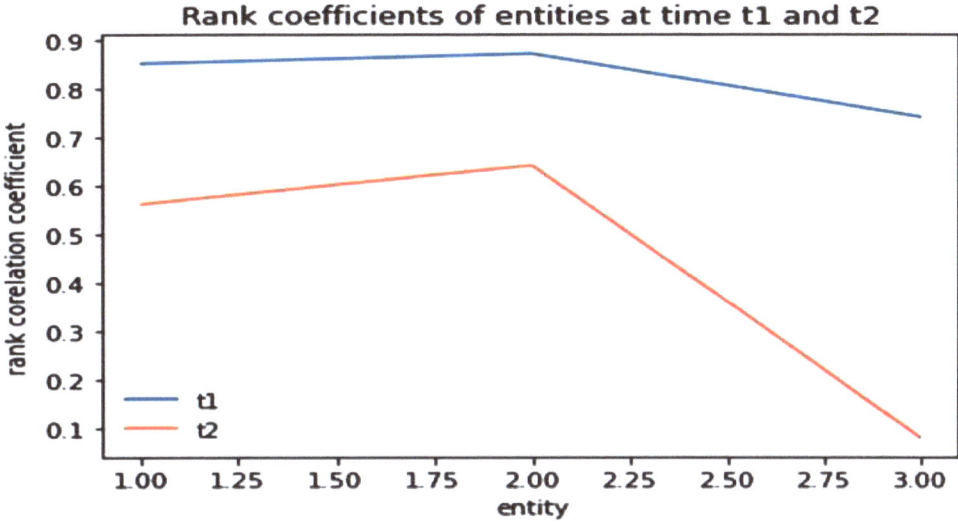

Fig. (6). Difference of rank coefficients over a time period.

CONCLUSION

A new authorization method and a two-way dual trust model are presented in the suggested work, which may be implemented in the cloud and an IoT setup. Trust is considered from both the provider's and the user's perspectives. The transaction is only carried out when a pre-set minimal limit is exceeded [11, 12]. In order to minimize biased feedback, trustworthiness is also estimated in the reputation calculation in addition to the feedback values. The measurement of the rank correlation method can prevent biased results from being generated by some malicious nodes that may exist in the environment. Malefic nodes should be eliminated at all costs since they could interfere with the system's functioning ability. This function is carried out through rank correlation in the suggested model. Trust values are also to be updated dynamically so that the changing behavioral pattern of the cloud environment can be tracked perfectly. Not only that, but the underlying IoT network devices can also avail trustworthy cloud devices in the said mechanism. The ultimate result is almost error-free data processing. By removing the biases, the system may function correctly and contribute to the emergence of a dependable and robust cloud-based IoT network environment.

ACKNOWLEDGEMENTS

The authors are grateful to their corresponding organizations for providing ample opportunities to carry out the research work seamlessly.

REFERENCES

[1]   R. Latif, S.H. Afzaal, and S. Latif, "A novel cloud management framework for trust establishment and evaluation in a federated cloud environment", *J. Supercomput.,* vol. 77, no. 11, pp. 12537-12560, 2021.
[http://dx.doi.org/10.1007/s11227-021-03775-8]

[2]   U. Ahmed, I. Raza, and S. A. Hussain,, "Trust Evaluation in Cross-Cloud Federation: Survey and Requirement Analysis", *ACM Comput. Surv.,* vol. 52, no. 1, pp. 19-37, 2019.
[http://dx.doi.org/10.1145/3292499]

[3]   H. Kurdi, and S.H. Ahmed, "A lightweight trust management algorithm based on subjective logic for interconnected cloud computing environment", *J. Supercomput.,* no. Oct, 2018.
[http://dx.doi.org/10.1007/s11227-018-2669-y]

[4]   P. Sun, "Research on cloud computing service based on trust access control", *Int. J. Eng. Bus. Manag.,* no. Nov, 2019.
[http://dx.doi.org/10.1177/1847979019897444]

[5]   M. Saima Mehraj, and Banday Tariq, "Establishing a zero trust strategy in cloud computing environment", *International Conference on Computer Communication and Informatics (ICCCI,* pp. 22-24, 2020.
[http://dx.doi.org/10.1109/ICCCI48352.2020.9104214]

[6]   G.S. Mahmood, D.J. Huang, and B.A. Jaleel, "A Secure Cloud Computing System by Using Encryption and Access Control Model", *Journal of Information Processing System,* vol. 15, no. 3, pp. 538-549, 2019.

[7]   C. Uikey, and D.S. Bhilare, "RBACA: role-based access control architecture for multi-domain cloud environment", *Int. J. Bus. Inf. Syst.,* vol. 28, no. 1, p. 91160, 2018.
[http://dx.doi.org/10.1504/IJBIS.2018.091160]

[8]   Authority Cloud Storage," *2019 IEEE Intl Conf on Parallel & Distributed Processing with Applications, Big Data & Cloud Computing, Sustainable Computing & Communications, Social Computing & Networking (ISPA/BDCloud/SocialCom/SustainCom)*, Xiamen, China, 2019, pp. 608-613.
[http://dx.doi.org/10.1109/ISPA-BDCloud-SustainCom-SocialCom48970.2019.00092]

[9]   F. Cai, N. Zhu, J. He, P. Mu, W. Li, and Y. Yu, "Survey of access control models and technologies for cloud computing", *Springer Nature,* 2018.

[10]   S. Kaushik, and C. Gandhi, "Capability based outsourced data access control with assured file deletion and efficient revocation with trust factor in cloud computing", *Int. J. Cloud Appl. Comput.,* vol. 10, no. 1, pp. 64-84, 2020.
[http://dx.doi.org/10.4018/IJCAC.2020010105]

[11]   M. Alhanahnah, P. Bertok, Z. Tari, and S. Alouneh, "Context-Aware Multifaceted Trust Framework For evaluating trustworthiness of cloud providers", *Future Gener. Comput. Syst.,* 2017.
[http://dx.doi.org/10.1016/j.future.2017.09.071]

[12]   V. Pandey, and M. Goswami, "Various challenges and trust issues in cloud computing for improvement of quality and services", *International journal on emerging technologies (Special issue NCETST),* 2017.

CHAPTER 8

Utilizing Graphical Representation and Deep Learning Models to Classify IoT Malware Network Traffic

Tarun Dhar Diwan[1,*], **H.S. Hota**[2] and **Amit K. Sharma**[3]

[1] *Govt. E. Raghavendra Rao P.G. Science College, Bilaspur, Chhattisgarh, India*

[2] *Department of Computer Science, Atal Bihari Vajpayee University, Bilaspur, Chhattisgarh, India*

[3] *Department of Computer Science and Engineering Technology, University of Maryland Eastern Shore, Princess Anne, Maryland, USA*

Abstract: Malware has emerged as a significant threat with growing infection rates and degrees of sophistication as the number of devices and technologies related to the Internet of Things (IoT) has increased and more are put into service. Without robust security procedures, many confidential records are left open to vulnerabilities. As a result, it is simple for cybercriminals to use this data to carry out various unlawful acts. Therefore, advanced network security mechanisms that are capable of executing a traffic analysis in real time and mitigating harmful traffic are required. These mechanisms must also be able to detect malicious traffic. We propose a revolutionary technique for IoT malware traffic analysis that uses deep learning and graphical demonstration to detect and categorize new malware more quickly. This will allow us to handle the difficulty that has been presented (zero-day malware). Due to the utilization of deep learning technology, the suggested method for detecting malicious network traffic operates at the package level, significantly reducing the time required for detection and producing promising outcomes. A dataset called "1000 pcap files of ordinary and malicious traffic that were collected from various network traffic sources" is created to evaluate our method's performance. This dataset is used to assess how well our method works. The experimental findings of the Residual Neural Network (ResNet) are highly encouraging, delivering a rate of accuracy for the identification of malicious traffic that is 95.09%.

Keywords: Intrusion detection system (IDS), Machine Learning (ML), Network, Security, Traffic.

---

* **Corresponding author Tarun Dhar Diwan:** Govt. E. Raghavendra Rao P.G. Science College, Bilaspur, Chhattisgarh, India; E-mail: tarunctech@gmail.com

H.S. Hota, Dinesh K. Sharma, Ayan Kumar Das & Ditipriya Sinha (Eds.)

INTRODUCTION

Internet of Things (IoT) devices have increased significantly across several industries, including manufacturing, healthcare, education, home automation, and smart cities [1]. According to the most recent forecasts, the number of linked IoT devices was anticipated to exceed 15.1 billion smart items by the year 2023 [2]. It is anticipated that this number will reach 29.4 billion across the globe by the year 2030. Additional studies have demonstrated that the next significant step toward realizing the promises of the Internet to make the world a much more interconnected community is establishing a network of connected "smart" gadgets [3]. Smart devices are computing equipment that collects, analyzes, and shares data. However, this technology also presents new threats to users' security and privacy, and despite appearances, it is less risk-free than one might think. IoT networks typically use low-cost devices (such as thermal sensors, monitoring cameras, and so on), which typically have limited resources and, as a result, have either poor or no safety built in them [4]. The execution of sophisticated safeguarding duties on such devices is limited as a result of these limits, and hostile actors have the potential to quickly breach those devices and participate in a range of illicit acts. Because of this condition, the safety and integrity of the individual devices and the network as a whole have been compromised. In this respect, recent research that was carried out by the cybersecurity firm Avast revealed that two out of every five gadgets that are connected to the Internet as part of the IoT are susceptible to attacks [5].

When an IoT device is hacked, the report substantiates that botnets are the most typical attack. Botnets can operate independently or be aggregated together to form a more extensive network proficiently, starting catastrophic Denial of service assaults. A case of a DDoS assault [6] was driven by the IoT and used unsecured IoT devices to carry out major security breaches. In the latter half of 2016 [7], an attack sweeping the Internet at the time lowered 100s of services, including DNS providers and GitHub. The Mirai botnet differs from other botnets in that most of its components are IoT devices rather than computers. These IoT devices include digital cameras, DVR players, temperature sensors, and many others [8]. According to the investigation's findings, this massive DDoS attack featured more than 400,000 compromised IoT devices, making it one of the most powerful DDoS attacks in the phenomenon's history.

Collections that include identified attacking patterns are relied on by the vast majority of the techniques that are used for identifying malware in network traffic [9]. This enables the incoming traffic to be checked against the specified malware patterns to detect possible attacks [10]. Since this is possible, sooner rather than later would be better. When it comes to identifying known assaults, these methods are pretty precise and very successful; nevertheless, they are primarily ineffectual when identifying unidentified and novel variants of developing problems, for there are no indications. Although such methods are exact and efficient when identifying known attacks, they could be more effective in detecting emerging threats. In addition, they call for a significant amount of resources and overhead, in addition to manual interventions, to keep the attack signatures current.

Consequently, they could be better for real-time network anomaly detection due to their lack of suitability. A significant amount of work has been put into overcoming these restrictions, and numerous behavior analysis or anomaly detection strategies have been developed. However, there is neither a method nor a system capable of detecting or adapting flawlessly to differentiate between legitimate and malicious traffic, mainly undiscovered and newly developed malware. As a result, in this body of research work, we offer an innovative method for classifying network traffic by using a graphical representation in association with a DL technique known as the Residual Neural Network (ResNet) [11]. Bin-Vis [12] is a visual representation tool used in this method, and it is used to capture incoming communications and then convert them into 2D images. After that, the system is educated to recognize and differentiate between possible malicious software and standard network data by utilizing a technique called ResNet. Because of this, detecting known and unknown assaults may be automated and completed more quickly.

This work expands our prior works in other studies [13, 14]. It uses ResNet and adds additional samples of malware and pcap files that are valid for the stages of training and testing. The study that was provided in the former paper [13] employed self-organizing incremental neural networks (SOINN) in order to identify malware executables rather than traffic, but the research that was published in the latter [14] utilized the convolutional neural network MobileNet in order to analyze IoT malware traffic [12]. Both types of research can be found in the references section of this article. In addition, the two strategies were evaluated using relatively small datasets, which limited the training possibilities of neural networks available to the researchers. This study evaluates the effectiveness of three alternative classifiers by applying them to a dataset that contains one thousand Bin-Vis images of genuine and malicious pcap files. These files were obtained from a variety of sources of network traffic. The investigational and comparison outcomes with the classifying modeling techniques found in these studies [13, 14] indicate that the ResNet50 algorithm provides the finest efficiency when tracking malware traffic, with an absolute accuracy of 95.09%. These findings were based on the ResNet50 algorithm's capability to identify malicious traffic flow.

The inclusive organization of this research can be broken down into the following sections: The previous studies conducted on malicious traffic investigation and categorization applying the ML method are reviewed in Related Work, which also contains a summary of those previous works. In the third section, we provide an overview of the suggested methodology and the dataset utilized in the tests to demonstrate the methodology's usefulness. The experiment's outcomes, an analysis of those results, and a comparison of those results to alternative methodologies are presented.

RELATED WORK

Signature-based recognition and behavioral or abnormality-centered recognition are the two primary groupings that could be utilized to classify the numerous techniques that are utilized for identifying malicious network traffic [15]. Since the beginning of network security monitoring, strategies that are based on signatures have been utilized for detection. They refer to databases that contain known attack signatures. These databases produce a trend for each distinct danger that defines its unique qualities. This is done to recognize the actual danger in the upcoming years. After that, the indication is checked against the incoming traffic in order to locate any potential assaults. Techniques that rely on signatures are efficient at identifying known attacks. However, they could be more efficient when detecting unknown attacks or new variants of existing attacks without signatures. Signatures can only recognize previously known threats [4, 10], and to stay current, attack signatures must be updated regularly. On the other hand, in addition to manual interventions, this could necessitate significant resources and overhead [4, 9].

Researchers are increasingly concentrating their efforts on strategies that involve behavior analysis or the detection of anomalies [16] since signature-based techniques have their limits. In this perspective, several researchers have advocated for the significance of ML in categorizing malicious activity and identifying intrusions. Several network-level anomaly detection systems have used the ML technique [17]. Several experts have advocated, in this particular scenario, the significance of ML in categorizing malicious traffic and identifying intrusions. These methods analyze the information available regarding traffic on a network by gleaning helpful information from it to differentiate malicious data from regular traffic. After that, they use various characteristics to generate the classifier to identify prospective assaults. Because the obtained fallouts are typically given in a binary form (that is, either usually or maliciously), it will classify separate data occurrences as either normally or abnormally occurring. For instance, a study titled "Comparing the Predictive Accuracy of Five Supervised Machine Learning Algorithms with Five Features Selection Sets Derived from

Four Previous Works in Android Malware Traffic Detection" [18] matched the analytical accuracy of 5 supervised ML techniques with five features: Naive Bayes, K-nearest Neighbor, Decision Tree, Multi-Layer Perceptron, and Random Forest classifiers. The outcomes of the experiments indicate that the multi-layer perceptron classifier, which makes use of the features selection set and derives from the features selection procedure, surpasses all other classification methods with an accuracy rate of 83%, a true positive rate of 90%, and a false positive rate of 23%. These figures were derived from the fact that the MLP classifier had the lowest rate of false positives (23%). The researchers of the study [19] investigated how well RNN can predict the behavior of network activity by representing it as a series of events that evolve. This was done to test the RNN's ability to recognize network traffic behavior. After the network traffic attributes were converted into a string of characters, RNNs were used to learn more about the traffic's temporal characteristics. The authors concluded that the RNN identification methods have issues with engaging with issues associated with traffic behavior that are not simply distinguishable and are some notable examples of imbalanced network traffic. This was based on the findings of the experiments that were conducted. One more recent piece of research [20] employed seven distinct ML algorithms on the widely used dataset "Kyoto 2006+," which includes 24 features [21]. The ensemble method integrates the six algorithms mentioned earlier. The findings of the experiments showed that the majority of the classification techniques presented an accuracy that was more than 90%, which was considered satisfactory.

Similarly, the authors of a study [22] proposed a self-learning approach to anomaly detection that can be modified to accommodate shifting network traffic patterns. They used neural networks known as Discriminative Restricted Boltzmann Machines (DRBM) that received training on normal data. The information on the unusual traffic emerged dynamically, allowing the DRBM classifier to recognize unusual traffic with a high degree of accuracy. Two separate sets of experiments were carried out to demonstrate how effective this strategy is. During the first test, they collected actual network logs from a clean and an infected network host. However, in the second one, titled KDD'99, they used a dataset that was open to the general public [23]. According to the authors, the classification algorithm achieved the highest level of accuracy with the initial run of the experiments (92%-96%). The authors [24] centered on recognizing anomalies in contexts where contradictory network environments arise by eliminating noisy data linked with insignificant attributes. Specifically, the authors were interested in identifying the presence of abnormalities. As a result, they selected the attributes to employ premised on the inclusion of several various ML algorithms. In the first step of the process, they identified grouped features by employing an unsupervised method called k-means clustering. After that, they ranked the characteristics using the NB method and the Kruscal-Wallis test [25]. Only elements important to the task at hand were selected during this stage according to their ranking. In the final phase, they put the characteristics chosen in the second step through the C4.5 decision tree classifier to see how well they performed. According to the authors' experiments' findings, minimizing the number of characteristics contributed to a reduction in the required amount of calculation, which, in turn, increased both the speed and accuracy of anomaly identification.

The authors [26] presented a transfer-learning approach to categorize network activity in new findings. This model used the maximal entropy (Maxent) approach [27] as its foundational classifier. In contrast to conventional machine learning techniques when used for traffic categorization, Maxent helps bring expertise from one area into another, allowing for consistent performance regardless of changes to the network's surroundings. This model's efficacy was measured using two separate traffic datasets collected at the University of Cambridge, with the latter yielding an average accuracy of more than 98%. Both datasets were collected at the exact location. The researchers of a study [28] suggested a semi-supervised way to identify malicious network activity by employing concentration approaches. These models are grounded on current breakthroughs in deep generative algorithms and nonlinear inferences methodology [29]; therefore, the researchers believed this method would be helpful. This method makes use of the density models. Utilizing the variational auto-encoder allowed the automatic extraction of representation aspects of the natural flows in a manner that was not supervised (VAE). Linked flows were then grouped into a latent feature space, resulting in a more accurate classification [38]. This strategy utilized only a few named flows, yet it obtained an accuracy of over 90%, which was quite pleasing.

PROPOSED APPROACH

Approach Overview

The proposed method for analyzing malware traffic in IoT devices includes the following two primary stages: 1st of which is finding the equivalent graphical representation of the network traffic collected and processing this visual representation by a trained classifying algorithm. These steps are illustrated in Fig. (**1**), which can be found here. Utilizing pcap files in the network traffic collection process ensures the sniffer can save packets captured to their respective locations. This includes previously collected network traffic (both normal and aberrant traffic). These pcap files are then replayed using tcp replay. The operation begins with creating several packet chunks, which are then given to the visual representation tool to convert into a two-dimensional image. This is done so that the process does not negatively impact performance. In the second stage, the collected pictures are analyzed using the ResNet50 [11] to match them to its in-depth training. This step takes place after the first phase. ResNet-50, a deep learning algorithm, has been used to classify images and has already undergone preliminary training. It accomplished this by utilizing a convolutional neural network, also known as a CNN or ConvNet, which belongs to the class of deep neural networks and is most commonly used for visual data analysis. The ResNet-50 neural network contained 50 layers and was generated utilizing 10 thousand images from a thousand distinct categories that are stored in the ImageNet datasets. In addition, the algorithms include around 23 million trainable attributes, proving a deep architecture and boosting the model's effectiveness in image recognition. The fundamental advantage of ResNet is that it enables the training of deep neural networks containing thousands of levels while simultaneously delivering appealing results. ResNet soon rose to prominence as one of the most widely used architectural frameworks for various uses for computer vision, including picture categorization, entity identification, and facial recognition [30] due to its powerful representational ability. This ability allowed ResNet to rise to the top of the popularity rankings quickly.

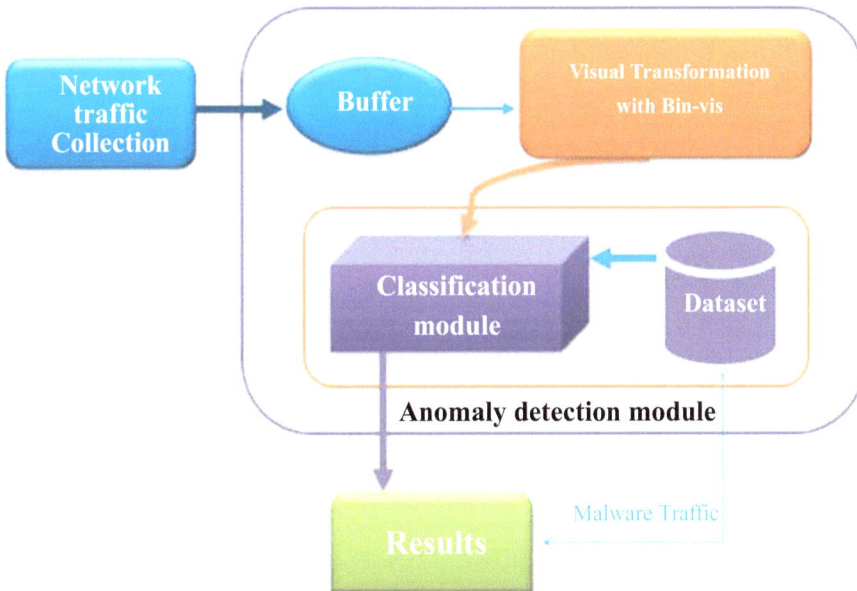

Fig. (1). High-level structure of the suggested method.

In our technique, the topological architecture of the neural network is generated during the training phase of the process. After that, during the testing stage, the gathered traffic is compared to the instances included in the database so that the classification may be carried out. The classifier will be trained using malware traffic that has previously been identified, and this will be done continuously in an attempt to increase the effectiveness of its recognition capabilities.

The Visual Transformation of the Network Traffic

Using the technique for visual representation known as Bin-Vis [12], the gathered traffic is then stored before being translated into RGB images. This tool is utilized on a massive scale, particularly by researchers in the field of information security, to display binary file structures in novel ways and to locate and analyze dangerous content [31]. The pcap chunk records are first saved in binary code during transformation. Subsequently, the appropriate RGB values are assigned to the files. The RGB values are mapped by evaluating every byte value in the pcap data to their corresponding value in the ASCII table. This is done in order to complete the procedure. This allows the RGB values to be mapped. This is done following the color scheme that was previously established. Bin-vis organized the various ASCII bytes into four distinct color categories, with printed ASCII bytes being given a blue color, control bytes being given a green color, and extended ASCII bytes being given a red color. Black and white colors denote both non-breaking and null spaces. The color grey also denotes null spaces. After that, the coordinates of each byte in the final RGB image are found by using a clustering technique [32] that is centered on space-filling arcs. This is done in order to find the coordinates of each byte color. This is done to ensure that geographically adjacent data are grouped together.

Compared to previous curves, this clustering approach does a better job of maintaining proximity between items in higher dimensional spaces, yielding superior RGB pictures for the classification phase. This is because preserving the locality between objects depends on the distance between the objects. The RGB image that is produced has a dimension of 784 bytes (1024 times 256).

The Hilbert space-filling curve was used to produce the Bin-Vis pictures, as shown in Fig. (**2**), for both normal and malicious pcap files [32]. These photos allow one to draw a positive conclusion about the results, as it is possible to distinguish between a valid pcap file and one that contains malware.

As can be seen in the pictures, most of the pixels in the photos of malware pcap files are either completely black or white. On the other hand, regular traffic can be distinguished from abnormal traffic by examining the arrangement of ASCII characters or colors over the picture.

Binary visualisation of normal pcap file

Binary visualisation of botnet pcap file

Binary visualisation of normal pcap file

Binary visualisation of backdoor pcap file

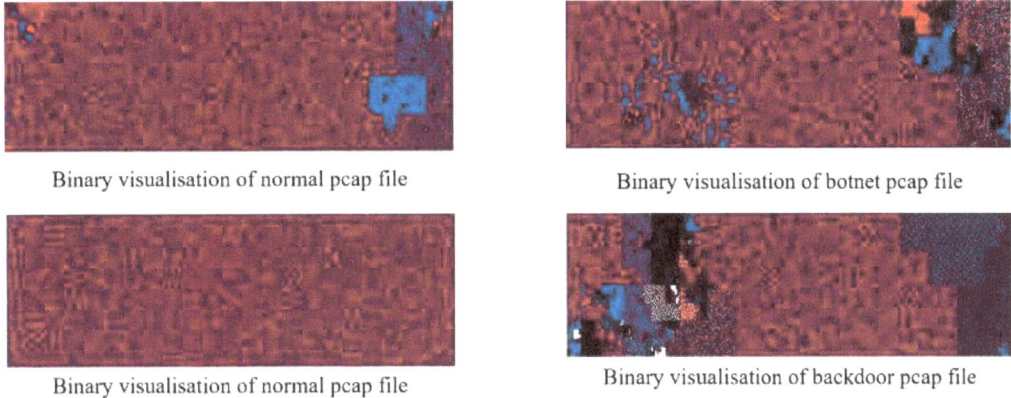

Fig. (2). The Hilbert space-filling curve was used to build binary visualization pictures of normal and malicious pcap files..

Data Collection

For training and validating the neural network, we prepared our dataset by using the proposed visual transformation approach. The dataset comprises a combination of 1,000 Bin-vis images of regular traffic and malware activity. These images were gathered from various sources of network traffic. Various sources, including the network of the Cyber-trust project, are represented in the standard PCAP files [34], which contain collected routine traffic. With the help of programs like Nmap and Wireshark, the traffic was gathered from various uncontaminated devices around the network [37]. The term "malware traffic analysis repository 1" refers to a collection that includes these three primary public sources of PCAP files containing malware. The harmful pcap files include genuine malicious traffic formed by various assaults, including trojans, botnets, Internet of Things-based attacks, backdoors, and so on. This file includes traffic that was maliciously manufactured. This data was captured as it was sent *via* the infected system. The percentage of fraudulent traffic samples that were found across the entire dataset is displayed in Fig. (**3**).

The ResNet algorithm was trained using 800 unique Bin-Vis, benign and malicious pictures, with a total size of 784 (1024*256) bytes. The pictures are divided into two categories: regular and malicious. Other Bin-Vis images, totaling an additional 200, were utilized to test the classifier. The testing set is meant to replicate unidentified network traffic that must be classified.

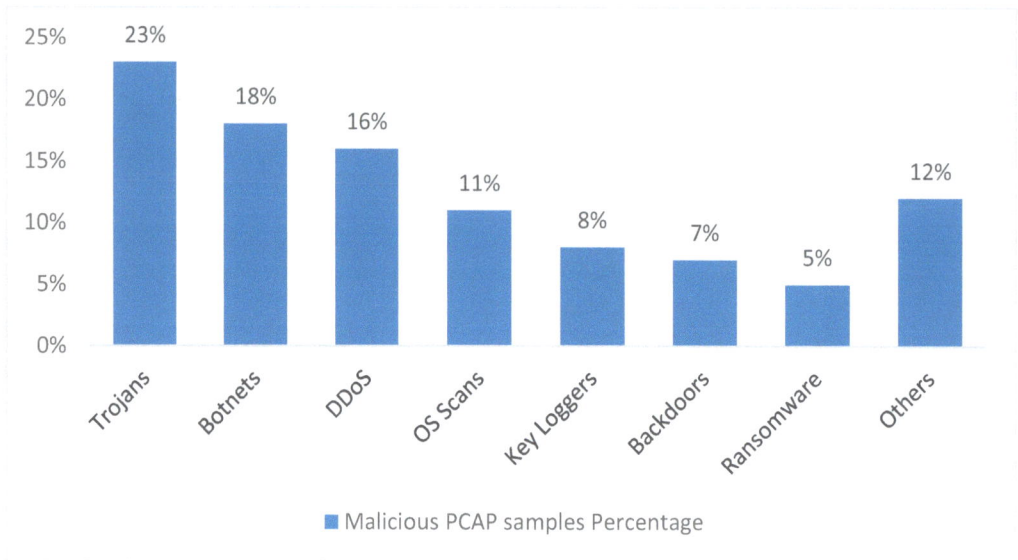

Fig. (3). Percentage of malicious traffic specimens determined by the malware type..

RESULTS OF EXPERIMENT

The findings of the tests conducted on the suggested technique to verify its effectiveness and reliability are reported in this part.

The performance measures are utilized in order to evaluate the classifier's performance (F1). The term "accuracy" refers to the proportion of all samples that can be correctly categorized as either normal or malicious. Precision, denoted by the letter "P," is the percentage of samples that have been positively categorized that are, in fact, positive. The proportion of correctly identified real samples is called recall, and the F-score is a weighted average of accuracy and recall. Precision is the number of abnormal samples that were correctly diagnosed. The equation that is used to calculate each metric is presented in Table **1**.

Table 1. Metrics employed to determine how well the proposed methodology worked.

Metric	Equation
Accuracy (A)	$A = (TP + TN) / (TP + TN + FP + FN)$
Precision (P)	$P = TP / (TP + FP)$
Recall (R)	$R = TP / (TP + FN)$
F 1	$F1 = 2 * ((P*R)/ P+R)$

The number of occurrences properly categorized as malicious traffic (TP), the number of cases correctly classified as regular traffic (TN), the number of cases wrongly categorized as malicious traffic (FP), and the number of cases wrongly categorized as regular traffic (FN).

Experimental Setting

Experiments were carried out using a pc that featured an Intel Core i7 processor operating at 3.80 gigahertz, 32 gigabytes of memory, and the Windows 11 Enterprise 64-bit operating system. We use an NVIDIA GTX 1060 graphics processing unit (GPU) containing 6 GB of RAM to speed things up. The Resnet50 learning algorithm was implemented with the help of the open-source Fastai Python library 4, designed for deep learning. Fastai is an artificial intelligence framework built on top of PyTorch and incorporates several of the most widely used techniques for categorizing images and processing natural languages.

Experiments Outcomes

In order to determine how reliable the suggested classifier was and how efficient the detection method was, several tests had to be conducted. The outcomes of the training and testing that was performed on the Resnet50 Neural Network are shown in Figs. (**4** and **5**), respectively. They are broken down into three categories: accuracy, training loss, and validation loss. The error loss, also known as the training and validation loss, is anticipated to decrease after each or multiple epochs. The error loss is calculated by adding up all of the mistakes committed to either the training or validation (also known as testing) sets during each epoch. When the validation loss is equal to or marginally greater than the training loss, the training of the NN ought to be interrupted so that the NN may be validated. This is done to compare the validation loss to the training loss. On the other hand, if validation losses are lower than the training losses, we need to continue training even though we already did (*i.e.*, under-fitting).

For all of our experiments, we set up the neural network to run for 50 epochs with a batch size of 6. Following the completion of the learning rate finder function, the value of the learning proportion parameter was set to 0.05. (LRFinder). Because of this function, there is no need to conduct a large number of trials in order to determine the best possible standards [33]. As can be observed in Fig. (**4**), after 50 iterations, Resnet50 attained an accuracy of 95.06%, with a validation loss of only 0.237579 and a training loss that was very similar to each other (0.23048). Accuracy scores varied from 91.22 to 95.33 percent throughout the earlier epochs, with the validation loss consistently lesser than the training losses.

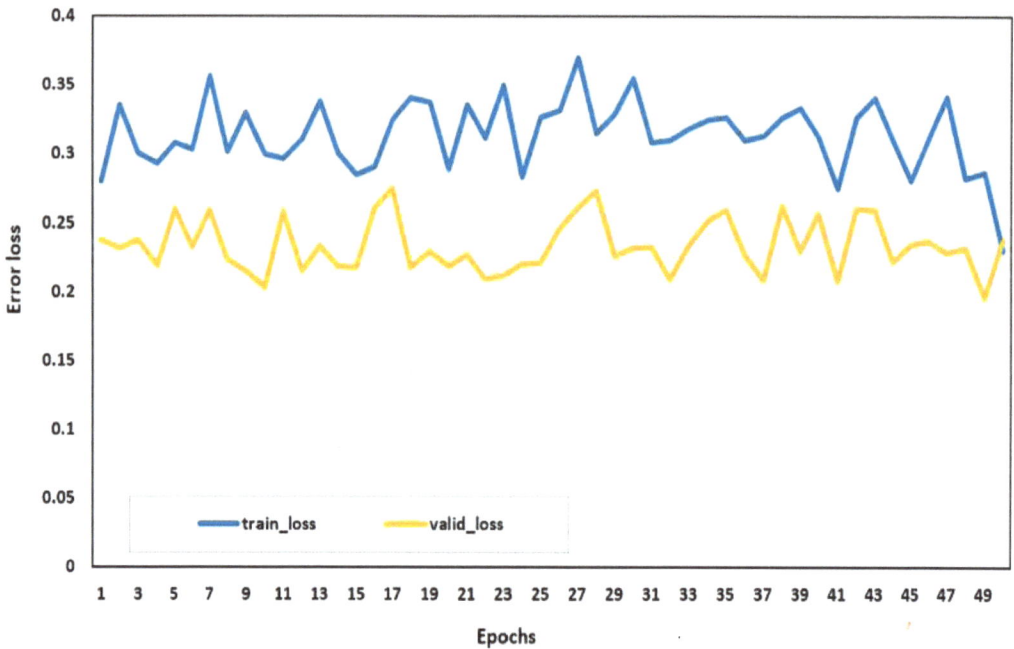

Fig. (4). Amounts of error losses that occurred during training and testing of the resnet 50.

Fig. (**5**) depicts the overall outcomes that were achieved by implementing the technique that was suggested. The strategy successfully achieved a global recognition accuracy of 95.09%, which is a high rate that fulfills the needed accuracy rate for utilization in practical applications. The fact that the classifier has such a high degree of accuracy suggests not just a high level of general trust in the process of pattern recognition but also that this level of confidence is widespread [35]. The rate of 96.13 percent shows this. The fact that the recall rate was lesser than the accuracy rate (95.06%) suggests that Resnet50 effectively identified the vast majority of the samples. Because acquiring FN, which happens when legitimate traffic is mistaken for malicious traffic, costs more than obtaining FP, which happens when legitimate traffic is mistaken for malicious traffic, accuracy in our line of work is more crucial than recall [36]. This is because the cost of obtaining FN is greater than that of obtaining FP, which occurs when normal traffic is misidentified as malicious traffic [39, 40]. Based on these statistics, the F-score number, also known as F1, comes in at 95.21%.

Extensive analysis of Resnet50 data

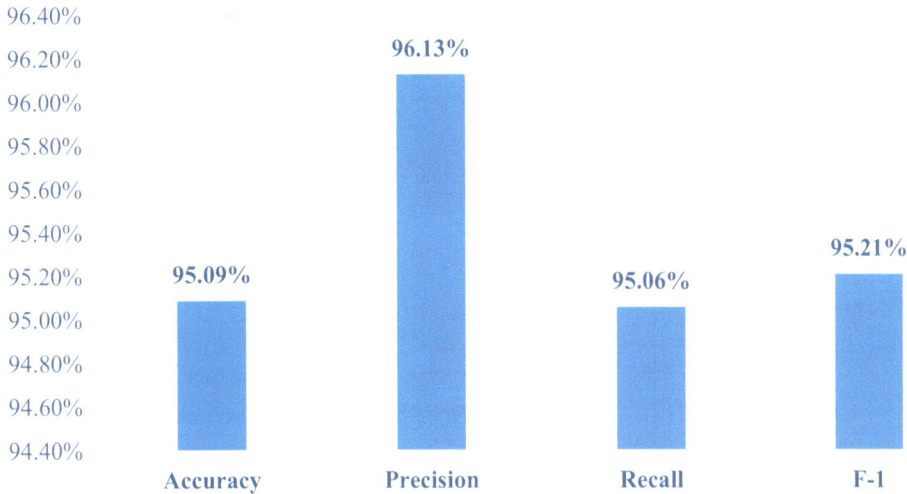

Fig. (5). Extensive analysis of Resnet50 data.

Comparison

A comparison was made between the training approaches used in the previous studies [13, 14] and the metrics mentioned in this segment to demonstrate the efficacy of Resnet in detecting malicious activity. SOINNs (Self-organizing incremental neural networks) were utilized to examine and identify malware payloads. SOINN is a well-known unsupervised machine learning technique with incremental capabilities that enables rapid learning by utilizing the nodes necessary for forming the neural network and deleting unnecessary nodes. In the study [14], a similar method is applied to Google's MobileNet convolutional neural networks.

After determining the optimal initial configuration for each classification model, the learning model was reinstructed using the newly generated dataset and evaluated using the testing dataset. Both the Residual CNN ResNet with 34 layers (ResNet 34) and the ResNet with 50 layers (ResNet 50) were put through their paces during these tests. The exact datasets are being used in the training and testing of each method. Table **2** contains the evaluation's results. The Resnet50 method has the highest accuracy (95.09%) and precision (96.13%) compared to other algorithms based on the collected data. Observations also indicate that using extra layers improves Resnet's performance (Resnet50).

Table 2. Evaluation with different learning methods.

Learning Algorithms	Accuracy	Precision	Recall	F-score
Resnet34	93.24%	94.16%	63.92%	73.80%
Resnet50	95.09%	96.13%	95.06%	95.21%
MobileNet	92.02%	92.07%	92.09%	92.18%
SOINN	92.07%	90.06%	95.02%,	93.04%

CONCLUSION

In this research, we presented a unique method for detecting malicious network traffic that uses machine learning and visual representation. With an overall accuracy of 95.09%, the trials and comparisons with other neural networks have shown that the ResNet50 is the most impressive neural network for identifying malware network traffic.

We want to use more data in the upcoming years to train and evaluate the neural network. This will allow us to make this work more effective. The accuracy of the classifier's predictions will, without a shadow of a doubt, see an increase as a direct consequence of this change. In addition, we have plans to include an ML component into IDS Suricata or snort. This will allow us to improve the security and prevention operations carried out by these IDS. Analyzing how well the suggested strategy works in realistic scenarios (such as how long it takes to generate a visual representation and classify it) is another future work that must be done, particularly for online training.

REFERENCES

[1]   M. Nobakht, V. Sivaraman, and R. Boreli, "A host-based intrusion detection and mitigation framework for smart home IoT using OpenFlow", *11th International conference on availability, reliability and security (ARES),* pp. 147-156, 2016.
      [http://dx.doi.org/10.1109/ARES.2016.64]

[2]   L.S. Vailshery, "IoT connected devices worldwide 2019-2030 | Statista", *Statista,* 2022. Available from: https://www.statista.com/statistics/1183457/iot-connected-devices-worldwide/

[3]   Statista Research Department, Ed., "IoT devices installed base worldwide Statista," *Statista*, 2015-2025. Available from: https://www.statista.com/statistics/471264/iot-number-of-connected-devces-worldwide/

[4]   N. Keegan, S.Y. Ji, A. Chaudhary, C. Concolato, B. Yu, and D.H. Jeong, "A survey of cloud-based network intrusion detection analysis", *Human-centric Computing and Information Sciences,* vol. 6, no. 1, p. 19, 2016.
      [http://dx.doi.org/10.1186/s13673-016-0076-z]

[5]   S.J. Philip, T. Luu, and T. Carte, "There's No place like home: Understanding users' intentions toward securing internet-of-things (IoT) smart home networks", *Comput. Human Behav.,* vol. 139, 2022.

[6]   M. Antonakakis, T. April, M. Bailey, M. Bernhard, E. Bursztein, J. Cochran, Z. Durumeric, J.A.

Halderman, and L. Invernizzi, "Understanding the mirai botnet", *26th USENIX Security Symposium (USENIX Sec. 17),* pp. 1093-1110, 2017.

[7]   C. Kolias, G. Kambourakis, A. Stavrou, and J. Voas, "Ddos in the iot: Mirai and other botnets", *Computer,* vol. 50, no. 7, pp. 80-84, 2017.
[http://dx.doi.org/10.1109/MC.2017.201]

[8]   G. Kambourakis, C. Kolias, and A. Stavrou, "The mirai botnet and the iot zombie armies", *MILCOM 2017-2017 IEEE Military Communications Conference (MILCOM),* pp. 267-272, 2017.
[http://dx.doi.org/10.1109/MILCOM.2017.8170867]

[9]   J. Garbis, and J.W. Chapman, "Intrusion Detection and Prevention Systems", *Zero Trust Security,* pp. 117-126, 2021.

[10]   D. Kwon, H. Kim, J. Kim, S.C. Suh, I. Kim, and K.J. Kim, "A survey of deep learning-based network anomaly detection", *Cluster Comput.,* vol. 22, no. S1, pp. 949-961, 2019.
[http://dx.doi.org/10.1007/s10586-017-1117-8]

[11]   K. He, X. Zhang, S. Ren, and J. Sun, "Deep residual learning for image recognition", *Proceedings of the IEEE conference on computer vision and pattern recognition,* pp. 770-778, 2016.

[12]   S. Ali, O. Abusabha, F. Ali, M. Imran, and T. Abuhmed, "Effective Multitask Deep Learning for IoT Malware Detection and Identification Using Behavioral Traffic Analysis", *IEEE Trans. Netw. Serv. Manag.,* 2022.

[13]   I. Baptista, S. Shiaeles, and N. Kolokotronis, "A novel malware detection system based on machine learning and binary visualization", *International Conference on Communications Workshops (ICC Workshops),* pp. 1-6, 2019.
[http://dx.doi.org/10.1109/ICCW.2019.8757060]

[14]   R. Shire, S. Shiaeles, K. Bendiab, B. Ghita, and N. Kolokotronis, "Malware squid: A novel iot malware traffic analysis framework using convolutional neural network and binary visualisation", In: *Internet of Things, Smart Spaces, and Next Generation Networks and Systems.* Springer, 2019, pp. 65-76.
[http://dx.doi.org/10.1007/978-3-030-30859-9_6]

[15]   Z.B. Celik, R.J. Walls, P. McDaniel, and A. Swami, "Malware traffic detection using tamper resistant features", *MILCOM 2015-2015 IEEE Military Communications Conference.,* pp. 330-335, 2015.
[http://dx.doi.org/10.1109/MILCOM.2015.7357464]

[16]   M. Ahmed, A. Naser Mahmood, and J. Hu, "A survey of network anomaly detection techniques", *J. Netw. Comput. Appl.,* vol. 60, pp. 19-31, 2016.
[http://dx.doi.org/10.1016/j.jnca.2015.11.016]

[17]   S.W.A-H. Baddar, A. Merlo, and M. Migliardi, "Anomaly detection in computer networks: A state-o--the-art review", *JoWUA,* vol. 5, no. 4, pp. 29-64, 2014.

[18]   M.Z. Mas'ud, S. Sahib, M.F. Abdollah, S.R. Selamat, and R. Yusof, "Analysis of features selection and machine learning classifier in android malware detection", *International Conference on Information Science & Applications (ICISA),* pp. 1-5, 2014.
[http://dx.doi.org/10.1109/ICISA.2014.6847364]

[19]   P. Torres, C. Catania, S. Garcia, and C.G. Garino, "An analysis of recurrent neural networks for botnet detection behavior", *IEEE biennial congress of Argentina (ARGENCON),* pp. 1-6, 2016.
[http://dx.doi.org/10.1109/ARGENCON.2016.7585247]

[20]   M. Zaman, and C-H. Lung, "Evaluation of machine learning techniques for network intrusion detection", *NOMS 2018-2018 IEEE/IFIP Network Operations and Management Symposium,* pp. 1-5, 2018.
[http://dx.doi.org/10.1109/NOMS.2018.8406212]

[21]   M. Ghurab, G. Gaphari, F. Alshami, R. Alshamy, and S. M. Othman, "A Detailed Analysis of Benchmark Datasets for Network Intrusion Detection System", *Asian Journal of Research in*

Computer Science, pp. 14-33, 2021.
[http://dx.doi.org/10.9734/ajrcos/2021/v7i430185]

[22]   U. Fiore, F. Palmieri, A. Castiglione, and A. De Santis, "Network anomaly detection with the restricted Boltzmann machine", *Neurocomputing,* vol. 122, pp. 13-23, 2013.
[http://dx.doi.org/10.1016/j.neucom.2012.11.050]

[23]   M. Tavallaee, E. Bagheri, W. Lu, and A.A. Ghorbani, "A detailed analysis of the kdd cup 99 data set", *Symposium on Computational Intelligence for Security and Defense Applications,* pp. 1-6, 2009.
[http://dx.doi.org/10.1109/CISDA.2009.5356528]

[24]   P. Louvieris, N. Clewley, and X. Liu, "Effects-based feature identification for network intrusion detection", *Neurocomputing,* vol. 121, pp. 265-273, 2013.
[http://dx.doi.org/10.1016/j.neucom.2013.04.038]

[25]   W.H. Kruskal, and W.A. Wallis, "Use of ranks in one-criterion variance analysis", *J. Am. Stat. Assoc.,* vol. 47, no. 260, pp. 583-621, 1952.
[http://dx.doi.org/10.1080/01621459.1952.10483441]

[26]   G. Sun, L. Liang, T. Chen, F. Xiao, and F. Lang, "Network traffic classification based on transfer learning", *Comput. Electr. Eng.,* vol. 69, pp. 920-927, 2018.
[http://dx.doi.org/10.1016/j.compeleceng.2018.03.005]

[27]   B. Duan, Y. Zhao, and H. Liu, "Maximum entropy principle and topological optimization of truss structures", *Computational Mechanics in Structural Engineering.,* pp. 179-192, 1999.
[http://dx.doi.org/10.1016/B978-008043008-9/50052-1]

[28]   T. Li, S. Chen, Z. Yao, X. Chen, and J. Yang, "Semi-supervised network traffic classification using deep generative models", *14th International Conference on Natural Computation, Fuzzy Systems and Knowledge Discovery (ICNC-FSKD),* pp. 1282-1288, 2018.
[http://dx.doi.org/10.1109/FSKD.2018.8686880]

[29]   D. P. Kingma and M. Welling, "Auto-encoding variational Bayes," *arXiv preprint arXiv:*1312.6114, pp. 1–14, Dec. 2013.

[30]   K. He, X. Zhang, S. Ren, and J. Sun, "Identity mappings in deep residual networks", *European conference on computer vision,* pp. 630-645, 2016.

[31]   S. Lui, "Binvis.io lets you visualise and analyse binary files", *Lifehacker Australia,* 2016. Available from: https://www.lifehacker.com.au/2016/02/binvis-io-lets-you-visualise-and-analyse-binary-files/

[32]   L. Zhou, C.R. Johnson, and D. Weiskopf, "Data-Driven Space-Filling Curves", *IEEE Trans. Vis. Comput. Graph.,* vol. 27, no. 2, pp. 1591-1600, 2021.
[http://dx.doi.org/10.1109/TVCG.2020.3030473] [PMID: 33048752]

[33]   L.N. Smith, "Cyclical learning rates for training neural networks", *Winter Conference on Applications of Computer Vision (WACV),* pp. 464-472, 2017.
[http://dx.doi.org/10.1109/WACV.2017.58]

[34]   G. Sargsyan, D.S Kavallieros, and N. Kolokotronis, "Security Technologies and Methods for Advanced Cyber Threat Intelligence, Detection and Mitigation", *Boston-Delft: now publishers.*
[http://dx.doi.org/10.1561/9781680838350]

[35]   X. Ai, T. Jena, S. Khan, R. Hughes, and V.K. Pallipuram, "A2Cloud-H: A Multi-tiered Machine Learning Framework for Cost-Effective Cloud Resource Selection", *Proceedings of the Future Technologies Conference (FTC),* vol. 3, 2021..

[36]   A. Bhujel, N.E. Kim, E. Arulmozhi, J.K. Basak, and H.T. Kim, "A Lightweight Attention-Based Convolutional Neural Networks for Tomato Leaf Disease Classification", *Agriculture,* vol. 12, no. 2, p. 228, 2022.
[http://dx.doi.org/10.3390/agriculture12020228]

[37]   R. Li, J.S. Johansen, H. Ahmed, T.V. Ilyevsky, R.B. Wilbur, H.M. Bharadwaj, and J.M. Siskind, "The

Perils and Pitfalls of Block Design for EEG Classification Experiments", *IEEE Trans. Pattern Anal. Mach. Intell.,* p. 1, 2020.
[http://dx.doi.org/10.1109/TPAMI.2020.2973153] [PMID: 33211652]

[38]   G. Bendiab, S. Shiaeles, A. Alruban, and N. Kolokotronis, "IoT Malware Network Traffic Classification using Visual Representation and Deep Learning", *6th IEEE Conference on Network Softwarization (NetSoft),* pp. 444-449, 2020.
[http://dx.doi.org/10.1109/NetSoft48620.2020.9165381]

[39]   J.R. Rose, M. Swann, K.P. Grammatikakis, I. Koufos, G. Bendiab, S. Shiaeles, and N. Kolokotronis, "IDERES: Intrusion detection and response system using machine learning and attack graphs", *J. Systems Archit.,* vol. 131, p. 102722, 2022.
[http://dx.doi.org/10.1016/j.sysarc.2022.102722]

[40]   I. Bernik, B. Markelj, and S.L. Vrhovec, "Advances in Cybersecurity", *University of Maribor,* 2017.
[http://dx.doi.org/10.18690/978-961-286-114-8]

CHAPTER 9

Optimum Utilization of Modern-Day Technology with Wearable Devices Using IoT

Nikhil Kaushik[1,*], **SVAV Prasad**[1] and **Arvind Rehalia**[2]

[1] *Department of Electronics and Communication Engineering, Lingaya's Vidyapeeth, Faridabad, Haryana, India*

[2] *Department of Information Technology, Bharati Vidyapeeth's College of Engineering, New Delhi, Delhi, India*

Abstract: IoT is a future-proof technology that is extremely capable of providing the required solution in real time for everyday life, healthcare, smart city, agriculture, automation industry, disaster management, *etc.* IoT is taking sensors, computing, and communication to the next level collectively. Due to the explosion of demand for services, the IoT platform provides customizable health services. Managing health records and patient's personal information can improve healthcare quality and efficiency simultaneously. For smart and safe usage, a unique identification is provided in IoT; in this way, large amounts of information are accessible to all. The solutions provided through IoT are more accurate and accountable. Wearable devices can help in dealing with various diseases with the ability to constantly monitor the present situation. One can even predict the worst condition to arrive and prepare for it or can even delay it or completely eliminate it. There are various devices that are already available that can be worn on hands and tell about blood pressure, temperature, step count, calories burnt, heart rate, sleeping hours, walking speed, *etc.* Wearable devices provide continuous monitoring at every place, like at home or office or while swimming and playing games. However, the accuracy and the ability to transmit the information to medical service providers in real time are also attained with the help of innovative IoT technology. The Immediate Health Monitoring System uses IoT, which enables it to monitor the patient's temperature along with the oxygen level in an instant; this system transmits the same information to the doctor or medical service provider at a distant location. If the values of the parameters change from the standard values, then an alert message is given to the medical service provider or the doctor concerned with the patient. This instant health monitoring plan based on IoT helps doctors effortlessly collect real-time numbers at their location, which is far from the patient's location. The next level in the healthcare industry can be achieved with the help of wearable devices, which are part of IoT.

---

[*] **Corresponding author Nikhil Kaushik:** Department of Electronics and Communication Engineering, Lingaya's Vidyapeeth, Faridabad, Haryana, India; E-mail: nikhil.sir46@gmail.com

H.S. Hota, Dinesh K. Sharma, Ayan Kumar Das & Ditipriya Sinha (Eds.)

Keywords: Biomedical sensor, Cloud platform, Healthcare, IoT, Instant, Sensor, Wearable device.

INTRODUCTION

Health monitoring plans based on modern technology like the Internet of Things (IoT) can be made, which can monitor the health of patients in real time. There are many smartwatches in the market that can monitor various health parameters, but accuracy and real-time response to the medical service provider are the key features that are achieved with the help of wearable devices developed using IoT technology [1]. This type of smartwatch can be connected to many other devices with the help of Bluetooth or Wi-Fi. Changing parameter values like temperature and oxygen level of the patient are sent to the medical facility provider or doctor to check the situation accordingly [2].

Wearable devices can help in dealing with various diseases by constantly monitoring an individual. One can even predict the worst condition to arrive and prepare for it or can even delay it or completely eliminate it [3]. If a condition arises when a certain parameter deviates from the values that come under the standard parameter values, then an alarm message is generated and provided to the concerned medical facility provider/doctor and important people associated with the patient [4]. The wearable device consists of a Spo2 sensor and a temperature sensor. The signals originating from these sensors are amplified [5]. These signals are then conditioned and made usable for the next step.

Using a microcontroller like Arduino, the data or information that is generated is forwarded to the cloud for storage and computational purposes [6]. A person's daily health data can be recorded with the help of wearable gadgets that are easy to wear and can be worn on the biceps, like a Sony Walkman device [7]. The security of the data generated and the space to keep that data are the two main problems that arise, although the cloud can be used as a solution to the space issue, and the security problem requires hard information encryption. These wearable devices capture a number of data that may be personal, so the information collected by these wearable devices is a cause of concern. Many countries have regulations on this, but still, there are many countries that do not have regulations over such information or data [8]. The security of information generated by wearable gadgets presents a significant challenge. Robust encryption techniques are indispensable to safeguard the integrity and confidentiality of this information. The lack of consistent regulatory frameworks across different jurisdictions further complicates the issue, underscoring the need for a harmonized approach to data privacy and protection in the context of wearable technology [9].

Methodology

IoT is playing an important role in the medical field as well; it helps in continuous and safe monitoring, guaranteeing both social distancing and the reduction of travel. An adaptive approach is utilized to analyze the performance of the user, which provides results that are reliable and more accurate for the assessment and detection of the pattern of complex actions compared to the old techniques used to monitor the patient. With the involvement of electronics in the field of medical science, there is a scope for the rapid adaptation of the system according to the requirement of the user or medical organization to better handle diseases and maintain healthy living [10]. There is also an advantage of automated execution of the scheduled task, which can be performed without failure because the IoT takes care of the sensor's signal and data, and those who are responsible for performing the required task are synchronized with each other *via* the help of the internet [11].

IoT technology is coupled to develop the proficiency of the healthcare structure [6], which is developed to be worn on the biceps, thus resulting in ease of utilization for the end user. There are numerous stages in this arrangement that involve proper management. For this to be realized into reality, microcontrollers like Arduino or Raspberry Pi deliver efficient results with the desired performance. The signals generated or produced by the sensors are in analog form. This analog signal is converted into digital form for further use. Afterward, the encryption of information is done before the storage of data is executed. Fig. (1) displays a flowchart, which shows the stages that have to be passed or followed by the system.

Module Information

A temperature sensor as well as a Spo2 sensor/oximeter consists of main sensors used in this system with microcontroller Arduino. Usually, in COVID-19, the oxygen level in the blood of a person infected is found to be radically low, so an oximeter is needed to continuously measure the oxygen level of a human suffering from COVID-19 and other such diseases where a medical service provider must be aware of the low blood oxygen level [12]. Along with this, the temperature of the human body also increases, which is also a sign of COVID-19 [13]. Hence, this system has provision for monitoring both oxygen level and human body temperature for immediate monitoring of patient's health. Bioelectrical signals are very low-amplitude and low-frequency electrical indicators that can be dignified from biological beings , for example, dogs, cats, cows, horses, humans, *etc.* Bioelectrical signals are caused by the complex self-regulatory system and can be measured through changes in electrical potential across a cell or an organ.

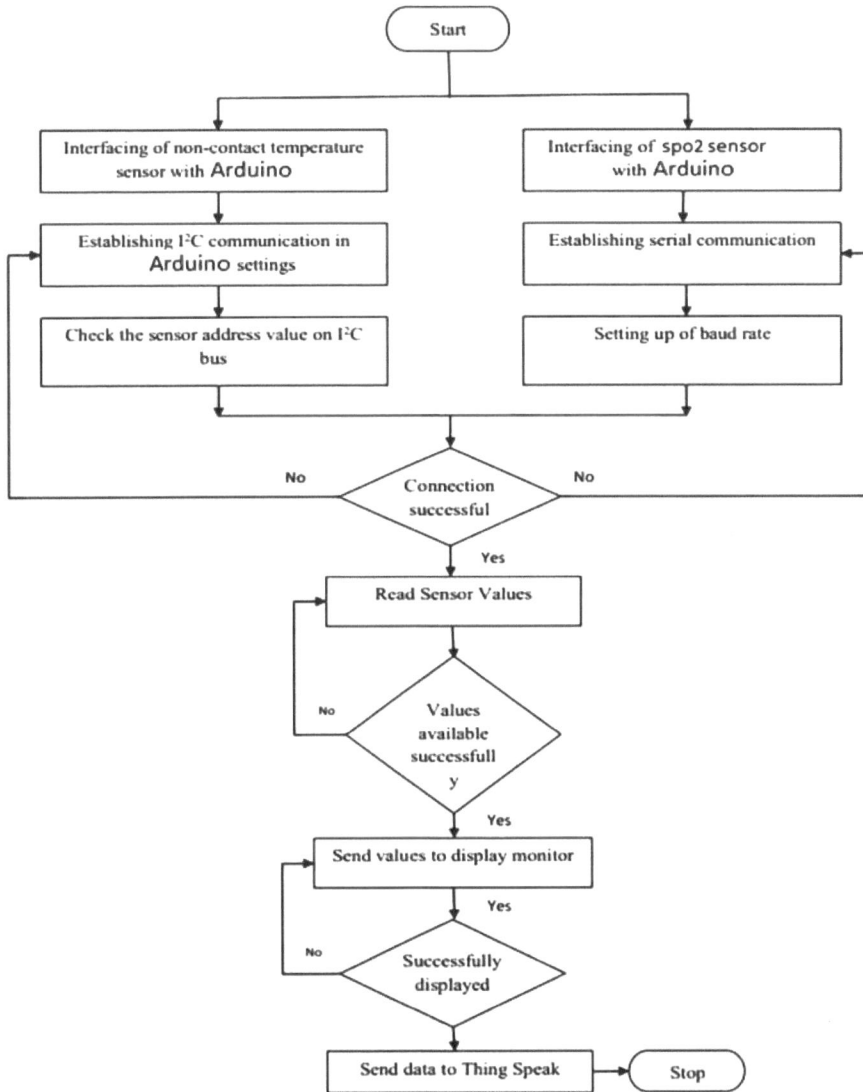

Fig. (1). Flowchart of different steps of the system.

The source of bioelectric signals is the activity of a single excitable neural or muscular cell. Bioelectrical signals are generated from the complex self-regulatory system and can be measured through changes in electrical potential across a cell or an organ. The biomedical signals are measured using invasive and non-invasive sensors. Both types of sensors, invasive and non-invasive, are wearable devices for health monitoring. The device we created is a non-invasive device with the ability to measure oxygen level and the temperature of the body on which it is used [5]. This wearable device provides continuous monitoring at every place, like at home and office or while playing several games. The internet connectivity and ability to customize have access to vast data, which improve efficiency over other methods with limited efficiency like questionnaires, *etc* [9].

Oximeter

MAX30100 is a proficient sensor; it has a stumpy power intake and extraordinary precision and permanence. This sensor has a really good capability to monitor the oxygen level of the blood, that too without invading the body. Its performance is really good, and it is used for its proficiency. It delivers the option for easy plug-and-play capability. The oximeter MAX30100 is shown in Fig. (**2**).

Fig. (2). Oximeter sensor MAX30100.

Temperature Sensor

In this system, the MLX90614 sensor is structured, which has really extraordinary precision. This measuring device has very little noise. It also has efficient digital signal processing with a 17-bit analog-to-digital converter, so it provides very accurate results. When this sensor is positioned near the body, this device starts to measure the temperature, and the best part is that this sensor is non-invasive. Also, it has the quality that no physical contact is required by this sensor for its functioning. It is very useful because contact can further spread the disease, so this also has the benefit of preventing further spread of the disease. The temperature sensor MLX90614 is shown in Fig. (**3**).

Fig. (3). Temperature sensor MLX90614.

Arduino

Arduino is a proficient, precise, fast, and balanced single-board microcontroller, which is approximately the size of a credit card (Fig. **4**). Linux can be utilized to run Arduino, and for the same purpose, Python can also be utilized. So, the functionality, as well as the dynamic range, of this small microcontroller is very useful in making compact modern-day devices. It can combine with a variety of sensors, detectors, and external devices to deliver huge productivity. The Arduino is shown in Fig. (**4**).

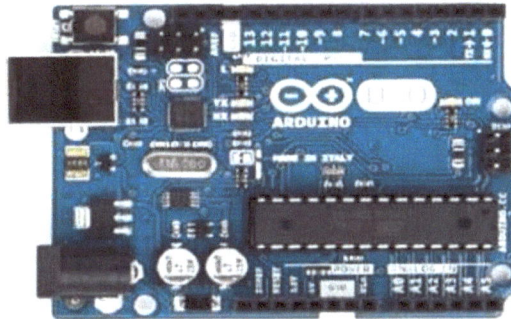

Fig. (4). Arduino the microcontroller.

Display

To resolve the issue of showing the result or information, a screen working on liquid crystal technology is employed in the instant health monitoring structure. The resolution of the screen is 240 × 320, which is an IPS panel. The SPI line involves the least GPIO pins for regulating its functionality. The display unit is shown in Fig. (**5**).

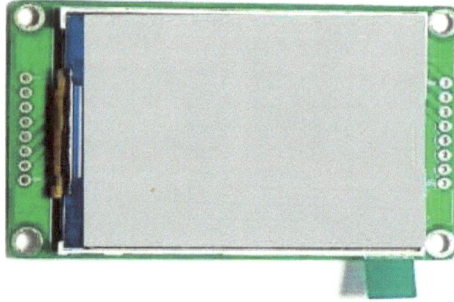

Fig. (5). Display unit.

Design of the Structure

With the help of IoT, the data collected can also be used and shared with hospitals or medical service providers so that they know the condition of patients, and in the case of an emergency, the medical facility provider can take the necessary steps like sending ambulance or sending a message to the family and friends of the patient to give certain medicine to delay or eliminate the worse condition to occur. Two sensors are used in the wearable device for temperature and oxygen levels [14]. The Arduino microcontroller basically has three main functions: capture the data, process it accordingly, and store the data. This information can also be displayed on the screen showing the parameters of the person who wears the device on the biceps. One of the main phases on which the working of the whole system depends is data collection or accumulation, which means that the accuracy and reliability of the system depend on how accurately the sensor is able to collect the data or information.

For data capturing, the outputs of the two sensors are provided to the GPIO terminals of the Arduino. For the purpose of providing power to the wearable device, two batteries of 1000 mah are used, which are charged by a power adapter that has an output of 5 V and 1 or 1.5 Amperes, or SMPS of similar rating can also be used. This way, the Arduino module, as well as powering various sensors, has an efficient power supply structure with low power consumption. On average, a maximum of 6 to 7 watts are consumed by the instant health monitoring system. The sensors used for measurement and data acquisition are IC-based with high precision, efficiency, and accuracy; hence, the power consumption is also low, and only some amount of power is lost in the form of heat energy.

Data Collection

Data collection or accumulation is one of the main levels on which the working of the whole system depends, which means that the accuracy and reliability of the system depend on how precisely the sensor is able to collect the data or information. For the information, the yields of both the two sensors are given to the GPIO terminals of the Arduino.

After making the necessary connections for the functioning of the system, a power supply of +5 V through battery *via* switch is provided to the wearable health monitoring system comprising of the microcontroller Arduino and two sensors (temperature and oxygen level) associated with it. Both the sensor *i.e.*, temperature sensor and oxygen level sensor, are placed on the human body, whose produced data or generated information is supplied to the Arduino microcontroller for further processing.

The temperature sensor (MLX90614) measures the ambient temperature and the temperature of the object, which is required to be measured. The interfacing stages of MLX90614 and the oximeter sensor are shown below:

- From the settings of interfacing in Arduino enabling I2C communication protocol.
- Download and install the packages for the oximeter sensor (MAX30100) and temperature sensor (MLX90614).
- Arduino is then connected to the oximeter sensor and temperature sensor.
- The sensor address value on I2C bus is confirmed by means of the command i2cdetect- y1.
- Address value is shown on the terminal after finding out the address value.
- Verify by moving your hand over the sensor whether its value or information is changing or not.

Storage of Information

Afterward, the capturing and processing of information/data succeeding important job left is the loading of data. ThingSpeak platform is utilized for the purpose of storage in this wearable health monitoring system, which is explained in the following steps:

- Login and formation of channel.
- Generating the API Key.
- With the help of .py extension, python codes are generated.
- Test the code.
- Check the output on screen.
- Watch data logging on the ThingSpeak site.
- Check on the ThingSpeak channel whether it displays different graphs corresponding to the provided changing values.

When the sensor delivers a signal to the Arduino, the microcontroller used in the wearable health monitoring device displays the values on the screen, and correspondingly, it saves the data on the cloud storage as well [15]. So, the doctors/hospitals that are away from the patient can easily access the data and make decisions accordingly [16].

System Result

The wearable device has the data collected by the integrated sensors, and for this device to be accurate and reliable, it must provide the result on the standard or quality of the device, which has been set by the system or device, which is accepted by the whole industry. So, the accuracy and effectiveness of the structure can be gauged by comparison of the measured data with the data generated by the commercial sensors that are available in the marketplace. The result of the temperature sensor used in the instant health monitoring system is compared with the device available in the market, and the percentage error is also shown in Table 1 below:

Table 1. Result of temperature sensor.

Number of samples	Room Temperature Measured	Actual Body Temperature	Body Temperature Observed	Relative Error (%e,)
MI	29° C	33 °C	34 °C	3.03
M2	28 °C	34 °C	35 °C	2.90
M3	29 °C	34 °C	34 °C	0.00
M4	30 °C	35 °C	36 °C	2.85
M5	29 °C	35 °C	35 °C	0.00

The computed maximum relative error was found to be 3.03. The placement of the sensor and environmental surroundings also affect the values generated by the sensor, but still, a satisfactory result is obtained by the setup.

One more sensor utilized by the wearable health monitoring device is the oxygen level sensor, whose result is compared with the device available in the market, and the percentage error is also shown in Table 2 below:

Table 2. Result of spo2 sensor.

Number of Samples	Actual SPO2 (in %)	Observed SPO2 (in %)	Relative Error (%E,
D1	98	98	0.00
D2	96	97	1.04

(Table 2) cont.....

Number of Samples	Actual SPO2 (in %)	Observed SPO2 (in %)	Relative Error (%E,
D3	97	97	0.00
D4	98	99	1.02
D5	95	96	1.05

The computed highest relative error was found to be 1.05. This indicates that the precision of the system for measuring oxygen levels is highly accurate. The image of the wearable health monitoring device, along with the basic scheme of the whole structure, is shown in Fig. (**6**).

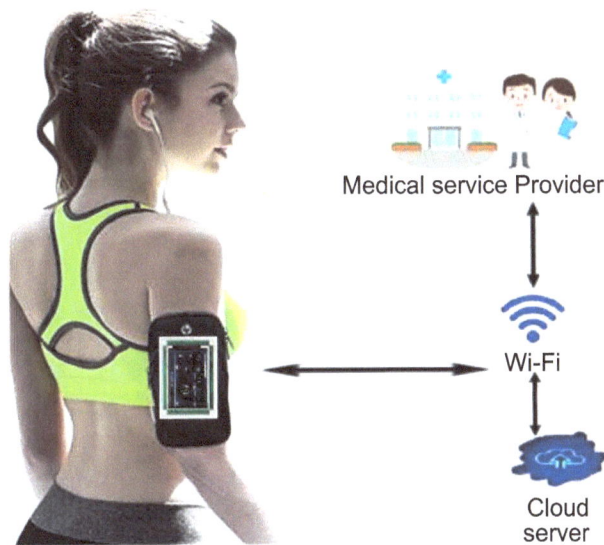

Fig. (6). Wearable health monitoring device in IoT environment.

The wearable health monitoring device is helpful for society, as there is an option for the vast utilization of this system for various critical medical situations, especially for COVID-19, but also for other diseases as well. Cloud technology is also there, which helps the doctors or medical facility provider to keep a check on the instant health of the person wearing this device accordingly [11]. The power consumption, as well as the price of the whole setup, is relatively very low, so almost everyone can use it, even people with low income.

CONCLUSION

The proposed instant health monitoring system provides the values of important parameters like temperature and oxygen level instantly, which are useful in monitoring the health of a patient even if the doctor or medical service provider is at a different place, which is far away from the patient. There is also the convenience of adding or removing the sensors to the system, which is helpful in monitoring the patient of various diseases, and its functionality does not just stop at pandemics like COVID-19, but the system can be modified to deal with other pandemics in future. This instant health monitoring system can be modified in the future to provide cutting-edge features as it is simple to add more sensors to the system. The system has the capability to avoid the reach of viruses by reducing face-to-face dealings of patients and medical service providers. Having technical officers at various hospitals who can teach medical doctors and supporting staff the efficient way to use the technology can yield the best maximum result.

The Wearable Health Monitoring System for Epidemic uses IoT, which enables it to monitor the patient's temperature along with the oxygen level in an instant; this system transmits the same information to the doctor or medical service provider at a distant location. It also enables us to look at the patient's current condition. If the values of the parameters change from the standard values, then an alert message can be given to the medical service provider or the doctor concerned with the patient. This instant health monitoring plan based on IoT helps doctors effortlessly collect real-time numbers at their location, which is far from the patient's location [11].

The utilization of cloud technology has made it possible to access the data at a place that is away from the patient, but still, medical facility providers can access the instant data. Also, the cost of the system and the running cost is also very low, which is helpful for low-income groups of society. The things that need improvisation for further improving the system is the security of the data generated, which is possible with the help of data encryption. The generated data or information can be secured from security breaches with the help of data encryption.

REFERENCES

[1]   P. Valsalan, T. A. Baomar, and A. H. Baabood, "IoT based health monitoring system", *Journal of critical reviews,* vol. 7, no. 4, pp. 739-743, 2020.

[2]   C. Senthamilarasi, J.J. Rani, B. Vidhya, and H. Aritha, "A smart patient health monitoring system using IoT", *Int. J. Pure Appl. Math.,* vol. 119, no. 16, pp. 59-70, 2018.

[3]   S. Cirani, and M. Picone, "Wearable computing for the internet of things", *IT Prof.,* vol. 17, no. 5, pp. 35-41, 2015.
       [http://dx.doi.org/10.1109/MITP.2015.89]

[4]   E. Guberović, T. Lipić, and I. Čavrak, "Dew intelligence: Federated learning perspective", *45th Annual Computers, Software, and Applications Conference (COMPSAC),* pp. 1819-1824, 2021.

[5]   M. Sparaco, L. Lavorgna, R. Conforti, G. Tedeschi, and S. Bonavita, "The role of wearable devices in multiple sclerosis", *Mult. Scler. Int.,* vol. 2018, pp. 1-7, 2018.
       [http://dx.doi.org/10.1155/2018/7627643] [PMID: 30405913]

[6]   M. Trombini, F. Ferraro, G. Iaconi, L. Vestito, F. Bandini, L. Mori, C. Trompetto, and S. Dellepiane, "A Study Protocol for Occupational Rehabilitation in Multiple Sclerosis", *Sensors,* vol. 21, no. 24, p. 8436, 2021.
[http://dx.doi.org/10.3390/s21248436] [PMID: 34960529]

[7]   A. Bahmani, A. Alavi, T. Buergel, S. Upadhyayula, Q. Wang, S.K. Ananthakrishnan, A. Alavi, D. Celis, D. Gillespie, G. Young, Z. Xing, M.H.H. Nguyen, A. Haque, A. Mathur, J. Payne, G. Mazaheri, J.K. Li, P. Kotipalli, L. Liao, R. Bhasin, K. Cha, B. Rolnik, A. Celli, O. Dagan-Rosenfeld, E. Higgs, W. Zhou, C.L. Berry, K.G. Van Winkle, K. Contrepois, U. Ray, K. Bettinger, S. Datta, X. Li, and M.P. Snyder, "A scalable, secure, and interoperable platform for deep data-driven health management", *Nat. Commun.,* vol. 12, no. 1, p. 5757, 2021.
[http://dx.doi.org/10.1038/s41467-021-26040-1] [PMID: 34599181]

[8]   X. Li, J. Dunn, D. Salins, G. Zhou, W. Zhou, S.M. Schüssler-Fiorenza Rose, D. Perelman, E. Colbert, R. Runge, S. Rego, R. Sonecha, S. Datta, T. McLaughlin, and M.P. Snyder, "Digital health: tracking physiomes and activity using wearable biosensors reveals useful health-related information", *PLoS Biol.,* vol. 15, no. 1, p. e2001402, 2017.
[http://dx.doi.org/10.1371/journal.pbio.2001402] [PMID: 28081144]

[9]   N. Sharma, M. Mangla, S.N. Mohanty, D. Gupta, P. Tiwari, M. Shorfuzzaman, and M. Rawashdeh, "A smart ontology-based IoT framework for remote patient monitoring", *Biomed. Signal Process. Control,* vol. 68, p. 102717, 2021.
[http://dx.doi.org/10.1016/j.bspc.2021.102717]

[10]   P.W. Huang, T.H. Chang, M.J. Lee, T.M. Lin, M.L. Chung, and B.F. Wu, "An embedded non-contact body temperature measurement system with automatic face tracking and neural network regression", *2016 International Automatic Control Conference (CACS),* pp. 161-166, 2016.
[http://dx.doi.org/10.1109/CACS.2016.7973902]

[11]   L. Hong-tan, K. Cui-hua, B. Muthu, and C.B. Sivaparthipan, "WITHDRAWN: Big data and ambient intelligence in IoT-based wireless student health monitoring system", *Aggress. Violent. Behav.,* p. 101601, 2021.
[http://dx.doi.org/10.1016/j.avb.2021.101601]

[12]   K. Kumar, N. Kumar, and R. Shah, "Role of IoT to avoid spreading of COVID-19", *International Journal of Intelligent Networks,* vol. 1, pp. 32-35, 2020.
[http://dx.doi.org/10.1016/j.ijin.2020.05.002]

[13]   A.I. Paganelli, P.E. Velmovitsky, P. Miranda, A. Branco, P. Alencar, D. Cowan, M. Endler, and P.P. Morita, "A conceptual IoT-based early-warning architecture for remote monitoring of COVID-19 patients in wards and at home", *Internet of Things,* vol. 18, p. 100399, 2022.
[http://dx.doi.org/10.1016/j.iot.2021.100399] [PMID: 38620637]

[14]   L.S. Kondaka, M. Thenmozhi, K. Vijayakumar, and R. Kohli, "An intensive healthcare monitoring paradigm by using IoT based machine learning strategies", *Multimedia Tools Appl.,* vol. 81, no. 26, pp. 36891-36905, 2022.
[http://dx.doi.org/10.1007/s11042-021-11111-8]

[15]   A. Manocha, G. Kumar, M. Bhatia, and A. Sharma, "IoT-inspired machine learning-assisted sedentary behavior analysis in smart healthcare industry", *J. Ambient Intell. Humaniz. Comput.,* vol. •••, pp. 1-4, 2021.

[16]   M. Otoom, N. Otoum, M.A. Alzubaidi, Y. Etoom, and R. Banihani, "An IoT-based framework for early identification and monitoring of COVID-19 cases", *Biomed. Signal Process. Control,* vol. 62, p. 102149, 2020.
[http://dx.doi.org/10.1016/j.bspc.2020.102149] [PMID: 32834831]

CHAPTER 10

An IoT-Enabled Automated Model for the Detection of COVID-19 Spread Using Deep Learning

Sanjib Roy[1,*], **Rishabh Kumar**[1] and **Radha Tamal Goswami**[2]

[1] *Department of Computer Science and Engineering, Birla Institute of Technology, Mesra - Patna Campus, Bihar, India*

[2] *Department of Electrical Engineering, Techno International New Town, Kolkata, West Bengal, India*

Abstract: COVID-19 was a global disaster for humans in 2020. It actually causes breathing problems, sneezing, and coughing. Early detection is essential to minimize the viral effects. RT-PCR test is not suitable against the rapid spread of coronavirus since it takes time to detect positive cases. Moreover, COVID-19 is a transmittable disease; therefore, there is always a chance of spreading the disease by RT-PCR method. Nowadays, radiographic images have already proven to be popular and alternate diagnostic tools in the context of disease prediction. Several research papers have already proposed different techniques using deep learning or CNN methods or transfer learning methods with radiographic images for automatic screening of COVID-19 disease. Unfortunately, most of these existing screening methods have either worked on small datasets or have produced the results with low accuracy. In this paper, an IoT-enabled automated screening model has been presented to classify the COVID-19 cases with the CNN-LSTM+Capsule network. The LSTM-Capsule network model not only diagnose the COVID-19 cases quickly but also maintains low hardware costs. The proposed model has worked on 280 COVID-positive and 290 normal patients' images taken from two benchmark datasets and tried to find out the spreading tendency of the virus by getting some realistic data from IoT sensor devices in the affected zone. The proposed model achieves an accuracy of 97%. Moreover, cross-validation is applied in this model to avoid over-fitting. This paper concludes that the proposed model gives an insight into the CNN-LSTM+Capsule network working for COVID-19 detection that helps get richer feature mapping from the radiographic images and further classifies the COVID-19 cases from the normal ones effectively. Moreover, the LSTM-Capsule network model has outperformed relative to other related works in the early identification of COVID-19 cases.

Keywords: COVID-19, Capsule network, Computer tomography, CNN-LSTM, IoT, X-ray.

* **Corresponding author Sanjib Roy:** Department of Computer Science and Engineering, Birla Institute of Technology, Mesra - Patna Campus, Bihar, India; E-mail: snjry2007@gmail.com

H.S. Hota, Dinesh K. Sharma, Ayan Kumar Das & Ditipriya Sinha (Eds.)

INTRODUCTION

The virus SARS-COV2 [1] is the source of the COVID-19 disease. It is very devastating as a contagious disease and spreads through air droplets from an individual's coughs and sneezes [2, 3]. No explicit prevention mechanism is available till now. Only isolation is the remedy for infected individuals [5, 6]. Generally, COVID-19 symptoms appear within 2 to 14 days, and the time-consuming nature of molecular tests demands alternative options for fast screening. This disease can be alternately analyzed by different radiographic such as X-ray and computer tomography images [7]. COVID-19-positive patients have some distinguishable clinical features, and due to this fact, both radiographic images help in detecting COVID-19 cases effectively by identifying these distinguishable clinical features [8]. The advancements in technology, sensors, and smart wearable devices have a great impact on our daily life. Tracking and quarantine of COVID-19-positive patients are possible, and suspected cases can be tracked and monitored by using these devices [9].

In various recent researches, one of the common AI-based methods, called deep technique, has been used for the differentiation of COVID-19 cases from normal ones. Apart from that, the mentioned techniques have been used in various research studies to get impressive results on classification. Especially, capsules consist of a group of neurons that accept and produce the output as vector as opposed to the values produced by CNN. The output of each neuron represents a different property of the same feature. The mentioned property enriches the capsule network to learn the features of an image. In addition to that, the capsule network also learns the deformations and viewing conditions of an image. It recognizes the parts of an image and then recognizes the whole entity. The features or output from CNN act as an input to a capsule. Based on the type of employed capsule, the features are processed and encoded. Based on the input, the network produces the output. The output contains a set of instantiation parameters and information about probabilistic features [12]. CNNs do not encode pose and angular information. On the other hand, the capsule network has the advantage of viewpoint invariance. As a result, it tends to accurately classify the images of the same object with different orientations. Moreover, in the case of max pooling operation, due to the movement of the most active neuron to the next layer, a lot of information is lost. It can be resolved by the routing-by-agreement method in the case of the capsule network [13].

The untouched issues and limitations of related works have encouraged authors to present an auto-screening deep model for COVID-19 prediction. In the present study, a deep model has been presented to detect coronavirus by using feature extraction through LSTM along with classification through the capsule network.

Different machine learning techniques have been incorporated as a classifier for comparing the attainment of the model against the capsule network. The major contributions are listed below.

- A deep technique has been presented for identifying positive patients with radiographic images.
- The proposed model introduces CNN-LSTM as a feature extractor and finds the best suite by using different classifiers to accomplish high accuracy values.
- The capsule network is utilized for binary classification.
- The statistical evaluation of the deep technique is based on radiographic images taken from two benchmark datasets, and the spreading tendency is justified by the collection of data from sensors that are deployed at the affected area.
- The statistical evaluation of the proposed model has been presented by comparing it with four other existing models on consideration of several evaluation metrics.

The remaining part of the paper is presented with relevant research on disease detection along with the proposed methodology and experimental results in the following subsections. Finally, conclusions are made with future research directions.

RELATED WORK

The most important primary treatment to avert the rapid escalation of COVID-19 disease is to screen patients with primary symptoms, and according to that, they are suggested to consult with a doctor. Nowadays, due to some limitations of RT-PCR tests, the hospital relies on medical imaging for those people who are suffering from COVID-19 symptoms, as the procedure is simple, accurate, and fast. As a result, radiographic images are widely used as alternative diagnostic tools for COVID-19 detection. At the same time, a significant burden for physicians has been created due to the fast transmission rate of COVID-19-positive cases. This situation can be handled by using different machine intelligence techniques, which have made remarkable progress in recent years, mainly due to two factors: continuously growing available data and increasing computing power. An automatic detection system [15] has been developed by using a transfer learning system comprised of 1427 radiographic images. The system has performed well in terms of 0.9678 accuracy, along with a sensitivity of 0.9866 and specificity of 0.9646. An automatic COVID-19 detection system [16] has been developed based upon different transfer learning models, where each of the transfer learning models has been used separately with radiographic images. The ResNet-50 that has been used in this system has produced the best result along with 97.5% accuracy among other pre-trained networks and has been used separately in this model. COVIDX-Net [17], another deep technique, has been applied with seven convolutional models to classify COVID-19 cases from radiographic images. Among these, VGG19 and DenseNet have shown a good performance by producing 0.89 f1-scores for normal cases and 0.91 f1-scores for positive cases. InceptionV3 has shown the worst-case performance by producing 0.67 f1-scores for normal cases. In another paper, a transfer learning multi-channel model [18] has been built on ResNet architecture for COVID-19 diagnosis. The ensemble model more accurately extracts the relevant features for each class with 0.94 precision and 100% recall value. InstaCovNet-19 [19], an integrated stacked deep model, has been presented with ResNet101, Xception, InceptionV3, and MobileNet. The model has produced 0.9908 accuracy on multi-class classification and 0.9953 accuracy on binary class. In one of the papers [20], a deep model has been developed for the discernment of COVID-19 cases using 1065 computer tomography scans. In this technique, Inception architecture has been modified along with different validation schemes. The internal validation has achieved 0.895 accuracy along with 0.88 specificity and 0.87 sensitivity. At the same time, the external validation has achieved 0.793 accuracy along with 0.83 specificity and 0.67 sensitivity. A computer-aided tool [21] has been introduced for identifying COVID-19 cases using the SVM classifier. SVM has shown remarkable performance with a small dataset of radiographic images with 0.988 accuracy.

Machine intelligence systems have strong contributions in the healthcare sector for the discernment of various diseases. Feature extraction or classification can be done through different machine intelligence procedures. In a study [22], COVID-Net has been proposed with x-ray images. An accuracy of about 0.933 has been produced by this model. Another model [23] has been proposed without any feature extraction method for identifying the positive cases. The model was trained with 125 radiographic images and finally produced an accuracy of 0.8702. A deep segmentation model [24] has been constructed for the identification of COVID-19 disease using 300 radiographic images. Another study [25] has been developed to produce a CNN architecture using 13,975 radiographic images for COVID-19 prediction. Finally, the model has produced an accuracy of about 0.942. On the other hand, a new diagnosis system [26] has been introduced to identify patients with COVID-19 symptoms and extract the facets of the new disease. In this system, FPN is used with an accuracy of about 0.942. On the other hand, a new diagnosis system [26] has been introduced to identify patients with COVID-19 symptoms and extract the facets of the new disease. In this system, FPN is used with ResNet-50 for the extraction of facets. The system has achieved an accuracy of 0.95 with a 0.87 F1 score. Another study [27] for COVID-19 detection has been introduced with CT images. Initially, pre-trained UNet was used for the segmentation of a patient's lung region. Finally, 0.901 accuracy has been achieved by this model. In another paper [28], an integrated model has been developed, where CNN architecture has been used for splitting multiple image cubes. Feature extraction has been done using ResNet18, which can accurately distinguish COVID-19 cases with 0.867 accuracy. A modified CNN [29] has been introduced with radiographic images. The concatenated architecture of Xception and ResNet50-V2 has been used for detecting COVID-positive cases. The architecture has achieved 99.5% accuracy. In another study [30], LSTM and GRU have been combined for COVID-19 detection architecture. The outputs produced by this model have been correlated for clinical purposes. The model has obtained 0.87 accuracy. In a study [31], a system has been developed to identify COVID-19 cases with radiographic images. ResNet-18, ResNet-50, SqeezeNet, and DenseNet-121 have been used separately to predict the result. The system has correctly identified COVID-19 cases with a 0.98 sensitivity rate. In another system named TLCoV [32], CNN, VGG16, and ResNet50 have been applied for the identification of COVID-19 cases. The model has achieved 0.9767 accuracy along with 0.9665 precision and 0.9654 recall.

Convolutional neural network (CNN) is one of the best architectures for disease detection systems. A lightweight ensemble architecture based on CNN [33] has been inculcated for classification purposes. CNN has been introduced to capture features and produce different ML classifiers to get the outputs. The model has produced about 0.90 accuracy. Another study [34] exhibits a CNN-based architecture named CovXNet model to produce an accuracy of about 0.974. A supervised technique [35] has been introduced to reduce the provision of labeling images manually. Resnet architecture [36] has been introduced for COVID-19 detection. The system has performed on kinetic datasets and produced better performance than any other superficial architecture. The acerbity of the disease has been projected with CNN architecture [37]. The system has worked on the lung dataset and produced an accuracy of about 96%. In another context, the authors [38] have presented a deep learning model along with IoT to prevent the spread of COVID-19 and also produced a very good scheme to deploy IoT devices to identify positive cases.

METHODOLOGY

In the present study, a deep model has been proposed as a useful detection technique to segregate COVID-19-positive cases from healthy ones. In this model, CNN-LSTM has been used to get richer information by extracting features from radiographic images, and binary classification is done through a capsule network. Finally, the system achieves up-to-the-mark performance. The flow of control of the proposed work is shown in Fig (**1**).

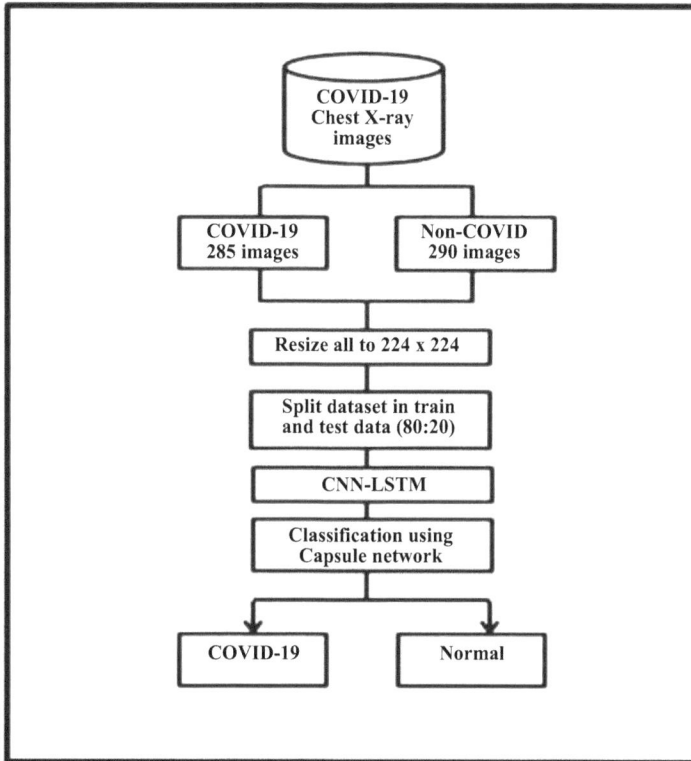

Fig. (1). Schematic flow control of the proposed model.

The entire indoctrination of the above mentioned system is built on two aggregated datasets of X-ray images of different dimensions. The images from the combined dataset are refined to 224×224 dimensions so that they can be well suited to CNN-LSTM. After that, the colored images are converted to 224×224×3. Then, the dataset is divided into 460 training and 115 testing data. The dataset for training purposes is fed to LSTM, where feature extraction is done. Finally, the capsule network works on the extracted features to segregate the positive cases from the healthy ones. The model has effectively classified the binary cases with an accuracy of 0.97. The system has also produced other qualitative performance metrics where each of the metrics has significant interpretation in disease detection.

The methodology section has been further divided into three sub-sections. The authors have given an insight into feature mapping using LSTM. They have also given importance to dynamic routing, where relevant features come to play a vital role in classification to get a better accuracy result.

Datasets Description and Preparation

Two benchmark datasets comprise 575 images, which are composed of the COVID-19 chest xray dataset [41] and the COVID-19 radiography database [42], including 285 COVID-19 positive images and 290 normal or other flu patients' images, as well as 145 healthy person's images and 145 viral pneumonia patients' images. The collected images are pre-processed to equal dimensions so that the images can be well suited to CNN-LSTM and capsule network. Four hundred and sixty training data and 115 testing data are used for further processing in this model. To make the final testing accurate, the dataset comprised of radiographic images remains of the same size.

Extraction of features using IoT-enabled LSTM

LSTM is an improved version of RNNs. It consists of three components, namely an entry section, an intermediate section, and an exit section. The parameters used with LSTM are given as X_t, which refers to the instant input, c_t and X_{t-1}, which denote the fresh and prior conditions, respectively, and h_t and h_{t-1}, which are used for the instant and former outcomes, respectively. The workflow of LSTM is shown in Fig (**2**).

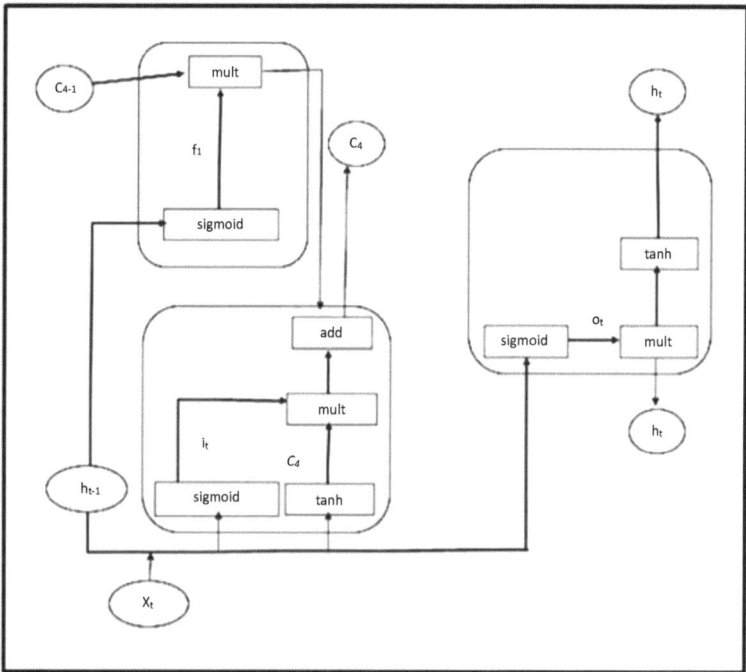

Fig. (2). Working principle of feature extraction through LSTM.

The previous output (h_{t-1}) and the current input (X_t) pass through the sigmoid layer to find the appropriate choice of information that must be added, which is shown in eq. (1).

$$i_t = \sigma\,(w_i.\,[\,h_{t-1}, X_t] + \, B_i)\tag{1}$$

The output (i_t) is fed to the tanh layer to get the new information based on X_{t-1} and X_t, which is depicted in eq. (2).

$$C_t = tanh\ tanh\ (w_i.\,[\,h_{t-1}, X_t] + \, B_i)\tag{2}$$

The output produced from eq. (2) is known as current moment information (C_t). Now, the memory information c_t and C_{t-1} are combined with sigmoid output w_i and bias (B_i) of LSTM in eq. (3).

$$c_t = f_t c_{t-1} + i_t C_t\tag{3}$$

The decision about whether the forget-related information will be added to the previous cell or not is based on probability, which is depicted in eq. (4).

$$f_t = \sigma\,(W_f.\,[\,h_{t-1}, X_t] + \, b_f\,)\tag{4}$$

The final output through LSTM is calculated over two following equations, *i.e.*, eq. (5) and eq. (6).

$$o_t = \sigma(\ W_0\,[h_{t-1}, X_t\,] + \, B_0)\tag{5}$$

$$h_t = o_t\ tanh\ tanh\ (c_t)\tag{6}$$

Working Principle of the Proposed Model

The working principle of the state of the work has been elaborately described through the architectural construction, which is depicted in Fig. (**3**). The images from the dataset are input through five convolutional layers using consecutive pooling operations. Then, LSTM is used for the uprooting of features from images. The relevant features from images and the real-time data collected from sensors are contrasted to understand the outspread tendency of the virus in the effective area. The convolutional approach can uproot the sophisticated features using simple computations. In contrast, the convolutional approach cannot identify the object correctly if the input images are of different sizes and are also oriented with different poses. Moreover, CNN drops some important information during the pooling operation. Thus capsule network is included in this present work by observing these limitations. The capsule network has the ability to evaluate the output in terms of vectors based on inputs. The strength capsule network is that it can identify identical objects even if they change by different orientations.

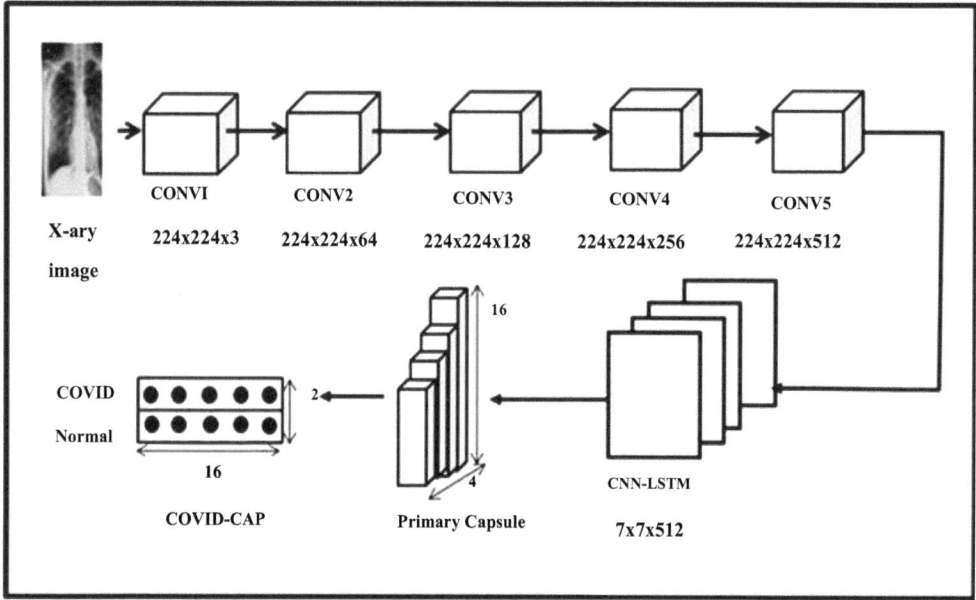

Fig. (3). Schematic layout of the proposed system using LSTM and capsule network amalgamation.

The extracted features containing reshaped images whose values are in vectors are put in the primary capsule layer. The prediction can be done through eq (7), where the feature values are presented through a weight matrix.

$$\hat{U}_{j\,|\,i} = W_{ij}u_i \tag{7}$$

The output produced as $\hat{U}_{j|i}$ is the anticipated feature vector, which can be attained by the multiplication of ith capsule's feature with the weight matrix Wij. In this context, each underneath capsule mitigates elevated capsule in its vicinity on the basis of $\hat{U}_{j|i}$ Based upon compliance, the features have been dispelled to the CONV-CAP layer, where dynamic routing comes into play for feature accustoming. The compliance (d_{ij}) is shown in eq. (8).

$$d_{ij} = c_{ij}\hat{U}_{j|i} \tag{8}$$

Where, c_{ij} is termed as coupling coefficient. The conjoin relationship between different level capsules initiates the capsule to dispel to the next layer based on the coupling coefficient, which is shown in eq. (9).

$$c_{ij} = \frac{e^{b_{ij}}}{e^{b_{in}}} \tag{9}$$

Where, b_{ij} is known as the log prior probabilities. The capsule of layer l is able to conjoin with the next layer capsule based on log prior probabilities, which is depicted in eq. (10).

$$b_{ij} = b_{ij} + \hat{U}_{j|i} \times v_j \tag{10}$$

The collection of extracted features of a particular capsule, say for j^{th} capsule, can be formulated as the aggregation of consensus of all other underneath capsules, as shown in eq. (11).

$$sum = \sum \quad d_{ij} \tag{11}$$

The final consensus (a_{ij}) is produced by scalar multiplication in eq. (12).

$$a_{ij} = v_j \times \hat{U}_{j|i} \tag{12}$$

Three hundred epochs are considered for training purposes in the present study with a learning rate of 10^{-3} to minimize the loss. The final consensus vector is constituted using the coupling coefficients C_{ij}, and the final output vector V is then classified in the COVID-CAP layer as COVID-19 positives and normal patients. The loss function is shown in eq. (13).

$$Loss = D_n \tag{13}$$

Eq. (13) suggests that the presence of a particular D_n is 1, otherwise 0 for absence.

EXPERIMENTS AND RESULTS

This section comprises configuration procedure for the experiment along with analyzing different performance metrics produced by the LSTM-Capsule network. Different ML techniques have also been tested on this model with the aim of finding the best feature extractor-classifier pair for prior detection of COVID-19-positive cases. The experimental results prove that the LSTM-Capsule pair has achieved the best performance. A correlative performance study has been conducted with the different ML procedures. Finally, an analytical comparative analysis has been made between the LSTM-Capsule network method with other related works.

Experimental Setups

The x-ray images are revised to 224x224 dimensions before being fed to five convolutional layers, followed by LSTM. The total experiment is done on a Linux system. x86-64 processor of 2 GHz speed along with 13GB of onboard RAM is used for experimental purposes. Also, online GPU is used along with Kaggle Notebook and Tensorflow for implementation purposes.

Evaluation Metrics

The performance metrics, along with associated terminologies, are defined below to evaluate the performance of the present study.

True Positive (TP): The end result of a system where it can able to prognosticate the positive class exactly.

True Negative (TN): The end result of a system where it can able to prognosticate the negative class exactly.

False Negative (FN): The end result of a system where it wrongly prognosticates the output as negative.

False Positive (FP): The end result of a system where it wrongly prognosticates the output as positive.

The aptness of the system to correctly identify the positive and negative cases among all possible cases is known as accuracy and is formulated in eq. (14).

$$Accuracy = \frac{True\ Positive + True\ Negative}{True\ Positive + True\ Negative + False\ Positive + False\ Negative} \tag{14}$$

The potentiality of a system to notify only the pertinent data points is known as precision and is also formulated in eq. (15).

$$Precision = \frac{True\ Positive}{True\ Positive + False\ Positive} \tag{15}$$

The potentiality of a system to notice all the pertinent cases within a data set is known as recall and is also formulated in eq. (16).

$$Recall = \frac{True\ Positive}{True\ Positive + False\ Negative} \tag{16}$$

F1-score is the combined result of recall and precision value, which in turn measures the system's accuracy using imbalanced data and is defined in eq. (17).

$$F1 - score = \frac{2*Precision*Recall}{Precision+Recall}$$　　　(17)

Correlative Performance of the Presented Model Using Different ML Classifiers

The present study uses 5 different ML classifiers in order to compare their performance with the capsule network. ML classifiers such as Support Vector Machine (SVM), Random Forest (RF), Decision Tree (DT), Multilayer Perceptron (MLP) and K-Nearest Neighbors (KNN) are used separately with the LSTM module, and comparative performance is noted in Table **1**. Table **1** reveals that SVM and MLP individually perform well among all other ML techniques. Both the mentioned ML techniques achieve almost the same accuracy as the capsule network. The graphical presentation of the correlative performance of the LSTM-Capsule system and other ML classifiers utilizing radiographic images is depicted in both Table **1** and Fig. (**4**).

Table 1. Comparative analysis of the proposed study by using different machine learning techniques as classifier.

ML Techniques	Performance Metrics			
	Accuracy	Precision	Recall	F1-score
Support Vector Machine	0.956	0.96	0.95	0.96
Random Forest	0.92	0.91	0.93	0.92
Decision Tree	0.81	0.85	0.77	0.81
MLP	0.95	0.96	0.93	0.94
KNN	0.93	0.93	0.93	0.93

F1-score interprets that the system effectively differentiates the positive and negative cases. In this context, the critical success index of 0.96 indicates that the proposed study effectively identified positive patients. ROC analysis is generally used for the assessment of the accuracy of the medical interpretation system. Based on probabilistic values, ROC maps the true positive rate in opposition to the false positive rate using various threshold points. If anyone arbitrarily chooses the decision criteria, then there will be a chance of distortion case. In this context, for choosing accuracy indices, the ROC gives the guarantee of avoiding distortion. Moreover, the infected patients and normal ones can be easily discriminated by using ROC analysis. In addition to that, AUC also improves the diagnosis performance by distinguishing normal and infected patients. The peak value of AUC suggests that the system can effectively discriminate the positive and negative classes. The pictorial representation of ROC/AUC curves is depicted in Fig. (5), which shows that the capsule network as a classifier performs better than other ML techniques for the proposed study.

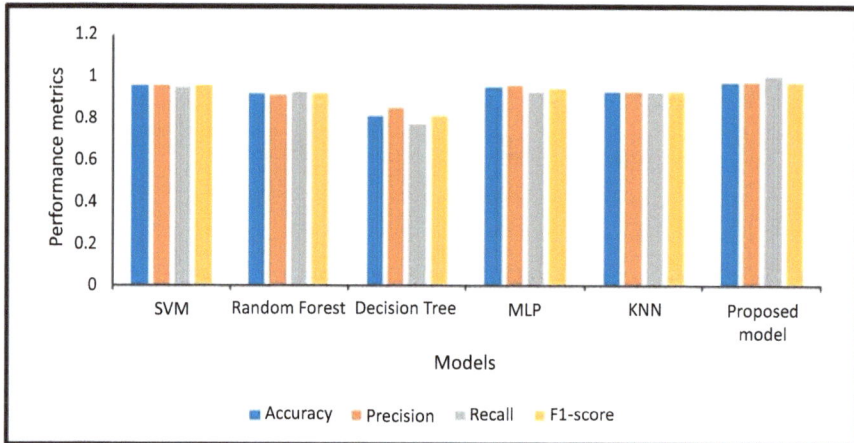

Fig. (4). Comparative analysis of the proposed model with other ML techniques.

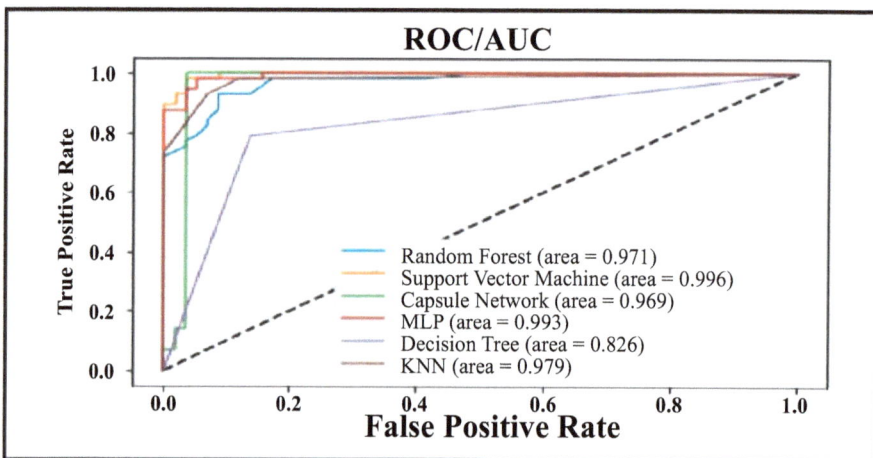

Fig. (5). ROC/AUC curve produced by the proposed model.

Comparative Analysis of the LSTM-Capsule Model with other Correlated Works

In the context of COVID-19 screening, the researchers produced great contributions in finding the different screening techniques. In a study [39], ResNet50 with SVM has been used for COVID-19 case classification. The combined technique accomplished well by achieving 95.38% accuracy. In another paper [40], the Inception transfer learning system produced 92.4% accuracy in the prior identification of COVID-19 positive patients. On the other hand [26], a deep system l was incorporated for the prediction of COVID-positive patients using 88 radiographic CT images. The system performed well, with an accuracy score of 0.86, along with 0.96 recall and 0.79 precision. Similarly, another paper [27] produced a deep model with computer tomography images for prompt identification of positive patients. The model produced 90.8% accuracy. The present study used CNN-LSTM for feature extraction from 575 x-ray images and then classified the binary classes using the capsule network. Finally, the proposed study produced 97% accuracy along with 0.97 sensitivity and 0.97 f1-score. The correlated analysis is shown in Table **2**, with a graphical depiction in Fig (**6**).

Table 2. Comparative analysis of LSTM-Capsule network with other subsisting works.

Existing Works	images	Techniques	Accuracy
[40]	x-ray	Deep learning method	0.924
[39]	x-ray	Transfer learning with SVM	0.9538
[26]	CT	Transfer learning	0.86
[27]	CT	3D deep network	0.908
Proposed model	x-ray	LSTM & Capsule network	0.97

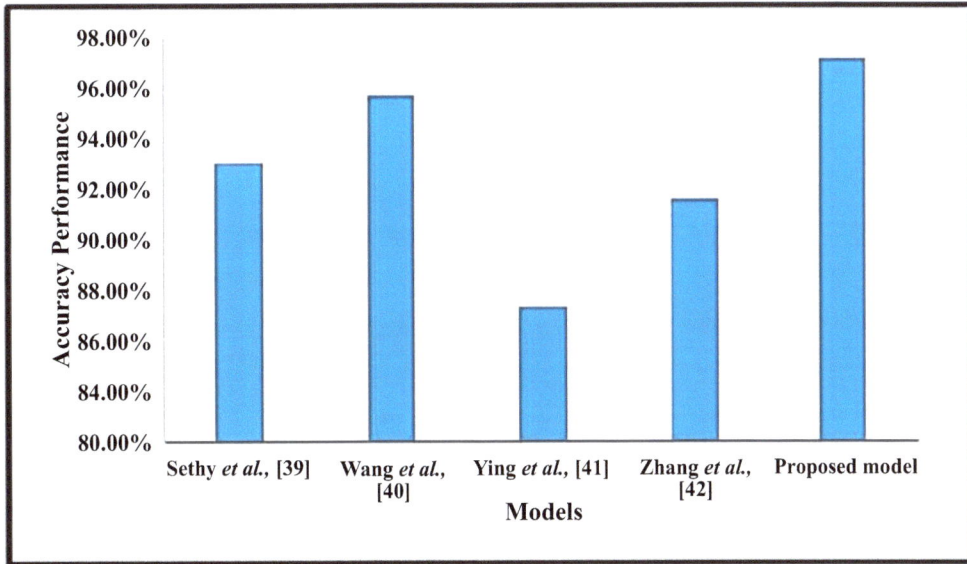

Fig. (6). Statistical comparative analysis of accuracy metric with different existing models.

CONCLUSION

In the present study, five machine learning procedures have been used independently as a classifier, and experimental results reveal that the LSTM-capsule network combination outperforms other techniques. The proposed study is examined on an X-ray dataset with an achievement of 97% accuracy. Thus, the LSTM-capsule network combination in this study is contemplated as the best feature extractor-classifier duo in COVID-19 detection. The statistical analysis reveals that the LSTM-capsule model outperforms four related works on COVID-19 detection with consideration of four different performance values.

The present study has speedup the automated screening process but has not been used for clinical study. Therefore, at this moment, the proposed study cannot be treated as a substitute for medical prognosis. Therefore, in this study, the authors focused on a substantial exploration of large datasets to obtain more accurate predictive outcomes.

ACKNOWLEDGEMENTS

We would like to express our sincere gratitude to all editors and reviewers for giving their esteemed time to review and provide valuable suggestions to incorporate in this book chapter.

REFERENCES

[1]   W. Guan, Z. Ni, Y. Hu, W. Liang, C. Ou, J. He, L. Liu, H. Shan, C. Lei, D.S.C. Hui, B. Du, L. Li, G. Zeng, K.Y. Yuen, R. Chen, C. Tang, T. Wang, P. Chen, J. Xiang, S. Li, J. Wang, Z. Liang, Y. Peng, L. Wei, Y. Liu, Y. Hu, P. Peng, J. Wang, J. Liu, Z. Chen, G. Li, Z. Zheng, S. Qiu, J. Luo, C. Ye, S. Zhu, and N. Zhong, "Clinical characteristics of coronavirus disease 2019 in China", *N. Engl. J. Med.,* vol. 382, no. 18, pp. 1708-1720, 2020.
[http://dx.doi.org/10.1056/NEJMoa2002032] [PMID: 32109013]

[2]   R.M. Pereira, D. Bertolini, L.O. Teixeira, C.N. Silla Jr, and Y.M.G. Costa, "COVID-19 identification in chest X-ray images on flat and hierarchical classification scenarios", *Comput. Methods Programs Biomed.,* vol. 194, p. 105532, 2020.
[http://dx.doi.org/10.1016/j.cmpb.2020.105532] [PMID: 32446037]

[3]   K. Tolksdorf, S. Buda, E. Schuler, L.H. Wieler, and W. Haas, "Influenza-associated pneumonia as reference to assess seriousness of coronavirus disease (COVID-19)", *Euro Surveill.,* vol. 25, no. 11, p. 2000258, 2020.
[http://dx.doi.org/10.2807/1560-7917.ES.2020.25.11.2000258] [PMID: 32186278]

[4]   E. Kwon, M. Kim, E. Choi, Y. Park, and C. Kim, "Tamoxifen-induced acute eosinophilic pneumonia in a breast cancer patient", *Int. J. Surg. Case Rep.,* vol. 60, pp. 186-190, 2019.
[http://dx.doi.org/10.1016/j.ijscr.2019.02.026] [PMID: 31229774]

[5]   G. Grasselli, A. Pesenti, and M. Cecconi, "Critical care utilization for the COVID-19 outbreak in Lombardy, Italy: early experience and forecast during an emergency response", *JAMA,* vol. 323, no. 16, pp. 1545-1546, 2020.
[http://dx.doi.org/10.1001/jama.2020.4031] [PMID: 32167538]

[6]   X. Jiang, M. Coffee, A. Bari, J. Wang, X. Jiang, J. Huang, J. Shi, J. Dai, J. Cai, T. Zhang, Z. Wu, G.

He, and Y. Huang, "Towards an artificial intelligence framework for data-driven prediction of coronavirus clinical severity", *Comput. Mater. Continua,* vol. 62, no. 3, pp. 537-551, 2020.
[http://dx.doi.org/10.32604/cmc.2020.010691]

[7]   Z.Y. Zu, M.D. Jiang, P.P. Xu, W. Chen, Q.Q. Ni, G.M. Lu, and L.J. Zhang, "Coronavirus disease 2019 (COVID-19): a perspective from China", *Radiology,* vol. 296, no. 2, pp. E15-E25, 2020.
[http://dx.doi.org/10.1148/radiol.2020200490] [PMID: 32083985]

[8]   G.Q. Qian, N.B. Yang, F. Ding, A.H.Y. Ma, Z.Y. Wang, Y.F. Shen, C.W. Shi, X. Lian, J.G. Chu, L. Chen, Z.Y. Wang, D.W. Ren, G.X. Li, X.Q. Chen, H.J. Shen, and X.M. Chen, "Epidemiologic and clinical characteristics of 91 hospitalized patients with COVID-19 in Zhejiang, China: a retrospective, multi-centre case series", *QJM,* vol. 113, no. 7, pp. 474-481, 2020.
[http://dx.doi.org/10.1093/qjmed/hcaa089] [PMID: 32181807]

[9]   U. Iqbal, and A.H. Mir, "Secure and scalable access control protocol for IoT environment", *Internet of Things,* vol. 12, p. 100291, 2020.
[http://dx.doi.org/10.1016/j.iot.2020.100291]

[10]   P.K. Sethy, S.K. Behera, K. Anitha, C. Pandey, and M.R. Khan, "Computer aid screening of COVID-19 using X-ray and CT scan images: An inner comparison", *J. XRay Sci. Technol.,* vol. 29, no. 2, pp. 197-210, 2021.
[http://dx.doi.org/10.3233/XST-200784] [PMID: 33492267]

[11]   J.P. Kanne, B.P. Little, J.H. Chung, B.M. Elicker, and L.H. Ketai, "Essentials for radiologists on COVID-19: an update—radiology scientific expert panel", *Radiology,* vol. 296, no. 2, pp. E113-E114, 2020.
[http://dx.doi.org/10.1148/radiol.2020200527] [PMID: 32105562]

[12]   M. Kwabena Patrick, and A. Felix Adekoya, "Capsule networks—a survey", *Journal of King Saud University-Computer and Information Sciences*, vol. 34, no. 1, pp. 1295–1310, Jan. 2022. Available from: https://www. sciencedirect. com/science/article/pii

[13]   A. Punjabi, J. Schmid, and A.K. Katsaggelos, "Examining the benefits of capsule neural networks", *arXiv preprint arXiv:2001.10964,* 2020.

[14]   H. Mukherjee, S. Ghosh, A. Dhar, S.M. Obaidullah, K.C. Santosh, and K. Roy, "Deep neural network to detect COVID-19: one architecture for both CT Scans and Chest X-rays", *Appl. Intell.,* vol. 51, no. 5, pp. 2777-2789, 2021.
[http://dx.doi.org/10.1007/s10489-020-01943-6] [PMID: 34764562]

[15]   T. Tuncer, S. Dogan, and E. Akbal, "A novel local senary pattern based epilepsy diagnosis system using EEG signals", *Australas. Phys. Eng. Sci. Med.,* vol. 42, no. 4, pp. 939-948, 2019.
[http://dx.doi.org/10.1007/s13246-019-00794-x] [PMID: 31482442]

[16]   A. Narin, C. Kaya, and Z. Pamuk, "Automatic detection of coronavirus disease (COVID-19) using X-ray images and deep convolutional neural networks", *Pattern Anal. Appl.,* vol. 24, no. 3, pp. 1207-1220, 2021.
[http://dx.doi.org/10.1007/s10044-021-00984-y] [PMID: 33994847]

[17]   E.E. Hemdan, M.A. Shouman, and M.E. Karar, "Covidx-net: A framework of deep learning classifiers to diagnose covid-19 in x-ray images", *arXiv preprint arXiv:2003.11055,* 2020.

[18]   S. Misra, S. Jeon, S. Lee, R. Managuli, I.S. Jang, and C. Kim, "Multi-channel transfer learning of chest X-ray images for screening of COVID-19", *Electronics (Basel),* vol. 9, no. 9, p. 1388, 2020.
[http://dx.doi.org/10.3390/electronics9091388]

[19]   A. Gupta, Anjum, S. Gupta, and R. Katarya, "InstaCovNet-19: A deep learning classification model for the detection of COVID-19 patients using Chest X-ray", *Appl. Soft Comput.,* vol. 99, p. 106859, 2021.
[http://dx.doi.org/10.1016/j.asoc.2020.106859] [PMID: 33162872]

[20]   S. Wang, B. Kang, J. Ma, X. Zeng, M. Xiao, J. Guo, M. Cai, J. Yang, Y. Li, X. Meng, and B. Xu, "A

deep learning algorithm using CT images to screen for Corona virus disease (COVID-19)", *Eur. Radiol.,* vol. 31, no. 8, pp. 6096-6104, 2021.
[http://dx.doi.org/10.1007/s00330-021-07715-1] [PMID: 33629156]

[21]   N. Absar, B. Mamur, A. Mahmud, T.B. Emran, M.U. Khandaker, M.R.I. Faruque, H. Osman, A. Elzaki, and B.A. Elkhader, "Development of a computer-aided tool for detection of COVID-19 pneumonia from CXR images using machine learning algorithm", *Journal of Radiation Research and Applied Sciences,* vol. 15, no. 1, pp. 32-43, 2022.
[http://dx.doi.org/10.1016/j.jrras.2022.02.002]

[22]   Z.Q. Linda Wang, and A. Wong, "COVID-Net: A tailored deep convolutional neural network design for detection of COVID-19 cases from chest radiography images", *arXiv preprint arXiv:2003.09871,* 2020.

[23]   T. Ozturk, M. Talo, E.A. Yildirim, U.B. Baloglu, O. Yildirim, and U. Rajendra Acharya, "Automated detection of COVID-19 cases using deep neural networks with X-ray images", *Comput. Biol. Med.,* vol. 121, p. 103792, 2020.
[http://dx.doi.org/10.1016/j.compbiomed.2020.103792] [PMID: 32568675]

[24]   F. Shan, Y. Gao, J. Wang, W. Shi, N. Shi, M. Han, Z. Xue, D. Shen, and Y. Shi, "Lung infection quantification of COVID-19 in CT images with deep learning", *arXiv preprint arXiv:2003.04655,* 2020.

[25]   L. Wang, Z.Q. Lin, and A. Wong, "COVID-Net: a tailored deep convolutional neural network design for detection of COVID-19 cases from chest X-ray images", *Sci. Rep.,* vol. 10, no. 1, p. 19549, 2020.
[http://dx.doi.org/10.1038/s41598-020-76550-z] [PMID: 33177550]

[26]   Y. Song, S. Zheng, L. Li, X. Zhang, Z. Huang, J. Chen, R. Wang, H. Zhao, Y. Chong, J. Shen, Y. Zha, and Y. Yang, "Deep learning enables accurate diagnosis of novel coronavirus (COVID-19) with CT images", *IEEE/ACM Trans. Comput. Biol. Bioinformatics,* vol. 18, no. 6, pp. 2775-2780, 2021.
[http://dx.doi.org/10.1109/TCBB.2021.3065361] [PMID: 33705321]

[27]   C. Zheng, X. Deng, Q. Fu, Q. Zhou, J. Feng, H. Ma, W. Liu, and X. Wang, "Deep learning-based detection for COVID-19 from chest CT using weak label", *MedRxiv,* 2020.
[http://dx.doi.org/10.1101/2020.03.12.20027185]

[28]   L. Brunese, F. Mercaldo, A. Reginelli, and A. Santone, "Explainable deep learning for pulmonary disease and coronavirus COVID-19 detection from X-rays", *Comput. Methods Programs Biomed.,* vol. 196, p. 105608, 2020.
[http://dx.doi.org/10.1016/j.cmpb.2020.105608] [PMID: 32599338]

[29]   M Rahimzadeh, and A. Attar, "A modified deep convolutional neural network for detecting COVID-19 and pneumonia from chest X-ray images based on the concatenation of Xception and ResNet50V2", *Informatics in medicine unlocked,* 2020.

[30]   S. Dutta and S. K. Bandyopadhyay, "Machine learning approach for confirmation of COVID-19 cases: positive, negative, death and release," *medRxiv*, preprint, Mar. 2020.

[31]   X. Jiang, "Feature extraction for image recognition and computer vision", *2nd IEEE International Conference on Computer Science and Information Technology,* pp. 1-13, 2009.
[http://dx.doi.org/10.1109/ICCSIT.2009.5235014]

[32]   A.K. Das, S. Kalam, C. Kumar, and D. Sinha, "TLCoV- An automated Covid-19 screening model using Transfer Learning from chest X-ray images", *Chaos Solitons Fractals,* vol. 144, p. 110713, 2021.
[http://dx.doi.org/10.1016/j.chaos.2021.110713] [PMID: 33526961]

[33]   H.S. Alghamdi, G. Amoudi, S. Elhag, K. Saeedi, and J. Nasser, "Deep learning approaches for detecting COVID-19 from chest X-ray images: A survey", *IEEE Access,* vol. 9, pp. 20235-20254, 2021.
[http://dx.doi.org/10.1109/ACCESS.2021.3054484] [PMID: 34786304]

[34]   T. Mahmud, M.A. Rahman, and S.A. Fattah, "CovXNet: A multi-dilation convolutional neural network for automatic COVID-19 and other pneumonia detection from chest X-ray images with transferable multi-receptive feature optimization", *Comput. Biol. Med.,* vol. 122, p. 103869, 2020. [http://dx.doi.org/10.1016/j.compbiomed.2020.103869] [PMID: 32658740]

[35]   S. Hu, Y. Gao, Z. Niu, Y. Jiang, L. Li, X. Xiao, M. Wang, E.F. Fang, W. Menpes-Smith, J. Xia, H. Ye, and G. Yang, "Weakly supervised deep learning for covid-19 infection detection and classification from ct images", *IEEE Access,* vol. 8, pp. 118869-118883, 2020. [http://dx.doi.org/10.1109/ACCESS.2020.3005510]

[36]   K. Hara, H. Kataoka, and Y. Satoh, "Learning spatio-temporal features with 3d residual networks for action recognition", *Proceedings of the IEEE international conference on computer vision workshops,* pp. 3154-3160, 2017.

[37]   S. Roy, W. Menapace, S. Oei, B. Luijten, E. Fini, C. Saltori, I. Huijben, N. Chennakeshava, F. Mento, A. Sentelli, E. Peschiera, R. Trevisan, G. Maschietto, E. Torri, R. Inchingolo, A. Smargiassi, G. Soldati, P. Rota, A. Passerini, R.J.G. van Sloun, E. Ricci, and L. Demi, "Deep learning for classification and localization of COVID-19 markers in point-of-care lung ultrasound", *IEEE Trans. Med. Imaging,* vol. 39, no. 8, pp. 2676-2687, 2020. [http://dx.doi.org/10.1109/TMI.2020.2994459] [PMID: 32406829]

[38]   M.H. Mir, S. Jamwal, A. Mehbodniya, T. Garg, U. Iqbal, and I.A. Samori, "IoT-enabled framework for early detection and prediction of COVID-19 suspects by leveraging machine learning in cloud", *J. Healthc. Eng.,* vol. 2022, pp. 1-16, 2022. [http://dx.doi.org/10.1155/2022/7713939] [PMID: 35432824]

[39]   P. K. Sethy and S. K. Behera, "Detection of coronavirus disease (COVID-19) based on deep features," *Preprint*, Mar. 2020.

[40]   L. Wang, Z.Q. Lin, and A. Wong, "COVID-Net: a tailored deep convolutional neural network design for detection of COVID-19 cases from chest X-ray images", *Sci. Rep.,* vol. 10, no. 1, p. 19549, 2020. [http://dx.doi.org/10.1038/s41598-020-76550-z] [PMID: 33177550]

[41]   K. Hara, H. Kataoka, and Y. Satoh, "Learning spatio-temporal features with 3d residual networks for action recognition", *Proceedings of the IEEE international conference on computer vision workshops,* pp. 3154-3160, 2017.

[42]   T. Yan, P.K. Wong, H. Ren, H. Wang, J. Wang, and Y. Li, "Automatic distinction between COVID-19 and common pneumonia using multi-scale convolutional neural network on chest CT scans", *Chaos Solitons Fractals,* vol. 140, p. 110153, 2020. [http://dx.doi.org/10.1016/j.chaos.2020.110153] [PMID: 32834641]

[43]   S. Roy, W. Menapace, S. Oei, B. Luijten, E. Fini, C. Saltori, I. Huijben, N. Chennakeshava, F. Mento, A. Sentelli, E. Peschiera, R. Trevisan, G. Maschietto, E. Torri, R. Inchingolo, A. Smargiassi, G. Soldati, P. Rota, A. Passerini, R.J.G. van Sloun, E. Ricci, and L. Demi, "Deep learning for classification and localization of COVID-19 markers in point-of-care lung ultrasound", *IEEE Trans. Med. Imaging,* vol. 39, no. 8, pp. 2676-2687, 2020. [http://dx.doi.org/10.1109/TMI.2020.2994459] [PMID: 32406829]

[44]   A. Mobiny, P.A. Cicalese, S. Zare, P. Yuan, M. Abavisani, C.C. Wu, J. Ahuja, P.M. de Groot, and H. Van Nguyen, "Radiologist-level covid-19 detection using ct scans with detail-oriented capsule networks", *arXiv preprint arXiv:2004.07407,* 2020.

[45]   A.F.M. Saif, T. Imtiaz, S. Rifat, C. Shahnaz, W.P. Zhu, and M.O. Ahmad, "CapsCovNet: A modified capsule network to diagnose Covid-19 from multimodal medical imaging", *IEEE Trans. Artif. Intell.,* vol. 2, no. 6, pp. 608-617, 2021. [http://dx.doi.org/10.1109/TAI.2021.3104791] [PMID: 35582431]

[46]   S. Heidarian, P. Afshar, A. Mohammadi, M.J. Rafiee, A. Oikonomou, K.N. Plataniotis, and F. Naderkhani, "Ct-caps: Feature extraction-based automated framework for covid-19 disease identification from chest ct scans using capsule networks", *ICASSP 2021-2021 IEEE International*

Conference on Acoustics, Speech and Signal Processing (ICASSP), pp. 1040-1044, 2021.

[47]   Available from: https://github.com/ieee8023/covid-chestxray-dataset

[48]   Available from: https://www.kaggle.com/tawsifurrahman/covid19-radiography-database

CHAPTER 11

Automated Identification of Cloud-IoT-Based Sensitive Data in a Dataset

Sudipta Chandra[1,*], Soumya Ray[2] and Kamta Nath Mishra[2]

[1] *Abzooba India Infotech Private Limited, Kolkata, West Bangal, India*

[2] *Department of Computer Science and Engineering, Birla Institute of Technology, Mesra - Patna Campus, Bihar, India*

Abstract: The Internet of Things (IoT) is a booming trend in the current automation industry and is estimated to cover a considerable share of the international market in the near future. Sharing of IoT data, especially data with a potential risk of sensitive data exposure, poses challenges to organizations. The rapid growth of IoT data is found in diverse applications, and it is connected to different hardware and software platforms. This leads to a major issue at the time of executing the application. Data identification is made through anonymization procedures and de-identification procedures before sharing with a third party. The detection of data points that have the potential to expose sensitive information can be a tedious task, especially if done manually. Automating the task helps make identification much easier when dealing with a lot of data sets, both small and large. The current solution has been envisaged with the intention of helping to identify potential leakage of sensitive information using an easy-to-implement framework, as well as a solution for detecting potential quasi-identifiers in data.

Keywords: Anonymity, Automated detection, IoT security, IoT-centric data privacy, Sensitive IoT data.

INTRODUCTION

IoT data today is undergoing increased adoption of cloud technologies due to the ability to buy processing power and storage on-demand. This exposes enterprise data to the outside world, and hence, novel big data security measures need to be taken to secure data from falling into the wrong hands.

Detection of IoT data points that have the potential to expose sensitive information can be a tedious task, especially if done manually. Automating the

---
[*] **Corresponding author Sudipta Chandra:** Abzooba India Infotech Private Limited, Kolkata, West Bangal, India; E-mail: sudipta.chandra@gmail.com

H.S. Hota, Dinesh K. Sharma, Ayan Kumar Das & Ditipriya Sinha (Eds.)

task helps make identification much easier when dealing with a lot of data sets, both small and large.

The current solution has been envisaged with the intention of helping identify and prevent the potential leakage of sensitive information. In this work, we suggest a framework for the analysis of data for privacy leaks involving an implementation methodology for probabilistic detection of potential quasi-identifiers. The framework also suggests optimizations to the probabilistic detection to support unclean data.

It is important to understand some related concepts before we dive into the main content.

IoT Based Data privacy

IoT-centric data may need to be shared with third parties for analysis, further research, and when organizations have data-sharing agreements. Privacy of individuals in the fields of healthcare, government, *etc.*, is important. The health conditions of an individual are private as they may lead to social and financial issues, bias, differential treatment in the workplace, *etc.*

Analytical processing done on data should not expose personal data for users or granular details that would lead analysts to trace back the data to the original details. Data mining and predictive analytics techniques need to implement privacy-preserving techniques, *e.g.*, masking sensitive data and other anonymization techniques.

Sensitive IoT Data

Any IoT data that has the potential to cause monetary loss, expose an individual to social and personal privacy issues, or even threaten their well-being (*e.g.*, physical security) can be classified as sensitive data.

Some examples of sensitive data are credit card numbers, bank account numbers, salary, healthcare-related information, *etc.*

Anonymity

The collection and dissemination of data are growing at an increasing scale; therefore, there is a need for the value of this data for research and business. In research, this data is required for classification and statistical and predictive analysis. Sharing and publishing the data along with specific information on individuals may put the respondent's privacy at risk.

Anonymity is related to identifying a user. In the absence of an individual's name, the person can be identified through the Voter's ID number, SSN number, *etc.* A person can also be identified by a combination of attributes, *e.g.*, age, gender, and location. This is, of course, possible when the published data can be joined/merged with data sets listing specific information on these identities.

Quasi-Identifiers and K-Anonymity

Quasi-identifiers are a combination of attributes that can be used to uniquely identify individuals by linking to external data. The concept of k-anonymity is used to resolve this issue. In this method, data is generalized or suppressed to reduce granularity. If a record k in a dataset is indistinguishable from at least $k - 1$ other records with respect to every set of quasi-identifier attributes, the dataset can be called k-anonymous.

In this context, we may define quasi-sensitive attribute values as a set of attribute values that may not be sensitive when used individually but have the potential to reveal sensitive information about an individual when used together [1]. This can be done using record linkage, *i.e.*, by merging information from two data sets using a common identifier.

MOTIVATION

Identification of IoT data attributes that may have sensitive data is important before release to a third party, and once identified, standard anonymization or de-identification procedures can be applied to prevent leakage of sensitive information.

Leakage of sensitive information to a third party or the outside world may lead to unwanted lawsuits, financial losses, security lapses, and individual privacy concerns. The current solution has been envisaged with the intention of helping to identify and prevent the potential leakage of sensitive information.

• The major focus of this paper is to suggest an easy-to-implement framework for the analysis of IoT data for privacy leaks as well as a solution for detecting potential quasi-identifiers in data.

• The contributions of this chapter are listed below:

• A framework for the analysis of data for privacy leaks is suggested.

• The framework suggests an implementation methodology for the probabilistic detection of potential quasi-identifiers.

• The framework suggests optimizations to the probabilistic detection to support unclean data.

• A custom prototype was developed to test the feasibility of the above framework. This prototype was meta-data-driven with reporting capabilities and user authentication.

IDENTIFICATION OF QUASI-IDENTIFIERS

Anonymity is related to identifying a user. In the absence of an individual's name, the person can be identified through the Voter's ID number, SSN number, *etc.* A person can also be identified by a combination of attributes, *e.g.*, age, gender, and location. This is, of course, possible when the published data can be joined/merged with data sets listing specific information on these identities.

Quasi-identifiers are attributes that can be used to uniquely identify individuals by linking to external data. The concept of k-anonymity [15] was introduced to counter this security issue. In this method, data is generalized or suppressed to reduce granularity. If a record k in a dataset is indistinguishable from at least k − 1 other records with respect to every set of quasi-identifier attributes, the dataset can be called k-anonymous.

While it is difficult to know the background information an adversary may have, it would be useful to predict potential quasi-identifiers so that appropriate actions can be taken to make the data anonymous.

There are several solutions to achieving k-anonymity – by masking the data, generalization, variance, or even substitution. This process is called the de-identification of data. Existing proposals for de-identification, though, do not suggest an easy way of automatically identifying the potential quasi-identifiers.

The below section summarizes some related work in this area.

Related Work

C. Du Mouza *et al.*, in their paper on the automatic detection of sensitive information from a database [38], suggest a rule-based approach along with a combination of natural language processing. Their methodology requires a human expert to specify rules indicating sensitive information. NLP is used to identify the attributes that are semantically close to the defined rules. A sensitivity score is calculated for each matching attribute, and the score is higher for the higher number of rule matches.

S. Lodha *et al.*, in their paper on Probabilistic Anonymity [39], came up with probabilistic detection of potential quasi-identifiers by establishing a connection between the number of distinct values for a combination of attribute columns.

R. Motwani *et al.*, in their paper, suggest ways of detecting quasi-identifiers using two natural measures for distinct ratio and separation ratio [40]. For large data sets, they suggest algorithms select samples and present algorithms to detect all minimum keys and henceforth derive quasi-identifiers.

A. Omer *et al.* present a selective algorithm [41] to identify a minimal attribute subset and evaluate its significance. They aim to find an attribute subset that is able to identify the maximum number of rows in the data set.

The Table **1** below provides a comparative analysis of the above-listed algorithms and methodologies:

Table 1. Comparison of algorithms for detection of quasi-identifiers.

-	Detection	De-identification	Basic Methodology	Limitations	Domain	Large Datasets
C. Du Mouza	Sensitive Information.	None	Generalized technique	Applicable for Single attributes.	Generic	Not Established
S. Lodha	Quasi Identifiers	Random Sampling	Probabilistic	Not fit for non-standardized data	Generic	Not Established
R. Motwani	Quasi Identifiers	Generalized Approach	Random sampling. Improvements to the greedy algorithm, which requires multiple scans of the table.	Approximation method adopted	Generic	Yes
A. Omer	Quasi Identifiers	Generalization	Generalization hierarchies and decomposition.	Heterogeneous Data	Generic	Not Established
N. Mohammed	Not Applicable	Privacy-preserving approach	Probabilistic, Distributed Anonymization	Probabilistic method	Healthcare	Yes

PROPOSED FRAMEWORK

The identification of data attributes that may have sensitive data is important before release to a third party. The identified standard anonymization or de-identification procedures can be applied to prevent the leakage of sensitive information.

Leakage of sensitive information to a 3rd party or the outside world may lead to unwanted lawsuits, financial losses, security lapses, and individual privacy concerns. The current framework has been envisaged with the intention of helping to identify potential leakage of sensitive information.

The proposed framework focuses on building an easy-to-implement solution for the analysis of data for privacy leaks as well as a solution for detecting potential quasi-identifiers in data.

Features

Listed below are the salient features of the proposed framework:

• The framework suggests an architecture and meta-data-driven system to easily add privacy detection algorithms.

• The framework suggests a generic system that can be implemented in a distributed environment wherein the processing can be on one server and the reporting from another.

• The framework can be extended to implement a HIPAA-compliant privacy leak detection system. All elements required to be detected for HIPAA compliance can be implemented as individual detectors and plugged into the system. The sample implementation illustrates some of these (*e.g.*, Pin Code detection, email address detection, detection of dates, *etc.*).

• The framework identifies a method to query the Wordnet database and find synonyms, *i.e.*, find words with similar meanings. Columns in the data set are matched against both the original keyword queried and the synonym identified. The data owner can take appropriate actions based on matches found. This can be beneficial if the data contains variations of the same value. In this case, they are taken as a singular value.

• The framework provides a mechanism to detect potential columns that can be quasi-identifiers. The framework leverages probabilistic detection to handle this situation [39].

• The framework suggests optimizations to improve accuracy:

• By similarity matching, calculate the distance between 2 strings and then calculate probabilistic anonymity. This can be beneficial for unclean data with typing mistakes and spelling mistakes. The distance threshold can indicate the acceptance of a variation in 2 values. Two similar values satisfying the threshold criteria are taken as a singular value.

- For continuous variables, the framework enables the user to ignore minor variances by specifying a variance threshold. This can be beneficial for values where minor differences may occur, which should be ignored, *e.g.*, GPS values specifying latitude and longitude - minor variance may be treated as the same location instance.

Compatibility to Data Governance

Healthcare Data Governance Laws like HIPAA (The Health Insurance Portability and Accountability Act of 1996) require data providers and owners to follow certain privacy-preserving precautions to ensure that a patient's personal data does not get leaked.

As part of HIPAA, identifiers like names, geographic information, and all elements of dates, telephone numbers, fax numbers, email addresses, account numbers, *etc.*, need to be de-identified (masked, grouped, or removed) for a data set to be compliant [39].

The current framework enables the addition of each individual detector with the detection logic, and they are automatically processed and can be reported for further action. Implementation of the detection of these individual identifiers is beyond the scope of this paper – though the prototype implementation can be used as a good starting point. The prototype implementation illustrates some examples of the detection of dates, email addresses, account numbers, pin codes, *etc.*, to illustrate the usage.

BASIC FRAMEWORK METHODOLOGY

For detecting privacy leaks at a row/column level, all values in the files are parsed, while this can be selected depending on the discretion of the implementation. Each detection algorithm is configured using metadata and can be turned on/off. The framework would detect this at run time.

Active detectors are initialized at run time and are run on a data value, and the results obtained are stored back in storage.

The Algorithm (**1**) below lays out the process for implementing the framework and integrating detection classes.

Algorithm 1: Detector Framework

1.	Load Global Configuration GLC from storage to memory
2.	Read all Detector Configurations D from the storage
3.	Initialize Data Source DS
4.	Generate a new Analysis Instance A and get a unique identifier A_{id}
5.	Set Analysis Status "In Progress" for A_{id}
6.	Read list of files F
7.	For each file F_i
8.	For each Detector D_j
9.	If D_j is Active
10.	Read Class Name for D_j
11.	Initialize D_j
12.	For each data value V_k in F_i
13.	Call detection method of D_j
14.	Store Results R_m in Memory
15.	Read Maximum Detector Count DC for Detectors from GLC.
16.	If Count (R_m) < DC
17.	Continue to V_{k+1}
18.	else
19.	Quit Detection
20.	End If
21.	End For
22.	End If
23.	End For
24.	End For
25.	Save R to Storage/DB for A_{id}
26.	Set Analysis Status "Completed" for A_{id}
27.	

Algorithm 1. Detector framework.

Detection of Quasi-identifiers

Detection of quasi-identifiers for small data sets should be a trivial task as a domain expert can easily identify the sensitive attributes on manual scan and infer possible quasi-identifiers on manual analysis.

For large data sets with a lot of attributes, the task can be overwhelming. While there is no fool-proof method of inferring potential quasi-identifiers, we can get an indication of the potential ones by probabilistic analysis. One such method was suggested by Lodha *et al.* [39]. In this work, we have attempted to provide an optimal implementation of the probabilistic determination of quasi-identifiers as part of the framework. The Algorithm (**2**) for probabilistic determination is formulated below:

Algorithm 2: Algorithm for suggesting potential quasi-identifiers in a data set

---

1.   Read file

2.   Iterate rows

3.   Calculate the number of distinct values n for the whole data

4.   For each column Ci in the column set C

5.   Add column to column combinations set U

6.   For all previous columns from U

7.   Create and add unique column sets with the new column C_i and previous columns-sets in U.

8.   For each column set calculate and store no of distinct values as n_c.

9.   End for

10. End For

11. CloseFile

12. For each column-set CS_i in U

13.   Start with column-sets with largest size

14.   Loop till k, where k is the size of the column set.

15. $D = d_1 * d_2 * \ldots d_k$

16.   End Loop

17.   If D < n then

18.   The maximum expected number of singletons is bounded above by D/e.

19.   Else if D >= n then

20.   The maximum expected number of singletons is bounded above by $ne^{-n/D}$.

21.   End if

22.   If CS_i is not a potential quasi identifier then

23.   All sub sets of CS_i are not potential quasi identifiers.

24.   End if

25. End For

26.

Algorithm 2. Algorithm for suggesting potential quasi-identifiers in a data set.

The above algorithm is explained step-wise below:

The first step is to construct a set of all candidate attribute sets. Essentially, this process can be stated as "from a set of all attributes A, what are the possible combinations of attributes available from A". Hence, if n is the number of attributes, and we choose maximum q attributes for each quasi-identifier, as per rules of combination, we have $\binom{n}{k}$ choices. To keep this manageable, we choose a small size for k (say 3). Then, we calculate the total rows (n) in the data set. This can be an expensive operation, so known attributes that have less potential to qualify as quasi-identifiers can be filtered out.

Improvements to Probabilistic Detection

Lodha's algorithm for probabilistic detection of quasi-identifiers [39] works well with data sets that have attribute values distinctly identifiable from each other.

However, consider the case of GPS coordinates. A latitude or longitude reading for the same location may be marginally apart for every instance. Unless we allow scope for considering an error ignorance threshold, the same location readings would be considered as multiple distinct values and hence lead to erroneous detection.

This affects the calculation of n_c in Algorithm 2. The improved algorithm needs to incorporate the modified logic for calculating n_c (Algorithm **3**).

Algorithm 3: Calculation of distinct column values count for String attributes

---

1.   For All values V for column C_i of column set C

2. T_i = Threshold for Column C_i

3. VS_i = All distinct values for attribute C_i

4.   V = Current value being processed.

5. HK_i = Least Key in VS_i Strictly Greater Than V.

6. LK_i = Greatest Key in VS_i Strictly less than V.

7. DH_i = Jaro Winkler Similarity Distance between HK_i and V

8. DL_i = Jaro Winkler Similarity Distance between LK_i and V

9.   if $DH_i \geq T_i$ OR $DL_i \geq T_i$ Then

10.   No Action Needed

11.   else

12.   n = n+1

13.   Add V to VS_i

14.   End IF

15.   End For

16.

Algorithm 3. Calculation of distinct column values count for String attributes.

The case may be similar to unclean data. The point of data entry may not always do a proper spell check for free text values, or similar data from multiple data sources integrated together may lead to unclean data wherein the same attribute value may be spelled slightly differently or slightly erroneously. Considering an edit distance threshold and integrating it into the algorithm have the potential to improve accuracy in such cases.

The algorithm for handling continuous attributes to consider attributes with marginal differences is presented below (Algorithm **4**):

Presented below is a sample of data used for analysis. Due to GPS imperfections, the identified latitudes for Norristown in 2 consecutive readings come up as 40.121 and 4.112. When used with a tolerance threshold of 0.01, both values can be correctly identified in the same bucket (Fig. **1**).

Algorithm 4: Calculation of distinct column values count for Continuous attributes

---

1. For All values V for column C_i of column set C
2. T_i = Threshold for Column C_i
3. VS_i = Sorted List of all distinct values for attribute C_i
4.   V = Current value being processed.
5. HK_i = Least Key in VS_i Strictly Greater Than V.
6. LK_i = Greatest Key in VS_i Strictly less than V.
7. DH_i = HK_i - V
8. DL_i = LK_i - V
9. if Abs(DH_i) <= T_i OR Abs(DL_i)<= T_i Then
10.   No Action needed
11.   else
12.   n = n+1
13.   Add V to VS_i
14.   End IF
15. End For
16.

Algorithm 4. Calculation of distinct column values count for Continuous attributes.

lat	lng	zip	twp
40.2978759	-75.5812935	19525	NEW HANOVER
40.2580614	-75.2646799	19446	HATFIELD TOWNSHIP
40.1211818	-75.3519752	19401	NORRISTOWN
40.112153	-75.343513	19401	NORRISTOWN
40.2534732	-75.283245	19446	LANSDALE
40.1821111	-75.1277951	19044	HORSHAM

Fig. (1). SEQ Figure * ARABIC 1 - Sample Values.

The below analysis results demonstrate the optimization effects before and after optimization. Before the optimizations in algorithm 3 or 4 are applied, we get results that do not reflect what should be the actual scenario (Fig. **2**).

QID Expectations

911.csv

Maximum Expected Fraction of rows that may be singletons

Column Set	Expected Fraction
[lat, lng, twp]	1
[lng, zip, twp]	1
[lat, lng, zip]	1
[lat, zip, twp]	1

Fig. (2). Results before.

Now, we define a tolerance threshold for the above columns as below (Fig. **3**):

algorithm_id	file_name	column_name	property_name	property_value	🔍 id *
8	911.csv	lat	VALUE_VAR_IGNORE	0.01	3
8	911.csv	lng	VALUE_VAR_IGNORE	0.01	4
8	911.csv	twp	STRING_VAL_DISTANCE	0.9	5

Fig. (3). Threshold values defined for sample analysis

After optimizing the algorithm as per 3 and 4 and considering the above tolerance threshold, we notice a considerable improvement in the accuracy of results (Fig. **4**).

QID Expectations

911.csv

Maximum Expected Fraction of rows that may be singletons

Column Set	Expected Fraction
[lat, lng, twp]	0.01
[lng, zip, twp]	0.02
[lat, lng, zip]	1
[lat, zip, twp]	0.01

Fig. (4). QID expectations.

SYSTEM PROTOTYPE

A sample implementation of the suggested framework was done to evaluate the concept. The above diagram illustrates the overall high-level system architecture of the suggested framework (Fig. **5**).

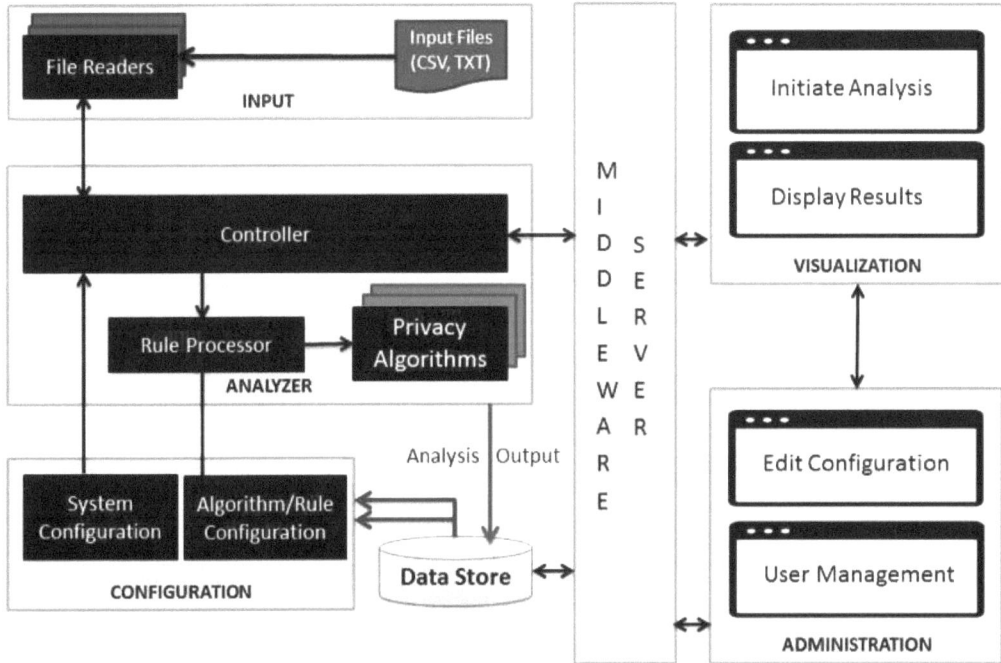

Fig. (5). System architecture of prototype.

The input module reads the source files, and the analyzer module reads the global system configuration and algorithm configuration from the metadata store. Once done, active privacy algorithms are run on each data item of a file, and results are stored in a JSON format in the DB. The Dashboard module displays the analysis output to the user, and the Admin module helps configure the system.

Input Module

The input module accepts data into the system in the form of CSV/TXT files. The location of the CSV files is configurable. The program will read all CSV/TXT files from the source directory one at a time. Privacy algorithms are run on a per-file basis. It is possible to configure the system to accept any file extension by setting configuration parameters.

Privacy Analyzer

The Privacy Analyzer module reads the data values from the file and runs the configured detection algorithms iteratively. Privacy algorithms can be added to the software by implementing the Interface: com.privacy.parsers.IPrivacyDetector and implementing the method: run detector.

For every new privacy algorithm implemented, there needs to be an entry in the algorithm configuration table.

Dashboard Module

The Dashboard module is responsible for showing the results of the analysis to the user. Initially, a summary is presented. When the user clicks on "Show Details," the results of that particular analysis run are shown to the user (Fig. **6**).

Analysis Status Summary

Analysis ID	Requested On	Start Date/Time	End Date/Time	Status	Additional Details	
2	2016-12-01 12:25:47.0	2016-12-01 12:23:32.0	2016-12-01 12:25:47.0	COMPLETE		Show Details
1	2016-11-30 17:32:11.0	2016-11-30 17:30:02.0	2016-11-30 17:32:11.0	COMPLETE		Show Details

Analysis Details

Ambulatory Surgical Measures-State.csv

Complications - Hospital.csv

Detection Results

Algorithm	Column Name	Value For Review
DateDetector	Measure Start Date	04/01/2012
DateDetector	Measure End Date	03/31/2015

Execution Time Taken

Duration (Seconds)	Started On	Completed On
95	Thu Dec 01 12:24:10 IST 2016	Thu Dec 01 12:25:46 IST 2016

Fig. (6). Analysis summary and details.

CONCLUSION

The current framework suggests an automated mechanism for running security algorithms on data. The goal is to detect potential privacy issues, and hence, the data owner is aware of the potential problems and can take corrective action. A probabilistic method of identifying the potential combination of columns that may lead to privacy leaks (Quasi Identifiers) when joined with public data is presented along with optimizations for unclean continuous and random data [44, 45].

There is scope for a lot of improvement and continued research. The framework can be enhanced to take corrective action in an automated manner. Currently, the prototype has been tested on publicly available data sets. There is scope for improvement, both in terms of performance and accuracy, when it can be tested on data of larger volume.

The framework can be extended to connect to actual Big Data stores like HDFS, Cassandra, *etc.*, by providing the appropriate enhancements. The process of detection can be optimized by using map reduction or even frameworks on top of map-reduce. The detection threads can be delegated to the point of data source, and hence, by in situ data processing, performance can be improved, and network overhead can be minimized.

ACKNOWLEDGEMENTS

This research work is supported by Birla Institute of Technology, Mesra, Ranchi. The authors would also like to thank the anonymous reviewers for their constructive comments and feedback on the chapter.

REFERENCES

[1]   P. Shi, L. Xiong, and B. Fung, "Anonymizing data with quasi-sensitive attribute values", *Proc. ACM CIKM*, pp. 1389-1392, 2010.

[2]   J. Dean, and S. Ghemawat, "MapReduce: Simpled Data Processing on Large Clusters", *Proceedings of 6th Symposium on Operating Systems Design and Implementation,* pp. 137-149, 2004.

[3]   K. Shvachko, H. Kuang, S. Radia, and R. Chansler, "The Hadoop distributed file system", *26th Symposium on Mass Storage Systems and Technologies, MSST,* pp. 1-10, 2010. [http://dx.doi.org/10.1109/MSST.2010.5496972]

[4]   J. Hurwitz, A. Nugent, F. Halper, and M. Kaufman, *Big Data For Dummies*. Hoboken, John Wiley & Sons, Inc., 2013.

[5]   BigDataWorkingGroup, "Expanded Top Ten Big Data Security and Privacy Challenges," *Cloud Security   Alliance,*   2013.   Available   from: https://downloads.cloudsecurityalliance.org/initiatives/bdwg/Expanded_Top_Ten_ Big_Data_Security_and_Privacy_Challenges.pdf [Accessed: 27-Feb-2016]

[6]   J. Heyens, K. Greshake, and E. Petryka, "MongoDB databases at risk – Several thousand MongoDBs without access control on the Internet," *Saarland Univ., Center for IT Security, Privacy and Accountability,* 2015.

[7]   KoanHealth, "mongoid-encrypted-fields: A library for storing encrypted data in Mongo," GitHub repository, 2012." Available from: https://github.com/KoanHealth/mongoid-encrypted-fields [Accessed: 05-Apr-2016]

[8]   Z. Xiao, and Y. Xiao, "Achieving Accountable MapReduce in cloud computing", *Future Gener. Comput. Syst.,* vol. 30, pp. 1-13, 2014.
[http://dx.doi.org/10.1016/j.future.2013.07.001]

[9]   F. Liu, X. Shu, D. Yao, and A.R. Butt, "Privacy-Preserving Scanning of Big Content for Sensitive Data Exposure with MapReduce", *Proceedings of the 5th ACM Conference on Data and Application Security and Privacy - CODASPY '15,* pp. 195-206, 2015.
[http://dx.doi.org/10.1145/2699026.2699106]

[10]   A. Z. Broder, "Identifying and filtering near-duplicate documents". vol. 1848, Lecture Notes in Computer Science, R. Giancarlo and D. Sankoff, Eds. Montreal, Canada: Springer, 2000, pp. 1–10.

[11]   S-H. Kim, and I-Y. Lee, "Data Block Management Scheme Based on Secret Sharing for HDFS", *10th International Conference on Broadband and Wireless Computing, Communication and Applications (BWCCA),* pp. 51-56, 2015.
[http://dx.doi.org/10.1109/BWCCA.2015.70]

[12]   A. Shamir, "How to Share a Secret", *Communications of the ACM1,* vol. 22, no. 11, pp. 612-613, 1979.
[http://dx.doi.org/10.1145/359168.359176]

[13]   R. Agrawal, and R. Srikant, "Privacy-preserving data mining", *Proceedings of the 2000 ACM SIGMOD international conference on Management of data - SIGMOD,* vol. 29, no. 2, pp. 439-450, 2000.
[http://dx.doi.org/10.1145/342009.335438]

[14]   Y. Lindell, and B. Pinkas, "Privacy-preserving Data Mining", *Crypto,* vol. 29, pp. 36-54, 2000.

[15]   P. Samarati, and L. Sweeney, "Protecting Privacy when Disclosing Information: k-Anonymity and its Enforcement Through Generalization and Suppresion", *Proc of the IEEE Symposium on Research in Security and Privacy,* pp. 384-393, 1998.

[16]   A. Machanavajjhala, D. Kifer, J. Gehrke, and M. Venkitasubramaniam, "L-diversity", *ACM Transactions on Knowledge Discovery from Data,* vol. 1, no. 1, p. 3, 2007.
[http://dx.doi.org/10.1145/1217299.1217302]

[17]   C.C. Aggarwal, and P.S. Yu, "A General Survey of Privacy-Preserving Data Mining Models and Algorithms,", *Privacy-preserving data mining, Springer US,* pp. 11-52, 2008.
[http://dx.doi.org/10.1007/978-0-387-70992-5_2]

[18]   D. Boneh, and M. Franklin, "Identity-Based Encryption from the Weil Pairing", *SIAM J. Comput.,* vol. 32, no. 3, pp. 586-615, 2003.
[http://dx.doi.org/10.1137/S0097539701398521]

[19]   A. Shamir, "Identity-Based Cryptosystems and Signature Schemes", *Lect. Notes Comput. Sci.,* vol. 196, pp. 47-53, 1984.
[http://dx.doi.org/10.1007/3-540-39568-7_5]

[20]   J. Baek, Q. Vu, J. Liu, X. Huang, and Y. Xiang, "A secure cloud computing based framework for big data information management of smart grid", *Cloud Computing, IEEE Transactions on,* vol. pp, no. 99, p. 1, 2014.

[21]   A. Sahai, and B. Waters, "Fuzzy Identity-Based Encryption", *Annual International Conference on the Theory and Applications of Cryptographic Techniques,* pp. 457-473, 2005.

[22]   A. Lewko, and B. Waters, "Decentralizing attribute-based encryption", *Lecture Notes in Computer Science (including subseries Lecture Notes in Artificial Intelligence and Lecture Notes in Bioinformatics),* vol. 6632, pp. 568-588, 2011.

[http://dx.doi.org/10.1007/978-3-642-20465-4_31]

[23]   K. Yang, X. Jia, and K. Ren, "Secure and Verifiable Policy Update Outsourcing for Big Data Access Control in the Cloud", *Transactions on Parallel and Distributed Systems,* vol. pp, no. 99, pp. 1-1, 2014.

[24]   J. Gao, S. Li, T. Zhang, J. Gao, and Y. Park, *A Sticky Policy Framework for Big Data Security,* pp. 130-137, 2015.

[25]   C. Gentry, "A Fully Homomorphic Encryption Scheme," Ph.D. dissertation, Dept. Comput. Sci., Stanford Univ., Stanford, CA, USA, 2009.

[26]   Z. Brakerski, C. Gentry, and V. Vaikuntanathan, "Fully Homomorphic Encryption without Bootstrapping", *Innovations in Theoretical Computer Science,* pp. 309-325, 2012.
[http://dx.doi.org/10.1145/2090236.2090262]

[27]   Z. Brakerski, "Fully homomorphic encryption without modulus switching from classical GapSVP", *Lecture Notes in Computer Science (including subseries Lecture Notes in Artificial Intelligence and Lecture Notes in Bioinformatics),* vol. 7417, pp. 868-886, 2012.
[http://dx.doi.org/10.1007/978-3-642-32009-5_50]

[28]   V.O. Waziri, J.K. Alhassan, I. Ismaila, and M.N. Dogonyaro, "Big Data Analytics and Data Security in the Cloud *via* Fully Homomorphic Encryption", *International Journal of Computer, Electrical, Automation, Control and Information Engineering,* vol. 9, no. 3, pp. 744-753, 2015.

[29]   C. Dwork, "Differential privacy", *Proceedings of the 33rd International Colloquium on Automata, Languages and Programming,* pp. 1-12, 2006.

[30]   K.M.P. Shrivastva, M.a. Rizvi, and S. Singh, "Big Data Privacy Based on Differential Privacy a Hope for Big Data", *2014 International Conference on Computational Intelligence and Communication Networks,* pp. 776-781, 2014.
[http://dx.doi.org/10.1109/CICN.2014.167]

[31]   J. Li, J. Li, D. Xie, and Z. Cai, "Secure Auditing and Deduplicating Data in Cloud", *IEEE Trans. Comput.,* vol. 9340, no. c, pp. 1-1, 2015.

[32]   A.W. Toga, and I.D. Dinov, "Sharing big biomedical data", *J. Big Data,* vol. 2, no. 1, p. 7, 2015.
[http://dx.doi.org/10.1186/s40537-015-0016-1] [PMID: 26929900]

[33]   C. Liu, J. Chen, L.T. Yang, X. Zhang, C. Yang, R. Ranjan, and K. Rao, "Authorized public auditing of dynamic big data storage on cloud with efficient verifiable fine-grained updates", *IEEE Trans. Parallel Distrib. Syst.,* vol. 25, no. 9, pp. 2234-2244, 2014.
[http://dx.doi.org/10.1109/TPDS.2013.191]

[34]   R. Hasan, R. Sion, and M. Winslett, "Introducing secure provenance: problems and challenges", *Proceedings of the 2007 ACM workshop,* pp. 13-18, 2007.

[35]   R. Agrawal, A. Imran, C. Seay, and J. Walker, "A Layer Based Architecture for Provenance in Big Data," in *Proc. 2014 IEEE Int. Conf. Big Data*, Washington, DC, USA, Oct. 2014, pp. 1–7.

[36]   M.S. Lin, C.Y. Chiu, Y.J. Lee, and H.K. Pao, ""Malicious URL filtering - A big data application," in Proceedings - 2013 IEEE International Conference on Big Data", *Big Data,* vol. 2013, pp. 589-596, 2013.

[37]   E. Yoon and A. Squicciarini, "Toward Detecting Compromised MapReduce Workers through Log Analysis," *2014 14th IEEE/ACM International Symposium on Cluster, Cloud and Grid Computing,* Chicago, IL, USA, 2014, pp. 41-50.
[http://dx.doi.org/10.1109/CCGrid.2014.120]

[38]   C. Du Mouza, E. Métais, N. Lammari, J. Akoka, T. Aubonnet, I. Comyn-Wattiau, H. Fadili, and S.S.S. Cherfi, "Towards an automatic detection of sensitive information in a database", *2nd International Conference on Advances in Databases, Knowledge, and Data Applications, DBKDA 2010,* pp. 247-252, 2010.

[http://dx.doi.org/10.1109/DBKDA.2010.17]

[39]   S. Lodha, and D. Thomas, "Probabilistic anonymity", *First ACM SIGKDD International Workshop, PinKDD 2007,* pp. 56-79, 2007.San Jose, CA, USA

[40]   K. Shirudkar, and D. Motwani, "Big-Data Security", *International Journal of Advanced Research in Computer Science and Software Engineering Research,* vol. 5, no. 3, pp. 1100-1109, 2015.

[41]   A.M. Omer, M. Murtadha, and B.I.N. Mohamad, "Simple and effective method for selecting quasi-identifier", *J. Theor. Appl. Inf. Technol.,* vol. 89, no. 2, pp. 512-517, 2016.

[42]   N. Mohammed, B.C.M. Fung, P.C.K. Hung, and C.K. Lee, "Centralized and Distributed Anonymization for High-Dimensional Healthcare Data", *ACM Trans. Knowl. Discov. Data,* vol. 4, no. 4, pp. 1-33, 2010.
       [http://dx.doi.org/10.1145/1857947.1857950]

[43]   C.C. Aggarwal, "On k -anonymity and the curse of dimensionality", *Proceedings of the 31st VLDB Conference,* pp. 901-909, 2005.

[44]   S. Ray, K.N. Mishra, and S. Dutta, "Big Data Security Issues from the Perspective of IoT and Cloud Computing: A Review", *Recent Advances in Computer Science and Communications,* vol. 14, no. 7, pp. 2057-2078, 2021.
       [http://dx.doi.org/10.2174/2666255813666200224092717]

[45]   S Ray, K N Mishra, and S Dutta, "Susceptible data classification and security reassurance in cloud-IoT based computing environment", *Sadhna Journal of Engineering Sciences, Springer,* vol. 46, p. 25, 2021.

CHAPTER 12

Blockchain and IoT-Based Smart Agriculture Supply Chain Management

Rishikesh[1,*], **Raj Vikram**[2] and **Arpita Srivastava**[1]

[1] *Department of Computer Science and Engineering, National Institute of Technology, Patna, Bihar, India*

[2] *Department of Computer Science and Engineering, ITER, Siksha 'O' Anusandhan, Bhubneshwar, Odisha, India*

Abstract: Blockchain is a widely recognized technology that has grown in prominence over time. It first gained popularity due to its use in Bitcoin. Because of its reliable security features, blockchain has been extensively employed in a variety of domains. The agricultural supply chain is one field where blockchain can be especially useful, as it provides benefits such as data immutability, transparency, and the ability to disregard middlemen. As a consequence of this, academics are working hard to figure out how to build a smart infrastructure for supply chain management that combines the security of blockchain with the promise of the Internet of Things (IoT). The primary goal of this study is to examine the structure and relationships of all entities participating in the agricultural supply chain. Smart contracts are crucial in such an environment. They are used to facilitate secure and automated interactions between various parties, such as farmers and consumers, farmers and delivery workers, and farmers and quality control authorities. These smart contracts ensure that every participant works in a coordinated manner. We used the remix IDE and the solidity programming language's smart contracts to create this solution. We compared blockchain transaction submission messages and node communications during the implementation phase. Customer messages, in particular, tend to be larger due to the inclusion of additional information such as registration, verification, purchase placing, and order confirmation. The authority's messages, on the other hand, are the smallest, as they merely demand the product's initial rating. This research intends to develop a robust and efficient agricultural supply chain management system that benefits all stakeholders by using the potential of blockchain technology and integrating IoT.

Keywords: Blockchain, IoT, Smart agriculture, Supply chain management.

* **Corresponding author Rishikesh:** Department of Computer Science and Engineering, National Institute of Technology, Patna, Bihar, India; E-mail: rishikesh.ph21.cs@nitp.ac.in

H.S. Hota, Dinesh K. Sharma, Ayan Kumar Das & Ditipriya Sinha (Eds.)

INTRODUCTION

The agriculture supply chain management system increases crop productivity and quality, as well as creates an infrastructure to sell agriculture products from farmers to customers. In blockchain-oriented agriculture supply chain management, because there is no third-party engagement in agriculture infrastructure, both farmers and customers get profit. Smart agriculture relies heavily on IoT. In smart agriculture, IoT sensors are utilized to gather information across the supply chain, and after that, data is processed. The IoT-based system often suffers from the risk of data tampering in the smart agriculture supply chain. A rogue network user can disrupt the IoT network, eavesdrop on data, and modify it. Product security in the supply chain for agricultural management can be enhanced through the transparency property of blockchain, where every user of the network has access to the shared ledger [3]. Another significant component is traceability. With the timestamp field in the metadata of the blockchain, one can track the origin of the product, the producer to which the product belongs, harvesting and production dates, and so on. When an unreliable producer or supplier joins the system and undermines the functioning of IoT-based smart agriculture, blockchain is one of the upcoming technologies that record the IoT data in blocks and make it tamper-resistant. The unalterable, tamper-proof character of the system enhances its integrity and secrecy. Cryptographic hashing is one of the crucial and fundamental attributes of blockchain technology. It is a ledger-based transaction system that upholds the confidentiality of user transactions and identification. The blockchain is explored in the current study in relation to IoT-based smart agriculture, which makes use of smart contracts to facilitate communication between farmers and consumers as well as between farmers and delivery personnel. The lack of a third party decreases product prices while simultaneously enhancing transaction security. The "Quality Assurance Authority" validates the quality of the product generated by the farmers and stores it in the *product* blockchain. Because of the immutability of blockchain, no one can mess with it. In the proposed architecture, a farmer smart contract is defined to retain the farmer's information. There are 'N' farmers, each of whom is capable of cultivating and selling 'M' crops. The farmer provides crop information as well as personal information to the government authority. The goal of the government authority is to provide a certificate based on the rating scale (which ranges from Low < Medium < Good). The farmer decides the crop's pricing and adds it to the available crop for sale based on the rating and other available things that are similar to the crop. There is always a chance that the farmer will act maliciously or deceitfully. The authorities will communicate the farmer's information to the IPFS in order to lessen that risk. Information about the farmer is hashed and preserved on the blockchain. Customers can place online orders and view the details of the crops offered by multiple farmers. Payment for the product should be handled through the payment contract. The farmer gets notified after the order is entered into the order contract. The farmer then arranges for the product to be sent with the assistance of an appropriate delivery associate. The consumer acknowledges receipt to the farmer, and the distributor also sends an appreciation notification. Simultaneously, an agricultural receipt message is delivered to the payment contract *via* the customer and distributor. The payments are subsequently credited to the beneficiary using the payment contract (Fig. **1**).

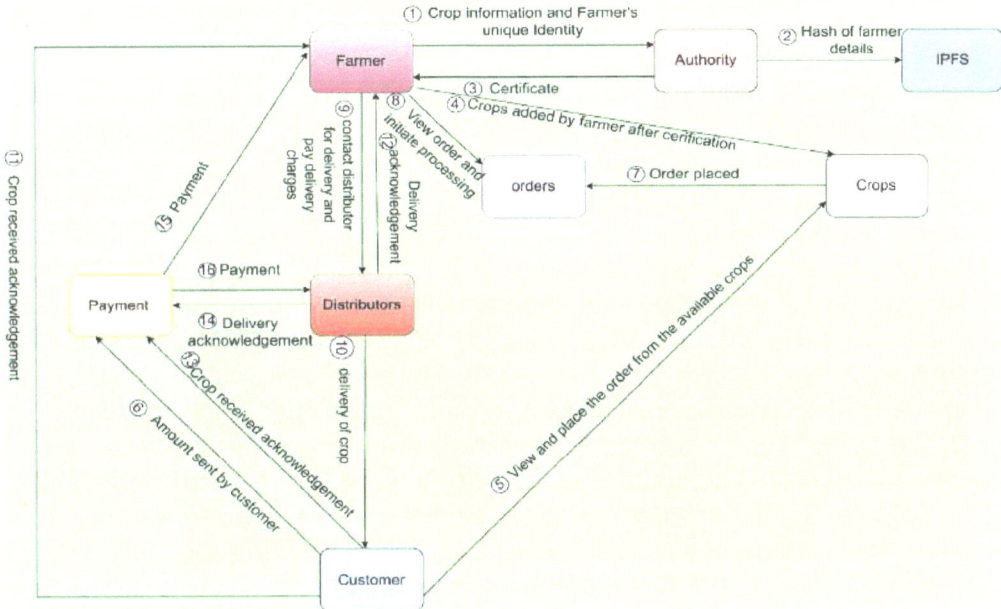

Fig. (1). Smart agriculture.

RELATED WORK

Blockchain is a network-wide shared data repository that maintains data as blocks of transactions, with each block containing a cryptographic hash that references it to the block immediately before it. Traditional databases can be distinguished from blockchain in the way that it manages information [1]. Blockchain eliminates the requirement for a trustworthy central authority by utilizing peer-t--peer node connections. The white paper "Bitcoin: A Peer-to-Peer Electronic Cash System" [2] revives this idea. Academic and corporate researchers are focusing on this technology using its enhanced security characteristics.

Several works have been proposed in numerous industries using this trending technology, including agriculture supply chain [1, 3], smart transportation [21], smart land registration [22], and many more. The supply chain for agricultural commodities ought not to be denied access to this technology. Several initiatives have been taken to make transactions reliable and transparent for all stakeholders involved in the supply chain, including farmers. Malik *et al.* [4] offer a three-tier production chain that is blockchain-based. The manufacturing process guarantees that data is provided to the end user. According to the authors' findings, the system is exceptionally fast and scalable to huge numbers of customers, as well as flexible to security concerns. The authors in a study [5] suggested a supply chain architecture by utilizing blockchain technology that is capable of managing supply chain stakeholders and the product production process. The technique is being used in the dairy business. The authors [6] discussed grain supply chain architecture. Multimode storage approaches are used to enhance blockchain storage efficiency. The reliability of data is not solved in this system, and it is still an issue. A private blockchain-oriented tracking system is proposed in a paper [7]. [8]. A study proposed AgroVita by using blockchain. A reliable traceability system ensures customer, farmer, and retailer empowerment. FoodTrail [9], a blockchain-oriented system, enhances the traceability of the harvest supply chain. The proposed architecture is composed of four layers. The approach eliminates reliance on third parties while simultaneously lowering implementation costs. The authors of a study [10] are concerned with the item's food safety and quality. In another study [11], a blockchain-oriented system is deployed on the Ethereum platform. IPFS is used as a repository to store transaction data hash values. A particular value of gas consumption is reported by the author that is required to execute the system. The authors of a research work [12] also utilized the IPFS technology to improve traceability in the soybean supply chain. The authors of a study [13] presented a blockchain-oriented system for tracking and monitoring the production, logistics, and land auditing processes. For food safety, a four-layer approach [14] of information, technology, management, and application is recommended. The authors of another study [15] illustrated a system that allocates a single QR code to a single item and encrypts the data with the AES encryption method. In a study [16], the authors explored a tracking system to manage the supply chain of fruits and vegetables. An on-chain and off-chain storage strategy is used to alleviate chain pressure. The authors of another study [17] suggested that a possible food-tracking system relies on blockchain and IoT connectivity. The Ethereum platform is used to maintain the suggested system. The authors of a paper [18] introduced AgriBlockIoT, which combines blockchain and IoT. In another paper [19], the authors created a supply chain management for rice that is currently being utilized by the Food Corporation of India (FCI). To store the data, the system uses an immutable digital platform [20]. A study proposed an agricultural product quality certification and distribution system based on factors such as transparency, security, and confidence from the perspective of a small farmer.

We deduced from the provided literature that the agricultural supply chain has been the subject of much research. However, the majority of studieshave focused on a particular food item that the farmer produces, while some studies have only addressed security or the complexity of the system. Nevertheless, there are lots of opportunities in this area. To show many-to-many linkages between farmers and crops, we designed the system. Numerous crops may be grown by a farmer, but they cannot be sold without a government agency's consent. The product is given a rating by the authority, and the farmer determines the price in line with the rating. The suggested strategy ensures that no one is malicious during the supply chain process by taking into account distributors and customers in addition to farmers by using an automated smart contract.

PROPOSED MODEL

To make the discussion clear, we have described the working individual contracts in detail. Fig. (**2**) shows the interaction of individual contracts and their associated variables and functions.

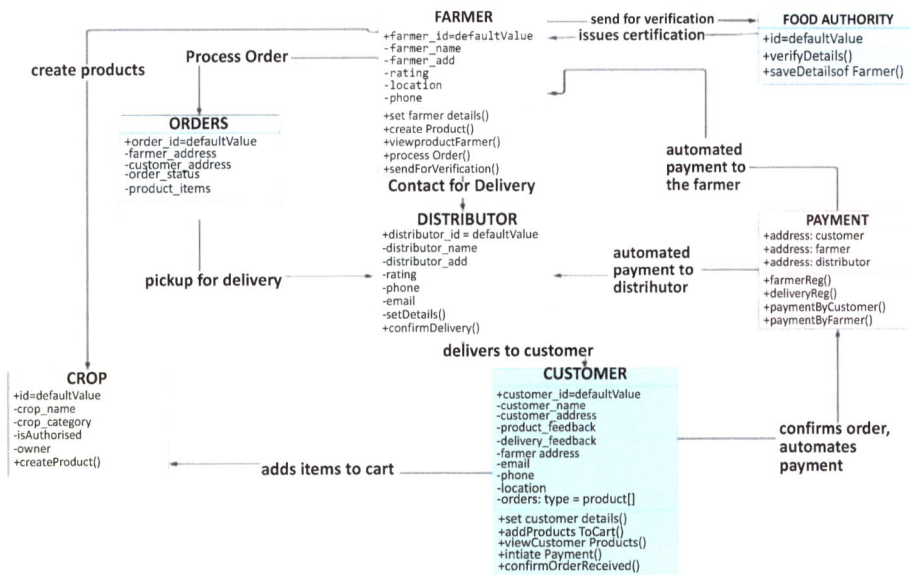

Fig. (2). Overall flow diagram of the proposed model.

Farmer Contract

The farmer first registers himself, and his entire information is logged in the *farmer* map and all of this information, including his or her name, email, phone number, and place of residence, is easily accessible to blockchain participants in order to keep the system transparent. Every farmer in the system is allocated a *farmerId*, a system-specific identifier that is used to map the farmer's information on the farmer map. Farmers can cultivate harvest products and make them available for purchase by the consumer through the blockchain-oriented online platform. The added product by the farmer is now put into the *FarmerProduct* map, which contains all the product details. *ProductId* is generated by the system that identifies the product uniquely in the system. The farmer can modify the availability of the product and can add and remove a product at any point in time from the online portal. Products can be seen through the *farmer* map using the farmer's address as a key. As part of the inspection process, the farmer sends a sample of the product to the food authority, who is then in charge of rating it on a scale that ranges from Low < Medium < Good and returns the results to the farmer. The farmer adds the price as well as the rate of the product with details of the farmer in the *FarmerProduct* blockchain. The customer is now able to purchase the product. The farmer confirms orders and selects the most appropriate distributors for the order. The orders are listed in the *order* map. The *OrderPrice* map stores the entire amount to be paid by the customer for that specific *orderId*. Algorithm 1 depicts the actions of farmer contracts. The algorithm is composed of five functions that carry out the tasks outlined above. Fig. (**3**) depicts the operation of a farmer's contract.

Fig. (3). Farmer's details.

Customer Contract

The customer enters their personal information when creating an account. Every consumer has a specific identification number called a *CustomerId*. Details about individuals can be found on the *Customer* map. Customers who register in the system can view and order the products by accessing the *FarmerProduct* blockchain. They can include products in their shopping basket, which are then recorded in the *Purchase* map of the particular customer. Customer *OrderPrice* map stores the price of their basket. Customers are able to explore the Products map, where they can see the products added to their shopping basket. After they initiate their order, it is sent to the farmer for approval. The payment or refund process is commenced upon receipt of delivery confirmation. All of these operations are linked to the *FarmerCustomerProduct* blockchain. The farmer makes an order object, puts all the products in the customer's basket, and sends the order object to the specific distributor address. Finally, the distributor delivers the order.

Algorithm 1

---

set farmer details ()

    if (farmer is not present in farmermap):

        | register farmer;

    else:

        | return error message;

create product ()

    if (farmer is present in farmer map):

        | set the product data associated with that farmer Id;

    else:

        | return error message;

viewProductsFarmer ()

    if (farmer is present in farmer map):

        | return list of farmer's products;

process Order ()

    if (farmer is present in farmer map and customer is in customer map):

        | new order will be created by farmer for customer and order will be taken

        | by distributor;

    else:

        | return error message;

sendForVerification ()

    send details of product and farmer to the authority;

Algorithm 1. The actions of farmer contracts.

Algorithm 2

setCustomerDetails ()

  if (caller is not in customer mapping):

    | register customer;

  else:

    | return error message;

addProductToCart ()

  if (caller is in customer mapping):

    | product with given product Id will be added to basket of customer;

  else:

    | return error message;

viewCustomerProducts()

  if (caller is in customer mapping):

    | customer can view basket;

  else:

    | return error message;

placeOrder()

confirmOrderReceived()

  if (caller is in customer mapping):

    If (customer confirms that he/she get the product having desired amount and quality):

    | Set order status to delivered;

    else:

    | Order Canceled;

Algorithm 2. The functional elements of a consumer contract.

Algorithm 2 depicts the functional elements of a consumer contract. Fig. (**4**) shows how a *customer* contract functions and how a consumer adds a product to his basket using the *ProductId*.

Fig. (4). Customer adds product to his basket with product id.

Product Contract

The products are produced and added to the online platform by the farmer. In this particular case, the *ProductId* is the distinctive product id. The product map contains a list of every product. The *FarmerProduct* blockchain keeps the farmer's information alongside their goods after receiving evaluations and approval from food inspectors. Customers can now add items to their baskets by simply inputting the *ProductId*.

Order Contract

Customers can place several orders from a single farmer by adding items to their shopping cart. The farmer assigns a delivery partner to each order after confirmation. The *order* map contains a list of all orders.

Distributor Contract

They can register by providing the required information. From the farmer, they are given numerous delivery orders. They are entitled to payment after delivery has been confirmed. The workings of a *distributor* contract are shown in Algorithm 3.

Payment Contract

The consumer commences the payment process. Payments are delivered to the farmers' and distributors' wallets following a successful delivery, subject to authentication by both the delivery partner and the customer. The exchange is verified by both parties, who then record it on the *FarmerCustomerPayment* blockchain. This makes it impossible for anyone to tamper with data. The workings of a *Payment* contract are shown in Algorithm 4. Fig. (**5**) depicts a payment denial in the event that the payment was initiated by the wrong address.

Algorithm 3

---

setDetails ()

    if (distributor is not registered):

       | farmer will register the distributor;

    else:

       | return error message;

  confirm delivery (orderId)

    order status set to delivered by distributor;

Algorithm 3. The workings of a distributor contract.

Fig. (5). Payment denial in case of wrong address initiating the payment.

RESULT AND DISCUSSIONS

A simulation is carried out using a Python-based simulator to test the performance of the proposed smart agriculture supply chain management system based on blockchain. Before being released on the Ethereum main network, smart contracts are authored in Solidity and tested for functioning in the Remix IDE. Python is used as a programming language in the simulation process to model existing frameworks and analyze graphs.

Algorithm 4

PaymentByCustomer()

    if (caller's balance is greater than equal to amount and caller is customerAddress

    and caller's value is equal to the amount and to is farmerAddress):

       | Payment to farmer;

    else:

       | return error message;

paymentByFarmer()

    if (caller's balance is greater than equal to amount and caller is farmer Address

    and caller's value is equal to the amount and to is distributor Address):

       | Payment to distributor;

    else:

       | return error message;

Algorithm 4. The workings of a Payment contract.

Experimental Setup

The experimental setup for our suggested model is shown in Table **1**.

Table 1. Experimental setup.

Components	Tools Required
Smart Contracts	Solidity
Blockchain Network	Ethereum Main Network
Integrated Development Environment	Remix (For deployment of contract.)
Simulation of Network	Python

Performance Analysis

Message Sizes Delivered by Various Entities

Fig. (**6**) displays the results of the comparison of the size of the blockchain transaction submission message and the message interaction between entities such as farmers, customers, distributors, and authorities during the proposed system's execution. When compared to other entities, the size of messages sent by customers is larger because, in addition to the messages for registration and verification, they also send messages for placing orders and receiving order confirmations. The message for authority is the smallest in size when compared to the others because it just transmits a registration message at first to register itself.

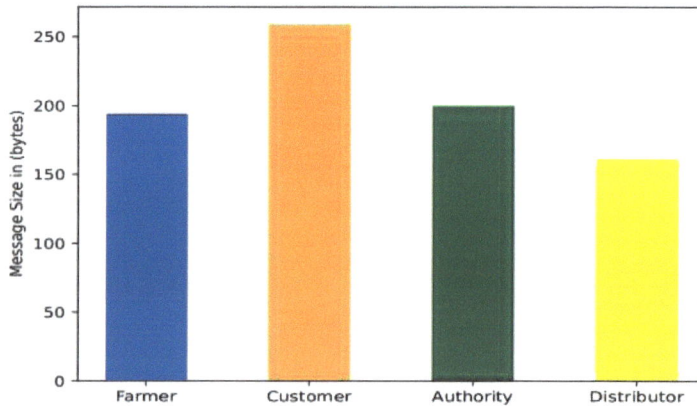

Fig. (6). Message size transmitted by different entities.

Gas Costs Comparison

Fig. (**7**) compares the quantity of gas utilized by storage contracts to that consumed by event-based contracts. Because these facts had to be carried out, we employed contracts to record specific information on the blockchain, such as farmer details, client details, and product qualities. In our contract, we divided the deployment and execution costs. A comparison of the gas fee was conducted utilizing both the events and all of the contract's transactions. Event-based contracts performed better than storage-based contracts in terms of code performance, cutting the transaction charge and significantly lowering the gas fee, as illustrated in Fig. (**7**).

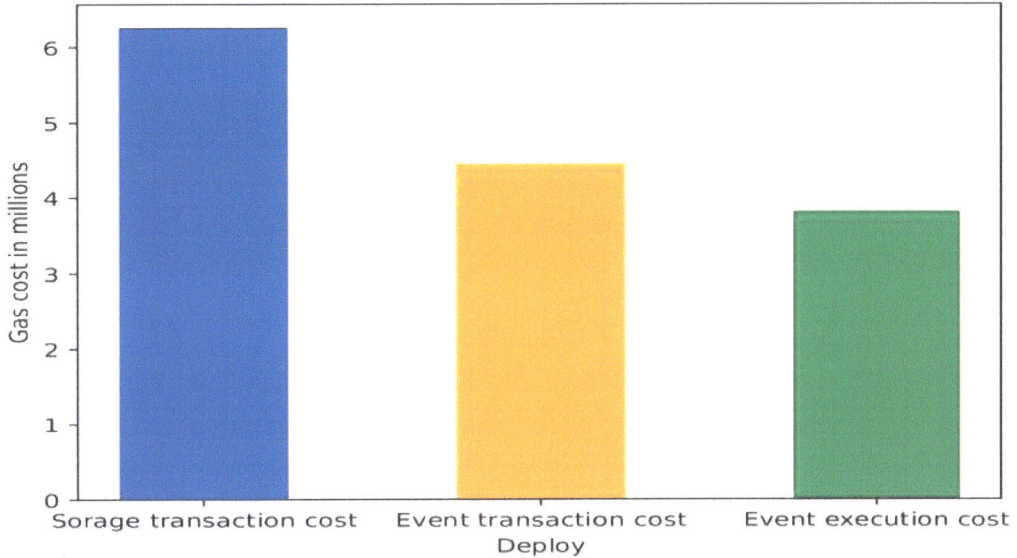

Fig. (7). Gas use by storage-based contracts versus execution-based contracts.

CONCLUSION

This article proposes a blockchain- and IoT-based smart agriculture infrastructure. By using this architecture, the number of middlemen who stand between the farmer and the consumer is reduced. That will have a positive effect on both farmers and consumers. The *FarmerProduct* map includes information on the farmer and their related products, whereas the *FarmerCustomerPayment* map includes information about the farmer, the consumer, and the payment. As a result, no one could possibly disrupt the transaction. Smart contracts are simulated on the Ethereum main network using Python programming to realize the functions of the proposed paradigm. Due to the fact that the customer additionally sends order placement and delivery confirmation messages in addition to the registration and verification messages, we have seen that the maximum message size is transmitted by the customer.

REFERENCES

[1]   H.H. Khan, M.N. Malik, Z. Konečná, A.G. Chofreh, F.A. Goni, and J.J. Klemeš, "Blockchain technology for agricultural supply chains during the COVID-19 pandemic: Benefits and cleaner solutions", *J. Clean. Prod.,* vol. 347, p. 131268, 2022.
[http://dx.doi.org/10.1016/j.jclepro.2022.131268] [PMID: 35287337]

[2]   S. Nakamoto, "Bitcoin: A Peer-to-Peer Electronic Cash System", *SSRN Electronic Journal,* 2008.

[3]   I. Ehsan, M. I. Khalid, L. Ricci, J. Iqbal, A. Alabrah, and S. S. Ullah, "A conceptual model for blockchain-based agriculture food supply chain system," in *Scientific Programming*, P. Gupta, Ed., vol. 2022, pp. 1–15.

[4]   S. Malik, S.S. Kanhere, and R. Jurdak, "ProductChain: Scalable Blockchain Framework to Support Provenance in Supply Chains", *17th International Symposium on Network Computing and Applications (NCA),* 2018.

[5]   F. Casino, V. Kanakaris, T.K. Dasaklis, S. Moschuris, S. Stachtiaris, and M. Pagoni, "Blockchain-based food supply chain traceability: a case study in the dairy sector", *Int. J. Prod. Res.,* vol. •••, pp. 1-13, 2020.

[6]   X. Zhang, P. Sun, J. Xu, X. Wang, J. Yu, Z. Zhao, and Y. Dong, "Blockchain-Based Safety Management System for the Grain Supply Chain", *IEEE Access,* vol. 8, pp. 36398-36410, 2020.
[http://dx.doi.org/10.1109/ACCESS.2020.2975415]

[7]   D. Prashar, N. Jha, S. Jha, Y. Lee, and G.P. Joshi, "Blockchain-Based Traceability and Visibility for Agricultural Products: A Decentralized Way of Ensuring Food Safety in India", *Sustainability (Basel),* vol. 12, no. 8, p. 3497, 2020.
[http://dx.doi.org/10.3390/su12083497]

[8]   S. Shaikh, M. Butala, R. Butala, and M. Creado, "AgroVita using Blockchain", *5th International Conference for Convergence in Technology (I2CT),* 2019.

[9]   H. Hayati, and I.G.B.B. Nugraha, "Blockchain Based Traceability System in Food Supply Chain", *International Seminar on Research of Information Technology and Intelligent Systems (ISRITI),* 2018.

[10]   V. Pandey, M. Pant, and V. Snasel, "Blockchain technology in food supply chains: Review and bibliometric analysis", *Technol. Soc.,* vol. 69, no. Mar, p. 101954, 2022.
[http://dx.doi.org/10.1016/j.techsoc.2022.101954]

[11]   A. Shahid, A. Almogren, N. Javaid, F.A. Al-Zahrani, M. Zuair, and M. Alam, "Blockchain-Based Agri-Food Supply Chain: A Complete Solution", *IEEE Access,* vol. 8, pp. 69230-69243, 2020.
[http://dx.doi.org/10.1109/ACCESS.2020.2986257]

[12]   K. Salah, N. Nizamuddin, R. Jayaraman, and M. Omar, "Blockchain-Based Soybean Traceability in Agricultural Supply Chain", *IEEE Access,* vol. 7, pp. 73295-73305, 2019.
[http://dx.doi.org/10.1109/ACCESS.2019.2918000]

[13]   G. Tradigo, P. Vizza, P. Veltri, and P. H. Guzzi, "An Information System to Track data and processes for food quality and bacterial pathologies prevention". 2019. Available from: https://ceur-ws.org/Vo--2400/paper-36.pdf

[14]   Y. Wang, and Y. Yang, "Research on Agricultural Food Safety Based on Blockchain Technology", *J. Phys. Conf. Ser.,* vol. 1606, no. 1, p. 012013, 2020.
[http://dx.doi.org/10.1088/1742-6596/1606/1/012013]

[15]   Z. Dong, J. Chen, Y. Chen, and R. Shao, "Food traceability system based on blockchain", *Proceedings of the 2020 International Conference on Aviation Safety and Information Technology,* 2020.

[16]   X. Yang, M. Li, H. Yu, M. Wang, D. Xu, and C. Sun, "A Trusted Blockchain-Based Traceability System for Fruit and Vegetable Agricultural Products", *IEEE Access,* vol. 9, pp. 36282-36293, 2021.
[http://dx.doi.org/10.1109/ACCESS.2021.3062845]

[17]   M. Kim, B. Hilton, Z. Burks, and J. Reyes, "Integrating Blockchain, Smart Contract-Tokens, and IoT to Design a Food Traceability Solution. 2018 IEEE 9th Annual Information Technology", *Electronics and Mobile Communication Conference (IEMCON),* 2018.

[18]   M. P. Caro, M. S. Ali, M. Vecchio, and R. Giaffreda, "Blockchain-based traceability in Agri-Food supply chain management: A practical implementation", *IEEE Xplore,* 2018. p. 1–4. Available from: https://ieeexplore.ieee.org/stamp/stamp.jsp?tp=&arnumber=8373021

[19]   Kakkar A, Ruchi. "A Blockchain Technology Solution to Enhance Operational Efficiency of Rice Supply Chain for Food Corporation of India", *Sustainable Communication Networks and Application* 2019; 24–31.

[20]   F.M. Enescu, and V. Manuel Ionescu, "Using Blockchain in the agri-food sector following SARS-

CoV-2 pandemic", *12th International Conference on Electronics, Computers and Artificial Intelligence (ECAI),* 2020.

[21]　M. Abdel-Basset, N. Moustafa, H. Hawash, I. Razzak, K.M. Sallam, and O.M. Elkomy, "Federated Intrusion Detection in Blockchain-Based Smart Transportation Systems", *IEEE Trans. Intell. Transp. Syst.,* pp. 1-15, 2021.

[22]　A. Sahai, and R. Pandey, "Smart Contract Definition for Land Registry in Blockchain", *IEEE Xplore,* 2020pp. 230-235. Available from: https://ieeexplore.ieee.org/document/91157 [http://dx.doi.org/10.1109/CSNT48778.2020.9115752]

Optimizing the Quality-of-Service Routing Mechanism Using Optimization Techniques for Software-Defined Network-Based IoT

Manisha Chandrakar[1,*] and **V. K. Patle**[1]

¹ School of Studies in Computer Science and IT, Pt. Ravishankar Shukla University, Raipur, Chhattisgarh, India

Abstract: The rise of IoT-connected gadgets has resulted in a deluge of information. Network bandwidth is heavily used due to the large amount of data being delivered to the cloud or fog. The IoT network could be vulnerable to network congestion. Furthermore, some IoT implementations need multimedia data transmission with various Quality of service (QoS) standards. Multinetwork information architecture (MINA) aims to satisfy various QoS criteria for different areas of IoT. While it can adapt to new network conditions, it cannot provide the quality of service required for critical IoT applications. This study proposes enhancing the software-defined network-based IoT network with the application-aware QoS routing algorithm (AQRA) and MINA to guarantee a wide range of quality-of-service (QoS) requirements for critical IoT applications. The best possible outcome was achieved by using the particle swarm optimization (PSO) method.

Keywords: Internet of Things (IoT), Quality of Service (QoS), Routing, Software-defined networking.

INTRODUCTION

Significant amounts of network bandwidth are consumed by the massive quantities of multimedia data generated by IoT devices. IoT devices operate at the same time and share the same networking facilities. Traditional IoT network design is not scalable or flexible enough to support massive amounts of data from IoT devices [1].

There is a chance that the Internet of Things may experience congestion. Software-defined networking (SDN) has emerged as a powerful tool for managing networks. The control operations of the controller are unified and isolated from

---
* **Corresponding author V.K. Patle:** School of Studies in Computer Science and IT, Pt. Ravishankar Shukla University, Raipur, Chhattisgarh, India; E-mail:patlevinod@gmail.com

H.S. Hota, Dinesh K. Sharma, Ayan Kumar Das & Ditipriya Sinha (Eds.)

network hardware. As a result, the controller incorporates global network vision as well as network programmability. IoT networking will be supported by SDN's unified regulation, which includes dynamic flow control and adaptive network resource management [2]. In an SDN-based IoT network, there are five distinct layers: Applications, networks, edges, perceptions, and controls.

The IoT's control layer includes an SDN monitor. There are three modules in the SDN controller:

1. Discovery topology application: This module discovers all the data-level network components and constructs the topology of the network.

2. Module for tracking network status: This module regularly watches and gathers the network state [3].

3. AQRA (Application-aware QoS Routing Algorithm) module: The planned AQRA operates as the module of the SDN controller. The AQRA allows network and edge layer compatibility to be managed *via* southbound API and even the reception of messages *via* Northbound API from the device layer.

Multiple QoS specifications, such as latency, jitter, packet error rate, and bandwidth, must be met by IoT applications when transmitting multimedia data. There are also mission-critical systems that include the transmission of emergency communications in IoT networks, such as gas detectors, smoke alarms, crisis sensors, and so on. If these types of messages are not sent in a timely manner due to network congestion, it can result in severe effects [3]. As a result, we must have QoS assurances to ensure that these messages arrive on schedule.

RELATED WORK

Some related works on IoT networking QoS improvements are studied here. The research that has been done in this field may be arranged into two distinct areas of study: architecture enhancement and algorithm enhancement.

Architecture Improvement

For the Internet of Things, the author outlined a network architecture based on software-defined networking. To talk about the issues of agility, scalability, and Quality of Service in the IoT, an architecture that integrates software-defined networking (SDN) with the data delivery service (DDS) middleware from the Object Management Group has been proposed [4]. By combining the software-defined network, storage, and protection, research proposed a software-defined focused IoT design to transmit, hold, and safeguard the information that is created by the IoT [5]. To address the scalability issue of the standard IoT architecture, the research proposes an IoT architecture with edge computing and a core network based on SDN design with an SDN-based fundamental network [6]. In order to provide modular IoT services, the author projected a classified fog computation manner for every fog node. Concerns with scalability and real data dissemination in the existing IoT architecture [7] are addressed by the authors of the suggested SDFN design for IoT, which employs SDN and fog processing.

Algorithm Enhancement

IoT-enabled SDN controller tracks available resources and a QoS-aware routing procedure grounded on a genetic algorithm (GA) to satisfy multiple QoS needs [8]. Nevertheless, there are some shortcomings in this work: QoS is not guaranteed for critical IoT applications; the cost function's static weights are unable to respond to the new network state; as the number of IoT devices on the network grows, in order to reduce network latency, load balancing should be taken into account. Unfortunately, MINA did not accomplish this. The authors suggested using edge computation for IoT networking to govern network congestion in regressive admission control [9]. The edge router uses the regressive admission control approach to track delay output until admitting streams of the network, ensuring decent efficiency for critical flows. Regressive admission control, on the other hand, only found one QoS requirement. Furthermore, it ignored the issue of low-priority flow starvation. A proactive flow deployment mechanism for Internet of Things devices that can recognize periodic network flow propagation cycles and mount the relevant stream admission into an SDN switch ahead of time [10]. The Ant Lion Whale Optimization algorithm chooses the cluster head using a fitness metric that takes latency and energy into account. The cluster member connection point that transmits data bytes to the sink node with the least amount of latency and the highest amount of energy is chosen as the cluster head [11].The author gave resource limits and high traffic volumes, maintaining the load on servers while at the same time ensuring the QoS of IoT congestion is an NP-hard task, and developed a revolutionary SDN-based IoT supervise and administration framework that offered load balancing and QoS because of this [12]. In contrast to PS-based schemes, LVS-based methods dramatically decrease controller synchronization costs by delaying the execution of effective multithreading amongst controllers until the demand on a specific server increases. In an SDN network with several controllers across multiple domains, this improves load balancing efficiency [13]. The practice experiment examined channel use, network delay, and packet delivery ratio. Improvements in packet prioritization, resource consumption, QoS assistance, and the performance of the (IPsec) security protocol were made in order to attain these metrics [14]. The goal of the traveling salesman problem (TSP) is to find an optimal solution. Metaheuristics, which have shown to be excellent TSP solvers, are required since precise algorithms cannot successfully solve the traveling salesman issue [15]. The search process has no memory, so it cannot be prevented from returning to areas that less frequently contain the global minimum; secondly, as the randomization used to generate a fresh trial does not take into account the knowledge obtained from the investigation, the search cannot be focused on more promising sites. To get around these two issues, the author suggests using the learning-enhanced simulated annealing (LESA) approach [16]. The issue with software-defined networks is monitoring and estimating available bandwidth. We highlighted how the cutting-edge methods for this new architecture make use of the additional features that are now available. The author analytically estimated the measurement inaccuracy due to OpenFlow's absence of a local timestamping mechanism, as well as the causes of problems caused by SDN and OpenFlow. The result is evident when compared to the real world. Additionally, these findings serve as a benchmark for (Available Bandwidth) ABW programmers eager to work in SDN environments, which call for an appropriate balance between accuracy, polling rate, and jitter (Table **1**) [17].

Table 1. Related Work.

S. No.	Author / Year	Objective	Mechanism
1.	Kavita Jaiswal, Veena Anand/2020	The objective of the research is an energy-efficient routing protocol. The protocol studies some constraints to select the optimal path [11]	IoT
2.	A. MontazerolghaemM.H.Yaghmaee/2020	Support for both load balancing and quality of service in an IoT management framework based on software-defined networking [12].	SDN
3.	Zehua Guo et. al. / 2014	An effective load-balancing strategy would reduce things like response time, resource use, packet loss, overuse, and so on [13].	SDIoT
4.	Sahrish Khan/2017	Represents a security architecture whereby a virtual switch is built into each node and used to link to a central domain controller [18]	SDN
5.	Haytham Qushtom/ 2017	Iimproving the quality of service (QoS) of sensitive data is the focus of a new delivery strategy that has been proposed [14].	IOT

(Table 1) cont.....

S. No.	Author / Year	Objective	Mechanism
6.	J. L. Herrera/ 2021	A distributed fog architecture for software development that takes into account both microservices and mobile edge computing technologies [20].	DD-FoG
7.	SamodhaPallewatta/ 2002	Proposed QoS-aware Multi-objective Set-based Particle Swarm Optimization (QMPSO) [19]	IoT
8.	Adewole A.P. / 2012	The simulated annealing technique and the genetic algorithm were used in this study in order to gain expertise using them by evaluating how well they performed on various test beds. Simulated annealing, according to experiments, has a shorter duration [15].	Genetic algorithm
9.	S. Sun / 2007	Method, assessment, and application of learning-enhanced simulated annealing to the registration of lung nodules are presented [16].	Machine learning
10.	P. C. A. Megyesi / 2017	Measurement of available bandwidth in SDNs presents a number of unique problems, and this article explores those issues and possible solutions [17].	SDN

APPLYING OPTIMIZATION TECHNIQUE FOR AQRA

The proposed QoS routing algorithm is detailed as follows for applications in SDN-based IoT networks. There are five parts:

(1) architecture of SDN-based IoT network.

(2) traffic classifications

(3) routing Simulation Annealing QoS

(4) input control of QoS-aware

(5) use of PSO to maximize the outcome.

There are three modules in the SDN controller:

Discovery topology application: This module discovers all the data level network components and constructs the topology of the network.

Module for tracking network status: This module regularly watches and gathers the network state.

AQRA (Application-aware QoS Routing Algorithm) module: The planned AQRA operates as the module of the SDN controller. The AQRA allows network and edge layer compatibility to be managed *via* southbound API and even the reception of messages *via* Northbound API from the device layer.

The AQRA is focused on annealing (SA), which is an approximately global search algorithm without being in the local maximum on a probability-based basis. The SA usually runs faster than the genetic algorithm (GA), as per the genetic algorithm used by MINA [8]. With population size, the GA runtime increases exponentially [20]. Due to its quicker runtime, the simulated annealing (SA) approach outperforms the genetic algorithm (GA) in addressing the route selection issue, making it more suitable for the Quality of Service (QoS) requirements of real-time responsive IoT systems. The attributes of the AQRA are:

- Adaptive cost feature weights must be adjusted to the existing state of the network to identify better routing routes.
- The SA method of search is memory-free and cannot thus stop revisiting areas with a lower probability of a global minimum [16]. When a state transition occurs, we look at the nearby path and the record path list to see if there are any new solutions to consider.
- Load balancing between routes shall be accomplished by choosing the route with the highest bandwidth available.

A QoS-aware admission management system is needed to guarantee the QoS conditions for high-priority applications. When the QoS criteria of critical applications (flows) are not satisfied, the QoS-aware admission control (AC) takes in. The fundamental idea behind quality-of-service-aware admission control is to limit the number of medium- or low-complexity flows that use a high-priority network resource. However, dropping low-priority flow packets so many times can lead to a hunger issue, which denies the low-priority flows. In order to prevent hunger, the AQRA reports in the flow info a drop counter (dc) and a drop chance (dp). When the flow notification Packet-in is sent, the dc will be initialized into 0.

PSO was conceived in 1995 by Dr. Kennedy and Eberhart as a heuristic global optimization technique. It is a population-driven search algorithm based on the animals, bees, or fishing simulation. PSO carries out a quest using an iteration-t--iteration swarm of particles. Every particle moves towards its previous best (pbest) location and best (gbest) global position in the swarm to find the optimum solution.

$$\text{pbest}(i,t) = \arg\min[\,f(P_i(k))\,]\quad, i \in \{1,2,3,.....N_p\}$$

$$\text{here}\quad k=1,.....t$$

$$\text{gbest}(t) = \arg\min[\,f(P_i(k))\,]$$

$$\text{arc}$$

$$\text{here } i=1......N_p$$

where t represents the current iteration number, f represents the fitness function, P represents the position, i represents the particle index, and N_p is the total number of particles. These equations are used to calculate the most recent changes in particle location P and velocity V:

$$V_i(t+1) = wV_i(t) + c1r1\,(\text{pbest}(i,t)\text{-}P_i(t)) + c2r2\,(\text{gbest}(t)\text{-}P_i(t)),$$

$$P_i(t+1) = P_i(t) + V_i(t+1)$$

To strike a balance between global and local manipulation, w in the preceding equation represents the weight of inertia, r1 and r2 are uniformly distributed random variables in the [0,1] interval, and c1 and c2 are positive constant quantities called "coefficients of acceleration."

After the discovery of delay, jitter, and packet loss ratio for average end-to-end flow performance and standard end-to-end flow performance for Mine, AQRA with/without history, and AC, the PSO optimization has been implemented in the proposed work (Fig. **1**).

The proposed QoS routing algorithm is detailed as follows for applications in SDN-based IoT networks.

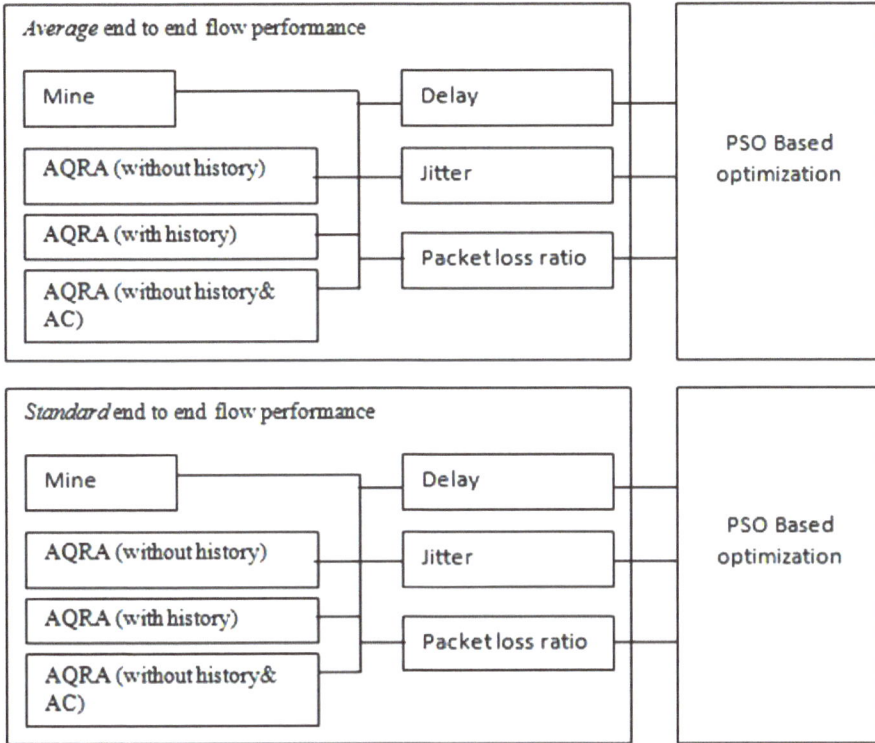

Fig. (1). Proposed models.

SIMULATION RESULT AND DISCUSSION

PSO-based optimization has been applied in previous studies. An Octave simulator was used for this work. For a given service, MINA only considers one QoS need. Its strength ratio of QoS is comparatively greater than the AQRA requirement (without history). However, AQRA's strength rate (with history) exceeds MINA's fitness ratio as AQRA takes into account historical explanations and the route with an extreme bandwidth usable. Moreover, AQRA (history & AC) will ensure that essential data transmission service QoS specifications are met by AC (Figs. **2-4**).

Table **2** displays the average complete transmission efficiency and standard complete transmission performance. In terms of delay, jitter, and packet failure, AQRA (with history) is 10.75, 11.88, and 10.82% stronger, respectively. This means AQRA will pursue better options thanks to its flexible cost function weights and load-balancing capabilities. The following table displays the estimated complete transmission output and standard deviation.

Table 2. Average end-to-end and standard end-to-end flow performance [21].

Quality of Service Parameter	MINA	Aqra (Without History)	Aqra (With History)	Aqra (Without History & AC)
-	Average	Standard	Average	Standard
Delay (ms)	99.82	39.27	92.28	38.83
Jitter (ms)	33.97	18.98	31.25	18.75
Packet loss rate (%)	0.057	0.056	0.053	0.054

Optimized delay:

Optimal solution found

Ans = 89.4575

Best objective value

Ans =   1.7034

Elapsed time is 0.871477 seconds

Optimized jitter:

Optimal solution found

Ans = 30.6403

Best objective value

Ans =   0.9443

Elapsed time is 1.525715 seconds.

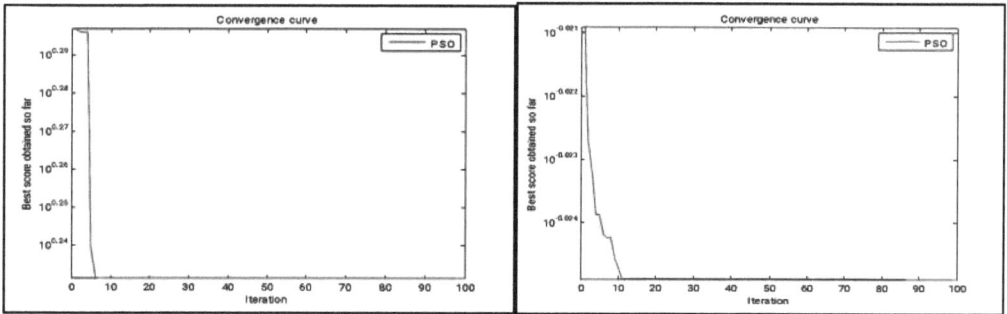

Fig. (2). Convergence curve for delay, jitter in case of average end-to-end flow performance.

Optimized packet loss rate:

Optimal solution found

Ans = 0.0541

Best objective value

Ans = 0.4795Ans

Elapsed time is 1.054186 seconds.

Optimized delay for standard end-to-end flow performance:

Optimal solution found

Ans = 39.0790

Best objective value

Ans = 0.6658

Elapsed time is 0.926122 seconds.

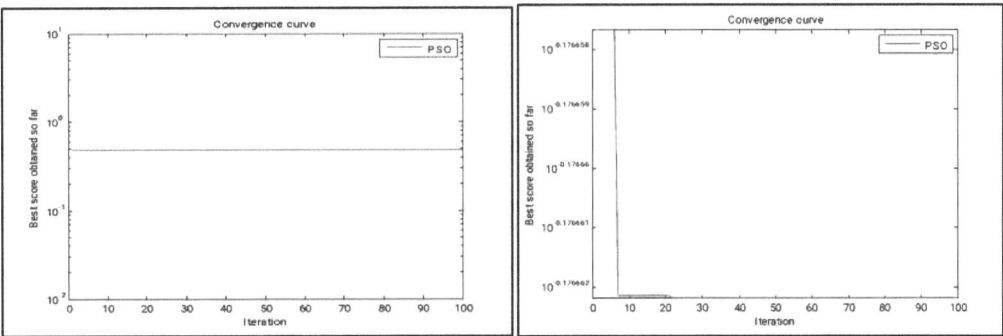

Fig. (3). Convergence curve for packet loss rate in case of average and delay for standard end-to-end flow performance.

CONCLUSION

IoT network optimization scales up traffic management greatly through reduced latency operational effectiveness and higher service experiences. The AQRA is designed to determine the most suitable paths through the network based on simulation annealing and flexible cost function weights. The assessment found that AQRA (with history and adaptive control) outperforms MINA in terms of QoS criteria. AQRA is superior to MINA in terms of end-to-end flow efficiency and has reduced standard deviation in delay, jitter, and packet loss rate. On top of that, AQRA may be executed much faster than MINA. The optimized values for average end-to-end flow performance are 89.4575 for delay, 30.6403 for jitter, and 0.0541 for packet loss. The optimized values for standard end-to-end flow performance are 39.0790 for delay, 18.7521 for jitter, and 0.2827 for packet loss.

Optimized jitter for standard end-to-end flow performance

Optimal solution found

Ans =   18.7521

Best objective value

Ans =   0.6650

Elapsed time is 1.284316 seconds.

Optimized packet loss ratio for standard end-to-end flow performance

Optimal solution found

Ans =   0.2827

Best objective value

Ans =   0.4797

Elapsed time is 0.910697 seconds.

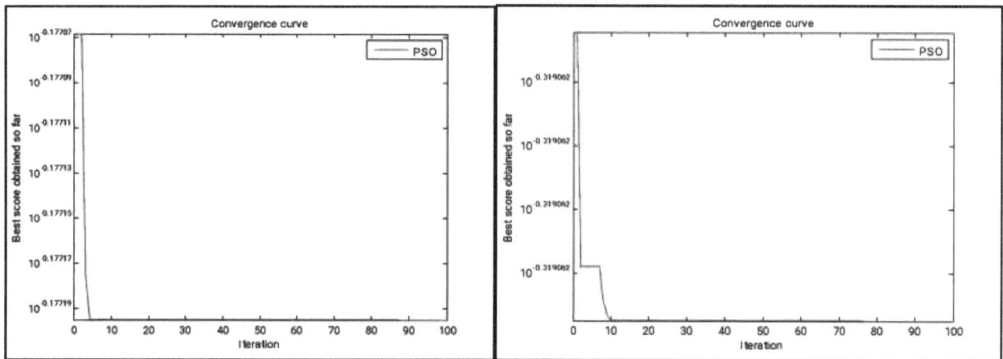

Fig. (4). Convergence curve for jitter, packet loss in case of standard end-to-end flow performance.

REFERENCES

[1]   Y. Liu, Q. Zhang, X. Xin, G. Cao, Y. Tao, and Y. Shen, "Dynamic bandwidth allocation for multi-QoS guarantee based on bee colony optimization", *IEEE Computing, Communications and IoT Applications (ComComAp)*, pp. 1-5.
[http://dx.doi.org/10.1109/ComComAp51192.2020.9398879]

[2]   G.Z. Imran, Z. Ghaffar, A. Alshahrani, M. Fayaz, A.M. Alghamdi, and J. Gwak, "A Topical Review on Machine Learning, Software Defined Networking, Internet of Things Applications: Research Limitations and Challenges", *Electronics (Basel)*, vol. 10, no. 8, p. 880, 2021.
[http://dx.doi.org/10.3390/electronics10080880]

[3]   H-C. Jang, C-W. Huang, and F-K. Yeh, "Design a bandwidth allocation framework for SDN based smart home", *Electronics and Mobile Communication Conference (IEMCON)*, pp. 1-6, 2016.

[4]   A. Hakiri, P. Berthou, A. Gokhale, and S. Abdellatif, "Publish/subscribe-enabled software defined networking for efficient and scalable IoT communications", *IEEE Commun. Mag.*, vol. 53, no. 9, pp. 48-54, 2015.
[http://dx.doi.org/10.1109/MCOM.2015.7263372]

[5]   Y. Jararweh, M. Al-Ayyoub, A. Darabseh, E. Benkhelifa, M. Vouk, and A. Rindos, "SDIoT: a software defined based internet of things framework", *J. Ambient Intell. Humaniz. Comput.*, vol. 6, no. 4, pp. 453-461, 2015.
[http://dx.doi.org/10.1007/s12652-015-0290-y]

[6]   X. Sun, and N. Ansari, "EdgeIoT: Mobile edge computing for the internet of things", *IEEE Commun. Mag.*, vol. 54, no. 12, pp. 22-29, 2016.
[http://dx.doi.org/10.1109/MCOM.2016.1600492CM]

[7]   S. Tomovic, K. Yoshigoe, I. Maljevic, and I. Radusinovic, "Softwaredefined fog network architecture for IoT", *Wirel. Pers. Commun.,* vol. 92, no. 1, pp. 181-196, 2017.
[http://dx.doi.org/10.1007/s11277-016-3845-0]

[8]   Z. Qin, G. Denker, C. Giannelli, P. Bellavista, and N. Venkatasubramanian, "A software defined networking architecture for the internet-of-things", *Proc. of IEEE Network Operations and Management Symposium (NOMS),* pp. 1-9, 2014.
[http://dx.doi.org/10.1109/NOMS.2014.6838365]

[9]   M. Jutila, "An adaptive edge router enabling internet of things", *IEEE Internet Things J.,* vol. 3, no. 6, pp. 1061-1069, 2016.
[http://dx.doi.org/10.1109/JIOT.2016.2550561]

[10]   P. Bull, R. Austin, and M. Sharma, "Pre-emptive flow installation for internet of things devices within software defined networks", *Proc. of 3rd International Conference on Future Internet of Things and Cloud (FiCloud),* pp. 124-130, 2015.
[http://dx.doi.org/10.1109/FiCloud.2015.87]

[11]   K. Jaiswal, and V. Anand, "EOMR: An Energy-Efficient Optimal Multi-path Routing Protocol to Improve QoS in Wireless Sensor Network for IoT Applications", *Wirel. Pers. Commun.,* vol. 111, no. 4, pp. 2493-2515, 2020.
[http://dx.doi.org/10.1007/s11277-019-07000-x]

[12]   A. Montazerolghaem, and M.H. Yaghmaee, "Load-Balanced and QoS-Aware Software-Defined Internet of Things", *IEEE Internet Things J.,* vol. 7, no. 4, pp. 3323-3337, 2020.
[http://dx.doi.org/10.1109/JIOT.2020.2967081]

[13]   Z. Guo, M. Su, Y. Xu, Z. Duan, L. Wang, S. Hui, and H. Jonathan Chao, "Improving the performance of load balancing in software-defined networks through load variance-based synchronization", *Computer Networks,* vol. 68, 2014pp. 95-109. Available from: https://www.sciencedirect.com/science/article/pii/S1389128614000814
[http://dx.doi.org/10.1016/j.comnet.2013.12.004]

[14]   H. Qushtom, and K. Rabaya'h, "Enhancing the QoS of IoT Networks with Lightweight Security Protocol using Contiki OS", *International Journal of Computer Network & Information Security,* vol. 9, no. 11, pp. 27-35, 2017.
[http://dx.doi.org/10.5815/ijcnis.2017.11.03]

[15]   A. Adewole, K. Otubamowo, and T. Egunjobi, "Article: A Comparative Study of Simulated Annealing and Genetic Algorithm for Solving the Travelling Salesman Problem", *Int. J. Appl. Inf. Syst.,* vol. 4, no. 4, pp. 6-12, 2012.
[http://dx.doi.org/10.5120/ijais12-450678]

[16]   S. Sun, F. Zhuge, J. Rosenberg, R.M. Steiner, G.D. Rubin, and S. Napel, "Learning-enhanced simulated annealing: method, evaluation, and application to lung nodule registration", *Appl. Intell.,* vol. 28, no. 1, pp. 83-99, 2008.
[http://dx.doi.org/10.1007/s10489-007-0043-5]

[17]   P. Megyesi, A. Botta, G. Aceto, A. Pescapé, and S. Molnár, "Challenges and solution for measuring available bandwidth in software defined networks", *Comput. Commun.,* vol. 99, pp. 48-61, 2017.
[http://dx.doi.org/10.1016/j.comcom.2016.12.004]

[18]   S. Khan, M. Shah, O. Khan, and A. Ahmed, "Software Defined Network (SDN) based Internet of Things (IoT): A road ahead," 2017, pp. 1–8.
[http://dx.doi.org/10.1145/3102304.3102319]

[19]   S. Pallewatta, V. Kostakos, and R. Buyya, "QoS-aware placement of microservices-based IoT applications in Fog computing environments", *Future Generation Computer Systems,* 2022, *131,* pp. 121-136.
[http://dx.doi.org/10.1016/j.future.2022.01.012]

[20] J. L. Herrera, J. Galán-Jiménez, J. Berrocal, and J. M. Murillo, "Optimizing the Response Time in SDN-Fog Environments for Time-Strict IoT Applications", *IEEE Internet of Things Journal,* vol. 8, no. 23, pp. 17172-17185, 2021.
[http://dx.doi.org/10.1109/JIOT.2021.3077992]

[21] G-C. Deng, and K. Wang, "An Application-aware QoS Routing Algorithm for SDN-based IoT Networking", *IEEE Symposium on Computers and Communications (ISCC),* pp. 00186-00191, 2018.
[http://dx.doi.org/10.1109/ISCC.2018.8538551]

CHAPTER 14

IoT-Based Data Security in Smart Farming Systems

G.S. Dhanush[1], **Devadri Bhattacharya**[1], **J.M. Adithya**[1], **G. Kushal**[1] and **M.R. Shrisha**[1,*]

[1] *Department of Electronics and Communication Engineering, B.M.S. College of Engineering, Bengaluru, Karnataka, India*

Abstract: Data security is crucial when interacting with internet-based networks, clouds, servers, *etc.* In today's world, the most prominent percentage of communication is internet-based. Using sensors like temperature and soil moisture sensors, the collected data is encrypted. The electronic gadgets transform the normal text into unintelligible cipher text, which is then stored in the cloud at the transmitting end. The AES128 key and hash code used on the transmitting side are used to decode data on the receiving side. In this process, if any unauthorized person tries to hack the data, they fail to get the original data since the data is in the form of cipher text. The application of IoT and 5G communication technologies introduces smart farming ecosystems to a wide range of cyber security risks and vulnerabilities. This type of cyberattack will cause economic disruption in nations with significant agricultural dependence. Hence, there is a need for data security in smart farming. In this paper, an efficient and easy way to encrypt the data using Cipher text is shown.

Keywords: Cipher text, IoT, Smart agriculture, ThingSpeak.

INTRODUCTION

Agriculture forms the major sector of India's economy; more than 50% of the population in most parts of the country practice agriculture. Agriculture is continuously evolving since Agriculture 1.0 *i.e.,* from the usage of manual farming to the usage of machinery in Agriculture 2.0, and is advancing towards Agriculture 3.0, with the application of embedded systems bringing about automation and precision agriculture [1]. Agriculture 4.0, which is also called smart agriculture or smart farming, is gaining the attention of researchers in recent days. It involves the usage of IoT, wireless sensor networks, Big data, AI/ML, and blockchain technology [2].

---

[*] **Corresponding author M.R. Shrisha:** Department of Electronics and Communication Engineering, B.M.S. College of Engineering, Bengaluru, Karnataka, India; E-mail: shrishamr.ece@bmsce.ac.in

H.S. Hota, Dinesh K. Sharma, Ayan Kumar Das & Ditipriya Sinha (Eds.)

Smart farming is farming using modern technologies and smart devices [3]. It aims to optimize farming practices using interactive electronic gadgets that communicate with each other *via* different wireless communication protocols like Bluetooth, Zigbee, NFC, Wi-Fi, LiFi, and 5G [4]. It involves the usage of electronic gadgets in farming and results in the collection of huge amounts of data and analysis of data, which is more useful for most of the stakeholders. The large amount of data that is collected and analyzed is called Big data. This has increased the chances of security risks.

Data privacy and data security are two major entities involved in smart farming. Data privacy involves the collection of data, analysis of data, storage of the collected data, usage of data more responsibly, and protection of data from third parties or unauthorized users. The selected architecture should ensure better accessibility of data, system integrity, authorization of data, and confidentiality of data [5].

In smart farming, more than a million smart devices are connected to IoT, and they communicate with each other, leading to security and privacy issues. The blockchain is a recent development that enables the security of data by using algorithms [6]. The combination of IoT with blockchain will result in increased efficiency and help secure data to a larger extent. The data is encrypted, and no third party can access the transactions except the authorized users.

PROPOSED METHODOLOGY

The block diagram as shown in Fig. (**1**) has two sensors linked to the Raspberry Pi to represent the IoT part (DHT11 temperature and humidity sensor and YL- 69 soil moisture sensor). The data is received and encrypted by the RaspPi chip using AES-128 Cipher Block Chaining before being sent to the ThingSpeak cloud [7]. The data is then read from the ThingSpeak cloud and decrypted using the AES-128 decryption cipher by the host server. Because the cloud does not represent the true values, there is no vulnerability in the event of an attack [8]. As a result, it will be difficult to determine true values if someone gains access to the cloud page in order to steal data because they will need to understand the key used in this method, and thus, security can be achieved and information protected [9]. This design is depicted in the figure above. The encryption and decryption flowchart is shown respectively in Figs. (**2** and **3**).

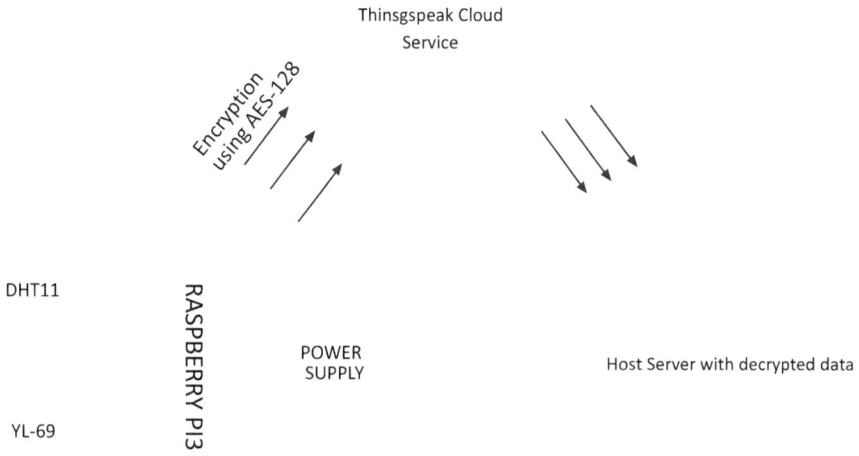

Fig. (1). IoT setup.

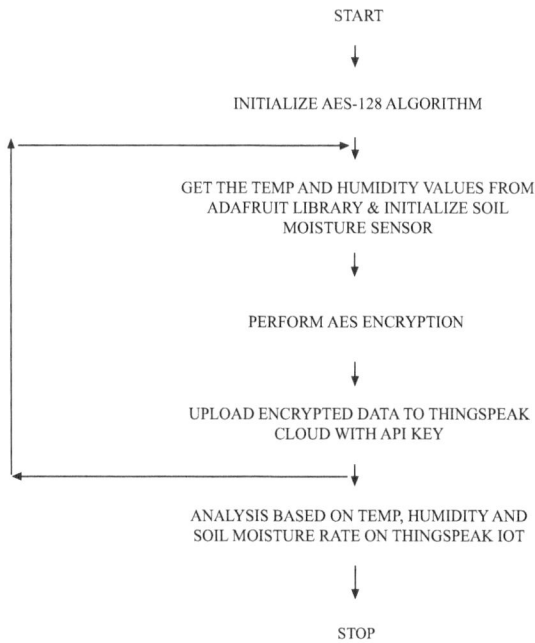

Fig. (2). Encryption flowchart.

Receiver Side: Before performing encryption on the transmitter side, the initialization of the AES128 algorithm is required to obtain the humidity and temperature data readings from the Ada fruit library; then the encryption password is entered, the AES128 algorithm is run, and hash code encryption is performed [10]. With the help of an API key, encrypted data is transferred to the ThingSpeak cloud for analysis depending on temperature and humidity.

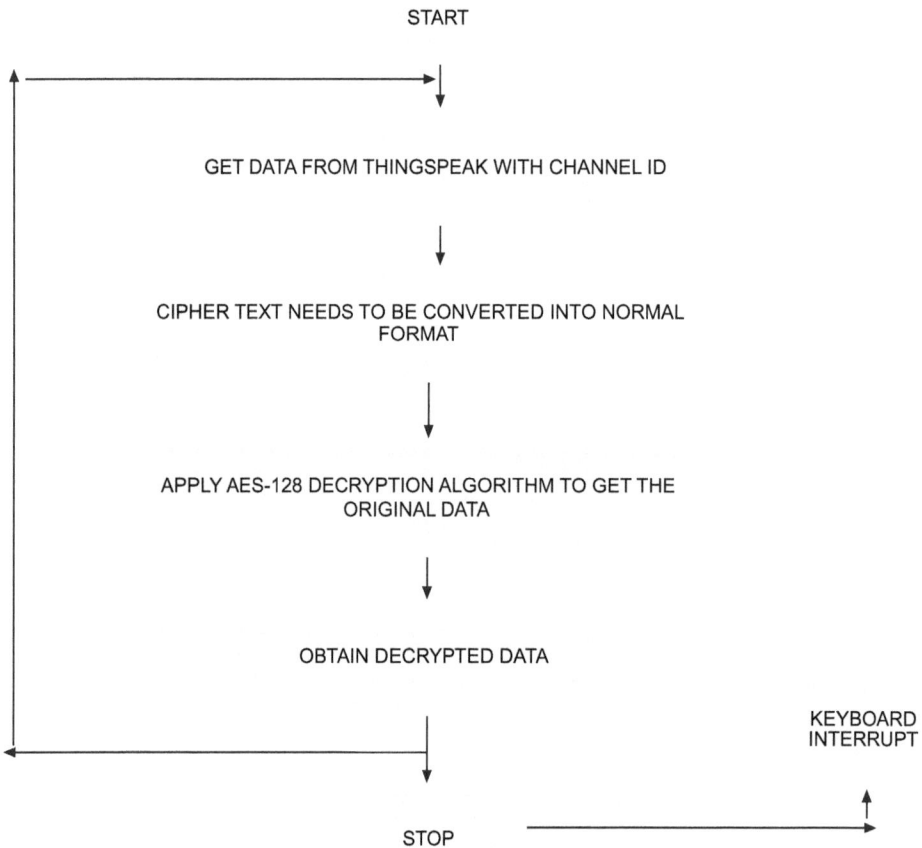

START

GET DATA FROM THINGSPEAK WITH CHANNEL ID

CIPHER TEXT NEEDS TO BE CONVERTED INTO NORMAL
FORMAT

APPLY AES-128 DECRYPTION ALGORITHM TO GET THE
ORIGINAL DATA

OBTAIN DECRYPTED DATA

KEYBOARD
INTERRUPT

STOP

Fig. (3). Decryption flowchart.

Receiver End: Decryption is done on the receiver side, but before that, the channel ID is required to retrieve the data from the item. To recover original data, the encrypted text must be transformed into plain text and then decrypted using the AES 128 technique. Finally, the original data is obtained.

PROJECT FLOW

A very popular symmetrical encryption algorithm shown in Fig. (**4**), AES128, also called the Rijndael algorithm, takes a viciously long time for a malicious software hacker to carry off a dictionary attack because the key is 128 bits lengthy and there are 14 hashes. It converts the individual blocks using keys of 128 bits and encrypts these blocks together to form cipher text. AES has a significant advantage in that it can be implemented in both hardware and software. Asymmetrical encryption is performed *via* Advanced Encryption Standards. It accepts a 128-bit block of data as input and performs a series of conversion steps to produce cipher text as the output.

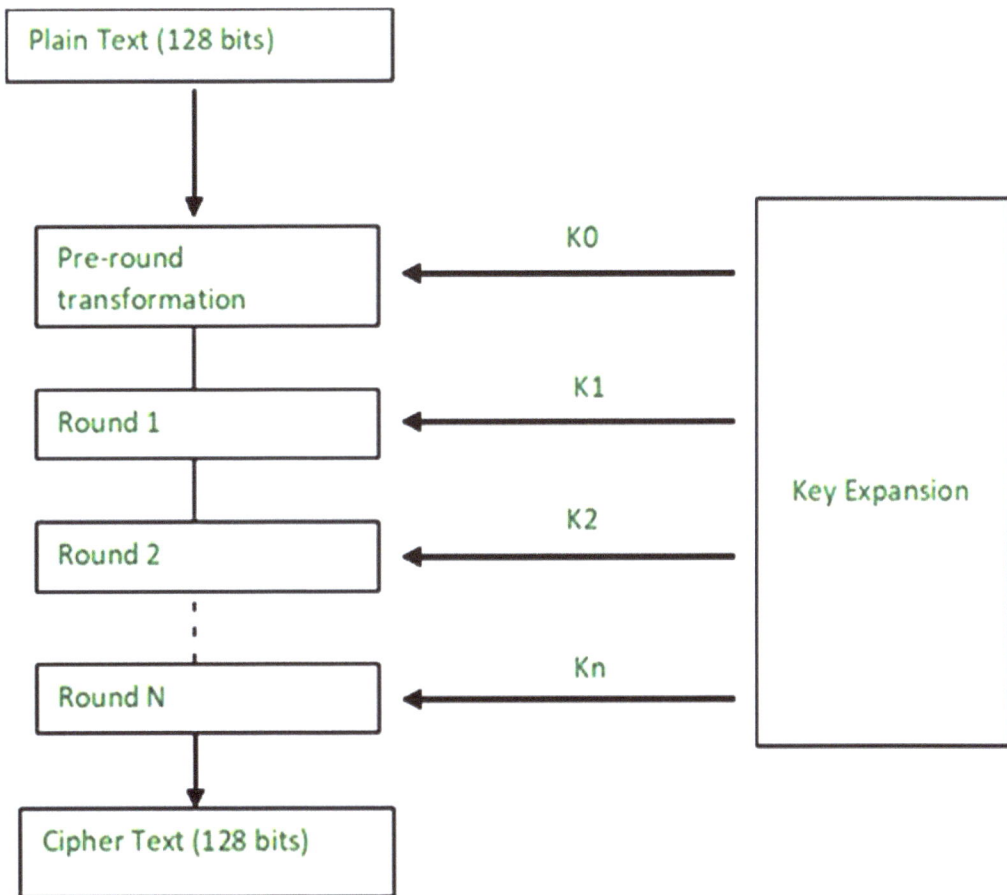

Fig. (4). AES Algorithm Block Diagram.

AES Working

Both the transmitter and the receiver need a copy of the secret key utilized by the AES symmetrical cipher, which uses the same secret key for both encryption and decryption. However, asymmetrical keys, which are useful for external file transfers, use separate keys for each of the two processes. The encrypted text is used in cipher text formats. The data in plain text is the data collected before encryption. Cipher text is classified into two categories: substitution ciphers, which substitute characters, and transposition ciphers, which require that characters be repositioned. The hash code (password) and secret AES key are used to encrypt the data being sent. During encryption, plain text is converted into cipher text, which does not allow the unauthorized user or hacker to hack the information [11]. In a similar fashion, the process is reversed for decryption, where the cipher text is converted to the original plain text. When it comes to decryption the cipher text is converted to original plain text as shown in Fig. (5).

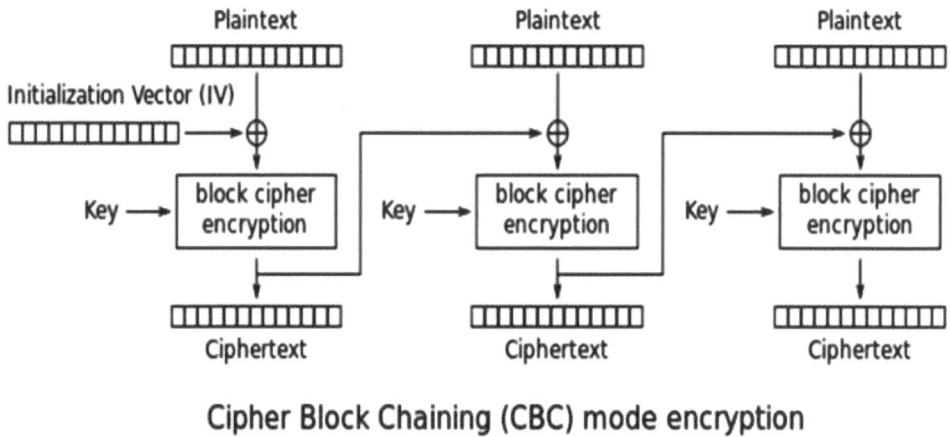

Cipher Block Chaining (CBC) mode encryption

Fig. (5). Cipher Block Chaining mode encryption for AES128.

RESULTS AND DISCUSSIONS

Output Without Encryption

On ThingSpeak, the output of each sensor obtained is shown in (Fig. **6**) with the indication of time and the output on Thonny IDE (Fig. **7**) on the Raspberry Pi system.

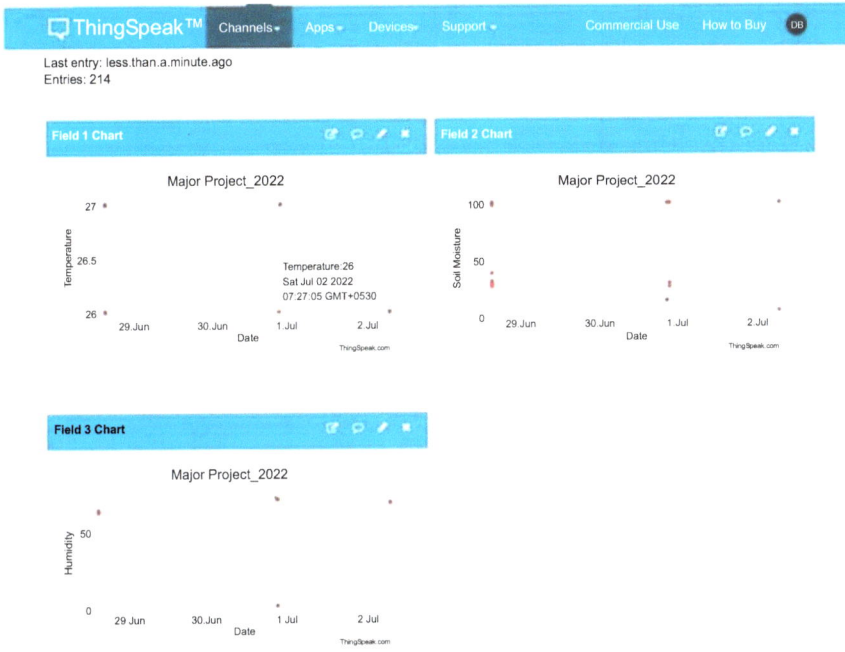

Fig. (6). Output on ThingSpeak without encryption.

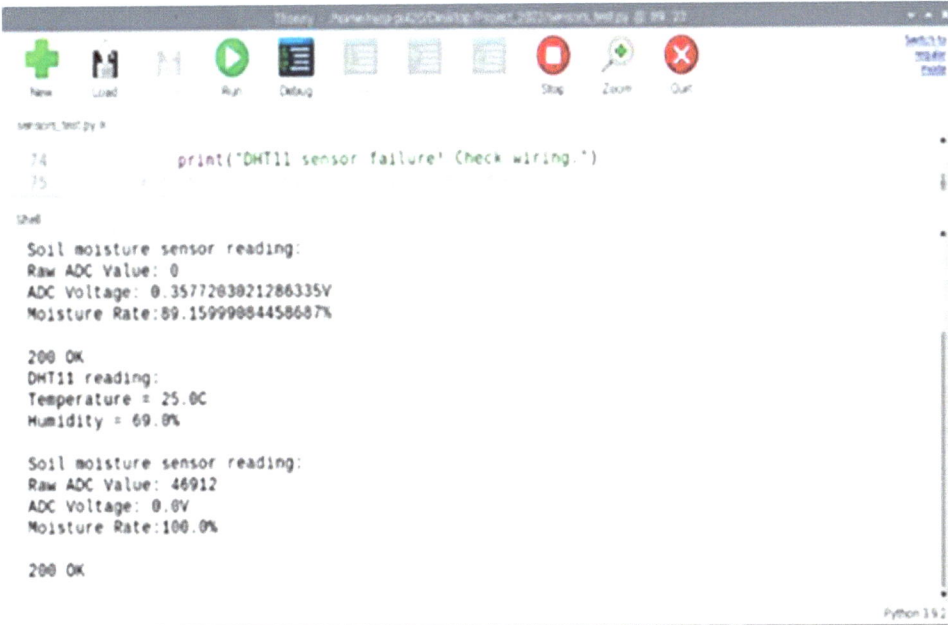

Fig. (7). Output for sensor values on Thonny IDE.

Output with Encryption

Here as seen in Fig. (**9**) the output in ThingsSpeak of each sensor with encryption obtained is shown in the graphs above with the indication of time and the output on Thonny IDE (Fig. **8**) on RaspberryPi system.

Output for Decryption

Here, in Fig. (**10**) on the host server, the values are obtained from the cloud and decrypted. The values are displayed only when the key is entered.

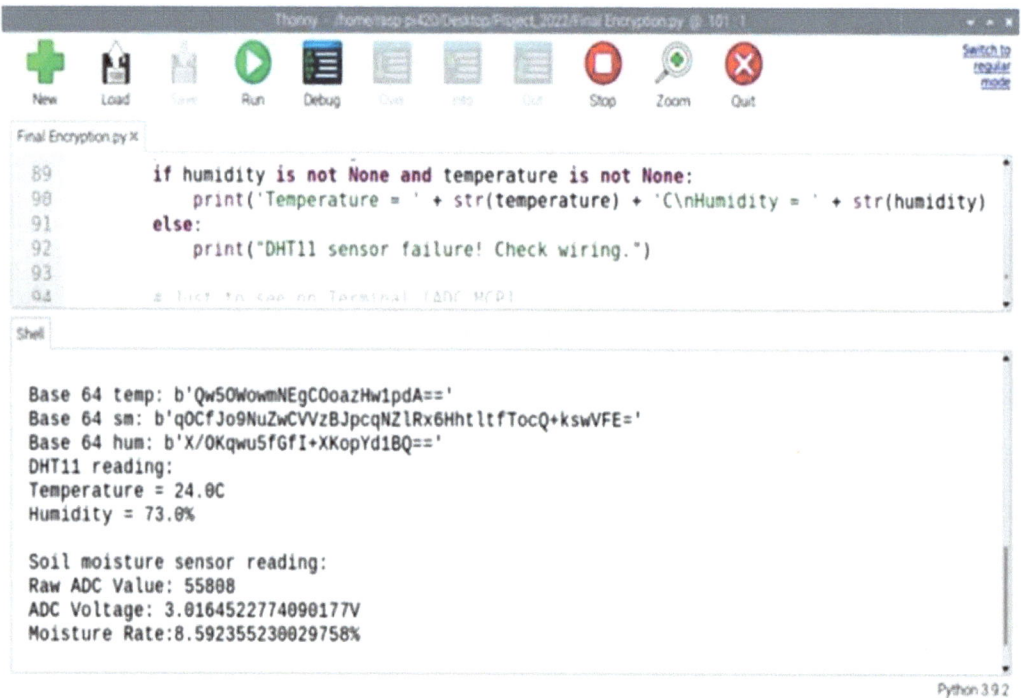

Fig. (8). Output for encryption on thonny IDE.

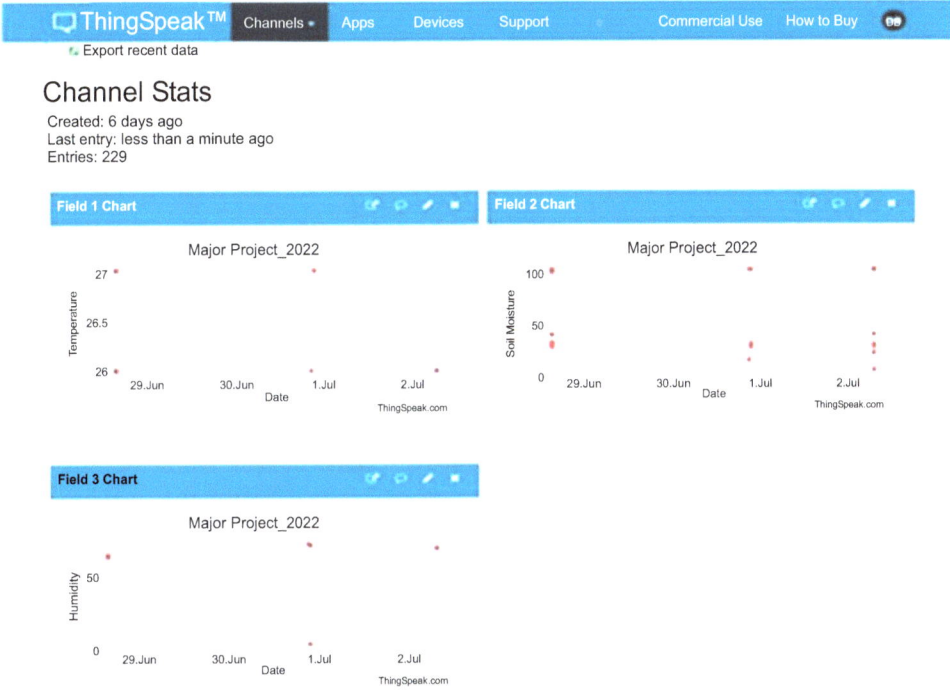

Fig. (9). Output on thingspeak with encryption.

Fig. (10). Output for decryption.

CONCLUSION

The paper presents the AES algorithm for the encryption and decryption of data using ThingSpeak. This helps in securing data that is prone to malefic attacks. Future work can be done by exploring other blockchain algorithms.

REFERENCES

[1] M. Amiri-Zarandi, R. A. Dara, E. Duncan, and E. D. G. Fraser, "Big data privacy in smart farming: A review," *MDPI*, vol. 2022, 2022.

[2] A. Vangala, A. K. Das, V. Chamola, V. Korotaev, and J. J. P. C. Rodrigues, "Security in IoT-enabled Smart Agriculture: Architecture", *Security Solutions and Challenges,* 2022.

[3] K. L. Raju and V. Vijayaraghavan, "IoT technologies in agricultural environment," *Survey (Lond.),* 2020.

[4] A. R. de A. Zanella, E. da Silva, and L. C. P. Albini, "Security challenges to smart agriculture: Current state, key issues, and future directions," *Array*, vol. 8, p. 100048, 2020.

[5] P. Kanakaraja, V. Sahithi, K. Ramyavani, and D. Richa, "Internet data security system using AES256 encoding technique," *International Journal of Recent Technology and Engineering (IJRTE)*, vol. 8, no. 4, 2019.

[6] M. Marwaha and R. Bedi, "Applying Encryption Algorithm for Data Security and Privacy in Cloud Computing", *IJCSI International Journal of Computer Science Issues,* no. 1, 2013.10.

[7] T. Popovic, N. Latinovic, A. Pešić, Ž. Zečević, B. Krstajić, and S. Djukanović, "Architecting an IoT-enabled platform for precision agriculture and ecological monitoring: A case study" 2017.

[8] A. Vangala, A. K. Das, and V. Chamola, "Security in IoT-enabled smart agriculture: Architecture," in *Security Solutions and Challenges*, 2022.

[9] K. Demestichas, N. Peppes, and T. Alexakis, "Survey on security threats in agricultural IoT and smart farming," 2020.
[http://dx.doi.org/10.3390/s20226458]

[10] M. Gupta, M. Abdelsalam, S. Khorsandroo, and S. Mittal, "Security and privacy in smart farming: Challenges and opportunities," *IEEE Access*, vol. 8, 2020.
[http://dx.doi.org/10.1109/ACCESS.2020.2975142]

[11] Laxmi S. Shabadi, and Hemavati B. Biradar, "Design and Implementation of IOT based Smart Security and Monitoring for Connected Smart Farming", *International Journal of Computer Applications,* no. 11, pp. 0975-8887, 2018.179

SUBJECT INDEX

A

Access Control 4, 38, 73, 104, 109, 136, 138

Accuracy 93, 98, 150, 156, 158, 159, 160, 165, 172, 173, 176, 178, 179, 180, 181, 186, 187, 189, 190, 199, 204, 209

Advanced Encryption Standards (AES) 242, 245

Agriculture 103, 115, 116, 117, 118, 120, 121, 122, 124, 129, 164, 213, 214, 215, 216, 217, 241, 242

Algorithm 58, 60, 61, 62, 63, 67, 69, 70, 71, 72, 93, 94, 96, 97, 98, 147, 149, 151, 152, 153, 157, 158, 159, 177, 180, 181, 187, 198, 199, 202, 203, 204, 230, 232, 233, 242, 245, 250

Anonymity 4, 35, 37, 51, 52, 195, 196, 197, 198, 203, 209

Attack 3, 4, 13, 16, 18, 23, 27, 33, 36, 52, 108, 113, 147, 148, 149, 150, 155, 159, 160, 214, 242, 245, 250

Authentication 4, 6, 8, 25, 26, 36, 37, 43, 73, 104, 109, 113, 153, 242

Automation 1, 2, 21, 25, 38, 80, 89, 105, 113, 120, 121, 122, 129, 164, 166, 176, 195, 241, 242

B

Bandwidth 27, 228, 229, 231, 233, 235, 237

Bitcoin 5, 7, 30, 32, 34, 36, 37, 41, 43, 44, 48, 49, 50, 53, 106, 213, 215, 236, 245

C

Capsule Network 176, 177, 179, 181, 182, 183, 184, 185, 187, 188, 189, 190

Cipher Text 241, 245, 246

Classification 63, 93, 96, 97, 147, 149, 150, 151, 152, 153, 154, 156, 158, 159, 160, 176, 177, 180, 181, 184, 187, 190, 196

Cloud Computing (CC) 20, 75, 104, 108, 135, 136, 137, 138, 145, 164, 170, 173, 174, 195, 230, 232, 233, 234

Communication 1, 2, 3, 4, 17, 21, 22, 23, 25, 26, 34, 35, 38, 40, 50, 51, 53, 61, 62, 69, 70, 73, 87, 109, 113, 117, 119, 123, 124, 126, 142, 147, 148, 154, 164, 165, 166, 167, 213, 214, 229, 231, 241, 242, 245, 246

Computer Tomography (CT) 176, 177, 179, 189

Confidentiality 3, 20, 109, 165, 242

Congestion 228, 229, 230

Consensus 1, 7, 10, 11, 12, 13, 14, 15, 16, 17, 18, 21, 30, 33, 34, 106, 107, 111, 236

Contracts 5, 6, 21, 23, 25, 42, 102, 107, 112, 113, 213, 222

COVID-19 166, 173, 174, 176, 177, 178, 179, 180, 181, 182, 187, 188, 189, 190

Cryptocurrencies 5, 30, 31, 41, 42, 43, 44, 46, 47, 48, 49, 50, 51, 52, 53, 106

Cryptography 6, 8, 36, 43, 106, 113, 214, 245

D

Decentralization 1, 4, 6, 30, 35, 39, 106, 113, 160

Decentralized 1, 3, 4, 5, 6, 10, 18, 25, 27, 30, 34, 35, 36, 37, 38, 39, 40, 41, 52, 53, 106, 108, 113, 120, 148, 160, 234, 242

Deep Learning (DL) 147, 149, 153, 157, 176, 177, 179, 180

Digital Ledger 6, 43, 106, 113, 214, 216

Distributed 3, 4, 6, 18, 25, 32, 35, 37, 38, 40, 50, 52, 53, 65, 74, 75, 104, 106, 108, 113, 118, 148, 232, 242

Drone 115, 116, 129, 133, 213, 214

Dynamic 19, 64, 68, 71, 72, 73, 135, 136, 145, 177, 181, 184, 229, 233, 245

www.ingramcontent.com/pod-product-compliance
Lightning Source LLC
Chambersburg PA
CBHW050819220326
41598CB00006B/264